War and the
Image of Germany

War and the Image of Germany

British Academics 1914–1918

STUART WALLACE

JOHN DONALD PUBLISHERS LTD
EDINBURGH

For Russell Stone and Nicholas Tarling

ISBN 0 85976 133 9

The publisher acknowledges subsidy from the Scottish
Arts Council towards the publication of this volume.

Distribution in the United States of America and
Canada by Humanities Press Inc., Atlantic Highlands,
NJ 07716, USA.

Phototypesetting by Quorn Selective Repro Ltd., Loughborough.
Printed in Great Britain by Bell & Bain Ltd., Glasgow.

Preface

I owe the idea for this book to a chance remark of Professor Geoffrey Best, then of the University of Edinburgh. His phrase 'the garrison intellectuals', to describe the phenomenon of almost universal support amongst leading European writers and academics for governments going to war in August 1914, led me on to investigate the attitude of British intellectuals. The war poets had been extensively studied, and other literary figures like Arnold Bennett, H. G. Wells and Bernard Shaw had all received detailed treatment. for the 1914–18 period. However, there was nothing like Klaus Schwabe's study of German academics during the First World War, and it was British academics who had begun to interest me. They had been as prominent as their German, French, and American colleagues in the work of wartime propaganda, but there also had been nothing in Britain to compare with Julien Benda's scathing postwar critique, *La Trahison des Clercs* (1927). Although an English translation had appeared the following year, Benda's book received curiously little attention in Britain. In the United States errant wartime academics were scourged by H. L. Mencken's young men in the pages of the *American Mercury*, in Germany Hans Wehburg's *Wider den Anruf der 93!* (1920) documented the national chauvinism of professors, but in Britain the academic community closed ranks. There was no inquest on whether historians or philosophers had been guilty of serious lapses in scholarly standards during the war years. It was this omission which initially I set out to repair.

The research for this book began in 1973 and rapidly grew beyond my concern with the academic profession during wartime. It had become clear that the German university system and German scholarship occupied a position of special prestige amongst scholars before the First World War. Britain was no exception to this, so that the war, when it came, involved painful reassessment by British scholars of German achievements. How was it that the nation of Kant and Hegel, Ranke and Dahlmann, had produced a band of professors so ready to justify every action of their government, including the invasion of Belgium? This question, or one like it, was to be repeated in another war, but even before then the spell of German *Wissenschaft* had been broken in August 1914. The considerable intellectual debt owed to Germany by British scholars was apparent from a reading of obituary notices, memoirs and biographies. Before the First World War the *Wanderjahre* after Oxford or Cambridge seem to have been the norm. In 1977 financial assistance from the *Deutscher Akademischer Austauschdienst* enabled me to consult matriculation records in order to

v

compile a list of British students at German universities before 1914.

Research for this book was completed in 1977. In the preceding five years I was helped by many people. I should like to thank Mr. E. V. Quinn, Librarian of Balliol College, for permission to use material from the A. L. Smith papers, and the following individuals: Dr. Paul Addison, Mr. Nicholas Barker, Mr. E. J. W. Barnes, Mrs. Sylvia Benians, Mr. Kenneth Blackwell (Bertrand Russell Archives), Mr. J. P. T. Bury, Mr. A. W. Chapman, Dr. David Coulton, Professor R. H. C. Davis, Mr. Owen Dudley Edwards, Professor Frank Eyck, Professor V. H. H. Galbraith, Dr. Martin Gilbert, Mrs. Mary J. Gregor, Dr. Cameron Hazlehurst, Professor Agnes Headlam-Morley, Mr. Michael Holroyd, Professor Victor Kiernan, Mr. James Klugmann, Professor L. S. Hearnshaw, Professor Jurgen Herbst, Professor F. M. Leventhal, Dr. Neville Masterman, Dr. J. A. Moses, Dr. R. C. Mowat, Dr. Peter Nicholson, Mr. W. B. Reddaway, Dr. Geoffrey Searle, Professor G. H. N. Seton-Watson, Dr. J. O. Stubbs, Mr. A. J. P. Taylor, Mr. H. N. V. Temperley, Professor Ulrich Trumpener, Dr. Alec Vidler, Mr. Jeffrey Weeks, and Mrs. Janet Weinroth.

The Librarians, Manuscripts Librarians and Archivists of the following institutions gave valuable assistance in my search for the papers of British academics: *Cambridge*: the University Library and the following colleges — Christ's, Churchill, Downing, Gonville and Caius, King's, Peterhouse, Pembroke, St. John's, and Trinity. *London*: the University Library and those of Bedford, Queen Mary, and University Colleges, the London School of Economics, and the Institute of Historical Research. Also the Royal Institute of International Affairs, the Royal Historical Society, the British Library, and the Public Record Office. *Oxford*: The Bodleian, Taylorian and Rhodes House Libraries and the following colleges — All Souls, Balliol, Christ Church, Corpus Christi, Exeter, Lincoln, Magdalen, Manchester, Merton, New, Queen's, University, and Worcester. *Other*: the university libraries of Aberdeen, Birmingham, Bristol, Glasgow, Hull, Keele, Leeds, Liverpool, Newcastle, Reading, St. Andrews, and Sussex; the John Rylands University Library and the Library of the Humboldt University (Berlin), the libraries of the University Colleges of Aberystwyth and Bangor; the North Yorkshire County Library and the International Institute of Social History (Amsterdam).

I would also like to acknowledge the financial assistance given in the years 1973 to 1975 by the University Grants Committee of New Zealand and the Auckland Grammar Schools Trust Board.

During the slow process of preparing my research for publication, I received much encouragement from my friends Alexander Murdoch and Roger Mason. John Tuckwell has been a tolerant and patient editor — his belief that a book would eventually appear, together with my well-developed feelings of guilt as each deadline passed, kept me plodding on. Finally, but not least, Paola Tinagli has been the best of friends, as well as a perceptive observer of British academics. What improvements I have been able to make to the final version are largely due to her.

Stuart Wallace.

vii

Contents

List of Abbreviations

AHR	*American Historical Review*
Annals AAPSS	*Annals of the American Academy of Political and Social Science*
Assoc.	*Association*
EHR	*English Historical Review*
IJE	*International Journal of Ethics*
J.	*Journal*
L.S.E	London School of Economics
Mag.	*Magazine*
Mthly.	*Monthly*
N.C.F.	No-Conscription Fellowship
N.Y.	New York
Philos.	*Philosophical*
Proc.	*Proceedings*
Quly.	*Quarterly*
Rev.	*Review*
Soc.	*Society*
TLS	*Times Literary Supplement*
Trans.	*Transactions*
TRHS	*Transactions of the Royal Historical Society*
U.D.C.	Union of Democratic Control

Introduction: Before the War

Professors we,
From over the sea,
From the land where Professors in plenty be;
And we thrive and flourish, as well we may,
In the land that produces one Kant with a K
And many cants with a C.

(H. L. Mansel), *Scenes from an Unfinished Drama Entitled Phrontisterion, or Oxford in the Nineteenth Century* (1852)

This is a study of the effect of the First World War on British academics. These 'university men' — there were very few women — were part of a profession which was beginning to take on something approaching its modern appearance in the years before the outbreak of the war. However, they did not yet constitute an 'academic class' as did their counterparts in Wilhelmine Germany. What has been called the 'pyramid of prestige' amongst British universities[1] — with Oxbridge at the top and provincial 'redbrick' at the bottom — slowed down the development of professional self-consciousness. The academic role model in Britain remained, to a large extent, the Fellow of an Oxford or Cambridge college, whose loyalty was first to the body of which he was a member, and in whose affairs he had a voice (the college), and only then to the University. Thus the largest and most prestigious universities, because of their collegiate structure, remained largely untouched by the new Association of University Teachers. In addition, the relative poverty, isolation and small size of most provincial universities and colleges also affected the development of the academic profession.[2] In Germany, by contrast, universities were numerous, well-endowed, with sizeable state grants, and were part of a 'competitive' system. It is true that there was some kind of 'pecking-order' which put Breslau below Bonn, and Bonn below Berlin, but, generally speaking the German system of higher education 'was based on a single type of university'.[3] In Britain there was greater differentiation, a more obvious hierarchical structure. Oxford and Cambridge

... had as yet few competitors, even among the newly-founded universities, so that a professorial chair at Oxford or Cambridge represented, as it long continued to do, the crown of academic achievement. A fellowship at a college provided a comfortable and civilised environment in which a serious scholar could work without too many calls on his time or too great an intrusion of outside anxieties or administrative demands.[4]

British academics were thus fewer in number, and less conscious of themselves as a distinct social group. In Britain, too, the boundaries

1

between university teaching and schoolmastering were still unclear —
there was movement back and forth between the English public schools
and the colleges of Oxford and Cambridge. The headmastership of a public
school, like Rugby, was certainly 'not inferior ... to the headship of an
Oxford college'.[5] At a lower level, university lecturers were paid 'little
more than ... secondary schoolmasters of three years standing, and less
than most'.[6] In Germany recruitment to the ranks of the professoriate from
the pool of assistants in an *Institut*, or from amongst *Privatdozenten*
(unsalaried lecturers), was a well-established practice by the 1870s. In
Britain the career pattern differed widely between the older universities
and the newer ones, but, generally speaking, achievement in research and
publication was still not the main criterion for academic recruitment or
advancement. 'Essayists, writers, brilliant public speakers and ad-
ministrators ... found their way to universities to a greater extent than in
Germany.'[7]

Allowing for these national differences, however, what has been said of
the German academic 'mandarins' might also be said of their British
counterparts: that they considered themselves 'members of a distinct
cultured segment of society'.[8] And yet, the 'higher learning' in Britain has
been neglected by historians, or rather, by British historians, since
American scholars have recently attempted to view the nineteenth-century
university in Britain in historical perspective.[9] Even before the First World
War there was in Britain no Thorstein Veblen or Friedrich Paulsen to
examine critically the state of the modern university.[10] The role of German
professors as 'educators of the nation' has received considerable attention,
both before 1914 and more recently. Since the Second World War this has
been because of the need to explain the failure of German universities to
offer significant resistance to Nazism.[11] In a similar fashion, the
phenomenon of McCarthyism in the United States in the 1950s prompted
at least one investigation of the American tradition of academic freedom.[12]
More recently, the role of the 'new mandarins' in formulating American
policy in Viet Nam seems to lie behind a study of American academics and
the First World War.[13]

What are the reasons for this neglect? It may partly be explained by the
later development and smaller size of the academic profession in Britain,
compared with Germany and the United States. But it seems also due to a
reluctance to treat universities, and those who work in them, as subjects
worthy of serious historical study. Yet universities have been an important
element in the 'cultural continuism' so characteristic of Britain. Perhaps
the continuism has in turn reinforced the tendency to forgo analysis of the
institutions which so successfully underpin it. The process works so

smoothly as to escape notice. Speaking of universities and associated cultural institutions in Britain, a recent observer has noted:

> The people whose work was in these institutions were not accustomed to think of themselves as 'intellectuals'. No form of corporate consciousness either drew them together or defined a social role for them as individuals. If the French intelligentsia formed a 'republican clergy', their English counterparts were decidedly Anglican in temper: aware of higher things but careful not to become tedious on that account, and not really in much doubt of the basic good sense of the nation and those who governed it . . . .
>
> 'Independence' here signified not a self-defining corporate invigilation of a transcendent general interest but the freedom to pursue one's particular (usually occupational) interest without ideological distraction or politico-juridical interference, in conditions where 'the Constitution' was not a redoubt to be defended or stormed, not even an arena of free civic activity, but a half-noticed, hardly changing country landscape.[14]

Before the First World War British intellectuals were a small group bound together by ties of kinship and shared assumptions based on intermarriage and common educational background (at the public schools and the older English universities). They constituted what Noel Annan has termed an 'intellectual aristocracy', 'wedded to gradual reform of accepted institutions and able to move between the worlds of speculation and government'. This emerging 'new class' lent a particular flavour to intellectual life:

> The influence of these families may partly explain a paradox which has puzzled European and American observers of English life: the paradox of an intelligentsia which appears to conform rather than rebel against the rest of society . . . the pro-consular tradition and the English habit of working through established institutions and modifying them to meet social needs only when such needs are proven are traits strongly exhibited by the intelligentsia of this country. Here is an aristocracy, secure, established and, like the rest of English society, accustomed to responsible and judicious utterance and sceptical of iconoclastic speculation. As a corollary it is also often contended that they exert a stultifying effect upon English intellectual life . . . .

The academic world overlapped with the 'aristocracy of the intellect' which had begun to form at the beginning of the nineteenth century. As Annan demonstrates, university chairs and college fellowships at Oxford and Cambridge were very often held by members of these families: 'the same names recurred as professors and tutors and schoolmasters; and by virtue of their affiliations their views on academic preferment carried weight'.[15] The two older English universities dominated the academic world, numerically as well as in terms of 'overwhelming academic and social importance'. Of the something under two thousand university teachers in Britain in 1900, about eight hundred worked in Oxford or

Cambridge.[16] In addition, many chairs in Welsh, Scottish, Irish and especially English provincial universities and colleges were held by former fellows of colleges in the two older universities.[17]

The political and ideological controversies of later Victorian and Edwardian Britain did little real damage to the close ties between the universities, the civil service (Home, Indian and Colonial), politics and the professions (including the Church):

> In a panorama emptied of profound intellectual upheaval or incendiary social conflict, British culture tranquilly cultivated its own private concerns at the end of the long epoch of Victorian imperialism. In 1900, the harmony between the hegemonic class and its intellectuals was virtually complete.[18]

However, after 1914 things were never to be quite the same again. The war set in train a series of changes 'of a less dramatic character' which 'began gradually to erode' the 'cultural monopoly' of Annan's aristocracy:

> The relative decline of the public schools and Oxbridge within an expanding educational system, the amelioration of the educational prospects of lower-middle-class children, the growth and diversification of State activity, the expansion of whole sectors of cultural production and the creation of new ones (publicity and cinema, for instance) together induced the formation of an intellectual stratum which, although still dominated by the old Victorian bloc, was necessarily of a different character. By the early 1930s, the national intelligentsia was more numerous, more disparate in social origin and occupational composition, and culturally less homogeneous than before.

One sign of this change was the growth of the academic profession, especially outside Oxford and Cambridge, and equally the growth of student numbers. By the mid-1920s the two older universities taught only one in three university students.[19]

The war also had one other major effect on British academics — it effectively demoted German universities from their former position as models for university reformers in other countries. Up until the 1870s German universities alone provided opportunities for scientific and scholarly research, and students from other countries (including Britain) flocked to them. Many of these individuals went on to academic careers in their own countries and carried with them 'the German model of cultivating research' within the university:

> The success of German research was attributed to the German university: first to its principle of 'unity of research and teaching', but also to its being a general rather than a specialised institution, and to its self-government. As a matter of fact ... the success of German research was due mainly to the intensive courses of training originally intended for teachers (seminars) and pharmacists (chemical laboratories) that developed far beyond their original purpose into university research institutes as a result of the intense competition between universities of the different German states.

These historical conditions notwithstanding, the fact was that the only system of research and training was the German one.[20]

As we shall see, some doubts were expressed before 1914 about the German model of university development, but it was the war which raised questions about the uses to which German scholarship were put. It was not just that scholarly ties were disrupted by war. The manifestoes of German professors in support of official policy came as a shock to many British scholars. The working-out of this problem forms the first theme of the following chapters. The second theme is a related one: the reaction of British academics to war, both as an intellectual problem requiring analysis and explanation, and as a personal problem requiring sometimes painful choices to be made.

In the sixty or so years before the outbreak of the First World War, the example of German universities and of German scholarship led to what has been called a 'knowledge revolution' in Britain, as well as in the rest of Europe and in North America.[21] While German philosophy and biblical criticism had profoundly influenced individual scholars in the late eighteenth and early nineteenth centuries, the second half of the nineteenth century saw 'institutionalization of the German influence' — the professionalisation of disciplines, the creation of new areas of study, and the reform of existing institutions.[22] Of course the transformation of values and institutions was uneven. Some British scholars who visited German universities before 1914 were repelled by the atmosphere, while others were greatly attracted by *Wissenschaft* — a word which described virtually a way of life. As Walter Metzger notes:

> The very notion of *Wissenschaft* had overtones of meaning utterly missing in its English counterpart *science*. The German term signified not merely the goal of rational understanding, but the goal of self-fulfilment; not merely the study of the 'exact sciences' but of everything taught by the university; not the study of things for their immediate utilities, but the morally imperative study of things for themselves and for their ultimate meaning.[23]

This belief, almost religious in intensity, was attractive to a generation of British intellectuals facing the erosion of traditional Christian beliefs. In much the same way, and at roughly the same time, the neo-Idealist philosophy of T. H. Green at Oxford provided another means of shoring up a system of values threatened by scientific discovery.[24]

Green's Germanophilia reminds us that the question of 'foreign influence' is never a simple one-way process. Green looked to German philosophy in order to reconstruct his beliefs. What was true for him was true for others:

For German intellectual achievements to be appreciated in Britain there had to be, to begin with, a predisposition to accept the fundamental assumptions behind the idea of the new knowledge. Simple contact and exposure are not sufficient; for these, as is well known, are frequently double-edged. They enforce national prejudice and insularity as much as they challenge them.[25]

Green was interested in reform of British education in general, rather than of the universities in particular, but amongst 'university reformers' the German example was a potent one. Mark Pattison, for example, sought to reconstruct collegiate Oxford on the model of a German university, complete with faculties, a graduated professoriate, and the research ethos.[26] However, research facilities were slow to develop in Britain, and up until the 1880s an increasing number of British students attended German universities, although never in the numbers that American and Russian students did. After 1890 the increase in the number of British students slowed,[27] but even in 1911 the Oxford historian A. J. Carlyle could claim that the 'position of the great German nation in philosophy, science and literature was so powerful that students were bound to study German and go to Germany if they were of any promise'. The list of those who did in fact go is a distinguished one.[28]

James Bryce, who later became one of the strongest supporters of the German idea of the university, in 1863 as a newly-elected Fellow of Oriel College, travelled to Heidelberg 'resolved to pass a semester studying law under von Vangerow' and perfecting his knowledge of German. Half a century later, as British Ambassador to the United States, Bryce remembered his *Wanderjahre*, and listed for a student audience at the University of Wisconsin the attractions of German universities: 'completeness of ... teaching organisation', 'instruction in every branch of knowledge', and 'the services' rendered 'to the prosecution of research'. The 'level of learning among the teachers', he concluded, was 'perhaps higher than anywhere else'.[29] Bryce could have added to this list the accessibility of the German university. Admission requirements were minimal, living costs were low, and, once matriculated, the student could wander from university to university in German-speaking parts of Switzerland and Austria-Hungary, as well as Germany itself, searching out the leading scholars in every field.

But, even more than these measurable attractions, it was the spirit of German scholarship which made German universities so attractive. Academic freedom (*lehrfreiheit*) and scientific method were the two features which Michael Sadler noted in his preface to the 1906 English translation of Friedrich Paulsen's classic work *Die deutschen Universitäten und das Universitäts-Studium* (1902):

The secret of the greatness of all institutions lies not in the form of their organisation, or even in their legal status, or in their financial resources, though of course each of these has an important bearing upon their efficiency and well-being, but in the spirit of their work and in the unwritten tradition of public service. It is the inner tradition of German university life, the spirit which animates and controls them, that most deserves study and excites our admiration. The German universities have become strong and great through untiring devotion to science, through belief in the power of education, through resolute defence of intellectual freedom, and through personal obligation to the claims of the state.[30]

During the First World War Sadler was to have second thoughts about academic freedom in German universities, but in 1906 his admiration was not at all unusual. The description of German scholarship by Lord Acton in the first issue of the *English Historical Review* (1886) is typical. He cited:

... the familiar type of German scholar ... the man who complained that the public library allowed him only thirteen hours a day to read, the man who spent thirty years on one volume, the man who wrote on Homer in 1806 and who still wrote on Homer in 1870, the man who discovered the 358 passages in which Dictys had imitated Sallust.[31]

This image of scholarly dedication had added meaning for someone like Acton who was a firm believer in the scientific nature of knowledge. As Charles McClelland has noted:

During the last half of the nineteenth century the definition of *Wissenschaft* had taken on some of the contours of a positivist ideology. If the extension of science and knowledge depended on hard, disciplined work rather than genius-inspired intuition, as the positivists believed, then every teacher could be a scholar. One need only read through one of the many late nineteenth century methods handbooks for evidence of the penetration of the concept of *Wissenschaft* as an edifice built of small blocks of research discoveries.[32]

In the same passage in his article Acton had also written of the Prussian university reformer Wilhelm von Humboldt forging 'the link between science and force by organising a university at Berlin', and it was this conception of the university as the symbol of (and contributor towards) national development and progress which proved so important in the development of British universities from the 1870s onwards. As German industry forged ahead there was a growing apprehension in Britain at what we might now call a 'laboratory gap'. Envious British eyes looked at the relatively ample German state assistance to higher education, compared to the meagre provision in their own country. In Germany state governments had revived or re-established older universities in the early nineteenth century, and continued to found new ones. In Britain this task was left, it seemed, to local initiative. Hartley Institution, Southampton (1862), Owens College, Manchester (1851), Firth College, Sheffield (1879), and

Mason College, Birmingham (1880) owed their foundation to the generosity of local manufacturers and merchants. These were all originally colleges of science only, as was the Yorkshire College of Science in Leeds (1874), started with money raised by public subscription. The colleges of the University of Wales at Aberystwyth (1874), Cardiff (1883) and Bangor (1884) had similar beginnings. Although financial assistance from the state to university colleges before 1914 has often been overlooked by historians,[33] there was clearly more reliance on local initiative or private benefaction in the establishment of new university colleges and the creation of new science laboratories at the older ones. It was concern at competition from German industry which lay behind the pleas for more government funding in Britain from academics like Sadler who had first-hand experience of German universities:

> At no earlier period in our educational history has German experience in organising intellectual activities had so close a bearing upon our needs. We find that what has long been going forward in German universities and technical high schools throws light upon the place of scientific research in industrial enterprise and national well-being. We see that German experience may guide us, by way both of warning and example, as to the right relationship between the university and the government or other public bodies from which most of the former receive an increasing proportion of their resources. As soon as we began to consider the true cost of developing the intellectual powers of the nation we realized that in the bold application of public funds to higher education and to free scientific education it was Germany which led the way.[34]

Was Sadler hinting at dangers in this government–university relationship with the phrase 'by way both of warning and example'? If he was, he did not elaborate. British observers appear not to have recognised the less admirable features of the status of the German professoriate as civil servants, for example the manifest discrimination against Jews and Social Democrats in filling chairs, particularly in Prussia which controlled nearly half of all German universities after 1870. Bryce was typical in his claim that the 'tradition of respect' for universities was strong amongst the university-educated German bureaucracy. This, he felt, was 'efficient protection'. To British eyes state control of German universities might seem 'excessive' but in practice it was not 'harmful'. Public opinion also protected 'freedom of teaching'.[35] If anything, the German example seemed more appropriate as the century wore on, for had not the decline of France and the rise of Germany been a striking demonstration of Acton's 'link between science and force'? The Battle of Sedan had been seen to be won in the lecture halls of Berlin and the laboratories of Giessen.[36]

However, the emerging British university system was by no means a replica of the German one. Eric Ashby has described what happened to German concepts of the university 'as they crossed the Channel'. Using the analogy of genetic mutation, he writes:

> Confronted with a different academic tradition in a different society, the German concepts were assimilated but transformed. One important reason was that there was no effective competition among British universities, such as existed among the universities in the German states. In Germany rivalry between universities stimulated them to adopt new ideas. In England higher education was dominated by the influence of Oxford and Cambridge: prestige was concentrated in these two centres in a way it has never been among the universities of Germany. And although the new institutions of higher education which were established in England were in part a protest against the exclusiveness of Oxford and Cambridge, nevertheless they had to live under the hegemony of these ancient universities. They acquired, by a process of social mimicry, some of the prevailing assumptions about higher education.[37]

Provincial university colleges, which had initially been established as scientific and technical institutions, added arts faculties (especially after the passing of the 1904 Education Act) and sought university status. The result was that they resembled neither German colleges of applied science (*Technische Hochschulen*) nor German universities. The strict institutional division in Germany between 'pure' and 'applied' knowledge did not apply in Britain, and even Imperial College (1907), established on the model of the College of Applied Science at Charlottenberg, became a constituent part of a reorganised University of London.[38]

At Oxford and Cambridge university reformers looked to German achievements in scholarship and traced them to 'the internal structure and organisation of German universities'.[39] But here too the result from the Royal Commissions of 1873–77, and the enacting legislation of 1882, was a fusion of German and British traditions. Jowett's compromise between the ideals of teaching and research, collegiate and faculty organisation, prevailed over Pattison's idea of professorial control of teaching designed to produce 'a professional class of learned and scientific men' on the German model.[40] However, despite the dominance of college tutors on the new faculty boards, research was increasingly seen at Oxford as reinforcement for professional status and a means of relief from the drudgery of teaching. 'Research ideals gained increasing acceptance as a valuable method of preventing the don from falling to the position of a mere schoolmaster.'[41]

At Cambridge the idea of a 'formal research mission' in university teaching was stronger, but even here it took time for the concept of research as 'a set of methods for pursuing basic knowledge', rather than simply a 'means of improving teaching', to become widely accepted.[42] The growth of research was also impeded by agricultural depression after 1875 which greatly decreased the revenue from investments so that few new chairs could be endowed and fewer fellowships were offered at Oxford and Cambridge. This meant that at the time when the function of the college fellowship was changing from being preparation for a career in the Church of England to providing support for teaching as a long-term activity, the financial basis for a growing academic profession was being whittled away, and with it the hope that it 'would offer opportunities for promotion analogous to those offered by the traditional learned professions'.[43] As time went on competition for chairs even outside Oxford and Cambridge became more fierce, and young men embarking on an academic career were often forced to choose between a long apprenticeship as a badly-paid lecturer or assistant to a professor in a Scottish university or in one of the new universities or colleges of England and Wales, or the hope of a university chair overseas.[44]

The status of non-professorial teaching staff outside Oxford and Cambridge was not unlike that of the German *privatdozenten*. Lecturers and Assistant Lecturers were the employees of the professors, paid by them and generally given *ad hoc* contracts. Few had tenure and generally their salaries were one third those of the professorial staff. In Britain, as in Germany, growing dissatisfaction with this situation led to the formation of professional associations in which lecturers took a lead.[45] Professors, on the other hand, had control of the teaching in their departments, and good salaries and security of tenure, although this varied from university to university. At Birmingham and Liverpool professorial power was consolidated after a struggle with governing councils consisting largely of hard-headed local businessmen and civic leaders. At newer universities there was occasional tension between professors and councils, but only at Nottingham did such disagreements take on the dimensions of a controversy over academic freedom.[46]

The most obvious examples of tension between academic staff and governing bodies concerned the right of professors to hold unpopular views outside the university. While Henry George and Single Tax had been the subject of discussion by university councils in the 1880s,[47] twenty years later it was growing labour unrest which led to friction. In October 1910 a letter appeared in *The Nation* alleging that in 'at least two northern universities' pressure was being brought to bear on lecturers if they associated themselves 'at all openly with any political party'. There was, it seemed, no attempt made to conceal the fact that these restrictions were made 'lest offence should be given to local magnates who have contributed or who may contribute to the funds of the University'. This, the writer noted, was in marked contrast to the 'opportunities for free political discussion ... in Oxford and Cambridge'.[48] In the same month the new London School of Economics faced a similar, but this time more explicit, threat from some of its 'local magnates'. The railway companies which contributed £1,000 a year to the School threatened to withdraw this unless Sidney Webb retired from the chairmanship of the Board of Governors, a course which he chose to save financial difficulties. Apparently his public statements on the Osborne Judgement had caused offence.[49]

Such incidents seemed to be more common in the United States where business endowment was on a larger scale, but according to J. A. Hobson, himself apparently the victim of prejudice against unorthodox views, even the level of private funding in Britain held dangers:

> The governors and the teaching faculty will meet them [the donors] more than half-way in their demand for safe teaching in all subjects where unsafe teaching might cause offence in rich and influential quarters.[50]

In a situation where professors espoused the cause of organised labour much could depend on the Vice-Chancellor. Someone like Sadler at Leeds was able to protect the right of academic staff to support municipal workers on strike in the city in 1913. Even in the case of the Professor of Economics, D. H. MacGregor, where it was more difficult to distinguish personal and professional statement, Sadler was able to assure local businessmen that dissent was worth defending:

> A muzzled University staff is a poor affair. But the forces in favour of silencing unpopular views as 'dangerous' or 'untimely', or 'likely to give offence to powerful friends' are always pressing and must be resisted.[51]

Sadler's knowledge of the German code of *lehrfreiheit* no doubt had something to do with his defence of his professors. However, in this instance the protection of extra-mural freedom of speech went beyond its original definition — the freedom of the teacher to investigate and discuss his subject without interference. It was this wider definition of academic freedom which was to come under attack during the First World War. The fact that there was no attempt to formulate a code of *lehrfreiheit* as in Germany, and as later in the United States, was as much an indication of the slow growth of professional self-consciousness as it was of the belief that 'academic independence' was less likely to be threatened in Britain, the reason usually given.[52] But in this situation self-censorship could easily pass unnoticed.

The problem of war, however, was a less immediate concern for most British academics before 1914. The gradual realisation that it did constitute an intellectual problem as well as a social phenomenon requiring analysis and explanation forms the second main theme of the present work. Before 1914 war was either considered a candidate for inevitable extinction as the 'horrors of military and naval invention' outran 'the endurance of man'[53], or as a survival in less civilised parts of the world — 'colonial wars in which white men slaughtered yellow men, or brown men, or black men, or wars between second-rate white men's states in the Balkans and South America'.[54]

The universities were no exception. Apart from the occasional debate in the Oxford Union, 'the living present' did not intrude. 'Industrial and technological developments were causing social transformations and disturbances. There were troubles in the Balkans and mutterings between the power alliances of Europe',[55] but the Oxford Modern History School officially noticed nothing after the Treaty of Berlin in 1878. Anything later than this date, even the cession of Thessaly to Greece in 1881, was considered politics not history.[56] As E. L. Woodward, an undergraduate between 1908 and 1913, remembered at Oxford, 'no one bothered much about anything after the battle of Waterloo':

> In these years ... the chief interests of those who would now be described as 'intellectuals' were either in social questions or in religion. There was not much interest in foreign affairs. Many of the dons were hardly less ignorant than the undergraduates about the public affairs of Europe, although they knew the mountains of Switzerland, the cathedrals of France and the ancient monuments of Greece and Italy .... I do not believe that there were half a dozen men in Oxford who realized the European significance of the Balkan wars. The Agadir incident happened in the Long Vacation; in the following Michaelmas term, there was a good deal of vague talk about a narrow escape from war. There was also a good deal of talk, equally ill-informed, about Germany and the bellicosity of William II. This talk rarely went beyond reproducing current newspaper articles. I do not think that anyone in my year was worried about the possibility of a general European war.[57]

Reminiscence over sixty years after the events described should be treated with caution, but the same note enters many memories of Oxford life. Young Cambridge was perhaps marginally less immured 'within the walls of a dead age' and the university was more likely to produce critics of British foreign policy than its sister institution. This was true of the 'Bulgarian Agitation' of 1876, Britain's equivalent of the Dreyfus Affair,[58] and the Boer War, even though critics were a small if vociferous minority. Indeed, the public opposition of university men to war in South Africa seems to lack some of the confident vigour of the earlier 'Bulgarian Agitation'. Even Cambridge with its stronger tradition of intellectual dissent was reluctant to criticise a government once it had gone to war, in 1899 as much as in 1914.

The potential difficulties for an intellectual in wartime are well illustrated in the case of Henry Sidgwick, Professor of Moral Philosophy at Cambridge. As legatee of John Stuart Mill's liberalism, Sidgwick had opposed British policy in 1876 over Turkish atrocities as immoral. However, South Africa was a question which directly affected British national and imperial interests, and here Sidgwick found the role of critic less congenial. He was perplexed by the difficulty in 'reconciling adequate security for England with effective independence for the Boers', but troubled also by what he termed his 'personal connection with the Government'. His wife was the sister of Arthur Balfour, Tory leader in the Commons, and so Sidgwick declined to lend his name to a protest petition circulated by a fellow-philosopher.[59] Ten years earlier Sidgwick had written of the definite limits to political dissent by 'the thoughtful and moral part of every community', and now events had confirmed this. Once war broke out it was 'doubtless right for most, if not all men to side with their country unreservedly', since not even the most critical intellectual 'should keep coldly aloof from patriotic sentiment'. Only before war broke out could such people be expected 'to make an earnest and systematic effort at an impartial view of the points at issue'.[60]

While Sidgwick attempted to give due consideration to both ethical ideals and national sentiment in wartime, his colleague John Westlake, Whewell Professor of International Law at Cambridge, was more concerned to provide justifications for British policy in South Africa. Writing one month after the outbreak of war, he freely admitted that British demands in the Transvaal were 'not founded on any legal right'. They were, he claimed, based on Britain's right to alleviate the 'intolerable' position of her nationals in the Boer republics. National ideals were 'always propagandist', that is expansionist, and hence admitted of 'no compromise'. But judging between the ideals of the Briton and the Boer, Westlake had no doubt that the 'racial' ideal of the latter was far inferior to 'the English ideal of a fair field for every race and every language accompanied by a humane treatment of the native races'.[61] Of course, this was exactly the kind of conclusion to which a later generation of academic liberals were led when they supported British entry into the First World War. However, in 1914 they had the incalculable benefit of apparent legal (as well as moral) rectitude which Westlake could not claim in 1899.

At Cambridge only two individuals argued publicly, in the Union, against the war. One of them, A. C. Pigou, was later to suffer as the result of his opposition to the First World War.[62] At Oxford there was opposition to the granting of an honorary degree to Cecil Rhodes who was widely believed to have been behind the Jameson Raid. However, Rhodes received his degree when the presence of the Prince of Wales at the ceremony ensured the threat of a proctorial veto was not carried out. The death of Rhodes in 1902 helped, as the university's historian put it, 'to dim and allay resentments' within Oxford, and the publication of his will with the scheme for scholarships disarmed his former critics. One of them, H. A. L. Fisher, even became a Trustee.[63] The Master of Balliol, Edward Caird, was unusual for his uncompromising criticism of the war, and he made himself very unpopular within the University by chairing meetings called to protest at the British policy of interning Boers in concentration camps. But he and Arthur Sidgwick, brother of Henry Sidgwick, were untypical figures in Oxford.[64]

The attitude of most Oxford dons to the war was summed up by an editorial in the *Oxford Magazine*. Under the heading 'Oxford's Duty to the Army', the editor commended conscription as a cure for the 'slouching gait of the average undergraduate, the slipshod dress of the many, the unconscious ignorance of anything approaching discipline of almost all'. This was not just another complaint about the younger generation but a suggestion that the university should train army officers. In the meantime L. R. Farnell, the Rector of Exeter College, was organising drilling, and the Professor of Logic commanding a volunteer 'Cycle corps'.[65] These were by no means isolated instances as volunteers corps were established at many other colleges and universities.[66]

There were more disturbing features of this patriotic revival. For example, when the German press began to criticise British policy in South Africa, there were suggestions that professors of German origin might be required to publicly express support for their adopted country.[67] In the event such proofs of loyalty were not required, but the whole episode calls to mind the persecution of German-born professors during the First World War. There were signs too that critics of official policy could expect a rough time from patriotic dons in any future war. Talk of 'dainty and self-indulgent moralists' who opposed the Boer War because they led an easy and isolated existence 'in the abstract and imaginary world ... of discussion and theory'[68] seems very like the criticism which individuals like Bertrand Russell had to face after 1914.

The damage done to Anglo-German relations by the Boer War was obvious enough, and it was to this that Germanophile academics directed their attention after 1900. An Anglo-German Friendship Committee (later the Anglo-German Friendship Society) was established in 1905, and it boasted many of the leading names in British academic life among its membership.[69] Manifestos of friendship were exchanged — the one side denying allegations of 'sinister designs entertained by the German people against England', the other assuring the Germans that the occasional diatribes of 'certain journalists' merely demonstrated 'their profound ignorance of the real sentiments' of the British people. 'For us, as between England and Germany', the British scholars wrote, 'there is no frontier to be defended .... A war between the two powers would be a world-calamity for which no victory could compensate either nation.'[70]

However, one of the German-born members of the British society, Karl Breul who taught at Cambridge, did warn his colleagues that all was not well in Germany. On a visit to that country he noted that Treitschke's idea of future Anglo-German conflict as an 'inevitable war of extermination between modern Rome and Carthage' was apparently 'much in vogue' with German students.[71] There were similar comments from other British academics who had attended Treitschke's lectures in Berlin or who had met German professors who 'exhorted the students to play football that they might be better able to fight England when the time arrived'.[72] Often these were memories coloured by the experience of two world wars, and it is rare to find before 1914 recognition of the degree to which extreme nationalism was commonplace within German universities.[73] War between Britain and Germany seemed unthinkable when the general assumption was that its prevention 'was to all intents and purposes a question of arbitration'.[74]

The belief that war between civilised states was obsolete was promoted within British universities by the 'International Polity Movement' begun by Norman Angell (Ralph Lane) with money provided by a business foundation. As one might expect, Cambridge had the largest number of 'Norman Angellites', but there were well-known exponents of the doctrine elsewhere: at Birmingham W. J. Ashley, in London L. T. Hobhouse, at Oxford Gilbert Murray. Not only did the 'Angellites' believe 'that international banking and the gold standard, respect for private property and the sentiment of the Stock Exchange, would survive all upheavals',[75] but they also suggested that the growing interdependence of developed economies had rendered obsolete the forceful settlement of international disputes. The Oxford philosopher, T. H. Green, had taught an earlier generation that the way to peace lay through Free Trade, but now Angell laid new emphasis on the economic unprofitability of war (and imperialism) for the victor state: 'Winning a war brought no advantages; therefore by implication losing a war brought no burdens'.[76]

Despite the rather simplistic economic analysis 'Angellism' was popular with serious-minded undergraduates and the younger Fellows at Cambridge where the Union carried a resolution declaring the futility of armed aggression. E. M. W. Tillyard, then a young Fellow of Jesus College, produced his own tribute to Angell's best-selling book *The Great*

Illusion (1910) by finding proof for its thesis in *The Athenian Empire and the Great Illusion* (1914).[77] R. M. MacIver, then a young lecturer at Aberdeen, also made extensive use of Angell's ideas in his standard work *Community* (1914). War between 'civilised peoples', he noted, was simply 'civil war':

> The development of common interests is making the institution of war between nations irrational and vain . . . . This is most obvious in the economic sphere, owing especially to the internationalisation of capital, so that one civilised community in destroying the commerce and capital of another, is destroying or injuring the investments of its own members. Again, as international trade grows, more and more members of each community live by the commercial prosperity of other communities and are necessarily ruined when that suffers.[78]

MacIver was fairly typical of liberal intellectuals in his belief that once the 'social conditions out of which war arose' had been transformed, and once international law had developed (as civil law had done within states) towards its final 'legislative stage', then civilised states could be free of war. But he was more aware than some of the need to recognise the role of conflict in society and to channel destructive impulses into 'ever less wasteful forms', such as 'the endless and fruitful struggle involved in the mastery of the environment and the conquest of essential evils'. Coming to much the same conclusion which Tillyard had in his examination of the Athenian Empire, MacIver saw war as a poor second to 'less wasteful forms':

> Apart from other considerations, the latter provide a better stimulus than the former. For war, from its destructive nature can spur a people only to occasional endeavour. Where war is the chief stimulus to solidarity its necessary intervals are full of danger. It is the warrior who, away from war, becomes luxurious and degenerate, it is the war-sustained people which, when it ceases to fight, falls into decadence simply because the more persistent stimuli involved in constructive effort cannot so effectively appeal to these.[79]

Although such ideas owed something to the writings of T. H. Green,[80] the influence of the American philosopher William James is unmistakable. His celebrated essay 'The Moral Equivalent of War' first appeared in 1910, the year in which Angell's *Great Illusion* was published, but it went far beyond the conventional wisdom of economic liberalism. Starting from the observation that 'Our ancestors have bred pugnacity into our bone and marrow and thousands of years of peace won't breed it out of us', James went on to sketch the outlines of a 'moral equivalent' to replace it. Instead of conscription for military purposes, James proposed 'a conscription of the whole youthful population to form for a certain number of years a part of an army enlisted against *Nature*'. Not only might this improve the quality of life for others, but, more importantly, 'military ideals of hardihood and discipline' would be inculcated into the nation's youth. This would help preserve 'in the midst of a pacific civilization' those 'manly virtues' which the 'military party' had feared might disappear if peace broke out. Essentially an optimist, James believed that 'patriotic pride and ambition in their military form' could be turned to more constructive purposes, since they were 'only specifications for a more general competitive passion'.[81] It was this scheme which the Principal of Manchester College, Oxford, had in mind when he reminded delegates to the Eighth National Peace Conference (1912) that they should recognise the 'fighting instinct' which was present 'more or less' in all people. If there were already university chairs in military history and lectureships in military science, why not similar endowments for 'industrial and commercial development and the history of peace'?[82]

There was little sign of this suggestion being taken up before 1914, and even James's ideas had less impact in Britain than one might have expected. Bertrand Russell acknowledged his debt to the American philosopher in his own search for 'a peaceful outlet for men's energies',[83] but the unpopularity in Britain of Pragmatism, the movement in philosophy to which James belonged, meant that his ideas did not reach many academic philosophers. The late development of psychology as an academic discipline in Britain meant that James's audience was further reduced.

Two early exponents of the fledgling discipline of social psychology, Graham Wallas and William McDougall, did tackle the same problem that James had, but more typical of the small group of liberal academics writing on the problem of war was Goldsworthy Lowes Dickinson, Fellow of King's College, Cambridge. It was Dickinson whom James had singled out as exhibiting in his writings the characteristic weaknesses of the 'socialistic peace advocates', namely a failure 'to realise the full inwardness of the situation', a failure to provide a 'substitute for war's disciplinary function' or to provide 'a *moral* equivalent for war'. 'The duties, penalties and sanctions pictured in the utopias they paint are all too weak and tame to touch the military-minded', James concluded. And it is true that, despite an undergraduate enthusiasm for drilling with the volunteer militia, Dickinson showed throughout his life a marked distate for the martial virtues which James saw as the 'enduring cement' of world peace.[84]

Dickinson's first writings on the problem of war in the years after the Anglo-Boer conflict laid great stress on the role of reason in the fight against militarism and imperialism. Men might not simply be 'reasoning animals', he wrote in July 1906, but on the other hand:

... it would be absurd to conclude that they cannot be influenced by reason. Slowly

> but surely, argument works upon us all, partly by confronting one passion with another and compelling a choice between them, partly by insisting on the consequences of actions, partly by pointing out incoherence and contradictions in the arguments by which we are accustomed to buttress our instincts.[85]

This belief animated all Dickinson's writings and especially his work after 1915 for post-war international organisation. As he wrote two years before the outbreak of the First World War, 'reason and imagination' were the only weapons available to the peace advocate. The role of the intellectual and the academic was thus to 'destroy illusions and reveal naked facts'.[86] It was an 'illusion', for example, that war was needed to cure defects in the nation's moral fibre. 'The disease of war is ... invoked to cure the disease of peace. But peace ought not to be a disease', Dickinson wrote in 1907. 'If our peace is cankered, that is not because it is peace, but because it is peace based on injustice and egotism.'[87] As for the supposed ideals of race, nation, empire and national honour, these arose from the ideology of the possessing class — from the 'monotony of life among well-fed people'. This was an echo of T. H. Green's judgement over thirty years earlier that the 'privileged class involuntarily believes and spreads the belief that the interest of the state lies in some extension without, not in an improvement of organisation within'.[88]

However, Green was writing in 1879 before the floodtide of imperialist fervour in the last two decades of the nineteenth century. But working-class jingoism and the new interest in crowd psychology were things Dickinson could not avoid twenty or so years later. The first Dickinson tended to excuse as 'a more pardonable kind of feeling' produced by the monotony of 'chronic overwork' and curable by social amelioration. For the peace advocate, as for the social reformer, 'the masses' were the 'last hope' for progress.[89] On crowd psychology Dickinson sought to provide his own moral equivalent. What was 'base in the life of the average man of business, or clerk or artisan, compared with that of the best soldier', was not 'the peaceableness of his occupation, but its lack of direct and conscious subordination to a common end'. 'In a community well organised and well moralised, such as the one the socialists conceive', Dickinson claimed, 'every occupation would be regarded as a public function, and performed in the spirit of public duty.'[90]

Dickinson's colleague when he lectured at the London School of Economics, Graham Wallas, was much less sanguine about hopes for world peace in the period before 1914. Dickinson had seen the Hague Conference of 1907 as a sure sign that mankind was becoming more peaceable and civilised, that history was now being seen as 'something to be transcended', not repeated. Wallas a year later saw Germany and

Britain possibly 'marching towards the horrors of a world-war merely because 'nation' and 'empire" were the categories used to make sense of 'an unintelligible universe'.[91] His book *Human Nature in Politics* (1908) had been greatly influenced by William James's *Principles of Psychology* (1890) which stressed the importance, not only of conscious actions (as in neo-Idealist theory), but also of instinct — a bundle of atavistic impulses. As Wallas's biographer notes: 'His disillusionment with the unrealistic assumptions of liberal-democratic thought had found a resolution in a new approach to politics based upon 'Darwinism' and 'the new psychology".[92] What Dickinson called Wallas's 'bio-psychological realism' was thus far removed from Dickinson's political dialogues which made 'the claim of reason seem more worthy of reverence . . .'[93]

Wallas seemed even less confident than James about the likelihood of finding a 'moral equivalent' for war. Like other liberals he could easily refute the arguments that war was necessary to improve 'the breeding stock', or that it could not be prevented by any system of international law.[94] But what of the argument 'that peace, even if it could be secured, would leave the warlike dispositions permanently unstimulated, and would therefore produce the nervous condition . . . called baulked disposition'? Would it not be impossible for 'man in such a condition' to 'live a life which anyone would call good'? This argument, Wallas felt, had 'more stuff in it'. And instead of James's vision of a civilian peace corps, Wallas could only offer the tentative suggestion that 'it would not only be more effective but more economical' if heroism, excitement and discipline of war and military life could be achieved by more direct means, rather than 'trusting that we may find them amongst the accidents and uncertainties, the fatigue and monotony of modern warfare'. Perhaps a general improvement in the quality of life for the mass of the population, together with 'some wholesome discipline' and temporary 'renunciation of ease and comfort' would be sufficient. But generally Wallas looked to increasing 'world consciousness' to replace outdated nationalism.[95]

In Wallas's book *The Great Society*, published only two months before the outbreak of war, are the following prophetic words: 'An internecine European war is the one enormous disaster which over-hangs our time . . . .' Gone was the optimism of nineteenth-century liberalism, what Wallas called the 'old delight in the 'manifest finger of destiny' and 'the tide of progress". Even 'the newer belief in the effortless 'evolution' of social institutions' looked far less certain. 'We are afraid of the blind forces to which we used so willingly to surrender ourselves', Wallas concluded rather pessimistically. Yet he remained a confirmed liberal who believed that human behaviour, as distinct from human nature, could respond to

environmental changes. This was 'the master-task of civilised mankind' —
to produce 'a harmony between themselves and their environment far
deeper and wider' than anything that could be found in existing society.[96]
In this he differed from the other Edwardian pioneer of British social
psychology, William McDougall, who, Wallas felt, tended to see rational
thought as 'a merely subordinate mechanism acting only in obedience to
the previous stimulation of one of the simpler instincts'.[97]

Yet the difference was a fine one, for McDougall's *Introduction to Social
Psychology* (1908) was no more pessimistic about the possibility of
European war than Wallas had been in *Human Nature in Politics*. The
'instinct of pugnacity', McDougall wrote, operated 'more powerfully' in
the present age 'than in any other in producing demonstrations of
collective emotion and action on a large scale'. And echoing Wallas's fears
for the outbreak of international conflict, he continued:

> In our own age the same instinct makes of Europe an armed camp occupied by twelve
> million soldiers, the support of which is a heavy burden on all the peoples; and we see
> how, more instantly than ever before, a whole nation may be moved by the combative
> instinct — a slight to the British flag, or an insulting remark in some foreign
> newspaper, sends a wave of angry emotion sweeping across the country,
> accompanied by all the characteristics of crude collective mentation and the two
> nations are ready to rush into a war that cannot fail to be disastrous to both of them.
> The most serious task of modern statesmanship is, perhaps, to discount and control
> these outbursts of collective pugnacity. At the present time custom is only just
> beginning to exert some control over this international pugnacity, and we are still
> very far from the time when international law, following in the wake of custom, will
> render the pugnacity of nations as needless as that of individuals of highly civilised
> states and physical combats between them as relatively infrequent.

Like Wallas, McDougall seemed to look forward to the time when
warfare would be 'replaced by industrial and intellectual rivalry'. Indeed,
there were already 'unmistakable signs' of this change. Wars between
'civilised nations' were 'tending to become mere incidents of their
commercial and industrial rivalry, being undertaken to secure markets or
sources of supply of raw material which shall bring industrial or
commercial advantage to their possessor.'[98] Trade warfare, which
McDougall regarded with such equanimity as an alternative to military
conflict, was not likely to appeal to Wallas who had broken with the
Fabians over the question of imperialism and tariff reform.[99] And there
was too an echo of Social Darwinist thinking in McDougall's writing
which was not present in Wallas's work. At one point, for example,
McDougall considered the possibility that military warfare would be
sublimated into less overtly violent forms and noted that this would 'end
what has been an important, probably the most important, factor of

progressive evolution, namely the selection of the fit and the extermination of the less fit (among both individuals and societies) resulting from their conflicts with one another'.[100] This passage remained in the many subsequent editions of the book during McDougall's lifetime (he died in 1938). In his writings in the 1920s McDougall continued to claim 'that war was the greatest instrument of natural selection among states and nations', 'the great antiseptic of national life'; the need for self-defence 'a bracing tonic influence without which nations must become relaxed in moral tone'.[101] Even his wartime service in the R.A.M.C., treating cases of shellshock in Edinburgh, did not shift him from these views.

McDougall went far beyond Wallas in his criticism of democratic values,[102] but he never espoused the cruder Social Darwinist arguments against attempts to abolish war. These were common even amongst academics; Wallas claimed that perhaps 'more than half of the professed historians and psychologists in Europe' believed in the rightness or inevitability of war, basing 'their arguments upon imposing biological and psychological generalisation'.[103] Apart from thoroughgoing Social Darwinists like Karl Pearson, Professor of Applied Mathematics and then (after 1911) of Eugenics at University College, London, Wallas was no doubt referring to the academic apologists of imperialism, like J. R. Seeley's followers.[104] But he may also have been referring to the writings of British neo-Idealist philosophers like F. H. Bradley and Bernard Bosanquet, especially in view of his long-standing rejection of the claims of that school of thought.[105]

Among British intellectuals before 1914 the influence of Hegelianism was every bit as important in arguments for the rightness of war as was the use (or rather misuse) of Darwinian ideas. In this connection F. H. Bradley's article on 'The Limits of Individual and National Self-Sacrifice' in the *International Journal of Ethics* for October 1894 is one of the best statements of the neo-Idealist position on war. Here Bradley, who unlike Bosanquet tended to express himself in unequivocal terms, launched an attack on the 'insincere professions' and 'sickening cant' of the 'Humanitarian' school. Against its claim for the equality and 'absolute value of individuals', Bradley pointed out that the real world was quite different: 'force rules the world, and ... self-assertion ... is a condition of welfare', he noted. And if 'the end' were 'the full development of human nature', then the end was 'superior to the individual' and it was 'right to act for this end to the best of one's judgement'.[106]

What then of the argument used by Wallas and MacIver that international law would develop (and was developing) as law within states had developed? Bradley had two objections. First, one simply could 'not argue in general from civic to international morality', from what citizens could or could not do, to what nations could or could not do. Secondly, 'analogy from civil life' did not reveal a picture of unlimited self-sacrifice. It showed, on the contrary, that 'within limits self-assertion ... [was] valid'. Bradley then reinforced these points (especially the first) in the following striking passage:

> A nation must aim at the good of mankind and at peace in the end; but, as things are, this principle will in some cases justify violence, and even extermination. For, beside the principle which establishes the end, there can be no absolute law; and the means to this end cannot be fixed beforehand. And such means certainly need not always consist in abstinence from aggression. Our first hope at the present is an international executive enforcing the morality of the best; but, if that is to exist, then the best must agree, and must be the strongest. And strength means war in reserve. We may look beyond this possibility to a better state of things, but the first seems the only road to the second. The meek will *not* inherit the earth, and a nation which claims morality must be ready to use force in defence of right.[107]

Bradley doubted therefore whether international law could 'be said really to exist', a point repeated by other neo-Idealist philosophers. Even where the existence of 'international morality' was conceded it was viewed as being quite different from individual morality, being of less importance and later growth. National life, wrote W. R. Sorley, the Cambridge philosopher, preceded international relations and nations possessed 'an independence and self-sufficiency ... not shared by the individual'. A nation's duty was 'to itself', a recognition of the patriotism (i.e. altruism) of its members rather than their selfishness. Morality (international and individual) did not depend upon sanctions, but law did. Without a 'superior power' to enforce international morality, international law was 'a dream of the distant future'.[108]

Such arguments would become important during the First World War when future international organisation was discussed, but in the prewar period war rather than peace was a talking-point amongst philosophers. Some, like D. G. Ritchie, Professor of Logic and Metaphysics at St. Andrews, went further than Bradley and attempted to assimilate Darwinian ideas to Idealist philosophy.[109] In an article for the *International Journal of Ethics* for January 1901 Ritchie referred to war as 'a harsh form of dialectic, a rough means of solving hard problems', but nevertheless it (or 'the genuine threat of war') was 'often the only way' to secure the desired end. This Ritchie defined as 'constitutional government and ... social progress', and he proposed to judge the rightness of war by weighing which of 'the conflicting forces' would be most likely to achieve this end. Not surprisingly, since this was written during the Boer War, it was Britain's opponents who were found wanting. Perhaps with the Boer republics in mind, Ritchie even concluded that the nation-state, so precious to radical liberals, was not 'necessarily the highest and final type of society'. Might not 'a few great 'Empires', in which self-governing federated communities control the less advanced races, represent a higher stage — more likely to be stable, less exposed to war and preparing the way for a federation of the world', Ritchie asked his readers. And later, in an apparent reference to the pro-Boers, he noted: 'The sympathy so often expressed for the weaker or smaller state, simply because weaker or smaller, is aesthetic rather than ethical: it is really a survival of that barbaric feeling about warfare which regards it as a noble sport'.[110]

No doubt the peace advocates were shocked by this piece of table-turning — usually *they* accused their opponents of harbouring outdated nostalgia for war. But Ritchie's definition of the just war must have seemed even more shocking. 'If we do not exactly say that all successful wars are just wars,' he had written, 'we admit that no nation is justified in engaging in war unless with reasonable prospect of success.' This was perilously close to the belief that Might was right, and during the First World War philosophers unsympathetic to Idealism would point to the similarity, especially in some of Bosanquet's writings, between the arguments used by the British and German followers of Hegel. However, one must admit that when they were not taking their arguments to extremes Bradley and Ritchie showed a grasp of international realities, especially unpalatable ones. It certainly simplified 'the internal problems of political society to isolate the state; but such simplification means abstraction from the actual truth of facts', Ritchie wrote. And with a wealth of historical data he attempted to demonstrate that war had 'ever been the maker of nations'.[111]

Yet it was true, as their critics alleged, that there was a fatalistic acceptance of war in the neo-Idealist position. While criticising as overpersonalised and 'not very scientific' the usual radical liberal explanation for the survival of war in civilised society (the machinations of ruling elites — what came to be known as 'secret diplomacy'), Ritchie equally left himself open to the charge of ignoring the possibility of reform of the international system. Ritchie did have a concept of 'human progress' but it was a game played by harsh rules, and ones established by the world's leading imperialist power which could disregard the rights of others:

> Nations exist for mankind and not mankind for nations; and when any nation, small or large, fails to serve the purpose for which nations exist, it has no moral right to block the onward movement of human progress, even while it may still have a certain quasi-legal status under the convenient fictions of International Law, until that status is altered by stern facts.[112]

This was very close to the ideas of German Social Darwinists like the historian Treitschke. Perhaps Ritchie was carried away by wartime hysteria, but he of course claimed that his explanation was a 'scientific' one. There was, he argued, 'everywhere an inevitable conflict between inconsistent types of civilization', and human nature and existing governments being what they were, this conflict could not 'always be kept in peaceful channels'.[113]

Ritchie died in the year following the signing of the peace with the Boer republics, but many of the other participants in this debate on the nature of war lived to see the outbreak of war in August 1914. Academic liberals like Wallas, Dickinson and L. T. Hobhouse worked to maintain British neutrality during the July crisis. Together with the economist J. A. Hobson, Wallas established the British Neutrality Committee at the end of that month. Leading members included well-known journalists and academics like F. W. Hirst, J. L. Hammond, G. M. Trevelyan and Gilbert Murray, Regius Professor of Greek at Oxford.[114] At about the same time Norman Angell was setting up the British Neutrality League with C. P. Scott, editor of the *Manchester Guardian*, and J. J. Thomson, Professor of Experimental Physics at Cambridge.[115] As the crisis deepened, letters began to appear in the press warning of the danger of British involvement in a war against Germany. On the first of August 1914, the day Germany declared war on Russia, *The Times* carried a 'Scholars' Protest Against War With Germany', with the signatures of nine people mostly connected with the University of Cambridge. These well-known scholars had decided to follow the cautious path sketched out by Henry Sidgwick fifteen years earlier in response to the Boer War, though now in more dangerous circumstances:

> We regard Germany as a nation leading the way in Arts and Sciences, and we have all learnt and are learning from German scholars. War upon her in the interests of Servia and Russia will be a sin against civilization. If by reason of honourable obligation we be unhappily involved in war, patriotism might still our mouths, but at this juncture we consider ourselves justified in protesting against being drawn into the struggle with a nation so near akin to our own, and with whom we have so much in common.[116]

This manifesto, with its admission of the limits of dissent if war broke out, was a good deal more cautious in tone than the spate of letters which appeared at this time in the *Manchester Guardian*. On the same day that the 'Scholars' Protest' appeared in *The Times* the *Guardian* printed a letter from Graham Wallas voicing his fears of the certain disastrous effects of a European war on the British working class. There could, he claimed, be a return 'to the general intellectual and moral stagnation of 1793 to 1815 during which the British working population, both in agriculture and manufacture, were brought down to a lower point of misery and hopelessness than at any other period of history'. Two days later the British Neutrality Committee reiterated its belief that Britain was under no obligation to assist France in the event of a Russo-German conflict. Russia was 'only partly civilised' and was 'governed by a military autocracy largely hostile to Western ideas of political and religious freedom'. Germany, by contrast, was 'wedged in between hostile states, highly civilised', with a culture that had 'contributed enormously in the past to Western civilisation', and was in addition 'racially allied' to Britain with similar 'moral ideas'.[117]

Ironically at least one of the signatories (Gilbert Murray) was to spend much of the war denying the truth of the last two (if not the first) propositions in the Neutrality Committee's manifesto. However, for the moment we can note that the Committee combined an idealistic appeal to the British Government to see that justice was done (especially to Belgium) and 'to act as arbiter in the general interest', with arguments of economic self-interest. Britain, the signatories wrote, could only remain 'the financial centre of the world' in peacetime. If war broke out London's functions as a centre of international finance 'would be temporarily and perhaps permanently transferred to the other side of the Atlantic'. This Angellite argument may have been directed at the hard-headed business-men of Manchester for whom the considerations of 'high politics' were indeed 'questionable':

> If we go to war, it will not be to defend any British right from violation: we do not even allege that Germany or Austria has wronged or affronted us in any way; we cannot even pretend to a sense of wrong. We shall attack them because, in a quarrel of a very complex issue in which we have no qualifications to act as judge, we presume to decide them ... or because on the basis of some cold calculation of high politics — which all the facts show to be of very questionable correctness — our security and interests render it opportune to do so .... [118]

Further protests from British scholars laid greater stress on the threat posed to 'civilisation' by war, although soon they would be talking of a war *for* civilisation. C. H. Herford, Professor of English at Manchester, warned of the possibility of a 'horrible crime against civilisation' unless 'this figment of 'honour' which binds us to intervene, not to save France from being crushed, but to enable her to make an unprovoked attack upon her neighbour with a better chance of impunity', was cleared away.[119] The fact that Herford had a German wife was to leave him in a very exposed position during the war, and his kind of francophobia was uncommon. More liberal academics would have agreed with G. M. Trevelyan's talk of a Russian peril to civilisation — Tsarist autocracy was a more obvious target than republican France. The aged Positivist E. S. Beesly, Professor of

History at King's College, London, while aware of the 'crime' of Germany in 1914, was unable to view with any pleasure the prospect 'of Cossacks harrying the land between the Oder and the Elbe as they did after Kunersdorf in the time of the great Frederick'.[120] Only a younger generation of liberal intellectuals nurtured on Tolstoy found it easy to slide into Russophilia, as we shall see later.

Whether the threat to 'civilisation' was defined as coming from without (Russia) or within (internal disorder resulting from the dislocations and deprivations of wartime), there was a widely-held liberal belief that British involvement in war would be 'criminal'. However, even before the German invasion of Belgium, some academics had brushed aside these moral objections. J. A. R. Marriott, history tutor at Worcester College, Oxford, and later a Conservative M.P., called for a closing of ranks at 'an hour so solemn'. Three days later, on the day Britain declared war on Germany, *The Times* printed 'A Scholar's Protest' which effectively answered all the previous talk of German *Kultur*. H. Stuart Jones, Fellow of Trinity College, Oxford, and, as he was careful to indicate, member of the German Imperial Archaeological Institute, pointed to that other Germany, the Germany of Treitschke and Bernhardi — two names which were soon to appear in every pamphlet and article on the war. Did the signatories of 'the Cambridge manifesto' realise that Germany was 'not governed by scholars, but by statesmen, who solemnly believe that might confers not only right but the duty of attacking the weaker [states]', Jones asked. Germany threatened France (which incidentally had also rendered services to scholarship) in language which no liberal should tolerate.[121]

At this point events overtook academic wrangling, leaving little room (even if the attempt had been made) for comparisons to be drawn between British behaviour in South Africa and German policy in Europe. By the tenth of August letters began to appear from the signatories of the Cambridge manifesto. The German invasion of Belgium had caused an almost complete change of mind. The first letter from J. Holland Rose, Reader in Modern History at Cambridge, and later one of the most prolific apologists for the British cause, spoke of the 'imperative need of repelling ... [German] aggression' before an 'honourable peace' could be possible. Professor Ramsay the classical archaeologist seemed to be uncertain as to the precise reason for Britain's declaration of war (he mentioned the 'invasion of Holland'), but went on to explain his reasons for recanting:

> The admiration which I feel for Germany as a civilising power in her own fashion (different from ours) is changed to dislike when she misuses her deserved influence in the world of thought to trample on law and right and to force the horrors of war on a

neutral state. The same reasons which made me sign make me now recognize that the cause of Germany is turned into an attempt to enslave Europe, which must be resisted at all costs .... I do not regret signing; it was right for us to seek justification before the world at large and in the memory of history by showing that we as a people desired by all honest means to avoid this war. My own private conviction that the war would be forced soon made me all the more resolute to show loathing for it.[122]

Not all recantations were so dignified. Bertrand Russell, who might have been expected not to have too much sympathy with liberal backsliders, remembered the collapse of the British Neutrality Committee in almost comic terms. But with limited knowledge of the often cynical motives behind official policy, there was a tendency in time of crisis to believe in the honesty of Sir Edward Grey, the Foreign Secretary, and to close ranks. Besides, as Howard Weinroth has remarked, it involved 'no great intellectual feat' to move from support for small nationalities in the Balkans to support for gallant little Belgium against German aggression.[123] In South Africa fifteen years earlier many liberal intellectuals had opposed British policy because it offended against this cardinal liberal principle, but in 1914 the German invasion of Belgium altered everything. As L. T. Hobhouse wrote to his sister Emily four days after the British declaration of war:

... there is no analogy between this and the Boer War. There we were doing a wrong — deliberately destroying two small peoples. Here we are fighting for France and Belgium which if beaten will be dismembered or annexed.[124]

It was not that Grey's foreign policy had been without fault. 'I still think that our adhesion to one side in the European alliance increased the tension and weighted the chances in favour of war', Hobhouse wrote later.[125] The Government had been wrong too in declaring war 'without exhausting every possibility of avoiding it', but, once in, national existence was at stake as it had never been in South Africa. 'Now we are in it seems ... useless to recriminate. Later on we can have it out with Grey', Hobhouse reassured himself.[126]

This collapse of liberal internationalism was of course not confined to Britain. Leading academics in the German peace movement, like the historian Karl Lamprecht and the scientist Wilhelm Ostwald, became convinced defenders of the German cause. In France the sociologist Emile Durkheim, who had been prominent in the Comité de Rapprochement Franco-Allemand, churned out wartime propaganda.[127] Amongst British liberals there may have been 'sorrowful acceptance' of the realities of international power politics but there was also a feeling of relief once Belgium had provided a clear moral issue and a justification for closing ranks.[128] No doubt academic liberals assumed that their ideals would withstand the test of war, and might even exert some influence on official policy during wartime. In reality the intellectuals appeared to provide no more than an outer coating for political decision-making. Yet the wartime writings of British academics are of interest since the First World War has all the trappings of a modern ideological conflict.

CHAPTER 1

'The Broken Fellowship'

It is the natural logic of the multitude that because we Englishmen feel it our duty at this moment to combat the German state to our last breath therefore Germany has never done anything of value for scholarship or letters. But that is just the kind of logic to which scholars should give no countenance. We surely need not be any weaker in our resolution to hold out till we have righted a great wrong and removed a great danger to our nation because we recognise the world's debt in science and letters to the researchers and writers of Germany.

'The Broken Fellowship', *Times Literary Supplement*, 4 Nov. 1915

For British scholars with ties of friendship and common intellectual endeavour with German colleagues the break in relations in August 1914 was especially painful. Some of them had German wives, and the war for them was, as the historian G. W. Prothero, himself married to a German, noted, 'a sort of civil war'.[1] Perhaps this feeling was best summed up by the economic historian W. J. Ashley. He had studied in Berlin under two great German economists Adolf Wagner and Gustav Schmoller, and was especially close to the latter. Early in the war Ashley was commissioned by Oxford University Press to write a pamphlet on *The War and its Economic Aspects* (1914). Despite the title Ashley spent the first part of this unburdening himself of his grief at the outbreak of hostilities between Germany and Britain. First he described the Germany of his student days:

For many years — from the time when I first went as a student to Germany — I have had a warm place in my heart for the German people. Like many other young Englishmen, it was in Germany that I first caught the infection of the scientific spirit that cares as much for widening the bounds of knowledge as for handing on knowledge already acquired; and what I saw of social intercourse in Göttingen and Dresden made me appreciate the *Gemütlichkeit*, the cheerful simple kindliness, which characterises so large a part of the people. I have believed that our two nations possessed many traits in common, and have had some common interests and duties; and I have done what I could to promote good understanding between them. And when the University of Berlin, in conferring an honorary degree, took occasion to describe me as a 'true friend of our nation', the epithet was not, I think, altogether undeserved.

But now the war, 'a special and personal grief' for Ashley, had broken the ties of scholarship and friendship:

It means the end, for many years to come, probably for my lifetime, of the hopes I have cherished of amicable cooperation between the two countries; the cessation — though that, in comparison, is but a small matter — of friendly inter-change of thought with men whose work for economic science and for social thought I have

29

long admired. And although I am convinced that the German Government and the German nation supporting it are profoundly in the wrong; though I am sure that it made a fatally unwise decision in determining at all risks, to back up — nay, to prompt — Austria; though I feel that it has quite misunderstood both the purposes and the temper of England; though I have not the slightest doubt that it is the bounden duty of every Englishman to do all that in him lies to bring about Germany's complete defeat; I am not going to deny to Germany the qualities which first called forth my respect, and I am not going, if I can help it, to pay any German the poor compliment of returning his 'hatred' .... .[2]

Despite his first-hand knowledge of German society and politics, Ashley was never involved in wartime polemics, confining himself to detailed analysis of the German economy at war. Among historians A. W. Ward followed the same path. He had been brought up in Germany until the age of sixteen and spoke German like a native. Like Ashley, his ties with German scholars were close. 'All through his life', wrote one of his colleagues, he 'was anxious to do all that was in his power to emphasise friendly relations between the land of his birth and that of his early education.'[3] As well known in Germany as in Britain as an historian of the first rank, Ward was uniquely equipped to be an intermediary between the scholars of the two countries. Just two years before the outbreak of the war he had spoken to the English Goethe Society of ties which transcended scholarship:

The service which German research and German sympathy have rendered to the study of Shakespeare during something like a century and a half can never be equalled, but they may, in some measure, be returned by the loving devotion of generations of Englishmen and Englishwomen to the study of Goethe. In these spheres of work and thought at least — in the payment of this mutual tribute to genius, and in this common acknowledgement of indebtedness for which there is no sinking fund — the cooperation and competition between Germans and Englishmen, is, we trust, destined to endure, as it is our heart's desire that the friendship they alike betoken may continue and increase in all the relations between the two peoples of the kinsmen.[4]

But war in 1914 put an end to all Ward's hopes, and to the Society, which was not revived until 1923. Although Ward publicly stated his belief that Britain's war against Germany was a 'righteous war', he too, like Ashley, never used his considerable knowledge of Germany to join in the attacks on her. Instead, he put together a long semi-historical paper on 'Securities for Peace' and 'retired into German history before the fall of Bismarck'. His *Germany, 1815–1890* which was published in three volumes between 1916 and 1918 showed no signs of the very real grief which the war had brought for Ward. Its tone, a reviewer noted, was one of 'serene detachment' and 'absolute impartiality'.[5] It was left to others to argue over the 'problem of German Kultur'.

How, then, could German policy be explained, or, as C. H. Herford, Professor of English Literature at Manchester, put it: 'How does it come ... that a nation standing, in very many respects, in the foremost ranks of civilised peoples, can openly resort in its warfare not only to practices, but also to principles which suggest a methodical and intellectualised barbarism?' For Herford this was a personal dilemma — his wife was German and his own ties with German scholars were very close. But his answer was a rare example of clear thinking among academic Germanophiles. As he noted, the usual explanation involved dividing 'the German people into two alien hosts'. On the one side were 'the thinkers, the idealists, the science-workers, the musicians, and the millions of kindly men and women' whose *Gemütlichkeit* so readily disarmed 'English reserve'. On the other side was the 'brutally aggressive military caste'. Usually this view took the form 'of postulating a fundamental contrast between Prussia and the rest of the German nation'.[6] This convenient division into 'good' and 'bad' Germans did not satisfy Herford, but it was a view commonly held. 'Of the two Germanys', the educationalist Sir Michael Sadler wrote to a friend, 'the one which you and we love is not responsible for this wickedness, except so far as it has not had the moral or physical courage enough to stab its Junkers in the face long ago'.[7]

Perhaps the foremost exponent of the 'two Germany' view was the scholar-politician, James Bryce, who identified German 'frightfulness' firmly with Prussia. 'There was nothing of this kind in Southern Germany when I knew it fifty years ago', he wrote in 1916. He just could not believe that 'the German learned class, or commercial class — or the people in any sense' had been 'persuaded by Treitschke, Bernhardi's system of doctrines, or had adopted the principle that State necessity justifies everything'. Soldiers might believe anything they wished, nor were 'most politicians much better'. But could the theologians and professors have really forsaken ethics or religion?[8] H. A. L. Fisher, whose lectures on *The War: Its Causes and Issues* Bryce had been criticising for such an indictment of German universities, was like Herford no 'good hater' of Germany. Indeed, he found 'no pleasure in contemplating the ruin of any civilised country under the processes of war', especially this 'struggle between the two great members of the Teutonic family' which was 'fratricidal and therefore peculiarly terrible'. And yet something was wrong with German professors. 'I am reminded', Fisher wrote to Bryce, 'that cultivated people can very soon sink to the lowest level of barbarism by the example of Görres who writing in the *Rhenische Mercur* in 1813 urged the destruction of Rheims Cathedral, of the Louvre and of Notre Dame'.[9]

This could not fail to strike home with Bryce who was, like Fisher, at that time involved in an official investigation of alleged German atrocities in Belgium, including the destruction of the university and historic buildings in Louvain. There was, too, considerable evidence that in their public utterances the 'organised masters of German science' endorsed German military policy; that they, like 'the enormous majority of the German people', not only passionately supported the war, but also justified, 'at the most with a regret for the loss of life, the sinking of the Lusitania and all the other expedients ... called into play for its successful prosecution'.[10] The manifestos of German scholars were specifically designed to show the solid support of professors for German policy and to reject the idea of 'two Germanys'. As ninety-three leading scholars announced in October 1914: 'The German Army and the German people are one, and to-day this consciousness fraternises 70,000,000 of Germans, all ranks, positions and parties being one'.[11]

What might be called the battle of manifestos in 1914 had begun with the *Address to Evangelical Christians Abroad* by thirty German theologians, including some of the names best known to the British public. Their rejection of the allegation of German atrocities, and their protest against 'unnameable horrors' committed against Germans living abroad, were answered by the address *To the Christian Scholars of Europe* from theologians associated with the University of Oxford. As one might have hoped, this last was couched in tones of Christian charity — no doubt to the Germans it seemed a case of British cant — the Oxford theologians claiming that German accusations arose from ignorance rather than from intellectual dishonesty:

> Some of us are specially bound to individuals on the list by personal ties of deep regard and admiration. Therefore we do our best to examine, with self-restraint and effort of impartiality which befits those whose business it is to sift the evidence and to look below the facts for their causes, the points emphasized or indicated by their signatories .... We hasten to express our belief in the sincerity and good faith of these protestations and disclaimers so far as they relate to the motives of those by whom the document has been signed .... Naturally we do not charge the signatories with stating the facts other than they saw them. But they wrote, we are quite sure, without having studied at first hand any adequate collection of the evidence.[12]

However, this claim for superior British wisdom did not impress the German theologians who fought back with *Another Word to the Protestant Christians Abroad* — as one of the Oxford divines sadly reflected, 'a most unworthy piece of special pleading'.[13]

Reading the reply of the Oxford theologians, one is immediately reminded of the criticisms directed at academic life in Wilhelmine Germany in the wake of the publication of Fritz Fischer's *Griff nach der*

Weltmacht (1961). The intrinsic shortcomings of German universities were clearly revealed in 1914, for those with eyes to see (the shortcomings of British universities escaped the notice of all but a few British academics). The Oxford theologians had noted, for example, the increasingly homogeneous (and imperialistic) ideology of the German professoriate and that 'no Social Democrat' could 'aspire to a professorial chair'. And they concluded:

> Of the existence and influence of this tendency the [German] signatories cannot be ignorant; and we do not know whether to be more grateful for their own implicit repudiation of sympathy with it, or more astonished at their ostrich-like attitude towards a state of things so notorious.

Normally they would not have held their German colleagues 'responsible for the theories of military writers like General von Bernhardi' any more than they would have expected to be held responsible themselves for 'the views of Lord Roberts'. But the German theologians had even denied the existence of aggressive imperialistic sentiments within Germany. How could they claim that Germany had 'not dreamed of depriving others of light and air'?[14]

On the other hand, the German claim, often to be repeated, that this was a war of *Kultur* against 'Asiatic barbarism' put some of the Oxford theologians in a rather difficult position. At least two of them (W. B. Selbie and J. E. Carpenter) had been signatories of a manifesto published in *The Times* after the Russian mobilisation of July 1914 (but before the German invasion of Belgium) protesting against British involvement in war on the side of the Tsarist autocracy. Even now the Oxford scholars thought it 'reasonable, in estimating German policy, to allow for the deep-seated nervousness in German minds', which was 'the outcome of the neighbourhood on their further border of the great mysterious northern Power with its huge population and the illimitable possibilities of its future'. Such language suggested similar nervousness in British minds. Certainly, it was claimed that the Anglo-Russian Entente in no way committed Britain to 'sympathy with some features of Russian internal administration'.[15]

This battle between theologians was pushed into the background by the publication of the most famous of German academic manifestos — that of 'the ninety-three' in October 1914. This 'Manifesto of the Intellectuals of Germany' became a byword among British and French intellectuals for the subordination of German scholarship to the dictates of state policy. It had been drawn up by Ulrich von Wilamowitz-Moellendorff, doyen of German classical philology and a man in frequent contact with British colleagues. The original signatories included most leading German scholars, and after energetic propaganda by the historian Dietrich Schäfer there were finally about 4,000 signatures attached to the manifesto — as Fritz Fischer points out, virtually the whole German professoriate.[16] 'As representatives of Science and Art' the signatories protested 'to the civilised world against the lies and calumnies' with which the Allies had been 'endeavouring to stain the honour of Germany in her hard struggle for existence — a struggle which has been forced upon her'. The 'lies' included the idea of German responsibility for the war and the 'criminal' violation of Belgian neutrality and of international law, allegations of atrocities against the Belgians (except under 'direct necessity') and finally the claim of the Allies that in fighting German militarism they were not seeking to destroy German civilisation. 'Have faith in us', the signatories asked the people of neutral states. 'Believe that we shall carry on this war to the end as a civilised nation to whom the legacy of a Goethe, a Beethoven, and a Kant is just as sacred as its own hearths and homes.'[17]

There is little doubt that this manifesto did immense damage to the reputation of German scholarship, in neutral as well as Allied states. Certainly for those with ties to Germany it was 'the most painful experience of their lives to find men', whose names they had been 'long accustomed to revere, showing themselves so blindly and bitterly partisan in their judgements'. If one took German 'pamphlet literature as a whole' and looked in it 'for anything like the sense of proportion, the objectivity and balanced judgement of true science', it was 'conspicuously wanting', noted one Oxford scholar. Why were there 'so few traces of German science' in the manifesto of the ninety-three? This question was beginning to be asked in the United States as well. J. W. Burgess, a political scientist at Columbia University and one of the few defenders of Germany among leading American academics, had by 1915 condemned the conduct of German savants. Even before American entry to the war in 1917 the American university community had turned against German propaganda — the manifesto of 'the ninety-three' had been the final blow to any hopes of critical voices being raised in German universities.[18]

Not surprisingly, the explanation for this sad falling-off from the ideals of *Wissenschaft* depended greatly on the extent of sympathy with things German. The simplest interpretation was that German academics had momentarily been 'swept away by a national impulse'. Alternatively 'the moral guilt of good men' could be considered lesser if weighed against the 'false political' and 'religious creed' so prevalent in the world in which they lived. Or perhaps Germany was 'a noble nation for a time *gone wrong*'. The qualities of greatness remained but they were 'unhappily blended'.[19] But for those less kindly disposed towards Germany, the manifesto of 'the ninety-three' had a different explanation: the German scholar was 'a singularly guileless and credulous person, entirely without political or constitutional training, and ready, as a believer in 'divine right and passive obedience', obediently to sign any statement submitted to him by his superiors'.[20] This explanation offered by an Edinburgh historian was echoed by many others who now pointed to the status of German academics as civil servants.

Whatever the exact reason for their fierce support of official policy, German scholars had effectively destroyed the credibility of the image of 'two Germanys' by October 1914. As C. H. Herford noted sadly:

> The relation between the things we honour and the things we abhor in the Germany of to-day, is too intimate to permit either of them exclusively to dominate any one region or class. They often appear to co-exist as different aspects of the same mind. And whatever demarcation could be discerned ... before the war, the war itself has all but completely effaced.

Herford had come as close as was possible for a British scholar steeped in German culture to a critical assessment of the German professoriate's role in creating the dominant ideology of the Wilhelmine ruling elite. The 'glaring' defects of modern Germany were 'rooted in a kind of fundamental rightness and nobility' — one could still discern 'the root of idealism from which even that which proudly called itself 'realpolitik' drew not a little of its vital sap'.[21]

Herford had also noticed an 'incapacity to value, and even to understand the mentality of other nations', and this defect in German scholarship soon drew the attention of other sympathetic observers. W. J. Ashley, for example, had found certain 'disquieting features' in the 'mental attitude' even of scholars he greatly respected:

> In academic circles the legitimate pride in German science seemed sometimes to have become almost an obsession and to have had the effect of shutting out of sight what was being done in other lands. It hardly seemed to be realized that what Germany had to teach the western world in the way of thoroughness and method had already been pretty well learnt, and that there were intellectual qualities of almost equal value, qualities of lucidity and discrimination and balance, which could perhaps be better learnt elsewhere — even in despised France. There was a curious national self-satisfaction which failed to perceive that the great new ideas, the waves of intellectual inspiration within and without the realm of scholarship and research, which were affecting the minds of this generation all over the world, were now almost all of them coming from other directions than Germany.[22]

With such doubts being expressed by academic Germanophiles it was not surprising that British scholars less sympathetic to Germany should now turn and attack German scholarship itself. A notable example of this occurred at the annual conference of the Classical Association in 1915. Its

President, W. F. Ridgeway, Professor of Archaeology at Cambridge, earned great applause with his claim that German contempt for Britain was, 'in no small degree', due to the attitude 'of British scholars, theologians, and some scientists, with some few exceptions, towards everything German'. The fact was 'that for the last two generations British scholars, British theologians and British men of science' had 'aimed chiefly at being the first to introduce into this country the last thing said in Germany, even though that might be only the worthless thesis produced by some young candidate for his doctorate'. What was worse, 'no one dreamed of inquiring whether the statements of the savant were correct or his arguments valid'.[23]

There were, one suspects, academic sour grapes mixed in with traditional British mistrust of research on the German scale, in Ridgeway's address. He spent much of it listing the difficulties encountered in finding a publisher for his criticism of Mommsen's work. But at the Classical Association conference there was general agreement that it had been 'that mass of Teutonic learning' which had 'encumbered and almost crushed classical study' since 1870.[24] Even the classicist E. A. Sonnenschein, a man by no means unsympathetic to German scholarship, wrote of it as 'one of the idols before which too many people in this country — including the writer of this paper — have bowed down'. As one of a persecuted minority during wartime — those of German origin or with German-sounding names — Sonnenschein's apologetic tone was understandable. It was clear that anyone with doubts about German scholarship (or perhaps old scores to settle) now felt free to voice them openly. 'I'm glad to be rid of the German incubus', the Professor of English Literature at Oxford wrote to a French friend. 'It has done no good, for many years, to scholarship; — indeed, it has produced a kind of slave-scholarship, though there are still some happy exceptions.'[25]

Mixed in with this reaction there was a certain streak of anti-intellectualism. Usually this was confined to the more lurid wartime pamphlets with titles like *Kaiser, Krupp and Kultur*, but occasionally it showed through in more serious pieces. A good example of this was the article by L. P. Jacks, Principal of Manchester College, Oxford, and a Nonconformist theologian. As he told his American readers, there was 'something . . . now moving in the philosophical and theological heart of Britain which, if pressed into utterance, would say, 'No more Kant, no more Hegel, no more Strauss, no more Nietzsche, no more Harnack, no more Eucken — for me!' There was in this, Jacks admitted, 'some insularity', but there was also 'a great deal of human nature'. Faced with 'the hideous crime committed on Belgium', things German 'stood discredited in the British mind'. Clearly this included German scholarship, as in another article at this time Jacks rejoiced that the 'age of German footnotes is on the wane'.[26]

Such blanket condemnations were not typical of British scholars (at least in their public pronouncements), and theologians in particular generally defended German scholarship. 'Only ignorance can afford to mock at German culture', wrote a Cambridge theologian early in the war. 'The man who has no debt to it to-day has no great intellectual debt to anybody. The contribution of no other nation is so great, and that let us ever greatfully acknowledge.'[27] However, the question of the relationship of British and German theology had aroused sufficient controversy for Oxford University Press to commission a pamphlet in their series on wartime issues. Its author, W. B. Selbie, Congregationalist theologian and Principal of Mansfield College, Oxford, was in no way anti-German. In fact he had signed one of the neutrality manifestos in July 1914. Selbie was not one to deny British 'indebtedness to Germany'. German theologians had 'worked so assiduously and thoroughly in all the various fields', their scholarship was 'so exact and their speculation so bold and far-reaching' that their writings inevitably dominated the field. British students came back from Germany 'imbued with the German spirit and method; and full of admiration for teachers like Harnack and Hermann, Troeltsch and Jülicher, Johannes Weiss, Seeberg and Loofs'.

But even as sympathetic an observer as Selbie felt that there was 'some ground for the apprehension' that British theology was 'coming to depend too exclusively on work done in Germany', and that native scholars were not always being given credit 'for the excellent and original work' they did. The appearance of the manifesto of the German professors had only served to remind Selbie of shortcomings already apparent in German scholarship — and here he quoted from L. T. Hobhouse's *Democracy and Reaction* (1904):

> It is learning divorced from its social purpose, destitute of large and generous ideas, worse than useless as a guide in the problems of national life, smothering the humanities in cartloads of detail, unavoidable, but fatal to the intellect.[28]

What Hobhouse termed 'the Germanisation of the intellectual world' was clearly a matter of concern to academic liberals like Selbie. Hobhouse, as we shall see later, had long been fighting his own battle against the German-derived neo-Idealist philosophy taught in many British universities, but his talk of those 'vast Teutonic treatises' which took 'the heart out of the English student'[29] reveals that he too shared the academic prejudices of some of his more conservative colleagues.

Those who had always claimed to have doubted the massive dimensions of the German research industry now felt that, with the war, the time had come to reassert older British traditions of scholarship. Gilbert Murray, Professor of Greek at Oxford, felt that the difference between the German and the British approach to classical literature was simply that the Germans aimed 'more at knowing: we at feeling and understanding. They are the professionals, we are the amateurs . . . . We are always aiming at culture in Arnold's sense, not Bernhardi's, they are aiming at research or achievement'.[30] Clearly even the cult of the amateur could assist in Britain's war effort. No one needed to be in awe of 'the German mind'. It was, as the historian J. W. Allen noted, 'at once powerful and dull': it was 'remarkably comprehensive', it had 'a great power of grasping complicated detail and a great faculty for the wide generalisation', but it was still 'extraordinarily lacking in fineness of perception, in intellectual subtlety and in humour'. These deficiencies were so great 'as to render German comprehensiveness almost futile'. 'They account for the odd stupidity which marks almost all German work', Allen concluded.[31] What more was there to be said? Clearly, German pedantry was yet one more manifestation of *Schrecklichkeit*.

The heights to which anti-German sentiment among British scholars could go is illustrated by a letter to *The Times* in December 1914 by the eminent Professor of Assyriology at Oxford, A. H. Sayce. Hobhouse was willing to concede 'the element of disinterested drudgery' as the German contribution to the 'international division of labour' in scholarship, but Sayce denied even this 'faithful, unrepaying service of the hard dry fact', as Hobhouse called it.[32] In science 'none of the great names' was German. Apart from Goethe, there were no great names in German literature. Kant was 'more than half Scottish in origin', and Schiller 'a milk-and-water Longfellow'. The German scholar could 'laboriously count syllables and words, and pile up volumes of indices', he could 'appropriate other men's discoveries in the interests of 'culture''', but beyond this he produced 'only theories' which took 'no regard of facts', which, because they came from Germany, 'must be regarded as infallible'. Not content with condemning German researchers to an existence as 'intellectual 'hewers of wood and drawers of water'' for their colleagues overseas, Sayce finished by damning the Germans for being 'still what they were fifteen centuries ago, the barbarians who raided our ancestors and destroyed the civilisation of the Roman Empire'.[33]

This was as bad as the worst anti-English pronouncements of German professors, but there was little criticism of Sayce's letter in the press. One Oxford colleague described it as an outburst full of 'wild theories and inconsistencies' but also emphasised his 'acutest pain' at the 'detestable ends' to which German scholarship was now being directed. Another, who was later to be one of the first to call for the resumption of scholarly relations with Germany after the war, reminded the readers of *The Times* that science was international. 'It ought to be impossible to think of Newton without also thinking of Kepler; or of Pasteur without thinking of Koch', he wrote. In its way this was a reply in the spirit of those British astronomers one hundred years earlier who had refused to allow war to interrupt the exchange of information with French colleagues.[34] But this was 1914 and not 1813, and Professor Ray Lankester, who strongly supported Sayce's charges against German science, had the last word — the 'delusion' of German superiority in scientific research was simply due to 'the irresponsible gush of young men' lately back from German universities.[35]

There is more than a suggestion of academic knives being sharpened in all this. The rights and wrongs of German scholarship had become convenient ammunition for older feuds. But it is clear that there was a general sense of doubt about the state of German universities and scholarship induced by the shock of the war, even in the minds of those formerly most sympathetic to Germany. What greater contrast could there be than that between Michael Sadler's preface to Friedrich Paulsen's *The German Universities* (1906), mentioned in the previous chapter, and his wartime reflections on German education? In the first Sadler, while not uncritical of certain aspects of the German system, obviously believed that in education the truth lay 'somewhere between the German system and the English'. In another essay of 1912 he seemed even less critical of German methods. Nine years later, however, in a contribution to a symposium on *German Culture* (1915), Sadler strongly criticised the 'one-sided excellence' of German education:

> Its elaborate organisation, triumphantly enforced by the State, has weakened its moral independence . . . . German education has paid the penalty for going to excess in the use of methods which, if employed in moderation, are salutary and wise. Its long tradition of mental discipline has exposed it to influences which have preyed on its fairness of mind and perverted intellectual passion into partisanship. Its conceptions of the claims of the State has led it to neglect the duty of disinterested reflection by means of which, in the past, German scholars have done signal service to the cause of truth and to the scientific progress of the world.[36]

The *lehrfreiheit* of German scholars, on which Sadler had laid such stress in 1906, was now revealed as something which masked the subordination of German professors to the state.

Of course this raised the question of whether German scholars could still be considered worthy of membership of learned societies in Allied countries. In May 1915 King George had deprived the Kaiser, the Crown Prince of Prussia and other German princes of their garter knighthoods. Might not this be a precedent for depriving enemy scholars of their more lowly privileges? This was the conclusion of the academies of Paris and Brussels, but not of the British Academy or the Royal Society. Nor did German academies and learned societies, 'with inconsiderable exceptions', deprive British scholars of their membership.[37] As we shall see later, universities, in the northern cities of England especially, were not able to withstand pressure to dismiss professors of German origin but of British nationality (let alone those of German nationality). Even in Oxford the Warden of New College was forced to defend his inclusion of German names amongst those on the college memorial to war dead.[38] But perhaps the most celebrated case involved the German Celtic scholar Kuno Meyer.

Meyer was a Professor at the University of Berlin at the outbreak of war, but up until 1911 he had been Professor of Celtic at the University of Liverpool and after that time honorary professor. For most of the war period Meyer was a 'travelling professor' in the United States, a position which gave him opportunities for subtle propaganda on behalf of Germany (as it did for visitors from Britain). It was Meyer who published a letter from an Oxford scholar (F. C. Conybeare) extremely critical of British policy in 1914, and it was this which brought him to the attention of his British colleagues. Meyer had also made disparaging remarks about Britain's ability to withstand an invasion, in a letter to the Vice-Chancellor of Liverpool University. This, together with his remarks on the future loyalty of the Irish, was enough for the University Council to act. Meyer was deprived of his honorary professorship and condemned for 'acting as an agent of sedition in imputing treason to loyal Irish soldiers now prisoners in Germany'. When it became known that Casement was working amongst Irish prisoners of war, Meyer was accused of using his time in Britain to secretly prepare the ground for Irish rebellion. His trips to the Aran Islands to study their dialect seemed especially suspect in retrospect. A Cambridge Celtic scholar called for Meyer to be deprived of the freedom of Dublin and Cork, previously given in recognition of his services to Irish studies, and the University of Wales was only prevented from stripping Meyer of his honorary D.Litt. by the discovery that their charter did not empower them to withdraw a degree once granted. However, Meyer's name (unlike those of Wilhelm Ostwald and Eduard Meyer who both wrote wartime polemics against Britain) did not again appear in the University of Liverpool calendar until after the war.[39]

The question of the involvement of scholarly bodies in the war was also a matter of discussion. Although he himself became heavily involved in wartime propaganda for the Allies, Lord Bryce was at pains to stress the need for bodies like the British Academy to chart a course of strict neutrality. In his Presidential Address to the Academy in 1916 he suggested that its policy should be not to let the war 'disturb the even tenor' of its activities. Meetings and public lectures carried on as before, the only change being suspension of the election of 'foreign men of letters' as 'Corresponding Fellows' — as Bryce put it, 'lest the judgement of their merits might be, or might be possibly seen to be, influenced by the political relations in which the country stands'. The more learned bodies were 'kept outside the passions of war the better for them and the nations', he concluded.[40] The difficult course which the Academy had to steer in wartime is suggested by an incident involving the French anti-war writer Romain Rolland. Originally invited to speak before the Academy during the celebrations for the tercentenary of Shakespeare's death in 1916, Rolland was asked later not to come presumably because of his growing notoriety after the publication of an English edition of his *Above the Battle* (1914). In the event the Academy's Book of *Homage to Shakespeare* (1916) had no Austrian or German contributors (the latter of whom especially had done so much for Shakespearean studies) although it had Chinese, Armenian, Indian, Burmese and Persian contributors.[41]

However, some British scholars were not satisfied with the cautious path urged by Bryce. Professor Ridgeway, whom we have already seen castigating academic Germanophiles, was not a man to forgo an opportunity to comment on issues of the day. An 'address of conventional order', he told the Classical Association, would be 'singularly out of place' during wartime. Instead he launched into an impassioned plea for conscription, citing the evidence of Athenian democracy to support his case (as the Angellites had used it for an opposite case before the war). Where Bryce had decided to say nothing in his address which might cause pain to a member of the British Academy reading it in 'ten or twenty years hence', Ridgeway considered that normal scholarly activities should be suspended for the course of the war. To 'hold annual meetings of societies as if the conditions were in no wise abnormal would . . . be highly immoral' since it could only convince 'the leading minds of Germany, not merely soldiers and politicians but the professorial and intellectual classes . . . that England was so besotted by cowardice, luxury and sloth, that she would fall an easy prey to any vigorous martial race'.[42]

Allowing for the special bees in Ridgeway's bonnet — conscription, the role of Quakers and Nonconformists in the peace movement, eugenics and the 'alien menace' (a thinly disguised form of anti-Semitism)[43] — his idea of mobilising scholars in the nation's cause was widely held. One of his successors as President of the Classical Association called upon members to do 'a useful piece of war work' for which there was a 'definite call' — namely, the creation of 'well-informed public opinion on the Greek situation'. By this Professor Ure meant support for the pro-Allied Greek Premier Venizelos against the allegedly pro-German King Constantine.[44] The dividing line between creating informed public opinion and disseminating propaganda was clearly a fine one. Yet classical scholarship did continue through the war years, despite Ridgeway's call for its suspension, and the *Classical Quarterly* (on whose Management Board Ridgeway sat) continued to publish summaries of important German research. This is perhaps a convenient point to turn to consider two other disciplines — philosophy and history — which were both affected by the war, though in different ways.

CHAPTER 2

Philosophers and the War

The war provided the most delicious opportunities for the philosophers. They are all agreed that the wickedness or virtue of a nation depends upon the metaphysical creed of its professors of philosophy, and that Germany is an awful example of the effect of the wrong creed. If they are opponents of Kant and Hegel, they find in these two the precursors of Bismarck, Treitschke, Ludendorff and Co .... If, like the bulk of our most patriotic instructors in mental and moral science, they have been in the habit of praising Kant and Hegel, they have a more delicate task to perform. They have to explain that these great and good men belonged to the old Germany which we all regret, and that the abandonment of them in favour of Nietzsche was what caused the invasion of Belgium.

Bertrand Russell, 'Philosophy and Virtue', *The Athenaeum*, 2 May 1919

What was the effect of the war on British philosophers? In some respects it was minimal. As the Professor of Philosophy at Birmingham put it:

Those whose business it is to read philosophical serials even in time of war must have been struck by the spirit of calm detachment with which the great problems of thought are discussed as though there were no such thing as war and politics. This is magnificent and is as it should be.[1]

Even if this sounds more like an air of unreality than a 'spirit of calm detachment', it may have helped G. F. Stout, a supporter of the war, and G. E. Moore, a member of the anti-war Union of Democratic Control, to continue to edit together the journal *Mind*. In its pages, throughout the war, abstracts of articles in German periodicals continued to appear — any falling-off in their number probably being due to difficulties in obtaining 'enemy' material rather than an intellectual embargo. Likewise in the *Proceedings of the Aristotelian Society* the name of the eminent philosopher and psychologist Wilhelm Wundt continued to appear as a 'Corresponding Member' despite the publication of his *Die Nationen und ihre Philosophie* (1915) which described the shallowness of British philosophy in the most impolite terms.

Some philosophers like Bernard Bosanquet, the leading British exponent of philosophical Idealism, eschewed public debate on the war, although privately he was in no doubt as to the rightness of the Allied cause. He refused to participate in organising a manifesto to represent the views of British philosophers 'who on the whole adhered to the tradition of great German idealists', being 'more desirous of shunning controversy' and spending his remaining years (he was 66 in 1914) on problems of logic.

43

He had 'made up his mind that the supreme duty of the non-combatant was to use his talents and opportunities . . . to the best advantage in his own field as far as the general distraction allowed'.[2] This reaction might be seen as a way of relieving the emotional strain of war, but it was also an indication of the dilemma of the philosopher in wartime. After science and mathematics, philosophy is one of the most cosmopolitan of disciplines. The tension between patriotism and any ideal of international scholarship was less marked than in the case of, say, historians, yet British philosophers were second only to historians as publicists for the Allied cause. While Bosanquet and the Oxford Idealist F. H. Bradley corresponded learnedly on 'the nature of play' through the war years, their colleague Sir Henry Jones, Professor of Moral Philosophy at Glasgow, wore himself out giving rousing speeches on recruiting drives up and down the country. An article by Jones with the title 'Why We Are Fighting' gives us some idea of what these might have been like:

> Our country can clothe itself in the splendid strength of the rectitude of its cause, and it will put the stern might of conscience into its strokes . . . . *This war has come upon us as a Duty*, and duty leaves no loose options either to a good man or an honourable nation.[3]

What greater contrast could there be than in the career of C. D. Broad, a man much younger than Jones, but one with an acuter sense of self-criticism? In a remarkable short autobiography he described forty years after the war his state of mind in 1914. He was, he wrote, neither a 'conscientious objector' nor a fervent supporter of war:

> . . . even if I had been convinced that it was my duty to enlist, I have little doubt that my physical cowardice would have led me to try to evade it. And even if I had been convinced that it was my duty to refuse to take part in the war, I have little doubt that my moral cowardice, in the face of popular obloquy and the disapproval of friends and relatives would have led me to conceal my conviction. I suppose that if no other way out of the dilemma had presented itself, I should have finally enlisted under the pressure of public opinion in the circles which immediately surrounded me.

But an alternative did present itself 'by which appearances were saved and 'honour', though 'rooted in dishonour', was satisfied'. Broad found work at the university where he had been teaching (St. Andrews) in the laboratory of the Chemistry Professor who was engaged in munitions research.[4]

At a less personal level, searchings of conscience are suggested in a lecture on the sensitive subject of 'War and Hatred' given by G. F. Stout, Professor of Logic and Metaphysics at St. Andrews under whom Broad had worked. At this time (1915) an official commission under Lord Bryce was investigating alleged German atrocities against Belgian civilians, and Stout noted that he tended to:

... skip such passages in the newspapers as those which describe German atrocities in Belgium. I refuse to read even official reports. I put myself off hoping that in the main they are not true, or that they are greatly exaggerated, or that they can be explained as to cast another light on them. Yet I have been gradually forced to believe in their reality by evidence which I cannot reasonably resist.

His reluctance Stout marked down to 'circumstances and education' — a scholar was singularly unfitted to comment on political affairs:

Persons of this type do very well so long as they live a sheltered life, spent, for instance, in study. But they are unfit to grapple effectively with certain forms of evil or really to appreciate their nature, or fully to recognize their existence.

While this fitted the popular image of the unworldly scholar (a role assumed readily by many academics), Stout had a more specific target in mind: those 'who, though they are by nature fully susceptible of angry sentiments, suppress them on principle, because they regard them as wrong and especially because they are afraid of giving way to hatred'. This was coded language for describing those, like Bertrand Russell, who refused to suspend critical judgement for the duration of the war. Stout, as the author of a standard *Manual of Psychology* (1899) and a pioneer in the new discipline, was ready to offer professional advice: 'some developed forms of the primitive emotion of anger' were 'necessary and right'. This meant 'resentment or righteous indignation' rather than 'hatred or malevolence', since as long as anger was not blind there was 'no general limit to its strength, persistence or intensity'. Such was 'enlightened anger ... free from the various forms of blindness which characterize hatred'.[5]

This injunction to set aside the precept to love one's enemy — it could after all never be 'a practical guide amid the stress and strain of daily life' — was a favourite argument of the more philosophically-minded apologists for the Allied cause. Whether or not retaliations were being called for, the concept of 'righteous indignation', 'that stern and disciplined mood in which the best of civilised men' might 'be expected to fight against injustice and oppression', fitted the official British presentation of its entry to the war as a defence of Belgian neutrality.[6] To argue, as Stout did, that it might 'sometimes be better to run the risk of being actuated by hatred than to run the risk of not feeling due resentment' was nicely attuned to the priorities of total war. For one thing it justified the official injunction to 'love your friends and hate your enemies', as Stout put it. It also provided ammunition against critics of official policy. In 'opposing the natural tendency to regard the faults all on one side, that of the enemy', they tended 'to run to the opposite extreme' and to make out that it was 'their own side' which was 'wholly or mainly or at least equally to blame in cases where an impartial consideration of the evidence would show the contrary'.[7]

This is an argument made familiar by its repeated use through the years, whether in politics or football. Bertrand Russell's answer to his old philosophy tutor (he had studied under Stout in his fourth year at Cambridge) is also familiar. As a critic of British foreign policy at least ten years before the outbreak of the war, Russell had long been defending himself against the charge of seeming to emphasise the faults on his own side and saying little 'about the faults on the other side'. The first was necessary because these faults were 'ignored by our compatriots' and the second 'because every newspaper and every professor throughout the country' was 'making them known'. Moreover, it was 'more profitable' to be conscious of one's own faults than the faults of the enemy: 'we can amend our faults if we become aware of them, whereas we can only increase hatred on both sides by proclaiming the faults of the enemy', Russell concluded.[8]

What, then, of the darker side of human nature? Russell, appearances to the contrary, was no stranger to this. As he wrote to his mistress in June 1915: 'The non-resistance people I know ... are so Sunday-schooly — one feels they don't know the volcanic side of human nature'.[9] He was aware, too, that his pleas for balanced judgement and for rationality in wartime might seem mere logic-chopping to some. 'I am willing to admit that disinterestedness itself may become a passion', he wrote in answer to an American critic:

> When a German is accused of having murdered a baby, and it turns out that he murdered a boy of twelve, I almost forget his crime in the desire to prevent injustice. I am conscious that if I belonged to a neutral nation I should reprobate the spirit of Germany wholeheartedly; but I am restrained by disgust at the orgy of self-righteousness that has swept over the British nation.[10]

Russell returned to this theme in 'Justice in War-Time: An Appeal to the Intellectuals of Europe', an article published in neutral Switzerland. In this Russell contrasted Leibniz's 'war in which philosophy takes no interest' with the present when 'philosophers, professors and intellectuals generally' undertook 'willingly to provide their respective governments with those ingenious distortions and those subtle untruths' by which it could be made to appear that 'all good' was on one side and 'all wickedness' on the other. How could one talk of 'moral reprobation'? It was 'nothing but an embodiment of hatred', and hatred was 'a mechanical product of biological instinct'. Righteous indignation merely prevented one having 'humane feelings towards the enemy' or 'nascent sympathy for his suffering'. And how could one talk of the war as a contest of Right over

Might (the two words were always capitalised)? Whatever philosophers might say, it was 'not being fought for any rational end' but simply because, 'at first, the nations wished to fight', and now because they were 'angry and determined to win victory'. 'Everything else' was 'idle talk, artificial rationalizing of instinctive actions and passions'.[11]

Russell's description of the belligerent states as dogs fighting in the street could not fail to infuriate every patriotic philosopher,[12] but at least they could console themselves that the weight of numbers was on their side. Among philosophers only the Pragmatist (one of the few in a British university) F. C. S. Schiller echoed Russell's scepticism as to the 'reputed influence of *pure* thought on human action'. In a review of John Dewey's *German Philosophy and Politics* (1916) tucked away in the pages of *Mind*, Schiller noted that this war, like all others, was really concerned with self-defence, property and national existence, rather than 'philosophic ideas'. It was these which were:

> ... the primary motives that send men to the battlefields, though at various times governments have eked them out by appeals to honour, glory, loyalty, religion, plunder and (now) 'nationality'. All this was as true of the Germans as of the other combatants.[13]

But although critical of British policy, Schiller (like G. E. Moore) never openly campaigned against the war. An obscure review might go unnoticed, but not participation in bodies like the Union of Democratic Control or the No-Conscription Fellowship.

However, the belief that wars involve 'philosophic ideas' proved durable for all Russell's or Schiller's scepticism. Thus we can find another British philosopher writing over twenty years later of another world war that it was 'as perhaps never before in the whole course of history, one between philosophies which differ fundamentally as to what man is and what he is here for'.[14] Philosophy and philosophers were in the front-line in 1914 as in 1939, although the search for the intellectual antecedents of conflict took a slightly different form in each case. In 1914 the dead historian Treitschke, Hegel and General von Bernhardi constituted the unholy trinity, with Nietzsche in reserve for those who wished to leave nothing to chance. The net could be cast even wider if, like L. T. Hobhouse, one was out of sympathy with most current trends in philosophy. For Hobhouse the most disturbing feature was the 'profound change of intellectual' and even 'of moral outlook'. The Victorians had believed in 'law and reason'; now the younger generation had 'come in large measure to believe in violence, and in impulse, emotion or instinct'. This erosion of values had been unwittingly begun by Victorian science which had destroyed both 'the ethical edifice' and 'the ideological superstructure' of Christianity, though it had intended to preserve the first. Now science itself had been eroded from within so that it no longer provided a basis for 'a mechanical view of the world', and biological theory was being 'interpreted as a justification for force and self-assertion'.

Who was to blame for this 'theory of revolt against law and morals', against 'intellectual' and 'moral restraint'? Hobhouse singled out the Pragmatists, like the American William James, Bergson and especially Nietzsche, 'a Pragmatist in everything but name'. These were the thinkers who emphasised 'the feebleness of reason, the arbitrary and unreal character of scientific law, the primariness of impulse, the superiority of instinct to rational purpose, the glorification of movement without vision'. They had pushed man 'back from reason to will' and in so doing had encouraged him to go back 'one step further on the line of retrogression from will to instincts, emotions and impulses' which man shared with 'brute creation'.[15] Hobhouse had put his finger on the reorientation of social thought charted much later by H. Stuart Hughes in *Consciousness and Society* (1958). The war seemed to confirm all his fears. As he wrote to his sister in the first month of war: 'All one's hopes for social and political progress are shattered once and for all . . . . We may write *Finis* to our work, and hope that civilization may rise again elsewhere'.[16]

Such acute pessimism matched that of Bertrand Russell as he contemplated civilised nations fighting like dogs in the street — James, as we have already seen, might have been less surprised at the 'instinct of pugnacity' (he had died in 1910). Supporters and opponents of official policy alike found alarming 'the naked assertion of the right of self-affirmation in the line that instinct and interest' prompted. Russell and Schiller believed, however, that no great principle (apart from national self-interest) was involved. Hobhouse, and others like him, pointed to the 'struggle of ideas underlying the great war'. While German philosophers raged against *Manchestertum* — the perfidious individualism of the British — their British colleagues discovered 'a deeper design, which was nothing less than the overthrow of the moral foundation on which Western civilization has been built up'.[17] Hobhouse had found that by immersing himself in the writings of Hegel, Nietzsche and Treitschke, 'reading their theories day by day to the refrain of the war news', he had become far less sceptical about relations between the academic and the practical'. And later in the war after a Zeppelin raid he noted:

> In the bombing of London I had just witnessed the visible and tangible outcome of a false and wicked doctrine, the foundations of which lay ... in the book before me .... In the Hegelian theory of the god-state, all that I had witnessed lay implicit.[18]

In 1914 Hegel's state rather than Nietzsche's 'blond beast' was at the centre of attention. It was widely believed that, 'more than anything else', it was 'the German theory of the State' which lay 'at the bottom of German aggression'.[19] The main features of this theory, repeated so often that they came to have an incantatory quality, were conveniently summarised by Hobhouse:

> The deification of the State and the belief that it is the supreme type of human organisation, the contempt for democracy, the unreal identification of liberty with law which simply puts every personal right at the mercy of the legislator, the upholding of war as a necessity, the disregard of humanity, the denial of the sanctity of treaties and of international law . . . .

It was this theory which Hobhouse found in all essentials in Hegel's *Rechtsphilosophie*. When it was combined with the destruction of 'the moral restraints against which power chafed' under the impact of Nietzsche, the results were disastrous:

> . . . while elsewhere the disruption of moral bonds produced political, literary, or artistic eccentricities which in the end were bound to correct themselves, in Germany it removed the feeble barriers which stood between an avalanche and a peaceful world.

Only in Germany had the twentieth-century revolt against reason created a state of mind which made for war.

This analysis of just where Germany had 'gone wrong' foreshadowed many of the later explanations offered for the rise of Nazism. Germany had apparently reacted against the ideas of the eighteenth-century enlightenment which 'sprang up in France, England, America and countries in sympathy with them'. Instead she 'developed a new variant in civilization — in point of fact a new religion', Hegelianism, 'the first completely reasoned answer to the democratic and humanitarian ideal'. Hobhouse was able to trace a line of descent from the 'humanitarianism' of Kant through the 'medium' of Fichte's 'idealistic nationalism' to Hegel's state philosophy.[20] Where Hobhouse led, others followed, and soon not even Goethe was spared the attentions of seekers after the source of German wickedness.[21] In later times the list would be extended even further to include Luther and other figures. In 1914 as in 1939 few remembered, as did a philosopher at University College, London, that it was unreasonable 'to hold anyone responsible, not only for his real views, but also for other people's distortions of them'. These were brave words, coming as they did in the course of a defence of Nietzsche.[22]

For armchair philosophers Nietzsche was a godsend. In a pamphlet entitled *The Germans: What They Covet* one Oxford historian offered a popular account of the philosopher couched in 'homely language':

This Superman was the special invention of a philosopher called Nietzsche, who spent his life railing against the 'superstition', as he called it, of Christianity, and against the virtues of pity, mercy and love, which are, he said, the most distinctive doctrines of that superstition. You need not remember anything else about Nietzsche except that he went stark staring mad before he died. But while he was going mad (and it would only be charitable to suppose that he was never very sane), he contrived to instil a good deal of his poisonous doctrine into those he bit.[23]

Small wonder that an enterprising bookseller in the Strand (no doubt with many unsold copies of Oscar Levy's translation of Nietzsche still on his hands) put a sign in his window proclaiming the conflict to be 'the 'Euro-Nietzschean' war'. Nietzsche, as Clive Bell remembered after the war, was a popular target for almost everyone,[24] but not so Hegel.

In 1914 what has been called 'Hegelianism modified by Anglo-Saxon caution' still held sway in British universities. Although by that time there were signs that the ground was shifting, the names of Bernard Bosanquet and F. H. Bradley still commanded respect. For 'philosophers generally they were 'the dominant figures even to those who opposed them''.[25] Theirs was a tradition of thought closely tied to Hegel; any wholesale condemnation of German philosophy was clearly dangerous. The task of a British Idealist or neo-Hegelian, like J. H. Muirhead, was thus to rescue what was worthwhile in the German philosophical tradition — anything up to the time of Hegel, perhaps even as far as Fichte. In his book *German Philosophy in Relation to the War* (1915) Muirhead set out to do just this: to prove that Hegelianism had been superseded by other less noble ideals in Germany; to prove Hegel innocent of the charges made against him; and to argue, as another philosopher put it, that there was 'indeed no true philosopher whose teaching can without violence be made to serve as a basis to the superstructure raised by Pan-German theorists'.[26] Whether Fichte could also be rescued from the charge of being an exponent of racist imperialism was a matter of debate.[27] But the rescue of Hegel was a matter of life and death for some philosophers.

Instead of the 'continuous development' of German philosophy from Hegel's 'great constructive effort of thought' to the present (as Hobhouse might have seen it, though in less flattering terms), Muirhead pointed to 'a reaction — a great rebellion and apostasy' after 1831, the year of Hegel's death. A reaction had set in when, 'going along with material expansion and the devotion to the special sciences it evoked', there arose 'a philosophy which sought to invert the old order and to read body and matter where it had read mind and spirit'. This new materialist school was at first 'content to rest its ethics on the humanistic tradition it had inherited from Idealism', but soon the latter 'had shrunk to little more than a hesitating note' and had fallen 'into the background in the popular mind'. When Social Darwinist thought came to Germany, the 'seed fell on ground prepared by a quarter century of materialist thought', of which Ernest Haeckel's *Riddle of the Universe* (1899) was perhaps the best-known example. Instead of being seen 'as only one among other agencies in development', the 'struggle for existence' had been 'exalted into the position of the supreme law of life'.[28]

Clearly Muirhead blamed not German Idealism and its conjunction with modern anti-materialist thought, but rather Materialism itself, especially when tainted by Social Darwinism. But did this explain why Germany was so different? Hobhouse thought not:

> Good philosophic idealists among us go about trying to prove that the reaction in Germany is modern and represents a sad falling-off from the idealism of Hegel. But the truth is that Hegel is the father and by long odds the serious champion of everything reactionary in the nineteenth century.[29]

To this Muirhead could only reply by drawing attention to the 'good' Hegel who, like Burke, had merely reacted against the anarchic individualism of the French Revolution. Hegel had 'felt that the time had come to vindicate the reality of the State as the 'substance' of the individual, family and national life'. He had been 'further convinced that justice could only be done in the unity of the State by a personal head as in a modern constitutional monarchy'. As for the claim that Hegel was the philosopher of Prussian militarism, there was textual evidence to show that he placed great emphasis on 'art, science, religion — all that goes to make ... the good life — for the full development of which the State' was the 'essential condition'.[30]

The anti-Hegelians, although fewer in number (at least among professional philosophers), seem to have had the better of the argument — not least since Muirhead's position was essentially defensive. It was also easier for some to accept that a German victory 'would be a world-wide advertisement for the State-philosophy of Hegel and its offshoots',[31] than to read the philosopher's work. But it also seemed that the bright young men of philosophy (mostly from Cambridge) were rejecting Idealism, and with it Hegel, as old-fashioned. Muirhead, Bradley and Bosanquet were of a generation which had been brought up with Victorian certainties — a belief in progress and western civilization, if not in orthodox Christianity. Russell and G. E. Moore, who started the Cambridge attack on Idealism in the 1890s, had both been born a generation later — time enough for them to have reacted, especially in rationalist and scientific Cambridge, against many of the values implicit in Idealism. C. D. Broad, a younger man who attended Russell's lectures at Trinity College, Cambridge, caught the mood:

The reactions of the clever young men following able and inspiring leaders, in an exciting attack on the orthodoxy of their immediate predecessors, are inevitably accompanied by a pleasant glow of intellectual contempt and *quasi*-moral indignation. We felt this strongly about such old fogies as Bradley and Bosanquet, to whom we must have appeared insufferably uppish and superficial; and we were no doubt often highly deficient in understanding and appreciation of what they had taught and of their reasons for it.[32]

The reaction against Idealism was also in some ways a reaction of Cambridge against Oxford, since Idealism was very much a product of the latter university. Edward Caird, T. H. Green and R. L. Nettleship had made Balliol a centre of the newly imported German ideas in the mid-nineteenth century. Later leading British Idealist philosophers — Bradley, Bosanquet, Muirhead, H. H. Joachim, D. G. Ritchie, William Wallace, J. A. Smith — were educated at Oxford where some of them also taught. Except for J. S. Mackenzie, and perhaps W. R. Sorley, the Cambridge Idealists were fewer in number and moved further from Hegelian orthodoxy. As Broad noted, 'Cambridge . . . had always been rather aloof from the current orthodoxy of Oxford and the Scottish universities'.[33] How far, then, was the reaction against Idealism a consequence of the war?

One recent assessment of the impact of the war is rather dismissive:

. . . [it] did not provoke in philosophy profound changes which echo on in subsequent years . . . . It may be that the xenophobia which induced worthy citizens to persecute dachshunds and German waiters in 1914 does have something to do with subsequent contempt in Anglo-Saxon philosophy for Hegelian idealism. But it is easy enough to demonstrate that an argued philosophical basis for such contempt existed at least a decade before the outbreak of war in 1914.[34]

This is certainly true in the sense that as early as 1899 G. E. Moore had attacked Idealist ethical theory in *The Nature of Judgement* and Russell had followed a few years later with criticism of Idealist metaphysics. However, two points need to be noted. Firstly, Oxford was still dominated by Idealism (even if Cambridge was not) in 1914; indeed, it had only just won its battle against an older, antithetical tradition. Using the evidence of past examination papers, G. G. Mure has pointed out that the logic of 'Aristotle, Bacon and Mill' formed 'a nucleus' which dwindled 'very slowly before the Idealist war of attrition until we reach the period of the Great War'.[35]

Secondly, we can say that the war, even if it did not 'provoke . . . profound changes', at least encouraged them. Indeed, the sceptical commentator previously cited appears to admit as much when he concedes that perhaps it could be 'more than insignificant speculation to suggest that the blood-letting of 1914–18 really had made if difficult to take seriously the idea that reality was a harmonious whole tending towards perfection'.[36] At least one Idealist philosopher, Sir James Black Baillie of Aberdeen, had his 'belief in Hegelian world-reason ... so deeply shaken as to be no longer susceptible of justification'. Under the meaningless destruction of world war he turned from 'optimistic idealism' to the study of human nature in an attempt to explain what had happened. This philosophical bankruptcy was what the Pragmatist F. C. S. Schiller had pointed to when he noted that the war had 'revealed that the actual world was a very different thing from the cosmic order' which Idealists had 'constructed in their minds'.[37]

The coincidence of attacks on Idealism and the war is particularly noticeable in the field of political theory. *The Metaphysical Theory of the State* (1918), Hobhouse's counterblast to Bosanquet's *Philosophical Theory of the State* (1899), appeared during wartime. Although Hobhouse had taken issue strongly with Idealist social and political thought from the time of the Boer War onwards, it was the war with Germany, as we have seen, which provided him with the opportunity to mount a systematic attack which would be noticed by a wider public. Hobhouse the philosophical Realist and political Liberal had found the conservative, not to say reactionary, implications of Bosanquet's writings deeply disturbing. The belief that 'the ideal' was 'realized in the actual world and in particular in the world of organised society' — that in fact that the social world was 'an incarnation or expression of the ideal' — meant to Hobhouse that there could be 'no question ... of realizing an ideal by human effort. We are already living in the ideal'.[38] The implicit quietism in such a belief was suggested by the title of one of Bradley's essays, 'My Station and its Duties' (1876). Even a later writer, far more sympathetic to Bradley than Hobhouse, notes:

> In political matters he was deeply conservative and reactionary .... Bradley was the implacable enemy of all utilitarian or liberal teaching; he could not abide pacifism or generalized humanitarian sentiment, and any belief in the natural equality of man or in the inviolability of life (whether political or religious in inspiration) he regarded as 'sentimental', 'degenerate', and 'disgusting' ....[39]

During the war, however, it was the Idealist view of the state 'in its external relations' which aroused most comment. Hobhouse, for example, felt that Idealism, in its confusing of the ideal and the actual, rested on 'mere generalisations of customs and institutions' which happened to be 'familiar'. Thus it set 'the State above moral criticism', constituted 'war as a necessary incident in its existence', condemned 'humanity' and repudiated the idea of a league of nations to maintain the peace. In short, Hobhouse concluded, 'we see in it a theory admirably suited to the period of militancy and regimentation in which we find ourselves'.[40] This last point hardly did justice to the subtleties of the Idealist position, but there was more than a hint of fatalistic acceptance of war in comments by one of its leading exponents:

> And what about war? It is certain to my mind, that evil and suffering must be permanent in the world, because man is a self-contradictory being, in an environment to which he can never be adapted, seeing that at least his own activity is always transforming it. And in principle there can be no reason for treating war as an exceptional case, as if presided over by a special devil apart from every other form of wrong. Neither the possibility of eradicating war, nor the incidental good that comes of it, can reasonably be discussed, as they commonly are, apart from the general problem of evil in the world. While man has a conscience, and things he values above life, and yet his conscience is liable to err, the root of war exists. Issues may arise between group and group which cannot be compromised. Within the state itself which is cited as the convincing analogy for a universal reign of law, both civil war and individual rebellion remain possible.[41]

An extreme example of what Hobhouse saw as the confusion of the real and ideal can be found in the attempts of Idealist philosophers to explain the slaughter on the Western Front in terms of good arising out of evil. An address by the Waynflete Professor of Moral and Metaphysical Philosophy to a conference on 'Progress and History' in 1916, the year of the battles on the Somme, can be taken as representative:

> This war is not an accident, nor an outburst of subterranean forces, but the act and deed of human will, and being so it cannot be merely evil . . . . Primarily and principally what is taking place, is a tremendous revelation of the potencies which in our nature — in that which makes us men — have escaped our notice and therefore, because unseen or ignored, working in the dark, have not yet been drawn upon or utilized. There has been and is still going on, an enormous increase of self-knowledge. At first this seems wholly an opening up of undreamt-of evil. Side by side there has come to us a parallel revelation of undreamt-of good. I must bear witness to my conviction that we are beholding a tremendous inrush or uprush of good into man and his world.

As rhetoric this was little different from the emotionally uplifting writings of historians with little conception of the intricacies of Hegelian thought. But the Waynflete professor, in denying the charge that such analysis was mere 'sentimental optimism', could claim that it was consistent with the Idealist belief in 'eternal progress'. The war was 'in its essence a victory over evil' since 'nothing' was 'wholly evil'. War, as Hegel had shown, should be accepted as giving rise directly to good.[42] War like tragedy had its part to play in human history, F. H. Bradley's younger brother noted. 'When I ask myself whether I wish for the total disappearance of war', he wrote in 1915, 'I answer 'Yes', if or when, uninterrupted peace can perform the office and generate the good of war'.[43] For someone with little sympathy for Idealism, like F. C. S. Schiller, such arguments seemed as meaningless as the war itself. The 'rational order of human affairs was shattered before their eyes and the belief that thought' controlled 'man's feelings' and determined his acts 'should have been among the first of the illusions swept away in the wreckage of war', but still the Idealists 'insisted on finding ideal reasons to which to attribute the catastrophe'.[44]

A more savage attack on Idealist political theory was launched in May 1916 at a joint meeting of the Aristotelian Society, the Oxford Philosophical Society and the Mind Association. In a symposium on 'The Nature of the State in View of its External Relations' Russell and two younger political philosophers, G. D. H. Cole (then a Fellow of Magdalen College, Oxford) and C. Delisle Burns (a University Extension lecturer), attacked the idea of a benevolent state resting on the consent of its citizens. At a time of mass death and military conscription the state seemed merely 'a collection of elderly middle-class gentlemen in control of power, gambling with the lives of their fellows'.[45] It was the 'intolerable' theories of 'Mr. Bosanquet or any Prusso-phil philosopher', Cole claimed, which denied the role of the 'individual citizen or the functional association' in the state. As the dilemma of the German socialists in 1914 had shown, men were 'bound together not by political or even national ties alone, but also by non-political bonds' which were 'no less compelling' in the obligations they imposed. Cole, as something of an *enfant terrible* and as a guild socialist, was concerned to cut the state down to size. It did not 'exhaust either the individuality or the organisable individuality of its citizens', nor was it 'greater than its citizens'; the state could not use people 'as mere pawns in its own game'. But it was also clear that the sovereignty of the state was relative in the sense that it was circumscribed by other states.[46]

Burns, who in the interwar period was to be a leading advocate of the League of Nations, followed a similar line of attack. Instead of Bosanquet's conception of the state as the 'supreme community', it was (judging by results rather than intentions) 'in its external relations ... obstructive to moral action'. There was thus a clear need for a world '*political* complex', and not just a belief in the 'sentimental unity of mankind', to assist the resolution of 'moral issues' between states 'by the use of moral criteria'.[47] This was unexceptional until Russell, who was by then involved in the No-Conscription Fellowship, tied the hopes of a new international order to more dangerous advocacy (at least, that seemed to be the implication) of resistance to state authority. Until the authority of the state over its citizens was questioned it was difficult to see a 'way by which each State could yield up a portion of its sovereignty to some international authority'.[48] Two months later Russell was fined in London 'for statements likely to prejudice the recruiting and discipline of His Majesty's forces'. Cole, however, was a relatively inactive member of the No-Conscription Fellowship and his attitude to conscientious objection was, as we shall see, equivocal. Burns worked in the Ministry of Reconstruction (1917–19), the Intelligence Division of the Ministry of Labour (1919–20), and, according to Margaret Cole, in M.I.5 during the war.[49] On the question, therefore, of the connection between thought and action, about which Russell had been so sceptical, the record is a rather contradictory one.

Russell's contribution to the symposium predictably attracted the most attention. In it he was concerned to tear away the 'mythology' in Idealist political theory which talked of the state 'as though it were an actual entity, something remote and god-like, vastly superior to its citizens and deserving of a quasi-adoration none of them deserve'. Such talk was 'mere superstition':

> The orders given by the State are in fact given by actual men, the purposes of the State are the purposes of certain people in office. There is nothing superhuman about these people. In most ages and in most countries they are composed of very common clay .... For this reason it must often happen that the purposes of the State are such as cannot commend themselves to men who have more humanity or more insight than most of their contemporaries. Such men, if they have courage, may easily find themselves forced to resist the State; any theory which would make it their duty to submit in spite of adverse individual judgement would take away something of human dignity and independence; it would savour of oriental despotism, and if successful would prevent the best men from growing to their full moral stature. The State embodies the wisdom of average men, and its institutions are clogged with the superstitions of the past. Those in whom any new wisdom is growing up, in whose minds the seeds of some future good is germinating, cannot but find themselves in greater or lesser degree out of harmony with established authority. For this reason, if for no other, the duty of obedience to the State cannot be made absolute.[50]

There is more than a hint of intellectual superiority in this, which critics were quick to seize upon,[51] but more importantly this extract confirms the impression that Russell and Bosanquet were speaking different languages, to their mutual incomprehension. For Russell the 'essence of the State' was 'the organisation of force':

> The main purposes of States in their external relations are the exploitation of what are called under-developed countries and the successful assertion of claims by the use of force against other States. These are precisely the purposes of highwaymen.

Bosanquet, on the other hand, approached 'the thought of the state':

> ... through familiarity with long self-sacrificing lives spent in service, or on behalf of the State, of the children of the poor, or from recollections of the change and opening of people's minds, within my own experience, from stolidity and resistance to welcome and intelligence in such matters as sanitation.

With his experience of work for the Charity Organization Society, Bosanquet felt able to claim that in such people the idea of the state was 'awakening'. By nature a reconciler of conflicting viewpoints, Bosanquet's reply to Russell was characteristically courteous. However, there must have been much in what Russell wrote which seemed repugnant to him, earnest Victorian that he was. Russell was of a generation which was influenced by the 'new psychology' of James and McDougall (and which was beginning to be influenced by Freud). This, as we shall see later, underlay his belief that the masses, craving security, were but 'impotent tools' in the hands of their rulers who used such irrational fears to satisfy their own need to dominate. 'Only passion can control passion, and only a contrary impulse or desire can check impulse', Russell concluded.[52] A neat solution but not one which commended itself to Bosanquet.

Although Russell had expressed scepticism about attempts to intellectualise the Anglo-German conflict, his reaction against Idealist theory cannot simply be seen as a theoretical justification of the campaign of passive resistance to authority in which he was involved with the No-Conscription Fellowship. His criticisms were also influenced by natural rights theory (resistance to authority),[53] ideas on future world organisation, and pluralist arguments for the rights of groups within the state.[54] In this he was expressing a view, which had been gaining currency before the war, that the state as it then existed fell between two stools: it was too small to properly regulate international conflict, and too big to allow proper 'consciousness of common interests'.[55] Equally, Russell's realisation of the importance of instinct in human nature may have come in part from his 'endeavour to understand popular feelings about the war', but it was also part of a wider movement of thought. There was, as Ernest Barker noted in 1914, 'a certain trend of anti-intellectualism' at work, and the experience of war would do much to strengthen it.[56]

CHAPTER 3

Historians and the War

Fortunately in the twentieth century, the conception that no historian has the right to be a patriot, and that he will best serve the interests of his country, if he try only to serve the interests of truth, has gained considerable ground . . . . The influence of Lord Acton had begun to make itself felt, not only in this country but in many others, and there have been signs that, wherever academic work could be carried out, free from state control or interference, historians were returning to the ideals of Ranke and his school. How far progress will now be checked it is impossible to say. But even if the value of historical work be lowered by false ideals of patriotism, it is yet better that it should be done badly than not at all. The difficulty increases indeed the responsibility of the historians of every country. No country can afford to neglect the study of its own foreign policy, without taking the risk that its ideals will be misunderstood and misconstrued. We must hope for enlightened patriotism.

C. K. Webster, *The Study of Nineteenth Century Diplomacy: An Inaugural Lecture* (1915)

British historians, practitioners of what A. W. Ward had called in 1913 'a great inductive science',[1] were less confident than philosophers about the influence of abstract concepts (the German theory of the state, for example) on policy. 'Nothing is more difficult than to estimate the influence of abstract theory upon action', another of them wrote in 1914. 'Political theories as such, are coherently conceived and held by very few persons anywhere.'[2] However, this proved no impediment to writing about the war. Although less flamboyantly nationalistic than their German colleagues, British historians were every bit as ready to adopt a 'role as educators of the nation'.[3] However, it is true that this task was generally conceived in characteristically modest terms — the British historian placing his skills at the service of 'national life' (to have mentioned the 'state' might have seemed too Hegelian). Thus we find A. F. Pollard in 1916, new editor of the journal *History*, setting out its objective as bringing 'the light of history to bear in the study of politics', a means of testing 'modern experiment by historical experience'.[4] The resulting 'war-history' by Pollard and many others has not hitherto received much attention. After the war there was even a certain amount of embarrassment about it. 'To treat of it would be a painful and almost indecent task', warned one of the formerly most prolific practitioners in 1923.[5] A less well-developed sense of decency, however, does allow us to pose the question of the extent to which these wartime writings influenced attitudes towards Germany and reinforced the self-image of Britain's role in Europe.

In 1914 the study of history in British universities had reached new heights of popularity. By the turn of the century the History Honours School at Oxford had outstripped the school of *Literae Humaniores* in size, although the prestige of the latter was probably still greater. At Cambridge the Historical Tripos had gained a considerable reputation under the guidance of Lord Acton (until his death in 1902), an historian well-known outside academic circles. In London A. F. Pollard was beginning his campaign for the establishment of an institute for historical research which might one day eclipse even the older universities as a centre of professional education. At Manchester T. F. Tout and James Tait had already achieved much of what Pollard desired for London. All the smaller universities and colleges in Britain had chairs of history before 1914, with the exception of St. Andrews (which still had only a lectureship) and Nottingham (whose status as a university college was still uncertain).[6]

Ten years before the outbreak of the First World War the last of the older generation of historians, the giants of the Victorian age who had been public figures as well as professional historians, had died.[7] Their ideas still lived on in their former pupils. Although history was still commonly spoken of as a 'science', unspoken assumptions about the past lurked behind inductive method as they had in the mid-nineteenth century. A. L. Smith, as a tutor in modern history at Balliol, coached many future leaders of the profession (like Lewis Namier), and 'in his history A.L. was, like everyone else, a disciple of Stubbs, who traced the Divine Purpose in the long evolutionary process which had ended in making England top nation'.[8] Mid-Victorian certainties, whether about Britain's world role or about the possibility of complete impartiality on the part of the historian, continued to hold sway. It was Acton's successor as Regius Professor at Cambridge who confidently claimed that a 'complete assemblage of the smallest facts' would 'tell in the end', and one of A. L. Smith's pupils who wrote that the historian 'needed . . . an intellectual detachment so complete that all hopes of humanity [would] fail to arouse a dominant emotion'.[9] The explicit commitment to 'scientific' history and the implicit belief in Britain's special role were not really questioned until after the war.[10]

One result of the quest for complete impartiality, and of underlying historicist assumptions, was that political history (especially in the guise of medieval constitutional history) dominated university teaching. There were documents and other records to provide 'the facts', and scholarly rigour was essential in order to deal with them — it was Bishop Stubbs himself who wrote that such history could 'scarcely be approached without an effort', as generations of readers of his *Select Charters* have found. Being remote from the present, such history encouraged scholarly impartiality.

As one of Stubbs's young men put it: 'The further back . . . that we carry our historical studies in point of time, the greater will be the educational value of the training'.[11] But for historians interested in nineteenth-century Britain, especially the period after 1870, the continual complaint was that documents were not being made available.[12] In that sense historians were not well-prepared for the role of semi-official apologists for the British declaration of war in August 1914. However, the mix of explicit and implicit commitments mentioned previously certainly explains the readiness with which many of them took the plunge into writing about the war.

Three weeks after the outbreak of the war members of the Oxford History School decided on the publication of an authoritative version of the British case against Germany. On the 14th of September *Why We Are At War: Great Britain's Case* appeared from the Clarendon Press. This was no mere pamphlet but a substantial volume of over 250 pages. It inaugurated a long series of 'Oxford pamphlets' on the war and, together with Gilbert Murray's *Foreign Policy of Sir Edward Grey* (1915), was to be one of the most widely quoted. Within a month it had reached a third edition, and by the end of 1914 it had gone through five further impressions and been translated into six languages. Its authors were some of the best-known history tutors in Oxford at that time: Ernest Barker and L. G. Wickham Legg (New College), H. W. C. Davis (Balliol), C. R. L. Fletcher (the Clarendon Press), Arthur Hassall (Christ Church), and F. Morgan (Keble).[13] In Germany, too, historians were busy at work on a weighty justification of official policy, published a little later, under the names of Otto Hintze, Hermann Oncken, Hermann Schumacher and Friedrich Meinecke, as *Deutschland und der Weltkrieg* (1915).

Like their German colleagues, the Oxford historians disclaimed any intention of writing propaganda. In fact, as professional historians they could claim to be impartial:

> We are not politicians, and we belong to different schools of political thought. We have written this book to set forth the causes of the present war, and the principles we believe to be at stake. We have some experience in the handling of historic evidence and we have endeavoured to treat the subject historically.

As if to substantiate this serious purpose, there were more pages of documents than there were of text. Authorised translations of the German 'White Book' and of extracts from the Austro-Hungarian 'dossier' on the Sarajevo assassination; extracts from the Russian 'Orange Book' (in French), from the dispatches of the British ambassadors in Vienna and Berlin, and from Grey's correspondence during the July crisis — all this suggested a well-educated, middle-class readership. Not only were there chapters on the diplomacy of the 1914 crisis and on the neutrality of Belgium and Luxemburg, but also on 'The Development of Russian Policy', 'The Growth of Alliances and the Race of Armaments Since 1871', and, inevitably, 'The New German Theory of the State'. The fact that the 'first-hand evidence' obviously presented a very partial version of events was quietly passed over, except in the case of the German 'White Book' which was damned as 'an official apology, supplemented by documents'.[14]

Why We Are At War also merited the same description, even if some of this British apologetic may have been the result of over-readiness to accept official papers at face value. Perhaps the historian's passion for 'facts' and his training amongst the documents were at fault here. The same could not be said, however, of many other examples of 'war history' beside which *Why We Are At War* seems sober and scholarly. For example, Ramsay Muir, Professor of Modern History at Manchester, published a similar study, *Britain's Case Against Germany*, in 1914, with the customary disclaimer: 'Despite the difficulty of maintaining an attitude of aloofness and impartiality during a great war, I have honestly tried . . . to see the facts plainly, and never to tamper with them'. But there the resemblance ends. Muir's account was far more sensational. His list of German 'crimes' rose to a crescendo with a description of the bombardment of Louvain as an 'unspeakable crime': 'Tilly's sack of Magdeburg is nothing to it; Alaric's sack of Rome fades into insignificance beside it'.[15] However, it is not the intention of this chapter to compile an anthology of lapses from scholarship — in much the same way that British academics ransacked the works of German professors in search of damning passages. It is useful, though, to examine what historical dimension was given to official policy.

Belgium, generally referred to as 'poor little Belgium', was the key. It was a godsend for the Asquith government. Its members, as Liberals, were 'prisoners of their own pacific images. Supporting a war demanded of them a reversal of life-time commitments. Belgium, as Asquith sensed, would relieve them of unbearable embarrassment'.[16] Staunchly Liberal historians, like J. L. Hammond and Ramsay Muir, sought to deny any suggestion of a British commitment before 1914 to give military assistance to France, and emphasised the German invasion of Belgium as the deciding factor.[17] But for the Oxford historians Britain's obligation to France was a 'matter of common knowledge', and for others France was as important as Belgium in Britain's decision to go to war — the danger to France was sufficient reason to intervene, the invasion of Belgium simply removed the 'last hesitation'.[18] Ernest Barker, one of the authors of *Why We Are At War*, felt able, when away from the sobering influence of his colleagues, to give free rein to his Francophilia in a pamphlet entitled *Great Britain's Reasons For Going To War* (1915):

> France, like England, is a democracy. France is one of the greatest democracies of the world. She is one of the greatest treasure-houses of European civilisation; she is one of the great seed-beds of liberal thought and ideas. Would England have been right to watch unconcerned, and without one proffer of any sort of aid, the crushing by military force of that democracy; the rifling of that treasure-house; the trampling down of that seed-bed? It is impossible to answer 'Yes'.[19]

Barker's pamphlet seems to have been written with a relatively unsophisticated audience in mind. The consequent dangers of over-simplification and distortion are well illustrated by R. S. Rait's *Why We Are Fighting Germany: A Village Lecture* (1914) which claimed, among other things, that Britain was fighting to defend French colonies which were only a mere 'stepping-stone to the possession of other colonies', namely British ones:

> The Germans want to seize colonies. The French have colonies, but not in very healthy climates. Great Britain has a great number of colonies and a large number of colonies and a large number of possessions scattered all over the world .... Germany's real aim is to seize not French colonies and dependencies, but British colonies and dependencies.

Clearly the Germans 'wanted to pick their victims off one by one, France this year and Great Britain a few years hence'. Britain, Rait concluded, should fight Germany because that country despised 'humanity' and everything that distinguished 'a fighting man from a ravening beast'.[20]

Not surprisingly the suggestion that, if France had been the first to violate Belgian neutrality, Britain would have accepted this with 'ready acquiescence' touched a sensitive nerve. Had not even the authors of *Why We Are At War* written that Britain fought 'in the noblest cause for which men can fight', 'the public law of Europe, as a sure shield and buckler of all nations, great and small, and especially the small'? 'Our cause, as one would expect from a people that has fought out its own internal struggles under the forms of law, is a legal cause', they continued. 'We are a people in whose blood the cause of law is the vital element.'[21] But the code of the gentleman, as well as that of 'public law', was at stake. 'How little the German Chancellor realized the Anglo-Saxon reverence for the sanctity of the plighted word', exclaimed another Oxford historian.[22] It is true that a younger colleague described diplomacy 'as a rule, a matter of business, not of sentiment', but then he was defending Italian neutrality before May 1915.[23]

This British emphasis on (one might say obsession with) legality and morality, which so infuriated the Germans, was not complete hypocrisy, according to a sympathetic American observer:

Each nation ... expresses its justification through the ideas which its past history has made most intelligible to itself — in terms, that is, of its own national philosophy. The English are traditionally Protestant, evangelical, and individualistic in their consciousness. Their moral defence instinctively takes a personal, a moralistic form. The blamelessness of their own conscience, the virtuousness of their motive — such as the defence of the sanctity of treaties and their pledged word — support them. Since their activities, as distinct from their consciousness, have been largely commercial and imperialistic, it is not surprising that the hypocrisy, the unctuous pharisaism of the British have become proverbial among the nations with another cast of thought. But since the emotion of good intent is a perfectly genuine phenomenon, the English are totally puzzled by the accusation. Nothing is more remote from their all too hearty and bluff straight-forwardness than conscious double-dealing.

The Germans were equally misunderstood, especially by the British, who showed 'intellectual unpreparedness' for the German mind at work justifying official policy. There was a 'hiatus between the German conception of themselves and the English reading of their mental and moral temper'.[24]

While there is much wisdom in these comments by the philosopher John Dewey, the long history of British intervention against small states did not go unnoticed, whether it was Denmark in 1807, the Boer republics in 1899, or Greece in 1915. Defence of the last must have sounded particularly unconvincing after condemnation of the German invasion of Belgium the previous year. J. W. Headlam, formerly of King's College, Cambridge, and now Historical Advisor to the Foreign Office, did his best in his pamphlet *Belgium and Greece* (1915):

> The neutrality of the two states was as different as black and white. For the neutrality of Belgium was the fulfilment of a solemn engagement, the neutrality of Greece was the violation of an engagement equally binding: if the one was a virtue, the other was a crime.

The Greek refusal to aid the Serbs as they had promised to do was 'a refusal sufficient to justify a demand that the nation which was guilty of it should be struck out of the society of civilised states'. Not noticing the considerable irony in this claim, Headlam further excused Allied invasion of Greece by claiming that Britain and France had only asked that their troops be given passage over Greek territory. This was exactly what the Germans had claimed in the case of Belgium in 1914. Headlam's words, 'never in the history of the world has a State been treated with such consideration', are worthy to stand beside the most self-serving German pronouncements.[25]

Usually the British case was presented in moral terms, as a demonstration that 'the call of Right' was 'higher than the call of blood'; as a defence of international law which transcended any notions of Teutonic solidarity (between Germany and Britain), or even of all the 'restraints' which 'humanity and civilisation' had been attempting to build up since the seventeenth century.[26] Just occasionally, though, it was commercial law, rather than international law, which provided the kind of argument likely to convince any waverers. It could be demonstrated that 'the inviolability of public faith' was 'not only of supreme importance in the political sphere', but that it also lay 'at the root of the whole mechanism of foreign trade and the international money market'. Not to have gone to the assistance of France would have led to 'a bankruptcy of external credit' and 'a feeling of doubt and insecurity throughout the money-markets of the world'.[27] This was the kind of argument which any audience of businessmen could understand, although no doubt it simply confirmed the view of German intellectuals, like Werner Sombart, that the British had the souls of shopkeepers.

More serious than the charge of a commercial mentality was the difficulty for British historians of justifying alliance with Tsarist Russia, especially when Germany claimed to be fighting on behalf of civilisation against 'Muscovite barbarism'. Since the British claimed that *they* were fighting on behalf of civilisation, explanations were in order. The authors of *Why We Are At War* attempted to provide some positive reasons, aside from common opposition to Germany. First, there was their 'common cause' of international arbitration and disarmament — the 1899 Hague Conference on the limitation of armaments had been called on the initiative of Tsar Nicholas II. Then there was their common interest in the independence of the Balkan states and their common opposition to German influence in Turkey. Lastly, there was the infant 'Russian constitutionalism' which 'not only coincided in time with the Anglo-Russian agreement of 1907, but [which] also owed much to the inspiration of England'. For his part the Regius Professor of Modern History at Cambridge claimed that Tsarist Russia had more in common with western democracy than did Germany. She had 'done more perhaps than any other of the great peoples in the interests of small nationalities'.[28]

There were hopes also of a deeper democracy within the peasant masses of Russia. Writers like Stephen Graham, who had written rhapsodically for years on 'Mother Russia', reached new emotional heights during wartime. The cult of Dostoyevsky gained new devotees. This was the background against which British historians began their 'rediscovery' of a Russia truly democratic in a way that left 'western constitutionmongers far behind the times'. This was how one of them described the process:

If by 'democracy' we mean merely a form of government, it is quite ludicrous to denounce Russia because our own particular arrangements do not or may not suit her. If, on the other hand, democracy means something vastly deeper and more important than forms of government, if it means a spirit, a point of view, and a quality informing the life and thought of a people, then the least I can say is that while I see a great deal of democracy in Russia, I do not see much of it in England. One might, indeed, go further and say that while, in that sense, England is the least democratic of European countries, and the most completely under the dominion of the superstitions of 'class' and 'rank', Russia is probably the most democratic of all.

Little difficulties, like Tsarist imperialism, anti-semitism and discrimination against national minorities, could be explained away as products of the 'Germanisation' of the 'central governing bureaucracy'.[29] This preference for the 'deeper democracy' of Russia, as we shall see later, also tells us something about attitude of British intellectuals to the industrialised society in which they themselves lived.

As for the role of Russia in the July 1914 crisis, British historians were inclined to give it the benefit of the doubt when apportioning responsibility for the outbreak of war. 'If Russia was the first to mobilize', wrote the authors of *Why We Are At War*, 'she took this step as a consequence of German threats.' And another historian noted of Russian obligations to France and Serbia, 'unless Russia meant to stand aside what else could she have done?'[30] What, then, of the role of Austria-Hungary, with whom Britain had 'been united for centuries by close ties of friendship and sympathy'? The alleged subordination of Habsburg to Hohenzollern interests, from the time of Bismarck onwards, suggested that Vienna was not primarily to blame in 1914.[31] This left Berlin (not until the 'revisionist' historiography of the 1920s and 1930s were Paris and London considered in any sense 'responsible' in accounts written in English) as the guilty party, and at the level of war-history the suspicion of a German plot was strong. As Ramsay Muir saw it:

The whole policy of Germany during the last five and twenty years is of one piece. Its enormous and constantly increasing military preparations; its far-reaching schemes of aggression in the Balkans; its attempts to stir up discontent in South Africa, and to assert a general protectorate over the Mohammedan subjects of the three powers with which it is now at war; its blusterous and bullying methods of diplomacy; its refusal to play a fair and honest part in the discussions of the nations, its eagerness to sow discord among the small and sorely-tried nations of the south-east, its readiness to disregard agreements, such as that of Algeciras, into which it had entered: — all this points to the same conclusion which is enforced by nearly all the political literature of these years, that the policy of the last quarter of a century has been one long and not overskilled preparation for the great bid for world power which was made in 1914 on so slight a pretext.[32]

Muir believed that he possessed 'moral certainty' — presumably something short of factual certainty — that all arrangements for war had been completed in Germany 'long before the Archduke's murder'. There was evidence that gun platforms had been secretly constructed at strategic points in Belgium by German agents; German coalers had taken up station a week before the assassination at Sarajevo; the Kiel Canal had been widened and the summer manoeuvres enlarged; German investors had rushed to sell Canadian Pacific stock in London. 'Is it, in the face of these facts, possible to deny that Germany had for some years been preparing to engage in war, and that even if the Archduke had never been murdered, war would have come this summer?', Muir asked his readers. There was more of E. Phillips Oppenheim or William Le Queux in Muir than in other historians, but even fairly level-headed colleagues could make wild assertions — for example, that prewar German societies which sought 'mutual good understanding' with Britain were but 'a blind behind which she [Germany] developed her devilish plots'.[33]

Paradoxically, what was written by British historians in the heat of battle was restated with considerable refinements, after a 'revisionist' interval of some forty years (1920–1960), by a new generation of German historians under the leadership of Fritz Fischer. The very title of his book *Griff nach der Weltmacht* (1961) calls to mind the claim by British historians nearly a half-century earlier that Germany was aiming at no less than world power and the destruction of the British Empire. Germany, to cover its own colonial failures, was planning 'to seize from the older colonising nations more attractive and profitable regions'. Conquest, 'supplemented by indemnities', would also solve other 'financial, industrial and commercial difficulties'.[34] Fischer's thesis that social and political pressures in Wilhelmine Germany disposed its ruling elite to risk war in 1914 can be found in early form in many of the writings of British historians — for example G. W. Prothero in 1916:

> The prospect of domestic revolution has driven rulers into foreign wars before now; and it can hardly be doubted that the spectre of Socialism and the menace of a revolutionary proletariat have contributed to make the great capitalists, the dominant military party and the Emperor himself, already inclined on other grounds to war, more ready to adopt this solution as an alternative.[35]

Prothero was one historian with a considerable knowledge of Germany. He had studied under Heinrich von Sybel (1873–4) and ten years later translated the first volume of Ranke's *Weltgeschichte*. However, apart from A. W. Ward, British historians had written little about Germany since Sir John Seeley's *Life and Times of Stein* (1878).[36] Interest in Germany did not go beyond a vague admiration for *Wissenschaft* and for the cultural Germany of Browning's 'tall old quaint irregular town'. It was this lack of interest in the social and political realities of the modern Reich which the Cambridge historian J. Holland Rose castigated in his lectures: 'Treitschke and Bernhardi are excused as freaks, alien to the German genius in its best form, as typified by Goethe, Kant, Schiller'. But Imperial Germany was 'not now the land of Goethe, Kant and Schiller. She is the creation of William I and II, of Roon, Moltke, Bismarck and Krupp; and she takes after her creators'.[37]

Despite this coupling of Bismarck with Prussian military power, the former chancellor was not treated with great hostility by British historians. A typical assessment was this one by the Manchester historian W. T. Waugh: '... unscrupulous enough and at times brutal enough: but there was in his diplomacy a coolness and restraint which stand in the sharpest contrast to the bluster and swagger of his would-be imitators'.[38] Similarly, Oxford historians saw Bismarck as the 'embodiment of the Fredrician tradition .... In the line of his defects, crimes or blunders, megalomania cannot fairly be placed. The intoxication of success, the fever of nationalist pride, never mastered his head'.[39] Charles Grant Robertson's *Bismarck* (1918) was also restrained in its assessment. Later, in another world war, the legacy of Bismarck would be scrutinised more critically, but for the present he was placed (with some vague misgivings) in the company of the 'good' Germans. However, the same could not be said of the historian Heinrich von Treitschke, whose monumental history of nineteenth-century Germany was appearing for the first time in English from 1915 onwards (it had been published in German between 1879 and 1894).

Treitschke was considered so important that several books were devoted to his life and writings. The one by the Oxford historian H. W. C. Davis managed to be reasonably fair-minded.[40] But there was no doubt that for British historians Treitschke and the 'Prussian School' of German history epitomised all that had gone wrong in German intellectual life after the 1870s. H. A. L. Fisher, writing with the bitterness of one who remembered the old 'good' Germany, penned this indictment of Treitschke and his followers in 1915:

> They have exalted material power and have belittled the empire of moral sentiments. They have applauded war as an instrument of progress and national hygiene. Holding that aggression is a symptom of vigour, and vigour the sign manual of political virtue, they have championed every violation of right which has subserved the aggrandisement of Prussia. They have scorned small states because they were small and have applauded big states because they were big. And in their violent and not unnatural reaction against the quietism and happy contemplation of that old and pleasant Germany for which Mozart wrote music and Goethe verse, ... they have exaggerated with Teutonic thoroughness the brutal side of politics as a thing much to be respected ... .[41]

Yet in Germany Treitschke had suffered neglect since his death in 1896. As a recent biographer notes, 'Germans were surprised to find the almost forgotten Treitschke singled out as one of the intellectual instigators of the war'. The new generation of historians, led by Erich Marcks and Max Lenz, looked to Ranke rather than Treitschke.[42] As J. W. Allen, one of the few British historians to recognise this development, noted: 'To the great majority of Germans, as to the great majority of Englishmen, Treitschke can be little more than a name'.[43]

While this may have been true, a number of qualifications need to be made. Firstly, the 'neo-Rankean' historians provided their own particular underpinning for German *Weltpolitik*, just as Treitschke had done earlier for Prussian foreign policy. Naval-building, colonial expansion, and, above all, rivalry with Great Britain were all encompassed in their view of Germany's mission in the world.[44] British historians had recognised these symptoms but misdiagnosed their cause. Secondly, in nationalist circles within Germany, writings of people like General von Bernhardi kept the ideas of Treitschke in circulation, reinvigorated by a dose of Social Darwinism. In Britain the rather mysterious figure of Professor J. A. Cramb fulfilled a similar role until his death in 1913, like Bernhardi sometimes acting as ghost-writer to top military men (in Cramb's case, Lord Roberts). It is difficult to estimate Cramb's influence before the outbreak of war, but during the war he became one of the most widely quoted experts on Treitschke and Bernhardi — the cover of his posthumously published lectures, *Germany and England* (1914), bore the words 'Treitschke Expounded', 'Bernhardi Explained'.[45]

John Adam Cramb (1861–1913) had travelled in Germany after taking a classics degree at Glasgow University (1885), attending Treitschke's lectures in Berlin as well as studying in Bonn. After a spell of teaching at Queen Margaret College, Glasgow (1887–90). he went to Queen's College, London, where he taught history for the rest of his life (1892–1913). Although he was styled Professor of History, the College was in fact a private girls' school. Inability to subscribe to Anglicanism had prevented his gaining a professorship at King's College, London. He was thus on the periphery of the university world, although he was a friend of Frederick York Powell, Regius Professor of History at Oxford, 1894–1904. He was also associated with Lord Roberts' campaign for compulsory military service and, perhaps as a result of this, he lectured from 1910 onwards at the Staff College, Camberley, and at other 'military stations' throughout Britain.[46] Some of these lectures formed the basis for his book *Germany and England*, a strange rambling series of reflections on the dangers of 'Pacificism' and on the 'tragic conflict' of Britain and Germany, rather than a systematic exposition of Treitschke's ideas. As one critic wrote, Cramb 'was himself strongly imbued with the spirit of the movement' of thought he had set out to expound.[47] The flavour of the book is caught by the last paragraph describing the inevitable future conflict:

> And one can imagine the ancient, mighty deity of all the Teutonic kindred, throned above the clouds, looking serenely down upon that conflict, upon his favourite children, locked in a death-struggle, smiling upon the heroism of that struggle, the heroism of the children of Odin the War-god![48]

Apart from the odd unfavourable comment, by A. F. Pollard for example, historians (like the authors of *Why We Are At War*) and philosophers (J. H. Muirhead for one) found nothing to complain of in Cramb's heady mix of Treitschke and Social Darwinism.[49] However, there were few who so clearly shared his belief in the inevitability of war as the Professor of History at Glasgow did. In an article entitled 'The War and the Races of Europe' D. J. Medley echoed Cramb's words on the impossibility of 'friendly rivalry', although laying the blame more at Germany's door:

> A rapidly-growing nation full of enterprise must needs find outlet for its energies or it will die of congestion. But if it can find salvation only at our expense, we must protect ourselves or become mere satellites of the rising power. Germany believes that there is not room in the world for herself and us at the same time.[50]

More usually Cramb was cited to explain some aspect of German policy while the policy of Britain, by contrast, was seen to be characterised by the quiet diplomacy of the Foreign Secretary Sir Edward Grey. 'The characteristics of Sir Edward Grey's diplomacy during the past ten years have been transparent honesty, and a disposition to be conciliatory which no rebuff could repress', concluded the Professor of History at Aberdeen. Even with the growth of German power, Grey 'neither thwarted nor opposed Germany's aspirations'. He 'took the German menace seriously, but met it with consideration and common sense'. 'Germany's almost insane hatred' of Grey was simply a 'confession of her knowledge' that he had 'presented the case against her in terms of civilisation itself'.[51]

Grey thus epitomised for British historians, and for many foreign ones, what John Dewey had described as 'the emotion of good intent', as well as the British sense of fair play. The defence of Belgium was evidence, it was thus claimed, of the 'natural tendency' of the British 'to side with the pigmy ... menaced by the giant'.[52] But there were of course good practical reasons for leaving other small invaded nations — those beyond the range of British sea power (Serbia and Luxemburg for example) — to be defended by someone else. Pitt's vindication of Dutch rights on the

Scheldt (1793) or Gladstone's defence of Belgian neutrality (1870) had more to do with British fears about a hostile great power controlling the whole of the Channel coast than with a general defence of the rights of small states. In the same way, the concern to maintain a 'balance of power' on the Continent was a policy of convenience for the British, rather than 'a political principle indispensable to the existence of International Law in its present condition'.[53] However, German historians pointing this out to their British colleagues were unlikely to have much effect. The 'balance of power' provided British historians with an opportunity to defend British policy 'by reference to history'. Parallels could be, and were, drawn between Kaiser Wilhelm II and Richelieu or Catherine II who had both tried 'tilting the balance for their own aggrandisement', or between the attitude to small states of Napoleon and the German Chancellor von Bethmann-Hollweg — had not the former referred to Switzerland and Holland as 'mere trifles'?[54] This idea was expanded upon by the Reader in Modern History at Cambridge, in a pamphlet for 'the young people of all English-speaking countries':

> ... the war we are waging now is not on behalf of some new-fangled notion. The independence of the Belgians and the Dutch has been a matter of concern to every British ruler who has had our interests at heart. That independence has been in turn threatened by the French, the Spaniards, again by the French, and now, lastly, by the Germans. If we go as far back as the reign of Edward I, we find that he tried to prevent the French conquering the people of Flanders .... [55]

For the Germans, who tended to write off the European balance as an outdated concept (at least in its existing form), the British stress on legality and morality seemed hypocritical. 'Public opinion in England is wonderfully responsive to cant', wrote the sociologist Ferdinand Tönnies. 'It is like a musical automat — one needs only to throw a cant phrase into the slot and the instrument begins to grind out a highly moral melody.'[56] This German habit of viewing unsentimentally the status quo — whether it was the European balance or the British Empire — in terms of *Realpolitik*, was rather embarrassing for the British. This was especially so in the case of empire, as the title of one of the Oxford pamphlets on the war makes clear. *Is the British Empire The Result of Wholesale Robbery?* posed a question which could only be answered defensively. Its author, the Beit Professor of Colonial History at Oxford, made the kind of case all too familiar in recent years as nostalgia for the days of 'the Raj' has blossomed: 'No doubt in the making of the British Empire, as in other human transactions, things have happened that one may wish might have happened otherwise'. But, if Britain had been 'fortunate in her opportunities, her use of them' had been 'assuredly not more unscrupulous than the use made of their opportunities by other nations'. This was a shaft aimed at those late entrants to the imperialist game, the Germans. The French, however, could be absolved from the charge of dirty-dealing. As two Oxford historians noted:

> No doubt the colonizing powers of Europe have sometimes alleged a grievance which did not exist, or have made a mountain out of a molehill, in order to justify the establishment of a protectorate. But each case must be judged on its merits; and we have no right to denounce France as a robber simply because she has become the protector of numerous uncivilised or half-civilised communities.[57]

It had been Treitschke who had portrayed Britain as 'a middle-aged burglar who desired to retire from business, and therefore proposed that burglary should cease'. Germany was the 'young and enterprising burglar, just starting a promising career'. There was thus 'a sense of outraged justice' in Treitschke's idea that Right was 'a question of might', the author of *Through German Eyes* (1915) conceded. In moral terms it was impossible to 'justify Great Britain's having painted red one-fifth of the habitable globe', but then nor could one 'justify the fact that A earns five times as much as B, but not one-tenth the income of C'. 'In this workaday world we have to be content with a rough kind of justice, and to acknowledge accomplished facts. We must live and let live.'[58] These were not sentiments likely to commend themselves to Treitschke's successors any more than arguments based on concepts of traditional morality or international law. Before 1914 they had argued that 'a war among the Great Powers themselves would provide the supreme test of the power and cohesiveness of the British as well as the Russian and other empires. This was because the colonial peoples would in such an event seize the opportunity to rise up in arms against their imperial masters because they had sensed their impending decline'. It was on this last point that the Irish Uprising in 1916 seemed uncomfortably like a confirmation of Max Lenz's predictions in *Ein Blick in das zwanzigste Jahrhundert* (1900).[59]

Ireland proved the sorest test of the British conception of empire and generally was passed over in silence. What was 'the outstanding mark of the British Empire?' It was 'the freedom of the people in it and the security which union gives', the Professor of Politics at Oxford concluded. The principle of 'unity through diversity' had been present in British policy as early as the eighteenth century, in former French Canada. This was something which the Germans just did not understand: 'Difficult as it may be for the logical, systematic German mind to realize it is still the fact that different kinds of patriotism may co-exist side by side simultaneously in the same man'. Far from being 'a machinery to enable the English to exploit a quarter of the globe', the British Empire was in fact 'a far-reaching and elastic structure, wherein the force of nationality' could have 'free development'. It was an example of 'union and peace' to set before the rest of the world. What, then, of those embarrassing exceptions — 'thrown in our teeth', as H. E. Egerton put it? Ireland and South Africa by no means disproved the general rule: nationalist aspirations were quite acceptable if 'compatible with the interests of the Empire as a whole'.[60]

All this had been written in the first two years of the war in answer to the kind of criticisms made by Tönnies in his book *Warlike England* (1915). Writing of British policy in Ireland, Tönnies had asked:

> Does Ireland, too, believe that the cause of law is the vital element in the blood of Englishmen? That England assumes with tenderness, out of courage of nobility, the protection of small nations? That it battles for them against militarism for the cause of justice?[61]

There were several ways of meeting such ironical use of British wartime propaganda. Ernest Barker specialised in telling comparisons of British Ireland and Prussian Poland. 'Prussian Poland' might be 'the Ireland of Prussia', but the difference was that the Polish loss of independence was still within the historical memory of the Poles. The 'sins of England towards Ireland', on the other hand, were committed between 1580 and 1780:

> ... although historians may find justification in the ideas of an age three centuries removed from our own for practices intolerable to a modern conscience, there is no justification that can wipe away the stain of guilt .... Prussia is pursuing the same sort of idea — the idea of plantation on land to be gained by compulsory expropriation — in the light of the twentieth century. Prussia does it with a less blundering cruelty, and with a good deal of fair-seeming modern argument .... But Prussia can hardly be excused for what she does in the twentieth century, however civilised or scientific her methods may be, by the fact that England did similar things in the seventeenth century.
>
> The true comparison ... is between the Ireland of to-day and the Prussian Poland of to-day .... While Prussia has been evicting the Poles, Great Britain has been settling the people of Ireland on the land.[62]

After the Easter Uprising even this kind of comparison became difficult, although Barker continued to make it in later editions of *Ireland in the Last Fifty Years*. It was always safer to make a general justification for empire, avoiding particular cases which might turn out unexpectedly. This provided historians of the British Empire, like E. A. Benians, A. P. Newton and J. Holland Rose, with arguments which were to prove of service again during the Second World War,[63] drawing on that rich seam of national mythology which is not yet exhausted. Benians's pamphlet *The British Empire and the War* (1915) is a good example of this strategy. First, the modest understatement: 'The English are not much given to introspection, nor are they gifted in explaining what they aim at or what they do'. Then, the appeal to the peculiarities of English history: 'They live by instinct, and advance by experience and their policy seems from hand to mouth, but it is an expression of national character, and is thus a continuous tradition'. But, under the stress of war, 'wherein Empires and the principles upon which they have been built are put to the test', the manner in which the Empire had rallied to Britain was proof enough of its true nature. 'Against the German ideal of Empire — the march of Teutonic culture over the earth' — the British Empire could be placed. It was truly one of 'those subtle and half-conscious compromises, through which the English achieve their full power of co-operation'. Germany, the 'nation of machines', could never understand 'the dominance of personality', the importance of 'individual resource and character' for the British.[64]

We began this chapter with the suggestion that the credo of strict historical objectivity did not easily coexist with prevailing historicist assumptions about Britain's world role. Perhaps it was this conflict which caused H. E. Egerton to pause momentarily in the course of his defence of British policy:

> Often the deeper our knowledge, the stronger becomes the case which can be made for the side which has failed and is therefore discredited. But there are limits to these grounds for cool-headed doubt and scepticism; and when the case of our adversary can be decided by his own admissions, it would be the merest pedantry to affect an attitude of uncertainty.[65]

Egerton had clearly regained his composure, disposed of his doubts. But had he followed the advice of the aged lawyer and historian A. V. Dicey 'to try to form an historical view of the war'; 'to look upon the war from something like the point of view from which it will be regarded by a fair-minded historian writing in A.D. 2000'?[66] Much of what has been quoted from the writings of Egerton and others suggests not.

CHAPTER 4

'The Peacefulness of Being at War'

During the last twelve months the life of Great Britain has been acquiring a unitary aim or purpose. The aim itself is warlike; but it has been attended with some increase of mental peace. When the war broke out we were living as a nation, without end or aim .... Whatever ideals existed had but a piecemeal acceptance: ... And beyond the relatively narrow circle where these ideals maintained their precarious dominion lay the vast dim populations, held together by 'group instincts', by geographical conditions, and by the necessities of the economic struggle for existence. Regarded from the moral point of view, the scene was one of indescribable confusion: it was, in fact, a moral chaos.

L. P. Jacks, 'The Peacefulness of Being at War', *Hibbert Journal*,
11 Sept. 1915

With the outbreak of war the universities and colleges began to change in appearance. Undergraduates and younger lecturers disappeared into the army and navy. For those left behind opposed to the war, this was an almost unbearable time. As Russell wrote from Cambridge after one and a half years of war:

The melancholy of this place now-a-days is beyond endurance — the Colleges are dead, except for a few Indians and a few pale pacifists and bloodthirsty old men hobbling along victorious in the absence of youth. Soldiers are billeted in the courts and drill on the grass; bellicose parsons preach to them in stentorian tones from the steps of the Hall.[1]

But for many other academics on the sidelines it was a time of something approaching exhilaration. 'It's going to be a good war, though some of us will have a lot to bear', the Professor of English at Oxford confided to a friend. 'I've often known this must come when I've heard the Germans talk about their destiny and their plans for achieving it. I'm glad I've lived to see it, and sick that I'm not in it.' This, it is true, was written in the first days of the war, but Walter Raleigh, unlike some, never wavered in his enthusiasm for war. Together with the Poet Laureate, Robert Bridges, and Gilbert Murray, Raleigh joined the Oxford Volunteers to 'rise at six every day to line hedgerows in the dark and 'advance in rushes' across the Oxford meadows'.[2] The young Aldous Huxley was also on hand to record in verse these academic manoeuvres:

The Volunteers in vomit-colour
Go forth to shoot the lamb of God,
Their leaden faces redden to a blazing comet-colour,
And they sweat as they plod.

Parson and poet-laureate,
Professor, grocer, don,
This one as fat as Ehud that, poor dear! would grow the more he ate
Yet more a skeleton

Some have piles and some have goitres
Most of them have Bright's disease,
Uric acid has made them flaccid and one gouty hero loiters,
Anchylosed in toes and knees.[3]

However, even the Volunteers had little idea of the realities of trench warfare. As the historian R. H. Tawney, by now a private in the Manchester Regiment, pointed out, the people at home had created for themselves an 'image of war', not as it was, but a 'picturesque' version which flattered their 'appetite for novelty, for excitement, for easy admiration', and for superficial emotion. 'The reality is horrible, but it is not as horrible as the grimacing phantom which you have imagined', Tawney told the readers of *The Nation*. The latter were presumably a serious-minded audience, but for most civilians the picture of cheery Tommies hunting down Huns like 'merry assassins' was more popular.[4] In this they were assisted by morale-boosting prose from historians which sought to convince the reader that the Western Front was some kind of gigantic playing-field. The national reputation for gifted amateurism and the 'clean rigour' of British games were contrasted to the Teutonic approach. The Germans, it was alleged, approached sport and life with the 'deadly concentration of a mind which never relaxes its rigour in play, the passionate earnestness of a combatant who has never learned in a mimic struggle to abide by limiting rules'. The 'tap-root' of the difference between the two nations lay in the British 'instinct for truancy' as against German 'docility'. The British just could not tolerate being 'set in a mental uniform and placed under spiritual drill'.[5] As Ramsay Muir put it, the basic antipathy was 'science over against sportsmanship; discipline over against self-government'.[6]

It was difficult for those at home to appreciate the new nature of 'total war', but it is also difficult to believe that a knowledge of wars in the past could not have suggested to these historians the hideous unreality of what they wrote. The usually level-headed J. W. Allen could be found claiming that young men at the Front were feeling 'for the first time in their lives' that they were 'wholly right with the world' 'doing their duty and nothing else'. 'In that consciousness' they were dying. If that were not 'happiness', then what could happiness be?[7] Yet at least one historian, T. F. Tout, received letters from former students at the Front which spoke of the other reality of 'putrefying corpses'.[8] However, the other 'image' was hard to shake — as late as April 1917 an audience at University College, London, heard that 'in the modern British system' soldiers were 'recognised as men not as inanimate pieces in a vast war game'.[9] Was it really so easy to explain the terrible losses of the previous year which were shortly (from May 1917) to lead to mutinies in first the French and then the British armies? When it came to self-deception, as well as the deception of others, British historians were not far behind their German colleagues. But more importantly, the war brought to the surface a series of images of society which had been partially obscured during peacetime. Although it is common to speak of these 'ideas of 1914' in Germany, their presence in Britain has been less often noted. There was, however, one perceptive observer of changes on the academic front.[10]

Jane Harrison, Fellow of Newnham College, Cambridge, was one of the relatively few women in a largely male profession. Perhaps this lent to her wartime writing a certain detachment as she observed the upsurge of nationalism amongst male intellectuals. The same 'watchwords' she noted time and time again in their articles and pamphlets: 'discipline, faith, simplicity, convention, law, obedience'. While there was not always the full-blown eulogy of war, which could be found in the writings of French or German intellectuals, there was a belief that war had its positive and creative side. The reaction against peace as 'a poor, emasculate and even effeminate business' had been 'less explicit' in Britain, though 'quite as anti-intellectualist, much less logical and theoretical'. 'War is savagery — a setback to civilisation — and yet, or rather because of this, it has for the quite young — say, for those under thirty — a singular charm lacking to the middle-aged.'[11] If British academics were any indication, the middle-aged were quite as ready to join Rupert Brooke in breaking free of the old orthodoxies. The forty-five year old Professor of Ancient History at Oxford was even able to see active service in the same theatre of war as Brooke. Sir John Myres commanded raids by small craft on the Turkish coast, where his 'ingenuity and buccaneering spirit served him no less than his detailed knowledge of the geography and people of the Asia Minor coast'.[12]

The war had, in fact, seen a closing of the generation gap. 'Ten years ago to mention the word 'duty' was to write yourself down a fogey', Harrison noted. Now everyone talked of 'Home and Country', 'Church and Army'. The creed of 'individualism' had been replaced by one of 'collectivism'.[13] This too was the view of that leading figure in the History Honours School at Oxford, A. L. Smith. The war, he told an audience at King's College, London, in 1916 had created an *union sacrée*:

War is indeed a mighty creator. It is an intellectual awakener and a moral tonic. It stirs men to think, and thinking is what we most lack in England. It creates a conscious unity of feeling which is the atmosphere needed for a new start. It purges away old strifes and sectional aims, and raises us for a while into higher and purer air. It helps us to recapture some of the lofty and intense patriotism of the ancient world. It reveals to us what constitutes a modern nation, the partnership between the living, the dead, and the yet unborn.[14]

This use of Burke's *Reflections on the Revolution in France* calls to mind the comment of Smith's aged colleague A. V. Dicey: '. . . as I think about the iniquity of Germany, and especially of the Kaiser, I am forced to understand the feelings of men like Burke and Nelson towards the Jacobins and revolutionists'.[15] But Smith's comments also indicated some unease with the liberal values of competitive individualism in prewar Britain. His contribution to the series of Oxford pamphlets on the war, *The Christian Attitude to War* (1915), explained this in greater detail:

The time has come to meet the old, narrow, exploded form of individualism in English thought by definitely developing that other aspect of life which is conveyed in the words Co-operation, Community, Corporateness. Our literature, our politics, our society, one might say our religion itself, is saturated with the conception of the 'individual'; in spite of the fact that, literally, there is no such thing among human beings as an individual; and that even if there were, it would still be more intelligent and profitable to regard him in his true character of a member of a community.

This theme of the recreation of a sense of community under the stress of war is something which is repeated in the writings of British academics, together with images of sacrifice, duty and morality. Much of the peacetime existence of British society was 'uglier, more fundamentally evil, more anti-Christian than even the cruelty, waste and idiotic folly of war', Smith noted. The New Testament had expressly denounced wealth rather than war, for the first was the 'more deadly corruption' for the 'soul of modern societies'. If the war could generate 'a mighty spiritual force', then it would have been 'worth its cost, not only in millions of pounds, but its cost in killed and wounded, in widowed and orphaned and childless'.[16] A noted Cambridge theologian referred to the war as a 'cleansing fire' after 'the accumulation of pestilential decay' of peacetime and hoped for a new world to 'spring out of the blood drenched ground'.[17] These were sentiments worthy of a Marinetti or a Péguy. A more authentically British note was struck by A. F. Pollard in August 1917:

The Prussian has so polluted the earth that the rest and best of mankind has to descend into the mire to cleanse the defilement away. The descent, the humiliation, and the suffering are not good things in themselves, but only as sacrifice. It is the spirit that matters and the purpose that sanctifies the squalor of the *via dolorosa*.[18]

It was almost as if the German jibe that the British were 'decadent money-grubbers, soulless individualists' had struck home. Werner Sombart's picture of shallow *Manchestertum*, underpinned by Benthamite Utilitarianism, in his wartime pamphlet *Händler und Helden* (Traders and Heroes) (1915) was not lost on Smith. The Germans wrongly 'thought their cause the cause of world progress', but was there not an element of truth in their criticism?

> We see they left out the good side of individualism, freedom, individual liberty, a priceless thing. But were we not in danger of leaving out discipline, unity, self-sacrifice, till the war recalled us to the elemental requisites of natural life?

Now the war provided an opportunity to combat "the gospel of self-interest' as the economists of the last century were wont to call it'.[19]

There had been signs of disquiet at the apparent moral vacuum at the centre of British life before 1914. The Liberal politician C. F. G. Masterman, the Anglo-Catholic Bishop of Oxford Charles Gore, and the political philosopher J. N. Figgis were all active critics of Edwardian society from a perspective which stressed moral as well as material shortcomings. Gore, who had been influenced by his old tutor at Oxford, T. H. Green, as well as by a High Church version of social Christianity, was especially prominent in the Christian Social Union to which A. L. Smith also belonged.[20] Well before the war Smith was writing of the need for a 'reconstruction of the sense of community' to replace 'rampant 'Manchesterdom''. Like Gore, Smith found Herbert Spencer's maxim 'Man versus the State' to be already in 1909 'a grotesque antithesis'. Vast forces lay dormant in 'the associative principle'. All that was needed was 'to strike the right balance between an extreme socialism, which might ruin production and culture, and a Mammonism which might provoke men to Anarchism'.[21] This form of Christian Socialism was socialist in the sense of rejecting *laissez-faire* individualism, but more obviously concerned with Christianising or moralising society. 'What was required was a wider recognition than Liberalism showed of the importance of the corporate life, of the social significance of the masses as such, and of the need for 'socialistic humanitarianism'.'[22] Some of these ideals were discovered during the war within peasant Russia, or at least within the writings of Tolstoy. The cult of the *moujik* reached new heights during the war, one Oxford theologian quoting with approval the maxim 'the kind heart of the Russian moujik is a more valuable asset to civilisation than the mighty brain of a German professor'.[23] The revolt against the intellect was as common during the war as the rediscovery of community. However, in Britain there was still some resistance to this trend by supporters of the war.

It had been L. P. Jacks, editor of the popular theological magazine the *Hibbert Journal*, who had coined the phrase 'the peacefulness of being at war' to describe the ideological truce which had been declared for the duration of hostilities. This was something not just to be tolerated, but something to be positively welcomed. The war had brought to Britain a 'peace of mind' it had not possessed for years, the consequence of wartime burdens everyone now had to bear:

> I doubt if there ever was a time when in general the minds of Englishmen were so agitated as they were in the few years preceding the war. Rest for our souls was hardly to be found anywhere. In religion, in philosophy, in politics, we were all at sixes and sevens, fighting one another in the name of our ideals, or striving to rouse the lethargic masses who cared not a button for any of our idealism; and often, it must be confessed, we were in a chronic state of irritation; and to make matters worse, a school of writers had arisen, represented by Mr. Bernard Shaw, who made it their business to irritate and, incidentally, to confuse us still further.

Compared to this aimlessness and confusion the war had brought a sense of 'mission'. Even 'the colossal expenditure of the nation's wealth' on war was a reason for 'peace of mind':

> Surely there is more ground for anxiety in the thought which forces itself upon us in time of peace that all this wealth we are accumulating in ever greater quantities has an unknown destination; that a thousand dangerous uses await it in the prevailing moral chaos .... This is what we see in normal times, and the spectacle is profoundly disturbing. Far less disturbing ... is that process of spending the wealth which we now have to witness.

'Better that the nation grow poor for a cause we can honour, than grow rich for an end that is unknown', Jacks concluded.[24]

This article by Jacks, together with a reply to it by Graham Wallas, was reprinted during the Second World War — Jacks was eighty years old by this time (Wallas had died in 1932). The problems for the liberal intellectual in wartime were to some extent the same in 1939 as in 1914. How far should criticism be suspended for the duration of the war? As a Victorian Liberal, Wallas probably shared much of Jacks's detestation of the state of Edwardian society (especially the social irresponsibility of the affluent classes). However, the rather complacent view of wartime consensus clearly stuck in his gullet. It was a state of mind which reminded him of the recruiting poster of 'a soldier's smiling face with the inscription, 'He's happy and satisfied, are you?''. It was also a 'state of mind ... rather more general and continuous in Germany than in England', especially working-class England. More importantly, the 'condition of 'peacefulness'' raised 'two interesting questions' for Wallas. Firstly, was it so supreme a 'human good' that it made 'war the best form of international relationship'? Secondly, if war were judged evil, should 'combatants and non-combatants ... surrender themselves to that peace of mind'? Not surprisingly, in view of his powerful critique of Social Darwinism in prewar writings, like *The Great Society* (1914), his answer to the first question was an emphatic negative:

> ... the 'peacefulness of being at war' is doomed by the nature of things to be transitory. If the world-war were to last in its present intensity for a whole generation, it would become a conflict of famished women and children fighting each other with their teeth and nails. It seems therefore reasonably certain that, if only for lack of men and materials, this war must in a comparatively few years come to some sort of end. The nations will then find that a large proportion of their best and bravest men are dead, while the degenerate or diseased are alive; that the slow development of the material conditions of a good life for the working classes has been checked; and that West European democracy is endangered, because military discipline in the presence of a group of exasperated enemies has become the supreme national need.

As a prediction of what would in fact happen this was not inaccurate. But to the second question Wallas' answer was more qualified. The value of 'absolute surrender of consciousness' was obvious for the soldier in the trenches; it was 'an anodyne' which few would grudge him and possibly 'an important source of military efficiency'. There might even be a 'certain military value' in a like surrender by non-combatants, but it was something in which Wallas just could not share:

> ... I cannot myself make, or desire to make, that surrender, because to do so would be to abandon as far as I am concerned any attempt to control by reasoned thought the policy of my nation. I should choose the unrest of thought because I desire that the war should come to an end the instant its continuance ceases to be the less of two monstrous evils, and because I believe that our national policy should even during the fighting be guided not only by the will to conquer but also by the will to make possible a lasting peace.[25]

With this article Wallas was clearly signalling to 'his German friends' who also hoped for a compromise peace. Wilhelmine Germany represented everything he opposed politically, 'a medieval aggressive dynasty wielding the whole material force of a fully conscious national machine-industry'. But, if it had not been for the war, 'this phenomenon would have been transient'.[26] There was a danger that, in fighting this immoral force, the Allies would be caught up in a military contest unguided by 'political thought' — the very thing which Bismarck had always sought to avoid.[27]

There was among liberal intellectuals, like Wallas or L. T. Hobhouse, a widespread fear that the violent forces unleashed in 1914 might well become self-perpetuating — that the war would become an end in itself. Wallas, the author of *Human Nature in Politics* (1908) and practitioner of the new science of social psychology, was perhaps more ready to come to terms with these new forces, to turn them to less destructive ends.[28] Hobhouse, initially more willing to support official policy in August 1914, seemed more pessimistic a year later. The greatest danger was Germany, he noted in 1915, but racism and imperialism were not 'the peculiar product of the German mind', as the Boer War had shown. The decline of respect for law and order in Edwardian Britain seemed a prelude to the war itself:

> It is the painfully won tradition of fear and self-restraint that man learns to impose on himself with so much effort which, being in a sense an artificial fabric, is ever liable to yield to the crude instincts of naked self-assertion which it scarcely covers, and with difficulty holds in.'[29]

In the last two years of war Hobhouse became increasingly disillusioned with the pursuit of 'total victory' by Asquith's successor as premier, Lloyd George. As a member of the 'Writers' Group', which included anti-war liberals like the economist J. A. Hobson, as well as supporters of the war like Wallas and Gilbert Murray, Hobhouse worked to prevent a punitive peace settlement leading to a continued 'economic war' against Germany once the fighting had stopped. During wartime, attempts to influence British government policy away from any desire to pursue imperialistic goals were largely a matter of organising signatures to manifestoes — 'a few big men ... with a couple of historians, and a bishop or two, and one or two respected and independent men in business and politics'.[30] Whether this would have much effect, even if lent respectability by the name of Lord Bryce, was of course another matter. There seemed little recognition in 1916 of what Wallas had called 'the supreme importance of controlling ... military action by political thought'.[31]

While the issue of future peace was debated, the much more pressing question of conscription also demanded attention. Britain alone in Europe did not have a policy of compulsory military service in 1914 (nor did the United States), although the schemes which did exist on the Continent might in reality be highly selective (for reasons of cost) or simply inefficient. The question of whether Britain should introduce conscription was one which clearly concerned liberals, but academics had been involved in the controversy well before 1914. At the end of the nineteenth century Oxford could boast the largest batallion of the 'Volunteer Force', forerunner of the modern 'Territorials'. Its organiser L. R. Farnell, Rector of Exeter College, later became an eager propagandist for the National Service League, established in 1901 to press for the introduction of compulsory military service. A Navy League (1895) also flourished, driven on by the organising skill of H. Spenser Wilkinson, soon to be first holder of the Chichele Professorship in Military History at Oxford (1909–23).

After the Liberal Government's reorganisation of the Army between 1906 and 1909, the universities were encouraged to establish Officers' Training Corps.[32] This, however, was still far short of full conscription. The National Service League campaign continued with the assistance of historians, like Professor F. J. C. Hearnshaw of King's College, London, and G. G. Coulton, the successor to J. A. Cramb as speechwriter for Lord Roberts, President of the League.[33] Evidence of opposition to these developments in universities and colleges is scanty, but there was a lively protest meeting against the establishment of a lectureship in Military History and Strategy at Manchester in 1905.[34]

The case for conscription was thus being argued by historians, among others, well before the debate between Wallas and Jacks over the 'absolute surrender of consciousness' by the individual citizen in wartime. Coulton, for example, specialised in arguments designed to appeal to Liberals like Wallas, or even to those further to the Left (the trade unions and the labour movement were generally hostile to conscription). Citing the case of Switzerland, he had long stressed that 'in history' compulsory service had 'been the usual note of democracies' while despots had 'preferred a paid army'. It was 'an obviously democratic principle that all the necessary burdens of the state should be shared as equally as possible among all citizens'. The Swiss short-service officer was less likely to be jingoistic than a career professional, and the whole system was essentially meritocratic. In the ranks conscripts received training in physique and character, and an opportunity to reach the top: 'while the millionaire might vegetate in the ranks, the artisan might rise to the highest military posts!' Any 'illiberal tendencies' apparent in Germany were 'mere local accidents easily separable from the essential principle of universal service' — this was an argument not repeated once war had broken out![35]

While Liberals might respond to the argument that John Stuart Mill had supported the idea of compulsory military service, or that this too could be no more voluntary than taxation, education or national insurance, the evidence of the support for compulsion from French socialists like Jean Jaurès was clearly directed at the British labour movement. The 'general spirit of a Nation in arms', Coulton wrote in 1917, was defensive. It could not be used in a war of aggression, nor could it be used to break strikes against the wishes of a large section of the population.[36] But while Jaurès had probably underestimated the negative conditioning of military service, Coulton had not. In 1906 he had strongly hinted at the usefulness of conscription for social indoctrination. Under the existing 'voluntary' system 'the ordinary British voter' had 'no direct reminder of his civic duties'. British schoolboys were 'never systematically taught what the

Fatherland' had done for them and what their 'reciprocal duties were in return'.[37] Such talk of 'Fatherland' could not, of course, be used during wartime, but it was a simple matter to illustrate the argument from English history. From the Anglo-Saxon fyrd, through the Assize of Arms of 1181 and the national levy of Tudor times, to the militia, it could be argued that, 'far from voluntarism being the immemorial tradition of the English race', it was 'a mushroom innovation established (and that only tentatively and provisionally)' in the nineteenth century. It was 'degenerate descendants of the Victorian era who, deluded by the pacifist prophecies of the Manchester School of politicians, forgot their martial traditions, shed their soldierly qualities, and relegated defence to the voluntarists'. In short, voluntarism was not a "heritage' to be proud of and to cling to', but a 'recent humiliation and disgrace, utterly unworthy of a race' which aspired to be 'imperial' and which claimed 'leadership among mankind'.[38]

Here the roles of historian and propagandist were clearly mixed; Hearnshaw and Coulton were definitely claiming historical expertise in this matter. Usually the advocates of conscription used a straightforward moral argument: by relying 'so largely upon pay and economic forces to provide men for her army' Britain had 'hitherto stood on a lower moral plane than the countries of the Continent'. There may even have been 'some justification for ... German contempt' of decadent Britain. After all, 'the chief cause of decadence of ancient Rome' had been 'the dereliction by the individual of his duties of active citizenship'.[39] Closer to home, conscription would also 'go far to reduce the huge crowds of betting, drinking, smoking and swearing crowds of spectators at races and football and other matches' while volunteers were dying at the Front.[40] And behind these moral strictures lay a simplified version of Idealist political philosophy: 'the right to call upon subjects to aid in the defence of the realm' was 'inherent in the very conception of sovereignty'. In evidence of this T. H. Green, Bradley, Bosanquet, Hegel (surprising perhaps) and, for good measure, John Stuart Mill were cited. It was the function of the state to secure, as far as it could, 'the good life of its citizens'. The 'logical and inevitable corollary' of this was that it was the 'duty of every citizen to support and safeguard the State'. 'True liberty' was primarily 'the liberty of the community or nation'. 'In comparison with that ideal the liberty of the individual' was 'of small moment'. If the nation was endangered, 'every member of it ought to offer his services (his life if need be) to ensure its survival'.[41]

The opponents of conscription were not slow to point out that such assertions opened the door to unbridled 'state absolutism' on the German scale. C. H. Herford and A. J. Grant, Professor of History at Leeds, were prominent opponents of conscription, as was the Cambridge theologian John Oman. All were supporters of the war against Germany, but not at the expense of individual consciences.[42] Too often the advocates of conscription showed little concern for conscientious objectors. The Cambridge economic historian William Cunningham, for example, repeated that familiar description of opponents of compulsion — individuals 'anxious to enjoy all the advantages of life in a community' while claiming 'a right to act on their own judgement, and to deny the General Will'.[43] Against this argument in wartime it was difficult to make much headway, unless one moved from Wallas's position of critical support for the war to Russell's stance of opposition, not just to conscription, but to the war itself. But, as we shall see, few academics were prepared to follow Russell into the path of civil disobedience organised by the No-Conscription Fellowship. As soon as it became apparent, late in 1915, that some kind of conscription would be introduced, it became increasingly difficult for those who supported the war to argue against a measure which appeared to promise its more effective prosecution. From supporters of conscription there was much talk of cleaning up the 'laggards' and 'slackers'. In June 1915 the heads of fourteen Oxford colleges wrote to *The Times* to call for an 'immediate announcement of forthcoming legislation to establish national service for the home, the workshop and the fighting line' to replace 'the voluntary go-as-you-please methods'.[44] This was much more than just military conscription, but by late 1915 even liberal supporters of the war were beginning to consider industrial conscription as well. This was true, for example, of L. T. Hobhouse and R. W. Seton-Watson, the latter at that time Lecturer in East European History at King's College, London.[45]

Against this background, those academics still concerned with the question of individual liberties concentrated on ensuring that the tribunals established under the Military Service Acts of 1916 to hear conscientious objections to conscription worked fairly. Liberals with very different views on the war — Lowes Dickinson and Gilbert Murray, for example — were to be equally exasperated by the 'extremism' of the authorities who allowed no exemptions at all, and of the 'absolutists' (objectors who refused even alternative non-military service).[46] But when it became clear that the Government was allowing the maltreatment of conscientious objectors, liberal academics rallied themselves and signed a protest manifesto published in the magazine of the No-Conscription Fellowship. This was a brave thing to do in October 1916 at a time when even less obviously anti-war organisations, like the Union of Democratic Control, were commonly labelled 'pro-German'. People like Murray, H. A. L. Fisher and John Maynard Keynes, who had connections in government circles, also made individual pleas on behalf of objectors.[47] However, these were honourable exceptions, and there were as many voices from within universities raised against the whole idea of conscientious objection. A. V. Dicey, so many of whose thoughts on the question of reprisals against Germany had contained good sense, supported moves to deprive objectors of their right to vote in national and municipal elections. Dicey also proposed the imposition of additional taxes upon these individuals.[48] As it turned out, the British Government restricted itself to taking away the vote from objectors for a period of five years — ironically the 1918 Representation of the People Act, which gave the vote to women over thirty years of age (and all men over twenty-one), was also the means of legislating this piece of vindictiveness.

Dicey, like others, had claimed that a false 'sentiment of political toleration' protected objectors from suffering the appropriate penalty for their lack of civic consciousness. This hardly squares with the treatment actually meted out to them, including the notorious 'Field Punishment Number One', otherwise known as 'crucifixion', which was not abolished until 1923.[49] What seemed to liberals to be 'extremism' or obstinacy on the part of objectors was likely to be construed in the worst possible way by those who had no sympathy with conscientious objection. The writings of reactionaries, like F. J. C. Hearnshaw or Professor E. V. Arnold of University College, Bangor, could easily be used to provide justification of the harshest kinds of treatment. 'The State does not and cannot submit the validity of its enactments to the private judgement of its subjects', Hearnshaw wrote in a book entitled, significantly, *Freedom in Service* (1916). The state had to demand 'implicit obedience'; the individual had to recognise that politically he had 'no separate existence'. The rights of individuals or groups, for which Guild Socialists like G. D. H. Cole argued (see Chapter 2 above), could not be weighed against those of the state. Hearnshaw proceeded on the assumption that error arose 'in inverse ratio to the magnitude and complexity of the respective organisms concerned': mankind was less likely to be wrong than the nation, the nation than class, class than the individual. As he noted in 1918:

> At the present moment ... the conscience of mankind is rightly asserting itself against the conscience of Germany; the conscience of the British nation is rightly asserting itself against the conscience of the I.L.P.; the conscience of the organised churches is rightly asserting itself against the conscience of the pacifist.[50]

It was a short step from this to the stigmatising of pacifists as 'degenerates, cosmopolitans and undesirables',[51] or, as a group of theologians put it, simply as 'foreigners'.[52]

The conscription issue was clearly an acid test for liberal values. Most academics appear to have opted for Jacks's 'peacefulness of being at war'. Perhaps this could even be said of the young historian R. H. Tawney, who had enlisted in the Manchester Regiment as a private on the outbreak of war. After being invalided back from the Front in 1916 and discharged from the Army (with the War Office making difficulties), Tawney worked with others on a memorandum for Lloyd George on 'the need for a new spirit in government and the conduct of the war'.[53] In reality it was part of an attempt by Lloyd George (in September still Secretary for War) to present himself as a more dynamic national leader than Asquith the Prime Minister. In language little different from that of Hearnshaw, the memorandum proposed first, under the heading 'National Obedience', 'That obedience to the considered decision of the Government should be rigidly enforced upon all sections of the Community'. The Home Front was to be fully mobilised with no half-measures, unhampered 'by the surviving poison of social prejudice and class interests'. While this meant an attack on war profiteering, corruption in the army and the waste of scarce resources, it also clearly meant clamping down on labour unrest:

> Most astonishing and shameful of all, we still see individuals and groups taking advantage of public necessities to forward their own self-interest at a moment when — as they know well — every exceptional pecuniary gain is quite literally the price of blood. It is detestable that the conduct of industry, any more than the manning of a fire-trench, should be the subject of haggling over the division of financial spoils wrung from our country in its hour of need. The soldier at the front expects from the civilian and from the Government a sense of obedience to duty and an enforcement of discipline as severe and as exacting as that to which he is himself accustomed. The call of duty should be imposed on all alike.

The final recommendation was for 'the age of liability to national service [to] be raised to 60' — for industrial as well as military conscription.[54]

Tawney fully supported these proposals, apparently not concerned with the rights of individuals or groups opposed to the war or to conscription itself. By this time (November 1916) he had moved from his prewar liberalism towards the ethical Socialism of his *Acquisitive Society* (1921). Other socialists, of course, did not share Tawney's readiness to see a vast extension of state power. Harold Laski, for example, supported Britain's entry to the war but not the imposition of conscription. Those, like G. D. H. Cole, who opposed the war also opposed conscription.[55] The difference was that Tawney had been a frontline soldier (one of the few survivors of his company). His experiences on the Somme had separated him from intellectuals behind the lines whose idealism was faltering under the impact of the heavy casualty figures of 1916. As he wrote in *The Nation* in October of that year:

While you seem — forgive me if I am rude — to have been surrendering your creeds with the nervous facility of a Tudor official, our foreground may be different, but our background is the same. It is that of August to November, 1914. We are your ghosts.[56]

Tawney, unlike the better-known soldier poets, like Robert Graves and Siegfried Sassoon, continued to believe in the 'ideas of 1914', although he conceded in December 1917 that he would be unlikely to 'get a hearing at a working-class meeting' speaking on 'the principles at stake. One would get laughed down'.[57] Tawney never lost this belief in the 'moral quality of war',[58] although in the last two years he came to believe that 'the loyalty which was given to the cause for which the War was undertaken' was being 'transferred to the War itself'. The end was 'no longer thought of as the reconciliation of enemies through the victory of a principle', but merely as 'the last trick to be snatched by the winner of a game of bluff and cunning'. Even the idealism of the frontline soldier, 'the generosity which would feel that the nation were contaminated if it snatched material advantages from the world's misery, the liberal spirit which knows that even among its enemies there is a better mind', was daily denounced as treason to the war dead.[59]

Much of what Tawney wrote during the war expressed ideas very similar to those of his old tutor at Balliol, A. L. Smith. Both men were members of the Christian Social Union and both welcomed the war as a counter to the peacetime ethic of possessive individualism. For Tawney military training — 'the conversion of a mob into an army' — was like 'organising an unorganised body of workers'. Smith pointed to 'the sense of brotherhood', of 'true Commonwealth' engendered by the war.[60] Where Smith talked of the 'corruption' in the soul of modern society, Tawney pointed to the 'cult of power' in capitalist society. The latter was exemplified by Prussia, but also by:

> ... the not very obscure analogy between a conception of politics which would trample on all moral laws in the pursuit of political power, and a conception of economic life which regards any kind of organisation as justified by its efficiency, and therefore holds that there are no moral principles upon which economic conduct need be based.

'The scale of values' which lay behind 'the claim of some Prussians to have a right to determine the future of 'weaker' or 'inferior' nations' was the same as the one which was 'realized in our industrial system', Tawney concluded.[61] But since the possibility of real change was greater in Britain, it was right 'to fight against Germany 'in order that the spiritual personality of nations may not be over-ridden by a machine''.[62] As rhetoric this was little different from the writings of historians like Ernest Barker.

D

The difference lay in Tawney's commitment to economic and social democracy through his membership of the Labour Party.[63]

Tawney's belief that the war could be used to usher in social change — that it really could be a 'war for democracy' — was the theme of his writings from 1916 onwards. In practical terms it meant convincing the labour movement 'that this war was their war, not an enterprise for which their rulers want their arms but not their minds and hearts'.[64] With this idea of a people's war he was twenty or so years too early. However, the Russian Revolution in October 1917 did raise the question of a compromise peace between the western Allies and the Central Powers. It is to the reverberations of this within the academic community that we now turn.

CHAPTER 5

The Question of a Compromise Peace

... a further prolongation of the war, with the turn things have now taken, probably means the disappearance of the social order we have known hitherto. With some regrets I think I am on the whole not sorry. The abolition of the rich will be rather a comfort and serve them right anyhow. What frightens me more is the prospect of a *general* impoverishment. In another year we shall have forfeited the claim we had staked out in the New World and in exchange this country will be mortgaged to America.

Well, the only course open to me is to be buoyantly Bolshevik; and as I lie in bed in the morning I reflect with a great deal of satisfaction that, because our rulers are as incompetent as they are mad and wicked, one particular era of a particular kind of civilisation is nearly over.

John Maynard Keynes to his mother, 24 December 1917

Advocates of a compromise peace were not common amongst British academics. The few that there were came from Cambridge rather than its sister university. While Oxford University Press produced a long series of patriotic pamphlets on the war (mostly written by members of the University), Cambridge became notorious for the *Cambridge Magazine*, an unofficial publication edited by the brilliant and eccentric undergraduate C. K. Ogden.[1] Begun in 1912, the magazine had achieved a circulation of 25,000 during the war, and a national reputation far beyond that of its sober rival the *Cambridge Review*. While never a pacifist magazine like the No-Conscription Fellowship's *Tribunal*, the *Cambridge Magazine* did open its columns to people like Bertrand Russell, Lowes Dickinson and Siegfried Sassoon, as well as to literary figures who supported the war, like Thomas Hardy, John Masefield and Arnold Bennett.[2] Another attraction was the 'Notes from the Foreign Press' which included material from the Central Powers. Perhaps this was sufficient for the charge of 'pacifism' to be made against it, although this would have been difficult to prove. The Professor of Archaeology at Cambridge, however, devoted much time to this task, complaining that every week Dickinson and others poured 'gentle streams of luke warm water upon patriotic enthusiasm'. The magazine's name was embarrassing for the University, and the Vice-Chancellor was at pains to deny that it was in any sense an official publication.[3] Other academics — many of them supporters of the war — sprang to the magazine's defence, but the criticism may have had something to do with the attack on its offices during Armistice Week.[4]

The unsavoury reputation acquired by the *Cambridge Magazine* (among the noisily patriotic) was shared by the Union of Democratic Control, a foreign-policy pressure group with strong Cambridge connections. The U.D.C. had been established in December 1914 by radical Liberals (like C. P. Trevelyan and the historian G. P. Gooch), anti-war socialists (like Ramsay MacDonald), and liberal intellectuals (like Norman Angell, H. N. Brailsford and J. A. Hobson). Lowes Dickinson and Russell, both of whom we shall examine in more detail later, organised the Cambridge branch which soon became the largest outside London. Once again Trinity College was heavily involved — no fewer than thirteen of its Fellows were members of the U.D.C.[5] The main objective of the Union was to oppose 'secret diplomacy' and to press for the 'democratic control' of foreign policy through Parliament. The rest of its programme was based on the assumption — as the Secretary of the Cambridge branch put it — 'then made by almost everybody, that the war must be won, and ... won fairly quickly'.[6] The U.D.C. was, in its avowed aims at least, not so much concerned with prewar British policy, or even with the war itself, as with any future peace settlement. It called for the holding of plebiscites before any postwar transfer of territory, the establishment of an 'International Council' of states, general disarmament and the nationalisation of the arms industry, and warned against 'economic war' against Germany after military hostilities had ceased. These were objectives which all good liberals, whether they supported the war or not, could support. One could hardly find a more 'respectable' supporter of official policy than Lord Bryce, yet his presidential address at the British Academy in 1915 was a clear criticism of 'issues of war and peace' being decided by 'the ruling few':

> How few are the persons in every state in whose hands lie issues of war and peace. In some of the now belligerent countries the final and vital decisions were taken by four or five persons only, in others by six or seven only. Even in Britain decisions rested practically with less than twenty-five, for though some persons outside the Cabinet took a part, not all within the Cabinet are reckoned as effective factors. It is probable of course that popular sentiment has to be considered, even in states more or less despotically governed. Against a strong and definite sentiment of the masses the ruling few would not act. But the masses are virtually led by a few and their common opinion is formed, particularly at a crisis, by the authority and the appeals of those few whom they have been accustomed to trust and obey. And, after all, the vital decision at the vital moment remains with the few. If they had decided otherwise than they did, the thing would not have happened. Something like it might have happened later, but the war would not have come then and so.[7]

Not all liberals shared Bryce's analysis of the outbreak of the war. R. W. Seton-Watson, for example, claimed that 'the foremost obstacle' to 'democratic control' was not so much 'the existence of an aristocratic caste or its alleged aversion to intruders from another class, as the boundless and dispiriting indifference of the masses' to the problems of foreign policy. If there were 'no keen and well-informed public opinion', A. F. Pollard wrote at about the same time, 'democratic control' would simply be 'a proposition that expert knowledge should be controlled by general ignorance'.[8] As self-appointed experts on foreign policy Pollard and especially Seton-Watson were eager that government should listen to them; 'democratic control' would simply get in the way. The existing foreign policymakers were not very efficient or well-informed, but they did not constitute a sinister class interest.[9] Further to the right politically, historians like F. J. C. Hearnshaw were even more sceptical about the possibility of creating well-informed public opinion. When Hearnshaw considered 'how unreasonable and bellicose uninformed public opinion' could become 'at times of excitement', he could only feel 'thankful' that hitherto foreign policy had been the preserve of an elite. And touching on something often ignored by U.D.C. writers, he noted:

> If it is a fact that from time to time unwilling and pacific peoples have been dragged or driven into war by bellicose governments, it is equally a fact that at other times cautious and reluctant governments (both autocratic and bureaucratic) have been forced into war by bellicose public opinion, or have with difficulty held back a populace less pacific than themselves.

But although this difference of opinion with the U.D.C. was a major one, what Hearnshaw objected to most was the assumption that all governments were, to some extent, responsible for the outbreak of the war. 'The war was not due to the 'European Anarchy', but to Austro-German design', Hearnshaw wrote in a reference to a well-known book by Lowes Dickinson. All states were not 'equally guilty', for two of them stood 'convicted as criminals'.[10] Once it was accepted 'that war was inevitable', then there was 'nothing left to justify mistrust' of British policy, another critic of the U.D.C. noted.[11] However, any confusion between a belief in the inevitability of war because of an anarchic international order, and a belief that 'secret diplomacy' had led to its outbreak, does not seem to have unduly troubled the U.D.C.

More serious was the fact that the U.D.C., although professing to avoid controversy on the origins of the war, was coming increasingly to be seen as an advocate of compromise peace. According to the secretary of the Cambridge branch of the Union, this characterisation was 'to a considerable extent justified'.[12] The fact that it was the unstated assumption which underlay much of U.D.C. writing on the war only served to lend credence to talk of the 'machinations of secret traitors' and a 'sinister' combination of 'secret diplomatists'.[13] What so enraged these critics, like G. G. Coulton whose *Main Illusions of Pacificism* (1915) exposed the 'Angellite' basis of the U.D.C.,[14] was that this body cast doubt on the official British version of the outbreak of the war, without giving any evidence for this scepticism. Unless there was an attempt to produce evidence, one of them claimed, any attempt to blame Grey for 'causing unnecessary bloodshed' was little short of treasonable. This from a Fellow of St. John's College, Cambridge, was an indication of the level of bitterness within the academic community. Matters had not been helped by the fact that the first public meeting of the Cambridge branch had been addressed by E. D. Morel, one of the most extreme opponents of government policy.[15] Later in the war Morel was equalled in his reputation as an uncompromising critic of government by Bertrand Russell, at that time Lecturer in Logic and the Principles of Mathematics at Trinity College, Cambridge.

The main body of British academics — at least of those who expressed themselves publicly — seemed to accept the war as 'an end in itself'. The intellectual brilliance of Russell or the tortured doubts of Dickinson (surely the most prolific of liberal 'dissenters') should not obscure the fact that for most academics (as for the public at large) the danger was not that the war would be pursued too vigorously, but rather the opposite. J. W. Allen's lecture of May 1915 was typical of many such arguments against the talk of compromise peace. 'The common will to peace' was 'really a negative thing', 'a mere revolt or a shrinking from the consequences of war'. A nation 'which refused war merely by reason of its natural fear and shrinking would be hopelessly decadent and doomed to disappear'. Aside from the moral justifications for 'relentless war' against Germany — for had not she 'made war upon the soul of man'? — there were the realities of war itself. 'There is only one thing of real importance, and that is to get Germany helpless. When we have done that we can be generous as we please', Allen concluded. The advocates of compromise peace implied (even if they did not say openly) that so far as the war was 'not quite immediately defensive', it had 'no rational purpose at all'. A peace based on agreement for 'the automatic avoidance of war in the future' (in other words a U.D.C.-type peace) was no substitute for one based on military victory.[16]

This in fact was the core of the objection of many to the U.D.C., and it also goes some way to explaining the sense of outrage felt by many academics at Russell's espousal of 'pacifist' sentiments. To say that war was irrational was to appear to patronise the fervently patriotic; to talk of compromise peace was to ignore the desire for revenge. An article by A. F. Pollard, 'The Temptation of Peace' (December 1916) took the U.D.C. to task for talking of 'peace and reconciliation without a thought of atonement'. In the name of 'ethics' the U.D.C. denounced 'all justice as revenge', and in the name of 'progress' pleaded for the *status quo ante bellum*. How could these people 'make peace with Miss Cavell's murderers, with the slave-drivers of Belgium, and with the perpetrators and accomplices of the Armenian massacres', Pollard asked incredulously. 'A nation's capacity for sacrifice in moral causes', not its readiness to make peace, was 'the test of its morality'.[17] Pollard's distate for compromise peace was echoed by other historians. The example of the war with Napoleon was often cited to highlight the dangers of such a course.[18] During the first three years of the war there was a sustained campaign in the press by academics to quash any talk of peace without total victory. The weight of academic expertise and influence was clearly marshalled against the U.D.C. and its fellow-travellers.[19] The dangers of this state of mind were clear to a slightly more detached observer like R. H. Tawney:

> The inertia, the apathy, the weight of custom and routine, which make it difficult to begin [a war], make it hardly less difficult to contemplate its being ended, and in proportion as the soldiers grow more pacific, the civilians grow more bellicose.[20]

However, during 1916 even some hitherto staunch supporters of the war began to grow weary. Typical of the growing apprehension over the consequences of any indefinite continuation of the war were the *War-Time Lectures* (1916) of E. V. Arnold, Professor of Latin at University College, Bangor. Arnold predicted that if the war went on much longer there was a definite danger of revolution at home and abroad (especially in the Austro-Hungarian Empire) leading to the establishment of left-wing revolutionary regimes. The defeat of the Central Powers would mean that 'the wild ideals and hideous cruelties of the French Revolution would be re-enacted: and the whole proud structure of German civilisation would crumble into nothing'. The Dual Monarchy would be split into a 'dozen petty kingdoms ... engaged upon mutual wars upon the model of the Balkan states'. The consequences for Britain were that it would become 'the helpless appendage of a European combination of States'. Events would show a certain degree of truth in this prediction, and it would be a mistake to write Arnold off just as a conservative Germanophile (he had been a Lloyd George liberal in 1910).[21] In November 1916 he wrote in A. R. Orage's *New Age* that Britain would have to face the facts about 'Pan-Germanism and Central Europe', for they could not be altered. It 'would be a crime to destroy' 'Berlin to Baghdad'. 'Why indeed, should we oppose ourselves to 'Central Europe'', Arnold asked. 'It is, to say the least, a half-way stage to 'All Europe''.[22] This was very different from the map of

Europe as envisaged by British historians, but Arnold now went even further and argued for negotiated peace.

In November 1916, a full year before the publication of the Lansdowne Letter (29 November 1917), it was not easy to call publicly for a negotiated peace, even if it were argued that this would best serve the interests of France and Belgium. Arnold had to phrase his suggestion carefully — 'even the bravest of peoples' might 'in the end be forced to yield to necessity'. But in a remarkable passage, Arnold dared to ask the very question which Bertrand Russell asked: 'If Germany were to conquer England, and admit Englishmen to its citizenship, should we individually suffer?' However, while Russell had asked his question in the course of an examination of the virtues of a course of passive resistance, Arnold's perspective was rather different. A German occupation would:

> ... preserve the English social system as it now exists from the violent catastrophes which now threaten it. As such we might expect it to be welcomed by the upper and middle classes, but viewed with suspicion by the well-to-do and powerful working men's unions. The course of events has shown that even in England material interests count for nothing with any class as against strongly roused national sentiment.[23]

The fact that Arnold seems to have escaped public abuse perhaps demonstrates that 'Lansdownism' was more politically respectable than talk of compromise peace from radical liberals or socialists. A year before the publication of his letter in the *Daily Telegraph* Lansdowne had been arguing privately for a moderation of war aims and a willingness by Britain to negotiate. As a result of this Lansdowne, an extreme Conservative, found his ideas being publicised by the U.D.C., rather to his alarm. Arnold, on the other hand, was readier to admit the similarity of his ideas to those of the U.D.C.[24]

Arnold's dire predictions of revolution in Britain were again aired in a series of anonymous articles in *The Times* in September 1917. The last of these opened with the claim that there was a 'revolutionary movement' which had 'long passed the stage of mere talk', and which had 'realized itself in formidable action':

> There has been no attack on the throne, no rioting in the streets, no destruction of visible property; but changes have already been brought about which are thwarting the efforts of the Government to conduct the war with efficiency, and if these changes go further they will bring the country into confusion.[25]

What Arnold was specifically referring to is made clear in his memorandum 'Labour in Revolt', circulated among members of the War Cabinet by Lord Milner, another reactionary (though not attached to the Tory party) with the idea of compromise peace in mind. Arnold identified a 'working-class movement', sharing the 'passionate revolutionary fervour' of Pan-Germanism and Sinn Fein, and quite distict from 'middle-class pacifism' or from 'lower-class' revolutionary activity in London's East End. This was a movement of the 'well-paid artisans' of Clydeside and the Midlands, of South Wales miners and dockers in general. The leadership was young and alienated from trade union bureaucracy, and much influenced by the Russian Revolution. The movement had 'humbled Government' and could impoverish the country with its demands, undermining 'confidence in lawful authority' and causing large-scale industrial violence. Clearly, something had to be done:

> The crushing of such a movement is one of the ordinary tasks of Government, and almost any method within reason, will crush it if carried out with decision and courage. But I do not myself believe that it can be done without serious conflict.[26]

Labour unrest and the growth of a radical shop stewards' movement continued to be a matter of concern for the rest of the war, although for the Government the worst was past until the Forty Hours Strike early in 1919 on Clydeside again raised the spectre of revolution. But for conservative academics like F. J. C. Hearnshaw the menace of Bolshevism came to overshadow even the war itself:

> It is more formidable than the Prussian attack made in 1914 because it is an attack made from within the country by those who enjoy the rights and privileges of the democratic franchise. But it is essentially the same as the Prussian attack, both in spirit and in method. It is a conspiracy by a militant oligarchy of pan-proletarians to establish a dictatorship over the community. Their Bernhardi is Karl Marx, and their modes of preparing for the class war are identical with those which the Germans employed .... Elaborate organisation, skilful formulation of plans, laborious accumulation of funds and munitions, secret diplomacy, insidious propaganda, careful manoeuvring for position, diligent search for a strategic pretext for declaring the conflict open, supreme disregard for treaty obligations — such are the methods common to Prussian fomentors of the last war and to the revolutionary projectors of the next war.[27]

Hearnshaw was perhaps unusually obsessed by such things, and there was something very like a 'Jewish-Bolshevik' conspiracy at the heart of his explanation.[28] He was clearly sympathetic, perhaps involved in, the attempts by Milner to establish 'patriotic labour' organisations around the paper *British Citizen and Empire Worker*.[29] However, his fear that the 'domestic truce' of 1914 was almost beyond hope of recall was a sentiment which was common in academic circles by 1918.

The last year of the war also saw another U.D.C. objective attain greater political respectability, the idea of a postwar league of nations. This, as we shall see, originated with a member of the Cambridge branch, G. Lowes

Dickinson, but soon became the common property of a wide range of liberal opinion from Lord Bryce to J. A. Hobson. Through Graham Wallas the so-called 'Bryce Group', which from September/October 1914 met privately to discuss the league idea, was in touch with Progressive intellectuals in the United States, some of whom were advisors to the government of Woodrow Wilson.[30] However, public debate was still 'hampered by the prevailing belief that the league movement was a stop-the-war movement, and that such action would be to the advantage of Britain's enemies'.[31] It mattered little that in Germany the league was considered to be a pro-Allied scheme. But there were also more fundamental objections to the idea of some 'International Council' for the settlement of disputes. J. W. Allen struck a sceptical note:

> I do not believe that any judicial or conciliation machinery could ever prevent war, or even really affect the probability of war. The most it would ever do would be to postpone a war: and it is doubtful whether postponement of war is ever a gain . . . . War is the logical, that is, the necessary, issue of a certain psychological situation. So far as that situation is created by governments, they are responsible for the war: but certainly it is never created by any single group of men . . . . Hardly ever, if at all, is the technical and diplomatic question upon which, formally, war is commenced, expressive of the cause of war, except very indirectly and incompletely. Often it is a mere pretext for war.'[32]

Allen was, of course, not only criticising the idea of conciliation machinery and the personalised explanation for war (the machinations of diplomatists and politicians) so favoured by the U.D.C., but was also repeating many of the objections to liberal internationalism expressed earlier by Idealist philosophers like F. H. Bradley and D. G. Ritchie. During the war the idea of a league of nations as part of a postwar settlement aroused either the scepticism or outright hostility of philosophers like Bosanquet or Sir Henry Jones. Bosanquet, for example, while admitting that the incidence of war might be 'immensely diminished by the reform of states, and their reconstruction in certain cases', was unimpressed by talk of international restraints or sanctions unless based on 'an organised moral world'. The comments by Jones were characteristically less subtle. As he told an Oxford audience in 1916:

> 'No nation', we are told by Mr. [H. A. L.] Fisher, 'has yet consented or in the present state of public ethics, is likely to consent to refer matters affecting its vital interests, independence or honour to an international tribunal.' I agree, and I go further. No nation ought to do so. A nation like an individual may consult its neighbours as to its duty, borrow light from its neighbours to see what it should do, but it cannot delegate the responsibility of choosing. There is a certain isolation and sacredness of soul in this matter of morality. We can send no proxies to meet duty or death.[33]

However, in the last two years of the war, especially after the entry of the

United States into the conflict in April 1917, the league movement took on new life. The Lansdowne letter in November of that year had raised the question of a postwar organisation to settle international disputes, as well as pressing for a statement of limited war aims. The league idea now became more respectable amongst those who could hardly be called liberal internationalists. The 'Bryce Group' had assisted in the establishment of the League of Nations Society in May 1915; now three years later more conservative academics established the League of Free Nations Association. In Dickinson's eyes it consisted of 'more 'reputable' people, known most of them ... to have been ardent supporters of the war, and good haters of Germany'.[34] Not surprisingly its vision of a postwar league differed significantly from that of the League of Nations Society which it tended to regard as 'a fad of liberal and religious idealists'.[35] The Society envisaged a league consisting of 'any civilised State desiring to join', but tended to be rather vague on the question of how to enforce its decisions. The Association, by contrast, clearly hoped that the existing wartime alliance against the Central Powers would continue as a basis of a strong postwar league wielding armed force.[36] As one of the governing council of the Association put it, the Allies were:

> ... already engaged on the purposes of a *league of peace* .... Germany's weapon must be broken in its hands. Germany, ... must, lose its trust in military force and seek greatness in some other way. It must learn to despise military ambition. It must recognise the political crudeness of the spirit and will to dominate.

Until that happened, until Germany renounced its 'barbaric ambition', it must be excluded from any league.[37] The writer was none other than Sir Henry Jones — the tone of self-righteousness is unmistakeable. Idealist theory was clearly elastic enough to encompass the league idea in this new form, one which did not imply any slackening of the war effort.

The seal of political respectability for the league idea was finally given when members of the government began to publicly advocate it. In January 1918 Lloyd George established the Phillimore Committee to report on the league idea. Among its members were two historians, A. F. Pollard and J. Holland Rose, who investigated the historical evolution of such schemes. Pollard's pamphlet, *The League of Nations: An Historical Argument* (1918), was one of the most informed contributions to the debate, albeit one which largely followed the harder line of the League of Free Nations Association. Elsewhere Pollard presented a case for considering the British Empire as 'the only permanent league of nations in existence',[38] but here he was more restrained, confining himself to arguing that a defeated Germany was in no position to ask for membership of a league of nations:

> Whether they are admitted or not, the League will, after the determination of Germany's frontiers, give them absolute security from attack, based on scraps of paper and independent of German arms .... She may even make a higher bid for the carrying trade of the world than before the war, and seek in remunerative triumphs of commerce and industry compensation for the loss of costly dominion.

From the perspective of the victor, Germany had to be content with its designated role as international hewer of wood and drawer of water. And as for the 'elaborate schemes on paper' for some international tribunal to act as arbiter in disputes:

> It would be better ... to consider the possibility of a League of Nations, formed simply for security rather than for the more ambitious ideal of justice. Order came before law, and law before justice ....
>
> The bare prevention of war may ... seem a poor substitute for justice. But some of these evils [bad government, oppressed nationalities] will be remedied by the terms of peace, and it is war with its horrors that we are most concerned to avert.[39]

Pollard's views corresponded closely to those expressed in the final report of the Phillimore Committee (March 1918), particularly the scepticism about the viability or usefulness of permanent international organisation. Pollard's preference for 'methods which develop naturally with experience', and which were directed towards more limited goals, was echoed by other historians and by international lawyers. The analogy of the growth of English law 'from case to case' was often cited in defence of this view, as were the lessons of the Vienna Settlement of 1815.[40] 'The first step towards permanent peace' was not 'the erection of a tribunal or the establishment of a super-State'. Rather, it was 'a simple treaty between as many Powers as possible not to make war upon one another'. What was needed was a realistic perception of what was likely to work. As a Cambridge critic of the U.D.C. put it:

> I do not believe that any League, however solemn, will suddenly change the nature of mankind, and (if I may so express it) humanize human societies once and for all. A higher morality is more likely to invent better machinery than a better machinery to create a higher morality. This does not imply that better machinery will not be helpful. The danger is that machinery devised in a moment of enthusiasm and responding to the aspirations of war-torn peoples may appear less satisfactory when enthusiasm has been cooled by time.[41]

However, the league idea in the sense of some continuation of the wartime alliance against Germany was finding favour with some members of the Government, like Lord Hugh Cecil, or with those closely associated with it, like General Smuts. In May 1918 these two individuals joined Bryce and the Archbishop of Canterbury in addressing a public meeting at Central Hall, Westminster. By October the League of Nations Society and the League of Free Nations Association were moving towards amalgamation. In the process the former body gave up virtually all its 'idealistic' programme, largely under the prompting of Viscount (formerly Sir Edward) Grey.[42] The policy of the resulting League of Nations Union was reflected in Grey's keynote address. The former target of the U.D.C.'s critique of 'secret diplomacy' had now become the first President of the Union dedicated to the ideal which the U.D.C. had done so much to promote, much to the disgust of radicals like J. A. Hobson. Although Grey denied that any league would be used as a weapon against Germany, he clearly contemplated the use of economic blockade against Germany, after the war, to encourage internal political reform. Until these had taken place, he did not feel that Germany could be admitted to any league.[43]

Undoubtedly the campaign for a League of Nations helped to revive the flagging ardour of liberal academics, like Gilbert Murray, who had become mildly infected by 'Lansdownism'. Those who had striven for future international cooperation from the first months of the war, like Lowes Dickinson and J. A. Hobson, were understandably bitter. And it is to Gilbert Murray that we now turn in order to examine the progression from enthusiastic support for the war to equally enthusiastic support for what had originally been an idea developed by intellectuals associated with the U.D.C.

CHAPTER 6

Gilbert Murray

> However badly we may have been or are yet likely to be domoralised by this war, that is a lesser evil than if all Europe were conquered by Germany. And even to be conquered by Germany now, after all we have suffered, would be a lesser evil than to have submitted to her without a struggle.

Gilbert Murray, 'The Turmoil of War' (1917)

> It is quite probable that the effects would have been less disastrous if we had stayed out and allowed Germany to become the complete master of western Europe, on more or less equal terms with U.S.A. and Russia.

Gilbert Murray to Bertrand Russell, 20th August 1955

Shortly before his death in 1957 Gilbert Murray set forth the ideals which had guided him as a scholar throughout his life:

> ... there has never been a day ... when I have failed to give thought to the work for peace and for Hellenism. The one is a matter of life and death for all of us; the other of maintaining, amid all the dust of modern and industrial life, our love and appreciation for the eternal values.[1]

Murray always maintained that the life of scholarship and the path of political commitment were inseparable. He did not have a political career like James Bryce, although he was asked several times to stand for Parliament as a Liberal. However, he was still a member of the intellectual elite, a generation after Bryce, which believed that privilege conferred certain duties. As one of his colleagues noted:

> He set his course by a tradition which was both Victorian and classical; to him it was unquestionable that, in peace as in war, the public call must be obeyed first, and that research, however laborious or entrancing, was a privilege of unclaimed leisure. He could not split his personality as to teach Greek without being a political animal.[2]

Another member of this 'intellectual aristocracy', who married Murray's daughter, described Murray's politics as those of 'aristocratic liberalism'. And, underpinning this belief in the social obligations of the rich and powerful was the legacy of Murray's classical studies — 'an unshakeable trust in reason' and a belief that 'extremism or fanaticism, even in a good cause' was 'a bad thing'.[3]

In fact, Murray was born in Sydney and spent his first eleven years 'down under'. At public school in England Murray first read the works of

Mill and Spencer, showing an early interest in liberalism which continued at Oxford. At university Murray, together with L. T. Hobhouse and Arthur Sidgwick (brother of Henry Sidgwick), started the Oxford Home Rule League in 1885.[4] When Murray came back to Oxford as Regius Professor of Greek in 1908, he was not only a leading classical scholar but also a politically active Liberal with radical pretensions. In 1912, for example, he presided over meetings organised by Oxford Fabians in support of striking municipal transport workers.[5] As an undergraduate at Oxford he had joined the Volunteer Corps, but during the Boer War Murray had written a scathing criticism of 'national ideals' in very much the kind of terms employed by Bertrand Russell during the First World War. The first sentence of his article, for example, read thus:

> If I had one remark and one only to make about National Ideals, it would be this: that the conscious and professed ideals are as straws in the wind; the unconscious or concealed ideals are the real forces that govern mankind.[6]

At this time Murray also contributed an essay on 'The Exploitation of Inferior Races in Ancient and Modern Times' to the book *Liberalism and Empire* (1902) edited by F. W. Hirst and J. L. Hammond.

When the Liberal Government came to power in 1906 Murray continued to criticise British foreign policy from a position somewhere to the left of the main body of the Liberal party. In the preface to his wartime defence of the Foreign Secretary, Sir Edward Grey, Murray described his position, before his change of heart in August 1914, as follows:

> I have always been unhappy about Morocco and Persia; profoundly unhappy about our strained relations with Germany; sympathetic in general towards the Radical and Socialist line on foreign policy; and always anxious to have the smallest Navy vote that a reasonable government would permit.
>
> I have never until this year [1914] seriously believed in the unalterable aggressive designs of Germany. I knew our own Jingoes, and recognised the existence of German Jingoes; but I believed that there, as here, the government was in the hands of the more wise and sober part of the nation. I have derided all scares and loathed (as I still loathe) all scaremongers and breeders of hatred. I have believed (as I still believe) that many persons now in newspaper offices might be more profitably housed in lunatic asylums. And I also felt, with some more impatience, that though as an outsider, I could not tell exactly what the Government ought to do, they surely could produce good relations between Great Britain and Germany if only they had the determination and the will.[7]

But now Murray admitted that 'on a large part of this question' he had been wrong. Addressing a meeting at the Essex Hall, London, in 1916, he asked: 'Have I any doubt in any corner of my mind that the war was right? I have none. We took the path of duty and the only path we could take.' Yet only fifteen years previously, as Murray also admitted, in that very hall he had spoken out against British policy in South Africa. 'I little imagined then that I should live to speak in favour of the policy of a much greater and more disastrous war', he concluded rather sadly.[8] What had caused this change of heart?

Undoubtedly it was the German invasion of Belgium which operated powerfully on Murray's conscience, as it did on the consciences of liberal intellectuals like L. T. Hobhouse, J. L. Hammond and Graham Wallas. Together with them Murray had signed neutrality manifestoes, but between the point of signing (26 or 27 July) and publication (3 August) Murray claimed to have been converted to support for the war by the published documents. 'The all told fundamentally the same story', he wrote in his defence of Sir Edward Grey:

> The statesman whom I had suspected as over-imperialist was doing everything humanly possible to preserve peace; the Power whose good faith I had always championed was in part playing a game of the most unscrupulous bluff, in part meant murder from the beginning.[9]

But even more than the documents, important though they might be, it was the figure of the Foreign Secretary which was crucial for liberal intellectuals returning to the fold. Forty years later Murray recalled 'that calm and irresistible speech of Grey's to Parliament on the third of August', 'a speech which he had not had time to prepare, but which yet seemed perfectly clear in its narrative and consistent in its reasoning'.[10] To an E. D. Morel or a Bertrand Russell, Grey was either a knave or a fool; to Murray he became the perfect embodiment of the English gentleman. All the cynical brilliance of Metternich, Talleyrand or Bismarck seemed:

> ... so utterly opposite to the characteristics of this quiet, able, unpretending Englishman of country tastes, simple in word and thought, a little tongue-tied and shy, learned in birds and good at fishing, and kindling quickly to warm sympathy in all questions of labour ....
>
> He seems so unlike a diplomat. The traditional qualities of the diplomat, the polished surface, the social brilliance, the narrow ruthless outlook, the skill in moving gracefully among traps and mines, the smiling falsehoods and *coups* of unscrupulous cleverness ....[11]

This was the reason that Murray could not understand the special venom reserved for Grey — no one seemed further removed from the world of 'secret diplomacy'. This 'queer delusion', Murray felt, was a reaction to the bipartisan approach to British foreign policy during the July crisis. The 'peril [was] so awful that wise men were mostly willing to measure their words and avoid the possibility of fanning any dangerous smoke into the flame'. This was the background against which Grey's policy had to be judged:

If here and there on some point of detail he has not driven as clever a bargain as he might; if he has not stood up to our friends Russia and France as defiantly as some of his less responsible critics would have done; and if, here and there, he has not pressed fearlessly forward in support of some weak nation to which British liberal sympathies went naturally forth; if under his guidance, with all our enormous naval expenditure and prestige, Great Britain has sometimes seemed to have little spare strength for the running of avoidable risks or the championing of disinterested causes; let those who criticize him who can still say he over-rated the danger. The rest of us will only be grateful for ever to one who through all these years of crisis acted justly and sought no aggrandizement, who kept faith with his friends and worked for a good understanding with his enemies, who never spoke a rash word to bring the peril nearer, and never neglected a precaution to meet it when it should come.[12]

As a eulogy of the Foreign Secretary this was not unusual, but for someone formerly so critical of British foreign policy this was really quite remarkable.

Murray in fact had fewer reservations about changing his mind than did many of his friends. He did not, for example, agree with 'a Radical friend' who claimed that, although "for the last twelve days" Grey had been "working for peace", British policy generally before 1914 had "been making peace impossible".[13] Murray also swallowed the Dual and Triple Ententes, Morocco and Persia. Even over Persia, where Radical criticism of Grey had been strong,[14] Murray concluded that even if he did not 'feel any enthusiasm' for Britain's record, it was still difficult to see how it could have been much better: 'After all it is not always the fault of the doctor if the patient dies'. His conclusion about Morocco was much the same, and he noted of the non-white world in general (and Ireland) that, while there were 'a few rusty spots on our large shield', it was not possible to 'have free institutions everywhere'.[15] His attitude to unrepentant critics of Grey, like H. N. Brailsford and Bertrand Russell, was that such writers were 'in their way high-minded, disinterested, courageous, and often very clever', but, for all that, 'impassioned advocates, not fair-minded inquirers'. 'Neutrality of opinion' was not the same as 'sincere and honest impartiality'.[16] To these two critics Murray was bound by ties of friendship and marriage — Brailsford and his wife were former pupils of Murray when he was Professor of Classics at Glasgow (1889–99), and Murray had married Russell's cousin, Lady Mary Howard. Relations between Russell and Murray, though on the surface friendly, were seriously strained during wartime. While professing not to charge Russell with being "the friend of every country but his own", Murray came pretty close to implying just this — ironically in view of the same charge being laid against him during the Boer War.[17] Russell for his part claimed that Murray's 'charmingly idyllic' account of Grey's foreign policy was written 'under the tutelage' of the

Foreign Office. And although Russell told Murray that their friendship still lived 'in the eternal world', he wrote elsewhere of Murray as 'a snivelling sentimental ass', 'as squashy as a slug'.[18]

Russell's comments tell us something of the bitterness of wartime divisions, but some of Murray's writings really do merit the charge of squashiness. An article of November 1916 for an American audience is a typical example. Against the background of the mud of the Somme, the best Murray could offer was the image of sacrifice:

> When I realize most fully the burden we are bearing, the ordeal of fire through which we are resolved to pass, I am not only proud of my country, I thank God that, if this awful event was to fall upon humanity — this awful evil to avert another yet more awful — that our country was called upon to stand in the very van of the battle and of suffering, and that we have not flinched from the task.[19]

However, the overwhelming impression conveyed by Murray's wartime articles and pamphlets is of a liberal conscience grappling with the problem of the evil of war. Murray was not a Sir Henry Jones arguing that out of the evil of war could come good. In his contribution to the Oxford series of pamphlets *How Can War Ever Be Right?* (1914) he noted:

> I have all my life been an advocate of Peace. I hate war, and not merely for its own cruelty and folly, but because it is the enemy of all the causes that I care for most, of social progress and good government and all friendliness and gentleness of life, as well as of art and learning and literature. I have spoken and presided at more meetings than I can remember for peace and arbitration and the promotion of international friendship. I opposed the policy of war in South Africa with all my energies, and have been either outspokenly hostile or inwardly unsympathetic towards almost every war that Great Britain has waged in my lifetime.

Murray could thus 'sympathize with every step' of the pacifist argument but still baulk at what seemed to be the acceptance of evil. It was a 'cardinal fact that in some causes' it was 'better to fight and be broken than to yield peacefully'. The 'mere act of resisting to death' could be 'in itself a victory'.[20]

However, Murray did not confine himself to the firmer ground of philosophical objection to non-resistance. He was soon on the slippery slope which leads from talk of 'national honour' to talk of the 'nobleness of war'. At the time of the Boer War he had written of patriotism as the practice of 'always admiring whatever you yourself happen to do', and national 'self-interest' as the basis of international politics.[21] Now Murray professed to see 'national honour' and 'dishonour' as 'real things'. No doubt a 'deal of nonsense' was talked about them, but they were real all the same. Their 'characteristic' was that they could not be bargained. Honour was 'simply that which a free man values more than life and dishonour . . .

that which he avoids more than suffering and death', Murray wrote in September 1914. What was true of individuals was also true of nations. Nations which did not follow this axiom were simply 'corrupt'. Belgium was therefore not merely a case of 'self-preservation' for Britain, but also a case of interest coinciding with honour. 'Dishonour would have brought with it a subtler and more lasting disadvantage, greater in its sum than immediate death', Murray concluded. His characterisation of the German invasion of Belgium as the attack of a 'wicked man' on a 'little girl' was well calculated to arouse righteous indignation. However, his description of war as having, like 'true tragedy', 'nobleness and triumph in it as well as disaster', was, as he himself conceded, 'dangerous ground':

> We must not begin to praise war without stopping to reflect on the hundreds of thousands of human beings involved in such horrors of pain and indignity that, if here in our ordinary hours we saw one man so treated, the memory would sicken us to the end of our lives ....

But still it was possible 'to see in this wilderness of evil some oases of extraordinary good'.[22]

While he was not quite as sanguine about war as the Idealist philosophers, Murray had fewer ties with German culture. Even fellow-Liberals like James Bryce and H. A. L. Fisher had more intimate contacts with German universities. Murray had never studied in Germany — the chance to study in Berlin under von Wilamowitz-Moellendorff being passed up in favour of marriage instead. This lack of contact or sympathy may account for a certain ferocity in Murray's attitude to Germany — certainly for his taking few pains to distinguish between 'good' and 'bad' Germans. In one of the first Oxford pamphlets on the war Murray outlined the necessities of war:

> We have now not only to strain every nerve to help our friend [France] — we must strain every nerve also to injure our enemy. This is horrible, but we must try to face the truth. For my own part, I find that I do desperately desire to hear of German dreadnoughts sunk in the North Sea. Mines are treacherous engines of death; but I should be only too glad to help in laying a mine for them. When I see one day that 20,000 Germans have been killed in such-and-such an engagement, and the next day that it was only 2,000, I am sorry.

When reduced to 'terms of private human life', Murray could see the tragedy of it all; 'Maass is with his regiment, and we shall do our best to kill him and after that to starve Ulf and Ulf's mother.'[23] But for Murray these were, as the Germans would have put it, 'a regrettable necessity'. Starvation in Poland, as the result of the British blockade of the Central Powers, was 'part of the normal means of war'. 'There was no choice.' It was not easy 'to think of actions much more horrible', but the alternative was 'something equivalent to helping the enemy'.[24]

If the war was accepted, then much of what Murray said was a realistic assessment of its consequences. However, far from a tone of *Realpolitik*, Murray's writing suggests an emotional enthusiasm for a moral crusade. Awkward facts about Russia were no longer welcome:

> Some English liberals seem to be sorry and half ashamed that we have Russia as an ally; for my own part I am glad and proud. Not only because of her splendid military achievements, but because, so far as I can read the signs of such things, there is in Russia, more than in other nations, a vast untapped reservoir of spiritual power, of idealism, of striving for a nobler life. And that is what Europe will most need at the end of this bitter material struggle.[25]

Similar Russophilia could be found in the writings of other academics, but Murray only two months previously had signed a neutrality manifesto which had referred to Russia as 'only partly civilised'; a power whose governing class was 'largely hostile to Western ideas of political and religious freedom'.[26] Such a *volte-face* was uncommon even by the standards of British liberalism — suspicion of Russia did not always evaporate with support for the war. Perhaps not surprisingly Murray began to keep company with members of the 'Fight for Right' movement, a patriotic ginger group.[27]

Murray, in common with many other Britons, was ready to believe the worst of Germany after the publication of the Bryce Report on alleged German atrocities in Belgium (1915). He knew of the evidence uncovered by the Commission even before it was published,[28] and continued to talk of the connection between German 'frightfulness' and preparation for war before 1914. At each stage Germany had gone 'outside the old conventions':

> The broken treaty, the calculated ferocity in Belgium and Northern France, the killing of women and non-combatants by land and sea and air, the shelling of hospitals, the ill-treatment of wounded prisoners; all the doctoring of weapons with a view to cruelty; the explosive bullets, the projectiles tinctured with substances which would produce a gangrenous wound; the poisoned gases; the infected wells. It is the same method throughout.[29]

As late as 1917 Murray was still referring to 'the great criminals and semi-maniacs in Germany and Austria'.[30] This was very far from the liberal view of the world that Murray had once held, but also some distance from the views even of other liberal supporters of the war, who more commonly laid at least some blame for the conflict on the state of international relations in Europe. A. D. Lindsay was typical of this latter group when he wrote:

> We recognize that for the general condition of Europe which made such a war possible we may, along with other nations, have been partly to blame, yet we hold that in the immediate situation we were guiltless and that it made most for the eventual peace of Europe that we should fight.[31]

Once his initial commitment to the war was made, Murray had to go on believing in the rightness of the Allied cause in public — that is, unless politicians were 'using the language of mere hypocrisy'.[32] Privately, however, Murray was beginning to voice his fears about the war as early as May 1915. In a letter to J. L. Hammond he wrote:

> The thing that I mind is the realization that it is not the higher England, the England of Freedom and moderation, that is fighting now; it is just England the mass of brute force and passion and cunning. And so, I suppose, it was bound to be .... I had hoped against hope that, for once, war would not necessarily bring oppression and reaction. But I fear it will be the Pitt business all over again .... We are a nation very like Germany without its discipline — a nation which scarcely deserves to win, or deserves it about as much as Russia does, because she was originally innocent.[33]

In public, however, Murray put on a brave face and told the 'Fight For Right' movement that, although militarism (in the form of Lord Roberts and Colonel Maude) did exist in Britain, it had as yet no political influence. Despite 'this froth or scum', which sometimes floated to the surface, Britain remained 'fundamentally true to her great traditions', 'a nation of 'white men', of rulers, of gentlemen'.[34] The role of the liberal intellectual, as he saw it, was thus to ensure that patriotism was not simply the preserve of the Jingo. The danger was that 'the many thousands of social reformers and radicals', who instinctively loathed war and had 'only been convinced with the utmost resistance, if at all, of the necessity of ... fighting' might 'from disgust and discouragement fall into the background'. That, Murray felt:

> ... would be the last culminating disaster. It would mean that the war had ceased to be a war for Free Europe against militarism, and had become merely one of the ordinary sordid and bloody struggles of nation against nation, one link in the insane chain of wrongs that lead to ever worse things.[35]

But how was it possible to decide the moment when the war had achieved its purpose — the 'deliverance of humanity from the power of the Sword'; 'freedom for all nations, and for all men and women inside the nations'?[36] Aside from difficulties in defining such intangible goals as these, Murray faced a dilemma common to many liberal supporters of the war. As he told the 'Fight for Right' movement in March 1917, anyone who prolonged the war 'one day longer' than was 'necessary for the establishment of the Right' would be 'more wicked than the wretches who caused the war'. Such an individual could see the consequences of his actions even more clearly than the rulers of Germany in July 1914. However, it was also not possible to wish for the war to be ended 'a day sooner' than 'Public Right' became the law of the civilised world once again: 'One is sometimes bewildered by this drag in two contrary directions, bewildered till it is hard to see clear'.[37] This bewilderment was evident in Murray's mild infection with 'Lansdownism' in January 1918, at a time when he was still counselling against peace talks. For a peace settlement not to be motivated by 'a mere grabbing or Jingo sentiment' there first had to be military victory; but would Britain's war aims to redefined in such a way as to prolong the war?[38]

Murray's efforts to keep British liberalism 'fully in touch with the war' seemed to have finally paid off a few weeks later, when Lloyd George's statement of war aims appeared. The 'Fourteen Points' of President Woodrow Wilson followed soon after. It now seemed to Murray that his fears of 'punitive tariffs, the crushing of Germany, annexations, war-indemnities, new naval stations, and the whole imperialist farrago' had 'disappeared into the bog of No-Man's Land'. There now seemed to be a real chance of the kind of peace settlement for which Murray had hoped from the first days of the war. It was Wilson who was now the 'leader of the Allied cause', a welcome counter to the 'Northcliffian Ministry' led by Lloyd George, and, one imagines, a replacement for Sir Edward Grey as Murray's epitome of political honesty. Indeed, there seemed to be no obstacle to a 'clean peace' except military stalemate. If the strain of war was 'prolonged beyond a certain point', it seemed 'almost inevitable that the common longing for peace among the suffering poor throughout Europe, reinforced by a vague but widespread conviction that, while their Governments can never agree, they themselves are agreed', would lead to a European revolution which could even affect Britain.[39] This fear of what Murray called a 'Bolshevik peace' was common to liberals and Fabians, like Beatrice Webb, to supporters of the war as well as critics, like Lowes Dickinson. However, Murray felt that revolution was less likely in Britain than the 'grave danger of political reaction'. As he wrote to E. D. Morel immediately after the war, the 'imminent and ghastly danger' was 'comparatively slight on the revolutionary side but very great indeed on the reactionary, protectionist, military side'.[40]

Arnold Toynbee has defined Murray's politics as those of 'aristocratic liberalism', a label which may describe his concern in the last years of the war, and during the interwar period, with the dangers of modern democracy. Early in 1916 Murray was predicting that 'political reaction' would 'not take the form of a mere wave of extreme conservatism', but that the 'real danger' would be 'a reaction against anything that might be called mellow and wise in politics' — 'a struggle between crude militarist reaction and violent, unthinking democracy'.[41] This had been the basis of his objection to the U.D.C. idea of 'democratic control' of foreign policy. Increased democracy was no 'substitute for character and wisdom', and could in fact lead to 'recklessness', 'unreason' and 'chauvinism'. It all depended on what was meant by 'the people' — the readers of 'the yellowest type of newspaper' or those who rose to 'the mind's eye' as one returned from 'a meeting of the Workers' Education Association or a particularly good trade union discussion'.[42] But, to be fair, this had also been part of the reason for his efforts on behalf of conscientious objectors persecuted by the Government.[43] Whichever way one looked at it, the price of Britain's entry to the war had been a marked diminution of moral purpose. 'It was part of the price we had to pay', he told the 'Fight for Right' movement. Total war meant that a 'high and austere duty' was handed over to agents who could not possibly perform it:

> ... to masses of very ordinary people, and not only of very ordinary people, but of stupid and vulgar and drunken and covetous and dishonest and tricky and cruel and brutal people, who will transform your imagined crusade into a very different reality.[44]

There was no disguising Murray's disillusionment — the distaste which sprang from lifelong teetotalism was the least of it. 'We want to democratise the country ... but we do not want to vulgarise it', Murray told an American audience in 1917, as he went on to defend royalty, the House of Lords (except for the Tory 'stranglehold') and, most of all, the English gentleman.[45] If there was a certain irony in these sentiments voiced by the son of a New South Wales politician, it went unnoticed. All around, the world as Murray and other genteel liberals had known it was crumbling. The war had exacerbated 'every kind of social instability' and fostered a 'habit of violence in public things'. There had been heroism and self-sacrifice, but the war had also revealed 'startling flaws' in the social order. Murray listed these in an address to the 'Civic and Moral Education League' in August 1919, beginning with the amount of 'hysteria' which lay so close to the surface, but including also:

> ... the defects of the governing machine, the immense power of the organised lie and the hideous tyranny of the advertisement; the thinness of the crust which separates civilization from savagery; and the rapidity with which human beings become inured to stories and even actions of cruelty, which not only have sickened them, but would have seemed incredible to them in the years before the war.[46]

Hence the importance for Murray of the League of Nations. He was one of those people for whom it 'offered all the advantages of revolution without its troubles. There need be no social upheaval, no abandonment of ancient values; simply a slight twist to the existing machine of international relations, and all would be well'.[47]

Throughout the 'twenties and 'thirties Murray continued to preach that the only way to international salvation lay through the League. As he told students at Aberystwyth in 1933:

> If our civilization is to be saved we must meet the campaign of violence by reason, by fairness, by accurate information, and by trust in the ultimate good will and good sense of the great mass of disinterested mankind.[48]

This work for the League and peace in the 'thirties is largely beyond the scope of this book, but we can note that Murray's approach to the League was in some ways a natural extension of his prewar liberalism. 'The parallel holds good between the governing and governed Britons on the one hand, and on the other between Great Britain and the lesser breeds without the law which Britain was to bring within the pale.' Such is the assessment of Salvador de Madariaga who worked closely with Murray during the 'thirties. For Madariaga Murray was motivated by a desire to apply the idea of the British Empire more widely as a basis of international organisation. 'The assumption, the subconscious attitude was that Britain would rule the waves of international assemblies as she ruled the waves of the sea; that she knew best what was good for the happiness of other nations.'[49]

Murray never ceased to regret the passing of the 'Victorian Cosmos' — life with values, public morality and respect for the law — and all his efforts were directed towards the recovery of that 'wholesome tradition ... of veracity, of consistency, of honesty and economy, and of intellectual competence' inherited from Peel, Salisbury and Gladstone. Murray claimed too that the war had caused 'a certain change of emphasis' in his attitude to political change, a new appreciation of true conservatism:

> Before the war I was a Liberal, and I believe now that nothing but the sincere practice of Liberal principles will save European society from imminent revolution and collapse .... Before the war I was eager for large and sweeping reforms, I was intolerant of Conservatism, and I laughed at risks. The social order then had such a margin of strength that risks could be safely taken. Now I feel a need above all things of qualities that will preserve civilization.[50]

This, and his belief in the League, saved Murray from the despair which afflicted that other Gladstonian Liberal L. T. Hobhouse after the war.[51] In a sense a certain consistency of beliefs (despite changes in emphasis) also prevented Murray from coming to terms with the problem of 'the cult of violence', although in the 'thirties he came to believe (as he had done during the First World War) that the League had 'to stand up against violence for the sake of right'.[52] His Cambridge contemporary Golds-worthy Lowes Dickinson, with whom Murray had disagreed so profoundly during the war, had similar hopes of the League, although he died before Nazi Germany presented the most serious challenges to it (Murray lived to fight another war on paper). But in other ways the two men were different. Dickinson, the retiring Cambridge don, invented the name 'League of Nations' and was one of its earliest supporters during the war. Yet, apart from a short term of service on the 'Committee on Intellectual Cooperation', Dickinson took no part in League affairs in Geneva in the 1920s. Murray, although he had hoped for some postwar 'Concert' during the early months of the war, did not publicly espouse the cause of the League until 1918 when, as we have seen, it had become the politically respectable thing to do. After the war Murray became the foremost League intellectual — Chairman of the League of Nations Union in Britain (1922–38) and President of the International Committee on Intellectual Cooperation at Geneva from 1928 onwards.

CHAPTER 7

Goldsworthy Lowes Dickinson

Yet still, after centuries of stumbling, reason is no more the furtive accomplice of habit and force. Force creates, habit perpetuates, reason the sycophant sanctions. And so he [Man] drifts, not up but down, and Nature watches in anguish, self-forbidden to intervene, unless it be to annihilate. If he is to drive, and drive straight, reason must seize the reins; and the art of driving is the art of politics.

Geoffrey Vivian in G. L. Dickinson, *A Modern Symposium* (1905)

The character of Geoffrey Vivian, 'a man of letters', in Dickinson's most famous book has been said to be 'the character whom he cast in the role of himself'. But from the time of the First World War until his death in 1932 Dickinson was also known to the public as a publicist for the League of Nations and author of *The International Anarchy* (1926), a book with an influence comparable with Angell's *Great Illusion* a quarter of a century earlier. As we have seen, Dickinson, like Murray, was involved in political affairs before 1914. Like Murray, he stood to the left of mainstream Liberalism. It was as the author of the then standard text on *The Development of Parliament During the Nineteenth Century* (1895) that Dickinson wrote a long series of letters to *The Nation* during the controversy over Lloyd George's budget in 1910. In fact, Dickinson's views had changed since the publication of the first edition of the book. In a new preface to the French translation (1906) he dissociated himself from his earlier criticisms of the House of Commons and his implicit support for the Lords. In 1895 he had been, as he put it, 'a kind of Socialistic Tory'.[1] As a young Classics Fellow of King's College, Cambridge, his views had been based on an equation of Plato's elite with English gentlemen: 'He took the Tories at their own valuation as aristocrats, and held with Plato that the best should rule'.[2] This description by another Fellow of King's would have fitted many others at Oxford and Cambridge at this time.

It was the Boer War which encouraged Dickinson to turn to Liberalism, and he began to see that 'Tory rule meant plutocracy, not as he had held aristocracy'.[3] As E. M. Forster points out, this was in a sense a 'return', since Dickinson had been influenced by the writings of Henry George as an undergraduate at King's. In fact, Dickinson had progressed through bell-ringing, reforming prostitutes, and the Church of England Temperance Society, to working on a co-operative farm (1885) started by Harold Cox, whom we shall later meet as a member of the wartime Bryce Commission on German atrocities in Belgium. At the time of the Diamond

112

Jubilee (1897) he succumbed to an infection of Jingoism (even considering
bicycling down to Spithead to see the Naval Review), before moving back
to the left via George's *Progress and Poverty*.[4] However, Dickinson's later
writings show traces of his earlier élitism, and he never quite lost a
fastidious horror of the working class whose cause he came later to espouse.
As his biographer notes:

> For the working classes as then existing he had little enthusiasm, and it was not until
> much later in his life that he established personal contacts with them. He had been
> brought up in a Victorian household, he minded h's being dropped, he knew he
> ought not to mind, still he did mind. And — a more serious aversion — he could not
> see that the working-class movement was proceeding in a direction which was either
> good or new .... He feared that there would be a levelling down, instead of a
> levelling up, and that the Many, in the process of making themselves comfortable,
> would throw away the pearl of great price which has been handed down to them by
> the Few .... Thus, although he came more and more to condemn our economic
> system and advocate drastic changes, he had no sympathy whatever with the
> Marxian who rejects Shakespeare and Tchekov on the grounds that they wrote for
> Capitalists.[5]

Dickinson's dislike of violence extended to the ideas of revolutionary
socialists: the case for 'social war' was undoubtedly stronger than any for
'international war', but 'no solution by force of the social question' was
possible 'even if it were desirable'.[6] There was in Dickinson's prewar
philosophy something of the fashionable literary anarchism of the London
salon. 'I have far more sympathy with Proudhon and with Kropotkin than
with Marx and the Social Democrats', he wrote in 1900.[7] In short, when
airing 'socialist' views, Dickinson would quote from Mill, Ruskin or
Whitman, but not from Marx.[8]

As far as international affairs were concerned, Dickinson's views seem to
have been a mixture of optimism about the prospects for peace and a vague
foreboding of future war. 'There may, indeed, be war between Germany
and England', he wrote in November 1907, 'but, if so, it will be because the
government and peoples of those countries have willed it; not because of
any necessity to be.'[9] But by August 1914, a few days after the outbreak of
war, Dickinson had exonerated the 'peoples', though not their governments, from blame. Writing in an obviously emotional state, he referred to
the death and destruction which would be the only certain outcome:

> Not one of the men employed in this work of destruction wants to perform it; not one
> of them knows how it came about that he is performing it; not one of them knows
> what object is to be served by performing it. The non-combatants are in the same
> case. They did not foreseee this, they did not want it, they did not choose it. They were
> never consulted. No one in Europe desires to be engaged in such work. We are sane
> people but our acts are mad. Why? Because we are all in the hands of some score of

individuals called Governments. Some score among the hundreds of millions of Europeans. These men have willed this thing for us over our heads. No nation has had the chance of saying No. The Russian peasants march because the Tsar and the priest tell them to. That of course. But equally the German Socialists march; equally the French Socialists. These men know what war means. They know what its effects must be. They hate it. But they march. Business men, knowing too, hating too, watch them march. Working men watch them march, and wait for starvation. All are powerless. The die has been cast for them. The crowned gamblers cast it, and the cast was death.

'Common men' were 'tools'. Their 'rulers' played on them 'like pipes'.[10]

The war was a terrible blow for Dickinson. There was a feeling of sheer helplessness for a man over fifty years of age who did not feel able to fight the Germans with his pen. As he wrote to a friend in November 1914:

> It would be easier to bear, and probably one would get the perspective better, if one were a young man who could serve, or had trained oneself for some function that might be useful now. But if one's whole life has been given up to trying to establish and spread reason, and suddenly the gulf opens and one finds the world is ruled by force and wishes to be so, one feels forlorn, indeed worse than forlorn.[11]

This despair was deepened by the ostracism which Dickinson experienced in Cambridge. He had misgivings about the tactics of the U.D.C. and joined reluctantly. But, having done so, he was elected President of the Cambridge branch. As such, he was an obvious target for super-patriots.[12] Being of a far more sensitive nature than Bertrand Russell, who was a much more open opponent of the war, Dickinson became a virtual recluse during wartime, confining himself to the writing of articles and pamphlets on the war. As he wrote later in May 1927:

> My sense of isolation from common opinion, my melancholy, and my clear sense of fact (for I must call it) caused me to retire altogether from such life as there was in the place. I lived and ate alone, when I was in Cambridge, and saw almost nobody. The long winter evenings still linger with me. Shut into my room, I seemed for a time to have shut out the world. My dim reading lamp, the rich red wallpaper, the flickering fire, were my background.

Later he moved to the more anonymous surroundings of London. But Dickinson was not persecuted like his colleague at King's, A. C. Pigou, as we shall see. 'I suffered nothing in Cambridge except a complete want of sympathy', he wrote later.[13] But this was bad enough for someone like Dickinson.

After the dismissal of Bertrand Russell from his lectureship at Trinity College (July 1916), Dickinson wrote bitterly that 'endowed semi-public institutions' were 'no place for genuine and independent minds': 'If you are honest and intelligent you must be a heretic and an outcast'.[14] However, compared to Russell, Dickinson was not cut out for the role of lonely rebel. 'Dickinson was a man who inspired affection by his gentleness and pathos', Russell wrote much later. And he continued:

> When he was a Fellow and I was still an undergraduate, I became aware that I was liable to hurt him by my somewhat brutal statement of unpleasant truths, or what I thought to be such. States of the world which made me caustic only made him sad, and to the end of his days whenever I met him, I was afraid of increasing his unhappiness by too stark a realism. But perhaps realism is not quite the right word. What I really mean is the practice of describing things which one finds almost unendurable in such a repulsive manner as to cause others to share one's fury. He told me once that I resembled Cordelia, but it cannot be said that he resembled King Lear.[15]

Another U.D.C. member was exasperated by Dickinson's 'fairmindedness' and described him as "wrinkled with scruples".[16] It was perhaps these 'scruples' which prevented Dickinson coming out as an opponent of the war like Russell, although he was never an advocate of pacifism.

One of Russell's 'unpleasant truths', with which Dickinson seemed never to have come to terms, was the problem of violence. Roger Fry echoed William James (whose comments on Dickinson we noted in the first chapter) when he observed that Dickinson's writings betrayed 'far too optimistic and naive' a 'conception of human nature'. They showed 'no notion of how much a primitive and prelogical mentality still survived in civilised man'. E. M. Forster was perhaps nearer the mark when he added that Dickinson did in fact realise this, but refused to face the 'consequences'.[17] It is possible to go even further: Dickinson was intellectually and temperamentally incapable of facing the consequences of a view of man which suggested, if not that war was inevitable, that some kind of violence was. The writings of Professor Cramb, he noted in November 1914, could not be answered: 'Those things lie too deep for argument. One is one kind of man or the other'.[18] And there Dickinson left matters, having no desire to read Cramb or anyone else like him. His reply to the crude Social Darwinism of the *Morning Post* was of the same kind. The newspaper had taken Dickinson to task for his criticism of the public school cult of games:

> The football match of which he is a horrified witness, is merely the microcosm of an even fiercer and more horrible struggle from which his sensitive nature instinctively veils itself. That unreflecting patriotism of which he complains is nothing but the tribal or racial instinct of self-preservation which exists in all healthy animals and all healthy flocks of animals. Mr Dickinson's quarrel is really with Nature. It is an offence to him that there should be 'violent instincts'.[19]

Against the advocacy of war as a rather rougher kind of rugger was it possible to argue in a serious fashion? As we shall see, the war pushed

Dickinson to the limits of his faith that argument could be conducted reasonably and that reason would prevail.

Since he was an early member of the U.D.C., Dickinson made the customary obeisance to the idea of 'democratic control' of foreign policy. As he wrote to the Professor of Political Economy at the L.S.E. in the second month of the war:

> Of course public opinion is anything but infallible. Yet I think that publicity in diplomacy, if and so long as diplomacy goes on, is essential. For one does have a chance of enlightening opinion, but one has none of enlightening foreign office officials and militarists and diplomatists.[20]

A few months later, in an article written for an American audience, Dickinson set out the U.D.C. view on the cause of the war:

> ... this war, like all wars for many centuries in Europe, was brought about by governments, without the connivance and against the desires and interests of peoples .... War is made — this war has been made — not by any necessity of nature, any law beyond human control, any fate to which men must passively bow .... Wars are made by governments acting under the influence of governmental theory.[21]

It was 'a diplomatist's war. None of the peoples wanted it, and none of them would have stood for it, if in some way they could have been jointly consulted in the light of the full knowledge of the facts'. When Italy entered the war (May 1915), this belief in the pacific nature of the electorate was shaken, but for Dickinson only momentarily. The hand of the Italian government probably had been 'forced .... by popular enthusiasm'. But if this were true, then for those who believed in the Allied cause it was 'an example of the sound instinct of the people defeating the erroneous calculations of the statesmen'.[22] Not even Dickinson was above having it both ways.

Dickinson was never as unequivocally opposed to the war as was Russell. In his first pamphlet on the war, for example, he began with the disclaimer that it was:

> ... not a 'stop the war' pamphlet. Being in this war, I think, as all Englishmen think, that we must go on fighting until we can emerge from it with our territory and our security intact, and with the future peace of Europe assured, so far as wisdom can assure it.[23]

Nor did Dickinson criticise Sir Edward Grey during the war — in public at least. In *The European Anarchy* (1916), the forerunner of his best-known book, *The International Anarchy* (1926), Dickinson even described him as 'probably the most pacific Minister that ever held office in a great nation'. 'I am not, and have not been, one of the critics of Sir Edward Grey', he concluded.[24] This was not very different from the treatment of Grey in the writings of Gilbert Murray. Why, then, were Dickinson's writings listed with those of Bertrand Russell by the War Office Censor by March 1917, and the National Peace Council forbidden to collect them on behalf of the Nobel and Carnegie peace organisations?[25] That he was a leading U.D.C. intellectual was perhaps reason enough — the War Office was unlikely to distinguish between the position of the U.D.C. and that of outright opposition to the war, and Dickinson's writings conveyed the impression that his support for the war was qualified to say the least.

In a way it seemed that Dickinson just could not make up his mind. In 1915, for example, he noted that:

> While ... it is unhistorical and unjust to pretend that Germany as such stands for domination, and the Western Powers for freedom, yet we may say with truth that a victory of the Western Powers, so far as their influence can reach, should make for freedom, while a victory of Germany will make for domination.[26]

A carefully weighed judgement which would have been unusual for a British historian during the war. Yet, only a few pages earlier, Dickinson had talked of the war as 'just one of the many wars for power and position'. And at other times Dickinson came close to the talk about the threat of *Kultur* common in the usual justifications of British policy.[27] Much of Dickinson's writing on the war was, as his friend Nathaniel Wedd put it, 'shorn of its rhetoric, just an impotent, helpless cry of the heart':

> Dickinson says we could not avoid making war and he hopes we shall win: but on the other hand he does nothing to help us to win and always talks of war as wicked in such a way as to imply that it is wicked of us to take part in it. The fact is that he is upset by the horrors of war and cannot stop to make his attitude logical or his position clear.[28]

It was this lack of 'tough-mindedness' in Dickinson which probably attracted him to the idea of 'international anarchy' as the cause of the war. It enabled him to account for the breakdown of peace in impersonal, even mechanistic, terms, and so to play down the element of individual responsibility on all sides. As he wrote to Leonard Woolf in the last month of the war:

> From these and most of the despatches, one gets a curious and disconcerting impression that none of the diplomats seriously wanted war, indeed that all feared it, but that the situation like a Greek fate was leading them into it.[29]

While Dickinson claimed to agree 'with the general view outside Germany that the final responsibility for the war at the last moment' rested with the Central Powers, he disputed 'with full conviction' the view 'universally held in England' that Germany had been 'pursuing for years past a policy of war' while all the other powers had sought only peace. The invasion of Belgium was not the culmination of long-term German policy, but merely 'an episode in a war already begun' — the previously bloodless warfare of competing states in an unregulated international system.[30] Belgium was thus only 'a contributory cause of British intervention', although Dickinson agreed (in public at least) 'with the general view' that it would have been 'neither right nor wise' for Britain to abstain after August 1914.[31] Privately, however, Dickinson wrote to Leonard Woolf in December 1918:

> ... I think nations really never go to war merely in defence of supposedly outraged international law, but always for their interests. We should never have gone to war merely because the Germans broke the treaty. And we should probably have aided and abetted France if she had wanted to break it.[32]

This was the kind of allegation made publicly by Russell and Morel during wartime; for Dickinson it was a conclusion painfully reached only at the war's end. But in the meantime, Dickinson pursued his explanation in terms of the 'state of fear and suspicion on both sides'. 'When there is such tension ... in the European situation', he argued, 'some Power or other will be tempted to precipitate the catastrophe, and some Power or other will always succumb to the temptation.' If it had not been Germany in 1914, it would have been Russia the following year. 'And some other year it might have been France or England. The war came out of the European states system, the system of states armed against one another, and dominated by mutual suspicion and fear.' So long as that system continued to operate, there would always be danger of war.[33] Britain was an exception to this but only because of its possession of an empire: 'As ambitious, as quarrelsome, and aggressive as other States, her geographical position has directed her aims overseas rather than towards the Continent'.[34] These views, expressed from the first months of the war, were Dickinson's lasting contribution to the postwar debate on its origins.[35]

After the first months of the war Dickinson seems gradually to have lost interest in the idea of 'democratic control', and to have spent less time working for the U.D.C. Unlike Russell, who also moved away from the apparent dead-end of U.D.C. theory, Dickinson did not move towards outright opposition to the war. Instead from 1915 onwards he became increasingly involved in agitation for a postwar league of nations, and generally kept company with 'the moderate liberals of the Bryce Group'.[36] Dickinson had called a meeting of Liberal academics, journalists and politicians as early as September 1914 to discuss the league idea, and in May 1915 was instrumental in the establishment of the League of Nations Society. It was Dickinson (or perhaps someone else in the Bryce Group) who first coined the term 'league of nations'. He was also an important intermediary between the Bryce Group, the U.D.C. and the League to

Enforce Peace, based in the United States. A recent American estimate is that, apart from the scheme for an international police force, 'Dickinson's ideas were the common denominator of early American and European peace programmes. Within the United Kingdom numerous internationalist, pacifist and reform organisations and Liberal and Labour party politicians propagated them'.[37] For all his 'tender-mindedness', Dickinson was no 'remote and ineffectual don'. As his autobiography makes clear, his greatest wish was 'to influence opinion and the course of events':

> I never wanted to write learned and scholarly works . . . . Whether I have been at all successful I doubt. Events can be influenced by thought, but only if the thought is more original than mine has ever been, and the personality behind it more massive. Voltaire and Rousseau did for France and Marx for Germany and the world what I should have liked to do for England.[38]

In one sense Dickinson was too modest — to the extent that the league movement had become politically respectable by 1918, he had succeeded in influencing 'opinion and the course of events'.

However, in the first two years of the war Dickinson's path was a lonely one. He was the only British representative at a meeting in the Hague in April 1915, held under the auspices of the *Anti Oorlog Raad* (Committee Against War), to discuss international law and the prevention of war. Since there were German and Austrian representatives at the meeting, the resulting *Organisation Centrale Pour Une Paix Durable* was severely criticised in the British press, although Dickinson was not mentioned by name.[39] Dickinson saw Grey, still Foreign Secretary at this stage, but he received little encouragement. However, no objection was made to Dickinson's plans for a lecture tour in the United States to publicise the league idea. This kept Dickinson out of Britain from February to April 1916.[40] The admirer of Kropotkin in 1906 now, nine years later, found international anarchy an indisputable *raison d'être* for international organisation. 'A league of Europe is not Utopia. It is sound business', Dickinson had written in 1914. And a year later: 'the ideal of the future is federation and to that ideal all the significant facts of the present point. It is idle for states to resist the current'.[41] The appeal of Dickinson's argument was neatly encapsulated by Sir Arthur Salter in his preface to the posthumous edition of *The International Anarchy* (1937): 'International anarchy is the cause of war; and international government, therefore, the indispensable condition of preventing it.'[42] But privately Dickinson feared that military stalemate might be the only way to peace, and that would 'never be accepted till everything else' had been tried in vain.[43] Clearly, there were limits to the power of reasoned argument.

When the war still continued after the terrible losses of 1916, Dickinson's worst fears seemed justified. He had now to recognise 'the fundamental fact' that men's actions were 'controlled more by passion than by reason'. Passion was 'aroused by abstract notions and words', and thus it became possible for men to sacrifice everything for causes which had 'no bearing on their real interests, whether material, moral or spiritual'.[44] It was not in the 'real interests' of the British people for their government to 'crush' Germany. True, she had 'behaved barbarously in Belgium' and at sea, but there were dangers in pursuing a policy of unconditional surrender. Any plans to punish the Kaiser and German officials, any talk of 'annual tribute' or annexation of German colonies, would nip in the bud the growth of a German peace party.[45] After the Economic Conference of the Allies in Paris (June 1916) Dickinson was especially worried by the possibility of 'economic war' against Germany once military hostilities had ceased. As he wrote to C. P. Scott, editor of the *Manchester Guardian*, there seemed 'only too much reason to fear' that the Allies were 'continuing the war, not to achieve their avowed objects, but to realize illegal schemes of conquest' which would 'leave the condition of Europe worse than before'. Perhaps even more alarming was the threat to civil liberties in Britain — the 'persecution of conscience' was a direct outcome of continuing the war for its own sake.[46] Lloyd George's advocacy of a 'knock-out blow' against Germany from September 1916 increased Dickinson's fears, and he devoted the greater part of articles for *The Cambridge Magazine* to citing historical evidence of the failure of such policies. The disintegration of the wartime alliance against Napoleon after 1815 was also useful to Dickinson in countering the arguments of the League to Enforce Peace for an anti-German alliance to continue after the war was won.[47] The revelations next year by the Bolsheviks of secret Allied treaties confirmed all Dickinson's worst fears that an opportunity for compromise peace had been missed. In a letter to Gilbert Murray he laid the responsibility for the demise of civilian control in Berlin, the result he felt of this missed opportunity, squarely at the door of Allied governments:

> For the sake of definition, not of controversy, I will say that I agree with you that once war had broken out, it was 'inevitable' that every means would be adopted, at every cost to everything, to win the war. Hence, if other governments offered their aid only on terms which were contrary to all their and our professions, our government could not refuse. This is all the hideous logic of war. But, on the other hand, it is equally 'inevitable' that effects should produce causes [sic]. And from the moment those treaties were entered into, our professions became insincere, and being known to be insincere by the decent people in the enemy countries, the possibility of a meeting point on a good 'league of nations' peace between the internationalists ... of all countries was ruined. No one could think worse than I do of the German military

party. They show what they are sufficiently now they are in power. The tragedy is that there [sic] were not in power until Brest-Litovsk, but only fighting for power. They would, I believe, have been defeated, if the allied governments had been able and willing to meet the policy of the Reichstag majority with sympathy instead of with blank negation.[48]

Dickinson overestimated the strength of 'pacific and internationally-minded elements' in Germany, and it is interesting to compare his analysis with that of his Cambridge colleague John Maynard Keynes. Keynes was sceptical of the usual liberal distinction between German government and people. Writing in August 1916 under the pseudonym 'Politicus', he claimed to see at least 'passive acquiescence' in the attitude of the German people towards their government's foreign policy:

> The idea that the German government is entirely freed from this influence and can make the people do exactly what it wishes will not bear examination .... Had the will for peace in Germany been wholehearted and strong and really widespread, it would not have been so easy to bamboozle the people in August 1914.

This had in fact been necessary. How, then, did this affect the advocacy of a compromise peace? Keynes felt that its proponents had to establish first that there *was* a military stalemate, and secondly that an early peace would prove 'durable', before they could 'hope to influence any important section of public opinion' in Allied countries. And he continued:

> So long as we think that there is a reasonable chance of 'crushing' Germany and 'dictating' terms, there is not the smallest doubt we shall insist on going on. On the other hand, even when we have finally made up our minds that there will be no decisive military victory, we shall refuse and rightly refuse to make peace, if we think it probable that it will be used by Germany for a policy of 'reculer pour mieux sauter'. We could at least hang on and let 'attrition' work for a year or two, until a different result became probable. Pacifists must show that a different result is probable now, and unless they can do that, the most convincing demonstrations of 'deadlock' are in vain.[49]

This was Keynes, if it was Keynes (the attribution of authorship is on circumstantial evidence only)[50], at his most cold-blooded. Yet even he, a year previously, had written of the Germans as not so different from other peoples. The 'general note' in Germany was one of 'moderation, sobriety, reasonableness and truth'.[51]

The secret treaties not only prolonged the war, but, in Dickinson's eyes, they were also 'largely responsible for the character of the Treaty of Versailles'. He fully accepted Keynes's denunciation of the penal aspects of the Treaty — the 'effect and presumably the intention' was to 'destroy Germany as a great economic Power' and to make her 'a helot nation'.[52] Yet Dickinson had to swallow it as a 'Hybrid Peace'. If he wanted to see

Wilsonian plans for international organisation come to fruition, the most he could do was press for far-reaching revision, and not rejection. Unlike many wartime supporters of Wilsonian ideas, he did not later desert the American President when the text of the Treaty of Versailles became known.[53] The 'territorial and economic provisions' may have been 'framed on the traditional lines of cupidity and fear', but over this 'monstrous fabric thus erected' the League was 'left to float, like a rainbow in the sky'. It was still 'an achievement which, at the outbreak of the war, would have seemed to most men incredible'. Criticism might be justified, but it had to be remembered that the League was:

> ... the creation of victorious states just emerged from a bloody and bitter war. And to expect this fact not to be reflected in the terms of the Covenant, and in the behaviour of the Governments, was to expect a cool magnaminity which victors have never been able to show.

This cool-headed analysis, unusual for the liberal left in 1920, was balanced by some vintage Dickinson as he attempted to explain how such a 'Hybrid Peace' had come about:

> To say that the Allied nations went to war in order to do what they have actually done may be unjust . . . . While certain generous conceptions haunted the upper storeys of men's minds, the currents of tradition, of habit, of half-avowed interest and ambition were sweeping them, all the time, along old channels.[54]

According to E. M. Forster, the war made Dickinson a supporter of the Labour Party. Certainly his analysis of the war in books like *The Causes of International War* (1920) and *War: Its Nature, Cause and Cure* (1923) made increasing reference to the 'social class' basis of British foreign policy. In fact, Dickinson argued that the war had accentuated this:

> The imperialism of the wealthy and aristocratic sections of the English, of the army, the navy, the church, the public schools, to a great extent the universities, is so direct, so simple, so unamenable to discussion and argument, as to resemble an instinct. There is no evidence that the war has done anything to it, except to enhance it. As to the League of Nations, these classes either are frankly hostile to it or they regard it as a device to consolidate the Empire by stabilising the *status quo* after it has been made as favourable as possible to British power.

Organised labour might offer support for internationalism, but, Dickinson felt, 'the passions, good and bad, of peoples' made them 'the easy dupes of imperialism':

> The 'people', the great mass, that is, of the uninitiated, who pursue their daily work and play, until the trumpet of doom blows from the heaven of their rulers, — these must be regarded as victims and dupes, not accomplices, in the great game. But though that be so, yet the masses must bear their responsibility, seeing that it is their passions, instincts and emotions that respond to the call when it is made.[55]

This was not so different from the position which Gilbert Murray had reached by 1920. Dickinson, with his references to the 'colossal egotism of the herd', had moved a considerable distance from simple preference for 'democratic control' — perhaps under the influence of writers on crowd psychology, like Wilfred Trotter whose *Instincts of the Herd in Peace and War* (1916) he had used in his book *The Causes of International War*.[56]

For Dickinson, then, prewar liberalism was dead, killed by the growth of national hatreds as much as by the conflict of Capital and Labour. War was 'the opposite of Liberalism', and Liberals when they waged it ceased to be Liberals. Like Murray he felt that there was more danger in 'the bitter intransigence of the possessing classes' than from any danger of 'Bolshevism' — except for Germany where the penal peace had provided fertile ground for such ideas. Yet, like Murray, his faith in 'public opinion' was at best qualified. It was 'precisely in the region of foreign affairs' that it was 'most malleable', for it was there that 'ignorance and indifference' were most complete. What Forster calls Dickinson's 'hatred of crowd psychology' was even stronger at the end of the war with the popular clamour for revenge in Allied countries. For this the governments only had themselves to blame — they had 'created a Frankenstein, and Frankenstein insisted on his pound of flesh at Versailles'.[57] And in a striking passage written for an American audience, Dickinson gave free rein to his disappointed hopes:

> One might compare nations to patients liable to outbreaks of homicidal mania, but normally sane, kindly, helpful and productive. Certain words, rashly spoken, are known to bring on the attacks. Wise and humane keepers would, therefore, avoid speaking to them.[58]

In his last major book, *The International Anarchy* (1926), Dickinson returned to the idea he had first developed during wartime. In a note of June 1927, added to his *Autobiography*, Dickinson wrote:

> I know that this is a good book — I believe it to be possibly the best book on the subject; because it is the only one I know which stresses the only important fact, that it is not this or that nation nor its policy, but the anarchy, that causes wars. The book was considerably and favourably enough reviewed, but it has not sold as much as a thousand copies. Another testimony to the general truth that truth is the last thing people care about.[59]

The next five years until his death in August 1932 did nothing to relieve his disillusionment — Europe was 'armed, suspicious, and covetous, even more than she was before the war'.[60] In a review of K. A. Bratt's *The Next War* (1930) he conceded that the younger generation were fighting new battles but that these, he feared, had little to do with the cause of peace. Bolshevism and Fascism, the 'principal manifestations of youth', whatever else they were, were 'movements towards war'.[61] Dickinson continued to believe in the League of Nations to the end, but a League with effective sanctions including the use of military force.[62] Despite all the criticisms it is possible to make of his conception of international politics, there was still underneath a visible strand of political realism. The same problems were approached in a different way by Dickinson's Cambridge contemporary Bertrand Russell. It might be said that Russell, to whom we now turn, was better able to come to terms with impulse (as opposed to reason), but had a less realistic conception of international politics.

CHAPTER 8

Bertrand Russell

... men of learning, by allowing partiality to colour their thoughts and words, have missed the opportunity of performing a service to mankind for which their training should have specially fitted them . . . . Men of learning, who should be accustomed to the pursuit of truth in their daily work, might have attempted at this time, to make themselves the mouthpieces of truth, to see what was false on their own side, what was valid on the side of their enemies. They might have used their reputation and their freedom from political entanglements to mitigate the abhorrence with which the nations have come to regard each other, to help towards mutual understanding, to make the peace, when it comes, not a mere cessation due to weariness, but a fraternal reconciliation, springing from realisation that the strife has been a folly of blindness. They have chosen to do nothing of this. Allegiance to country has swept away allegiance to truth . . . . The guardians of the temple of truth have betrayed it to idolaters, and have been the first to promote the idolatrous worship.

Bertrand Russell, 'Justice in War-Time' (1915)

Russell's writings during the war on British foreign policy reflect a liberal idealism which would have seemed unexceptional in time of peace, even from the pen of Gilbert Murray. In his reply to the latter's defence of Sir Edward Grey, Russell noted that all the standards by which historical judgements were arrived at had suddenly been cast aside in August 1914:

We perceive that in previous wars among the great powers similar views have been held on each side, to be unanimously discarded by subsequent historians: and we do not believe that what has always been false before has now suddenly become true.[1]

A quarter of a century earlier Henry Sidgwick, who had taught Russell at Cambridge, had made a similar plea for careful and balanced assessment of the justifications offered by contending parties in international disputes. But once war had broken out, he had felt that the 'thoughtful and moral part of every community' could not be expected to 'keep coldly aloof from patriotic sentiment'.[2] Russell, however, insisted that the intellectual's duty remained exactly the same even after his country had gone to war. 'There is no reason to expect an unusual degree of humane feeling from professors', he wrote in 1915, 'but some pride of rationality, some unwillingness to let judgement be enslaved to brutal passions, we might have hoped to find.' But, alas, it was a vain hope. The 'ingenious distortions' of German international lawyers, and the 'subtle untruths' of British historians, were but two examples of the general failure of intellectuals on both sides 'to resist the process of self-deception to which their Governments invited them'. What 'little attempt at truth' there had been was 'almost wholly

125

confined to Socialists, who had none of the educational advantages which proved so unavailing among professors'.[3]

Since there was little influence he could exert on Germany, Russell proposed to concentrate his energies on criticising the foreign policy of his own country, for here there was 'far more hope of reform'. Such hopes would be 'utopian in regard to Germany'. It was:

> ... important that England, the birthplace of liberty and the home of chivalrous generosity, should adopt in the future a policy worthy of itself, embodying its best, not deviously deceptive towards the hopes of its more humane citizens .... above all because I love England ... I wish to make the English people aware of the crimes that have been committed in its name, to recall it to a temper in which peace can be made and preserved, and to point to a better national pride than that of domination.[4]

But this order of priorities for the intellectual in wartime, which seemed logical enough to Russell, aroused bewilderment in people like Gilbert Murray. Writing of Russell's apparent failure to feel any moral indignation at the invasion of Belgium, Murray asked:

> ... if this is the sort of language, or anything like the sort of language, he would have used if England had done what Germany did? Suppose our fleet had treacherously seized Antwerp, suppose a tenth part of the devastation and outrage which Belgium has suffered had been ordered by our officers and committed by our men? I feel sure that, in that case, Mr Russell and I would have been standing on the same platform; my language would probably be stronger than it is now, but Mr. Russell's would be utterly unrecognisable.[5]

But while Belgium, as we have seen, had been a crucial moral issue for Murray, for Russell it merely exposed the hypocrisy of great power politics. The invasion had shown Germany 'at its worst' but it had not shown Britain in a very favourable light either. In words borne out by later research by historians, Russell remarked:

> ... if the Germans had not attacked Belgium there would have been more resignations in the [British] Cabinet and less unanimity of public opinion, but the Government would have found it impossible to stand aside while France was crushed. France, not Belgium, was for us the decisive factor.[6]

Given Russell's rather jaundiced view of the nation state, there was reason enough to see a difference merely of degree, rather than of kind, between British and German foreign policy:

> Stripped of Parliamentary verbiage, the fundamental fact about the European situation is that all the Great Powers of Europe have precisely the same objects — territory, trade and prestige. In pursuit of these objects no one of the Great Powers shrinks from wanton aggression, war and chicanery. But owing to the geographical position of Germany and our naval supremacy, England can achieve all its purposes by wars outside Europe, whereas English and Russian policy has shown that

Germany cannot achieve its aims except by a European war. We have made small wars because small wars were what suited our purpose; Germany has made a great war because a great war was what suited Germany's purpose. We and they alike have been immoral in aim and brutal in method, each in exact degree which was thought to be in the national advantage.[7]

There was a certain logic in all this, although Russell was obviously begging the question of whether Germany's 'aims' were not potentially more destructive. Russell's ideas on the international system rested on two assumptions. First, that 'Germany had as good a right to an Empire as any other Great Power, but could only acquire an Empire through war'. Second, that peace could no longer be maintained by 'a static conception of international relations'. As Russell noted in 1916: 'In a world where nations grow and decay, where forces change and populations become cramped, it is not possible or desirable to maintain the *status quo* for ever'. If peace was to be preserved, nations had to 'learn to accept unfavourable alterations of the map without feeling that they must first be defeated in war, or that in yielding they incur humiliation'. This was as true of Britain as of any other power — perhaps truer, since Britain was the model which Germany sought to emulate:

The mood in which Germany embarked upon the war was abominable, but it was a mood fostered by the habitual mood of England. We have prided ourselves on our territory and our wealth; we have been ready at all times to defend by force of arms what we have conquered in India and Africa. If we had realized the futility of empire, and had shown a willingness to yield colonies to Germany without waiting for the threat of force, we might have been in a position to persuade the Germans that their ambitions were foolish, and that the respect of the world was not to be won by an imperialist policy. But by our resistance we showed that we shared their standards . . . . So convinced were we of the sacredness of the *status quo* that we never realized how advantageous it was to us, or how, by insisting upon it, we shared the responsibility for the war.

As Russell reminded his American audience: 'Germany had no good ground for envy; we had no good ground for resisting whatever in Germany's demands was compatible with our continued existence'.[8] This is very suggestive of later 'revisionist' explanations for the outbreak of the war and of the intellectual justifications for appeasement of Germany in the postwar period. Russell was to support the latter policy at least up until 1938.[9]

However, we can also see in Russell's writing on international politics during the First World War a tendency to attach little importance to concepts like 'national interest' and 'balance of power'. In Morocco, Russell, like H. N. Brailsford and E. D. Morel, considered that British policy had been quite without justification. Britain 'ought to have met

Germany's desire for school-boy triumphs with the tolerant smile of an elder brother'. Instead, Lloyd George's Mansion House Speech (July 1911) had reduced British foreign policy 'to the German level'. At times like this it seemed that Russell had, not only a healthy scepticism about national honour and the like, but also little real conception of just how deeply ingrained such concepts were in the minds of people. It probably did not matter that the Germans cherished 'a desire to own African swamps' of which Britain had 'a superfluity'.[10] But his claim that the 'only things worth fighting for are the things of the spirit' showed a certain insensitivity to the hopes and desires of ordinary people.[11] It was this feature of Russell's wartime writing which one historian, perhaps unfairly, linked to his talent for logical thought:

> The morality of peace is the strongest weapon of the pacifist, and there is no assumption more common or more confident in that school of thought than that the conscientious objector is the superman of pure reason and a paragon of virtue; if all men reasoned as they do there would be no war, and the prevalence of war is due to animal instinct and low rationality. That, no doubt, is true as an abstract proposition, and it is not a mere coincidence that the intellectual protagonist of pacifism in England is an expert in the field of mathematical abstraction.[12]

Of course Russell *was* at pains to present the pacifist alternative as an eminently reasonable course of action. The emotional rhetoric of religious pacifism was as foreign to Russell as conventional patriotic sentiment. Only rarely would exasperation break through the logic of his argument.[13]

What Britain should have weighed in considering its reaction to the German invasion of Belgium, Russell felt, was not 'the legal fact that a treaty was broken', but rather 'the fact that a terrible cruelty was inflicted on an unoffending nation'. The 'question which England had to consider was, not whether Germany had committed a crime', but whether she 'should do anything to mitigate the bad consequences of that crime by going to war'. 'If we had not come in the Belgians would in all likelihood not have resisted the German army', Russell claimed. 'In return for a free passage and for our neutrality, the Germans would have respected Belgian independence, and Belgium would have been spared almost all it has suffered.' And, in confirmation of this analysis, Russell could point to Luxemburg. It was also under international guarantee, but it was 'impossible to compare its sufferings with the devastation, murder, and rapine ... inflicted on Belgium'.[14] Russell's assumptions about German policy towards Belgium look rather unrealistic in the context of recent historical scholarship.[15] However, Russell did have a point when he noted 'a certain unreality' in official explanations for Britain's involvement. As he wrote in answer to an American critic:

> If the faithful observance of treaties were a frequent occurrence, like the observance of contracts, the breach of a treaty might be a real and not merely a formal ground for war, since it would tend to weaken the practice of deciding disputes by agreement rather than by armed force. In the absence of such a practice, however, appeal to treaties is only to be regarded as part of the diplomatic machinery.[16]

Britain was thus guilty of hypocrisy, but more than this it had also encouraged Belgian resistance, and terrible suffering had resulted. If this were not to be repeated (and, in the case of Luxemburg, newly inflicted) when the tide of war began to go against Germany, some kind of compromise peace would be essential. 'The obligation of honour towards Belgium' was 'more fully discharged' if the Germans were 'led to evacuate Belgium by negotiation' rather than if they were 'driven out at the cost of destroying' whatever they had left unharmed.[17]

As we have seen, the advocacy of a compromise peace had been severely criticised, not only by the 'good haters' of Germany, but also by people like Maynard Keynes. What, then, of Russell's arguments for Belgium to allow the free passage of German troops? This would have been rejected out of hand by most observers, and it is rare to find anyone who considered the proposal seriously enough to raise real objections. The historian G. G. Coulton was one of the few, in his book *The Main Illusions of Pacificism*:

> It would be impossible to find any purely *moral* plea which would justify the Belgians in ... opening the back door to let Germany loose upon the weakest frontier of France, especially since that frontier had been left comparatively unfortified in reliance upon a treaty of neutrality which created, not merely a Belgian privilege, but also a corresponding Belgian duty. Secondly what valid reason has Mr Russell for supposing that Belgium, by betraying her trust, would in fact have avoided the horrors of invasion? In any fairly equal war, Belgian soil would have become the main battleground. Not only would the English and the French have had the right to go and meet the Germans wherever they could find them, but they would also have been justified in inflicting direct punishment upon Belgium for her treacherous breach of neutrality.[18]

The emotional reference to Belgium 'betraying her trust' was to be expected. But Coulton's description of the probable consequences of this in the policy of the Allies towards her is uncomfortably close to the argument used (rather dishonestly) by the Germans to justify their harsh treatment of this small state. The position of a powerless neutral occupying strategically important territory was unenviable; Russell's suggestion had not really resolved the terrible dilemma for a small state between powerful neighbours. One critic suggested that Belgian non-resistance might lead to an even greater decline in respect for the neutrality of such states.[19] Coulton himself pointed out that there was only 'one contingency' which could have '*saved* Belgium from martyrdom', and only one other which 'could have *mitigated* her martyrdom'. Neither of them would help Russell's case. Firstly, if 'the Germans, with Belgian connivance, had cut their way through to Paris, and had ended the war as brilliantly as in 1866 or 1870, then the Belgians would ... have lost little besides their honour'. But, in the long term, could Russell, 'as an impartial student of politics and morals', contemplate so complete a German victory 'with anything but horror?'[20]

Russell was no pro-German as many of his detractors believed. As he wrote many years later, 'the successes of the Germans before the Battle of the Marne were horrible to me. I desired the defeat of Germany as ardently as any retired colonel'.[21] His wartime pamphlet on the foreign policy of Sir Edward Grey was clearly the source for this:

> I consider that either a serious weakening of England, France, and Italy, or a serious strengthening of Germany, would be a great misfortune for the world. I wish ardently to see the Germans expelled from France and Belgium, and compelled to feel that the war has been a misfortune for them as well as for the Allies. Those things I desire as strongly as the noisiest of our patriots .... And if any Power is to be supreme at sea, it must be better for international freedom that the Power should be England, whose army is too small to be a danger, rather then Germany, which has by far the most powerful army in the world. On these broad grounds, if I belonged to a neutral country, my sympathies would be against Germany.[22]

This remarkable admission, even allowing some overstatement for the sake of winning over an audience, shows us a Russell perhaps not so far removed from Lowes Dickinson after all. For all Russell's ability to state 'unpleasant truths', he too was torn between a belief that the rulers of Britain were 'accomplices in abominable crimes against humanity and freedom', and a desire for an Allied victory.

Coulton's second 'contingency' raised even more serious criticisms. What would Belgium have gained from allowing passage to German troops 'if the Allies had been more successful from the first'? If there was 'practically nothing to choose between the German soldiery and Allied soldiery', then the Belgians would 'have gained nothing, even in the material sense'. Russell could only prove one part of his case by disproving another:

> Mr Russell cannot mitigate the martyrdom of Belgium, even in theory, except by postulating the excessive inhumanity of German military methods, as compared with those of the Allies; and that is precisely what he cannot afford to do; for it would bring down the whole U.D.C. fabric about his and Mr Dickinson's ears. The embarrassment of so distinguished a thinker in face of so simple a problem is surely a fair measure of the unsoundness of his general thesis.[23]

Coulton's gleeful exposure of what he felt was a logical flaw in the argument of a master logician was rather unfair. Although Russell believed that the ends of German foreign policy 'were exactly similar' to the ends pursued by British foreign policy, and that Britain had been more willing to provoke war in 1911 than Germany three years later, he still conceded that 'the sins of England' sank 'into insignificance beside the German treatment of Belgium'.[24] This ambiguity certainly did not make Russell's arguments for a policy of non-resistance, if the Germans invaded Britain, more credible.

These arguments were presented in articles in the *Atlantic Monthly* and the *International Journal of Ethics* between August and October 1915. Significantly, both were American periodicals; there would have been few journals in Britain willing to risk printing Russell's deliberate taunts to London's clubland. Here one could cite, for example, Russell's argument for the advantages of 'tribute' levied by a victorious Germany over the alternative of prolonging the war if the Allies were losing: it would be cheaper in lives and money, as well as a means of taxing 'the idle rich'. Since 'tribute' would logically consist of 'the total economic rent of the land and natural resources of England', 'wages and other earned income could not be diminished without diminishing the productivity of English labour, and so lessening England's capacity for paying tribute'. Of the potentially demoralising effects of such levies Russell did not seem to be aware — perhaps could not be, since the experience of 'reparations' was in the future. But it was a more sophisticated version of the argument which A. L. Smith had found amongst British workers, that they would not 'be any worse off under German rule'. As for the possible loss of colonies to Germany, this could only be a blessing in disguise, since it would remove from Britain the taint of imperialism — 'a canker of corruption and immorality'.[25] The history of reparations levied on Germany at the end of the war, together with the loss of its colonies, was soon to show just how inadequate Russell's argument was. However, more important than this was his general case for non-violent passive resistance.

It is important to remember that Russell, despite impressions to the contrary, never held that this was appropriate in all circumstances. Although he was often accused of holding 'the extreme Quaker doctrine of non-aggression',[26] Russell saw his own position as quite different from that of Tolstoy or the Quakers. Where they judged conduct in terms of its inherent morality, he judged 'conduct by its consequences':

> The principle that it is always wrong to employ force against another human being ... has always been rejected by the great majority of mankind as inconsistent with the existence of civilised society. In this, no doubt, the majority of mankind are in the right. But I think that occasions where forcible resistance is the best course are

much fewer than is generally believed and that some very great and important advances in civilization might be made if this were more widely recognised.[27]

This 'consequentialism' had only recently replaced Russell's earlier 'intuitionist' view of ethical questions. Russell had formerly been greatly influenced by G. E. Moore's *Principia Ethica* (1903) which had argued that an individual knew by intuition what was 'good', good being an objective feature of the universe (hence the position was also termed 'objectivist'). Thus a right action was one which produced the most good. His *later* position (which could be termed 'subjectivist') meant that logically he could not say the war was unjustified on purely moral or rational grounds, because he was presenting his 'feelings' rather than ethical facts. It meant also that he could not logically argue that passive resistance was the objectively correct course. However, this did not prevent Russell from presenting reasoned arguments 'to clarify' those 'feelings'. As he wrote in an article entitled 'The Ethics of War': 'the fundamental facts . . . in all ethical questions are feelings; all that thought can do is to clarify and systematize the expression of these feelings'.[28] However, there was a certain ambiguity in Russell's writings, as Alan Wood and others have noted. He 'did not always keep strictly to his opinions as a philosopher. He constantly wrote as if 'good' and 'bad' had some objective meaning'.[29] This encouraged critics to accuse him of exaggerating 'pure reason'. But perhaps one of the most perceptive criticisms came from T. E. Hulme.

Hulme was with the Royal Marine Artillery on the Western Front (where he was to be killed in September 1917) when he published his objections to Russell in the pages of the *Cambridge Magazine* and (even more forcefully) in the *New Age*. Hulme had come to St. John's College, Cambridge, with an exhibition in mathematics in 1902. He was sent down in 1904, possibly for hitting a policeman in May Week, but continued to attend the lectures of W. R. Sorley and J. McT. E. McTaggart, both philosophical Idealists. The French philosopher Henri Bergson (Hulme first met him in 1907) exerted an even greater influence and Hulme wrote a series of articles on him for the *New Age* between 1909 and 1912, as well as translating his *Introduction to Metaphysics* (1913). Hulme's other translation, of Sorel's *Reflections on Violence* (1915), is still in print today. However, it was as a defender of Bergson's philosophy that Hulme first crossed swords with Russell. The two men were poles apart philosophically. To Hulme, Russell's views were 'the result of an entirely commonplace and uncritical acceptance of the *liberal* ideology' that had prevailed since the eighteenth century. Russell's ethical ideas were those of a 'rationalist humanitarian'; Hulme sought a 'more tragic system of ethical values'. There was much that was unfair in Hulme's attack on Russell, and some abuse, but he did see that Russell's subjectivism in ethics 'debarred' him from saying that 'pacifist impulses' were '*better* than the low atavistic instinct behind the opposed ethic'. The most Russell could say was 'that he *prefers* pacifist instincts', Hulme rightly concluded. Earlier Hulme had talked of Russell's 'insufferable complacency' which was 'so satisfied that its own ideals' were 'the *inevitable* ideals of man — that opposition appears almost pathological and is regarded with tolerant pity'.[30] This was rough treatment, though not as rough as that received by Clive Bell.[31]

In an article 'The Kind of Rubbish We Oppose' Hulme noted that while Russell always gave 'many Reasons' why wars were evil, he only described 'Impulses that made them justifiable'. Russell never seemed 'to admit that any real Reasons' could exist among supporters of the war. This avoided 'the necessity for any tedious examination of the actual arguments' used by opponents by depriving them 'at one stroke of all validity'.[32] No doubt one of the passages in Russell's lectures to which Hulme most objected was his denial that the war was concerned with real as opposed to imaginary principles. Man's 'sense of right' or of 'public good' was very subjective. As Russell wrote in 1916:

> It is sheer cant to speak of a contest of might against right, and at the same time to hope for a victory of the right. If the contest is really between might and right, that *means* that right will be beaten. What is obscurely intended, when this phrase is used, is that the stronger side is only rendered stronger by men's sense of right. But men's sense of right is very subjective, and is only one factor in deciding the preponderance of force.[33]

It all depended very much on their 'own impulses and passions, a subjective thing, much influenced by prejudice and class-interest and accidents of geography or education'. 'Ethical notions', Russell told the Aristotelian Society in the same year:

> . . . are very seldom a cause, but almost always an effect, a means of claiming universal legislative authority for our own preferences, not as we fondly imagine, the actual ground for those preferences.[34]

For Britain the war was not a contest of principles — it was 'trivial for all its vastness'. 'No great principle' was at stake, 'no great human purpose' was involved on 'either side'. 'The supposed ideal ends for which it is being fought' were 'merely part of the myth'. It was 'legitimate to make war in order to end war', but there was 'no reason to think that this war had any such purpose'.[35]

Nor was this a war of self-defence in any simple sense. As Russell explained to a pacifist conference in Caxton Hall, London, in July 1915:

> Everywhere, the war is regarded as a war of self-defence. And, whatever may have

been true of its origin, it has become, from the moment of its outbreak, in actual fact a war for self-defence.[36]

The war, which had begun with an aggressor state and a victim state, had rapidly become a war of self-preservation on both sides. This had been recognised too by Maynard Keynes who sympathised with the dilemma in which the German socialists were placed in August 1914. At first they had opposed government policy:

> But when it was generally believed that the enemy had set foot beyond the frontier, how could a party which represented a third of the German nation take the responsibility of active and practical opposition to those whose business it was to defend the country? It is the horrible paradox of war and the perpetual scourge of peace parties in all countries, that when once war is joined it is for *all* nations a war of defence — a scourge of which those who, I will not say love war, but hate lovers of peace, do not spare the use.[37]

Here Maynard Keynes was expressing a view of the war very similar to that popularised by his Cambridge friend Lowes Dickinson; Russell characteristically put it in more provocative form.

Russell rightly considered that if 'the right of self-defence' were 'unreservedly admitted', then 'no effective theoretical opposition to war' was possible.[38] However, his own conditional pacifist position still left the thorny problem of deciding which wars were justified and of the efficacy of passive non-resistance, especially if 'rightness' was to be judged by consequences. Russell felt that wars of principle might in some cases be justified, and that wars of self-defence, if against an inferior civilisation, were justified, as were wars of colonisation when judged solely by 'results'. The claim of 'principle' should be approached 'very sceptically'. Civilised communities were justified in 'defending themselves against savages' since this would preserve civilisation, but defence against another civilised state would merely harm civilisation. Wars of colonisation were 'totally devoid of *technical* justification' and were 'apt to be more ruthless than any other sort of war'. But they at least had 'the merit, often quite fallaciously claimed for all wars, of leading in the main to the survival of the fittest'. It was 'chiefly through such wars that the civilised portions of the world' had been extended. This dispensation, however, had acted only in the past. Since 1870 such wars had really, like the First World War, been for prestige and plunder.[39]

This last point was not unlike that made twenty-five years earlier by Russell's former teacher Sidgwick: that 'nations most advanced in civilisation' tended to 'absorb semi-civilised states in their neighbourhood, as in the expansion of England and Russia in Asia and of France in Africa'. Such expansion, Sidgwick had felt, could not 'be altogether condemned' since it seemed 'clearly conducive to the general happiness that the absorption should take place'. But conditions for legitimacy were difficult to define and conflict among civilised states very probable.[40] With this Russell no doubt agreed, just as he apparently shared the Social Darwinist assumptions underlying Sidgwick's approval for white men's wars against 'lesser breeds'. British liberals could also support imperialist ventures though their definition of the 'civilisation' to be bestowed upon subject peoples might well differ markedly from that of clubland conservatives. The things in life which really mattered, Russell noted, were 'not subject to force' and could be 'defended without the help of armies and navies'. This was especially true of wars of self-defence where 'both the right and the duty' of resistance, as it was conceived, resulted from 'too material a conception of human and national welfare'.[41] Although Russell would have denied that the civilisation which he wished to preserve was that of a small privileged elite,[42] would the mass of the population have shared his priorities? But, perhaps more importantly for our purposes, was it true that what was of 'real value could not be endangered if a merely passive resistance were offered to the invader'?[43]

One could agree that many of the 'evils' suffered by an invaded country were 'due to the resistance offered to invasion', but Russell also envisaged a disarmed Britain, 'after a generation of instruction in the principles of passive resistance', being able to make German rule, after invasion, quite impossible. As he wrote in reply to an American critic:

> A nation sufficiently numerous and strong to resist successfully by force of arms will also be able, if it chooses, to resist by the method of strike, by mere refusal to obey. No one seriously supposes that the Germans would undertake to govern England, even if we had no army and navy. The mere political difficulties would be insuperable.

'Passive resistance would discourage the use of force [by the invaders] by arousing a sense of shame in the aggressive nation', for there would be absolutely no pretext for aggression. The German High Command 'could not congratulate themselves upon their military prowess'. 'To the soldierly mind, the whole expedition would be ridiculous, causing a feeling of disgust instead of pride.' Within Germany the 'opposition of whatever was not utterly brutal' would be aroused. By this time, 'if all Englishmen still passively resisted, administration by Germany would be impossible ... after shooting a few, the Germans would have to give up the attempt in despair'.[44]

Russell was concerned to present passive resistance as a realistic alternative. 'Much the same conditions — large population, public spirit, power of organisation — are required for passive non-obedience as are required for success in armed conflict', he noted, but the 'fortitude and discipline' needed were probably even greater.[45] Russell was to be less confident on this point as the result of observing Nazism in the 1930s. As he wrote in 1967, non-resistance:

> ... depends upon certain virtues in those against whom it is employed. When Indians lay down on railways, and challenged the authorities to crush them under trains, the British found such cruelties intolerable. But the Nazis had no such scruples in analogous situations. The doctrine which Tolstoy preached with great persuasive force, that the holders of power could be morally regenerated if met by non-resistance, was obviously untrue in Germany after 1933. Clearly Tolstoy was right only when the holders of power were not ruthless beyond a point, and clearly the Nazis went beyond that point.[46]

However, as late as 1936 (a year before the Nuremburg Laws) Russell maintained his earlier view of the usefulness of disarmament and passive resistance in the face of Nazi attack:

> The attractiveness of a life given to more interesting things than mere physical power cannot fail to have the kind of influence that it has often had in the past, and what is harsh and silly in the Nazi philosophy is more likely to be overcome in this way than by even the most victorious war .... A great civilized nation, in the absence of all stimulus to hatred, cannot long remain in the mood which has put the Nazis in power. With the fear of war removed, bullying would soon lose its charm, and a liberal outlook would become common.[47]

Such views were not uncommon in the 1930s despite warnings as to the true nature of Nazism. Even in 1915 at least one critic pointed to potential difficulties for the policy of passive resistance. If the intention was to defend that which was held to be good, and if it was 'the determination of the enemy to perpetrate that which one holds to be evil', then there were:

> ... only two alternatives: To yield, with the expectation that these good things will be destroyed, or to resist in the hope that they may be preserved, albeit at great cost and in diminished measure.[48]

During the First World War Russell seemed to pin more hope on peace through a 'central government of the world' wielding armed force, although he continued to stress that this had 'no bearing upon the question of whether non-resistance would be a good policy, if any nation could be induced to adopt it'.[49] This concept of strong international government — perhaps a 'Council of Powers' — continued to interest Russell, however. Like Robert MacIver, Russell made an analogy between this and the 'internal orderliness of the civilised community'; like Lowes Dickinson, Russell talked of 'the present international anarchy' and the 'tragic chain of violence' which had led to the war. But, more than either of them, Russell sought to come to terms with 'the herd instinct'. In an essay of 1935 entitled 'Some Psychological Difficulties of Pacifism in War Time' Russell admitted that the war had been an educative experience for the pacifist. Before 1914 they had not known of 'the wiles of the herd instinct', which were less obvious in peacetime:

> We did not realise that it is stimulated by the cognate emotions of fear and rage and blood-lust, and we were not on the look-out for the whole system of irrational beliefs which war-fever, like every strong passion, brings in its train.[50]

On the evidence of Russell's published writings, this change of heart had begun with the war itself. His letter to *The Nation* of August 15th 1914 spoke of the play of 'forces of national greed and national hatred — atavistic instincts, harmful to mankind at its present level, but transmitted from savage and half-animal ancestors':

> ... a whole population, hitherto peaceable and humane, precipitated in a few days down the steep slope to primitive barbarism, letting loose in a moment the instincts of hatred and blood-lust against which the whole fabric of society has been raised. 'Patriots' in all countries acclaim this brutal orgy as a noble determination to vindicate the right; reason and mercy are swept aside in one great flood of hatred; dim abstractions of unimaginable wickedness ... conceal the simple fact that the enemy are men, like ourselves neither better nor worse .... [This hatred was] concentrated and directed by Governments and the Press, fostered by the upper class as a distraction from social discontent, artificially nourished by the sinister influence of the makers of armaments, encouraged by the whole foul literature of 'glory' and by every text-book of history ... .[51]

Russell's first reaction to the war was thus a mixture of conventional U.D.C. theory combined with a realisation that the war had been welcomed (initially at least) by large sections of the population. Not surprisingly, therefore, he did not believe that future world peace was simply a matter of establishing machinery for its enforcement. Russell had been influenced by instinctualist psychology, and he may well have read McDougall and Trotter — his use of the term 'herd instinct' suggests at least an indirect acquaintance with the latter. Certainly he had read Bernard Hart's little book *The Psychology of Insanity* (1912), which was designed to present the ideas of Freud — 'probably the most original and fertile thinker who has yet entered the field of abnormal psychology' — to the general public.[52] Russell may also have read an article on 'War and Sublimation' by Freud's disciple Ernest Jones in the *International Review* (Zürich), the journal in which one of his own articles had been published earlier the same year, 1915. Certainly, Jones's argument was echoed by Russell in his *Principles of Social Reconstruction* (1916):

> The old primitive passions, which civilization has denied, surge up all the stronger for repression. In a moment imagination and instinct travel back through the

centuries, and the wild man of the woods emerges from the mental prison in which he has been confined. This is the deeper part of the psychology of the war fever.[53]

The visible world conflict was thus rooted in man himself:

> There is in all men a disposition to seek out occasions for the exercise of instinctive feelings, and it is this disposition, rather than any inexorable economic or physical fact, which is at the bottom of the enmities between nations. The conflicts of interest are invented to afford an excuse for feelings of hostility; but as the invention is unconscious, it is supposed that the hostility is caused by some real conflict of interests .... The cause of this absence of harmony between our instincts and our real needs is the modern development of industry and commerce .... [In] the modern world our economic organisation is more civilised than our emotions, and the conflicts in which we indulge do not really offer that prospect of gain which lets loose the brute within us.[54]

However, Russell found it surprising that 'so primitive a feeling' as 'herd instinct' could 'attach itself to somewhat artificial aggregations such as modern States or even alliances of States', and he was not satisfied with merely a simple biological explanation for war. He recognised the 'idealistic' motivations — for national honour as much as for power, wealth, prestige, and the 'sheer desire for excitement'. There was 'a passionate devotion to the Nation, conceived as an entity with a life of its own'. The 'impulse of heroism for the welfare of the nation' was 'more widespread than any other kind of subordination to something outside self, with the sole exception of parental affection'. It was 'by far the noblest of motives' making for war and it could not 'be combated by merely material considerations'.[55] This conclusion, perhaps a surprising one given Russell's contempt for 'national ideals', inevitably drew him towards the same search for a 'moral equivalent' for war as that undertaken earlier by William James. The latter was the only person to face the problem 'adequately', but his solution Russell found inadequate. Perhaps 'no adequate solution' was possible; all Russell himself could offer were 'partial solutions' — peaceful outlets for men's energies which cumulatively would diminish the 'force' which made for war. Indeed, Russell sounded rather like James with his talk of 'imagination and love of adventure' being catered for by 'intensification' of political life in a world state, and his argument for the necessity for conflict in human society, separated, where possible, from evil and hatred.[56]

It was not enough to show, as Angell had done, that wars did not benefit the capitalist and financier. The 'international character' of modern capitalism might point towards the need for peace, but Russell noted, 'the brute within us refuses to face this disappointing fact, and turns upon those who bring it forward with savage accusations of unmanliness or lack of patriotism'.[57] Russell equally rejected the argument 'that better economic conditions' would 'of themselves make men happy'. 'Socialism as a panacea seems to me to be mistaken in this way', he wrote in 1916.[58] But, on the other hand, he was also sceptical of the idea, common amongst peace advocates, that national pride could simply be transformed into some wider, international patriotism. Patriotism was 'in essence religious, like the impulses that lead to martyrdom'. It could only be 'adequately combated by a wider religion, extending the boundaries of one's country to all mankind'. But such extension eroded the 'primitive gregarious instinct underlying patriotism', and it became — 'except in a few men gifted with an exceptional love of power' — 'a very pale and thin feeling' when compared with the 'devotion' that led men 'to face death willingly on the battlefield'.[59] This, then, was the nub of the matter:

> The economic and political forces which make for war could be easily curbed, if the will to peace existed strongly in all civilised nations. But so long as populations are liable to war-fever, all work for peace must be precarious; and if war-fever could not be aroused, political and economic forces would be powerless to produce any long or very destructive war. The fundamental problem for the pacifist is to prevent the impulse towards war which seizes whole communities from time to time. And this can only be done by far-reaching changes in education, in the economic structure of society, and in the moral code by which public opinion controls the lives of men and women.[60]

These changes lay within the realm of practical rather than utopian expectation:

> No hostility is more instructive than that of cat and dog, yet a cat and a dog brought up together will become good friends. In like manner, familiarity with foreigners, absence of journalistic incitements to fear and suspicion, realisation that their likeness to ourselves is much greater than their unlikeness, will entirely prevent the growth of the impulse to go to war. The desires for triumph and power can be satisfied by the ordinary contests of football and politics unless the nation's pride is embodied in large and efficient armaments. The feeling that war is the ultimate test of a nation's manhood depends upon a rather barbarous standard of values, a belief that superiority in physical force is the most desirable form of superiority. This belief has largely died out as between individuals in a civilised country, and it seems not Utopian to hope that it may die out as between nations . . . .[61]

Maynard Keynes said of Russell that he 'sustained a pair of opinions ludicrously incompatible. He held that in fact human affairs were carried on after a most irrational fashion, but that the remedy was quite simple and easy, since all we had to do was to carry them on rationally'.[62] Russell may have had this *bon mot* in mind when he described Keynes's wartime work at the Treasury as advising the Government on how to achieve 'the maximum slaughter at the minimum expense'.[63] There was some truth in each of these unkind remarks. Russell found himself impaled on the horns of a philosophical dilemma; Keynes found himself dining with Lloyd George. Which was the worse fate? Each in their way expressed the wartime problems of liberal academics, as did, less starkly, the paths taken by Gilbert Murray and Lowes Dickinson. All four men expressed fears for the fabric of civilised Europe, but none more strongly than Russell who saw, not only the horrors of modern warfare, but also a return to the Dark Ages. Not only was the war 'perpetrating moral murder in the souls of vast millions of combatants', but it threatened also the 'universal exhaustion' of Europe:

> Heroism is succeeded by a merely habitual disregard of danger, enthusiasm for the national cause is replaced by passive obedience to orders. Familiarity with horrors makes war seem natural, not the abomination which it is seen to be at first. Humane feeling decays, since, if it survived, no man could endure the daily shock . . . . [The] small stock of very unusual energy that makes mental progress . . . is being wasted on the battlefield . . . . [If] the war lasts long, it is to be expected that the great age of Europe will be past and that men will look back to the period now coming to an end as the later Greeks looked back at the age of Pericles. Who then is supreme in Europe will be a matter of no importance to mankind; in the madness of rivalry, Europe will have decreed its own insignificance . . . . The collective life of Europe, which has carried it on since the Renaissance in the most wonderful upward movement known to history, will have received a mortal wound which may well prove mortal.[64]

Here Russell approached the reality of war and its significance for Europe more closely than any of his detractors. For someone whose philosophical horizons had been extended by Georg Cantor's *Mannichfaltigkeitslehre* and Gottlob Frege's *Begriffsschrift*, it seemed 'the politics of Bedlam' which decreed that all Germans were now mortal enemies. In July 1900 he had gone with Alfred North Whitehead to the International Congress of Philosophy in Paris. His meeting with the mathematician Giuseppe Peano was, Russell later wrote, 'a turning point in my intellectual life'.[65] But now the war had interrupted plans for a similar congress in London in 1915, and it seemed difficult in the midst of world conflict to envisage a time when scholarship would again become international. Even when the first steps were made towards reconciliation between scholars of the belligerent states after the war, the publicly expressed misgivings of some of their number were proof enough that the 'collective life of Europe' had received a wound — though not a mortal one as Russell had feared.

CHAPTER 9

Wartime Pressures on Academics

May I plead . . . with the great local authorities, and especially those of England and Wales; and with the Lord Mayors and Councils of our cities; and with the Education Committees of our Counties, that they will have patience with us University people, and with other teachers, and will not, in their natural desire for smoothness, endeavour to force us to repress unpopular opinions or to expel those among us who have unusual thoughts or sharp, unwary tongues? . . . . In hours of great excitement some eager eyes 'see red' and red alone. But a University, if you give it freedom, does not all 'see red' at the same time.

M. E. Sadler, 'The Universities and the War' (August 1916)

The dismissal of Bertrand Russell from his lectureship at Trinity College, Cambridge, is perhaps the best-known case of the infringement of academic freedom in a British university during the First World War — or at any time since. It was not an isolated case, although there appear to have been no other dismissals in Cambridge during the war. However, there is evidence of pressure being exerted against dons believed to have pacifist leanings. Sydney Cockerell, Director of the Fitzwilliam Museum and 'supernumerary Fellow' of Jesus College, suffered great unpopularity amongst his colleagues for his 'supposed pessimism' about the war. His Fellowship lapsed in 1916.[1] Even at Trinity College, where the U.D.C. found support among the younger Fellows, G. H. Hardy found that life for the honest doubter could be 'unpleasant', and this experience contributed to his decision to take up an offer of the chair of Geometry at Oxford after the war. He did not return to Cambridge until 1931.[2] Dickinson suffered no more than isolation as the result of his views on the war, but his colleague at King's College, A. C. Pigou, was actively persecuted by some fellow Cambridge economists, as we shall see later. Newnham College was also identified by the patriotic dons as a nest of U.D.C. sympathisers — especially by Professor Ridgeway who disliked the presence of females in Cambridge anyway.[3] At Oxford the number of U.D.C. members and sympathisers was smaller, although here there occurred the first of several cases of persecution.

F. C. Conybeare was one of the most eminent British-born scholars of Armenian culture. He had been a Fellow of University College, Oxford (1880–87), but, being possessed of private means, he was able to resign his Fellowship. However, Conybeare continued to live in Oxford, and his name remained on the list of the Faculty of Theology as listed in the university calendar. He was regarded as one of Oxford's leading scholars. He was also the writer of more controversial works, such as *The Dreyfus Case* (1898), which defended the Captain on the basis of private information, and *The Historical Christ* (1914), which led to his resignation from the Rationalist Press Association. In short, his views were probably not unlike those of his Oxford colleague Gilbert Murray, and his reaction to the outbreak of war was initially favourable:

> In August, September and October I felt so sure that England had all the right on her side and Germany all the wrong, that I hardly troubled to read the diplomatic documents . . . . At the beginning of October my attention was first drawn to the [German] Emperor's correspondence with the Tsar, and I realized that he had made a sincere effort for peace in the days July 28–31 . . . . I am not the man to see clearly the point in favour of the enemy and to conceal it.[4]

Next he turned for documentary evidence to M. Philips Price's *Diplomatic History of the War* (1914), a book 'temperately written without bias or flag-waving' — significantly Gilbert Murray had described it as 'somewhat hurried and inaccurate, as well as a little morbid in its surmises'.[5] On the basis of this Conybeare reached his own conclusions on the July crisis. The Archduke Franz Ferdinand was 'a sensible fellow' with a sensible policy of conciliating the subject nationalities of the Empire. For this display of good sense he was murdered by the Serbians. The Austrian ultimatum was thus quite justified and the difficulty of the German position understandable. 'I quite realise what a testy, obstinate, authoritative and somewhat senile old gentleman' the Wilhelmstrasse 'had to deal with', Conybeare wrote of Franz Joseph, especially when he was 'aided by that arch-oppressor the Magyar Tisza'.[6]

But Conybeare was concerned mostly with Grey, the minister who had secretly 'mortgaged' the Royal Navy 'to France *unconditionally*'. With the Triple Entente Britain was 'as much lashed to *Russia's* chariot wheels as France'. Although Grey wanted peace, he had 'set himself to follow Sazanof who . . . had him in his waistcoat pocket'. Sazanof had wanted war. 'The more Germany yielded, the more provocative and imperious he became.' But Grey was also at fault. He did not tell the British cabinet or parliament of Lichnowsky's conciliatory proposals (using the excuse that they were unofficial) because he knew that they would accept them. So far this was a fairly typical U.D.C. interpretation of events. What really got him into trouble was his claim that Grey had 'tricked' Britain into war. It was, Conybeare claimed, worse than the case of the Ems telegram since 'Grey had acted more criminally than Bismarck ever did'. Parliament had 'been utterly hoodwinked' over 'this sinister business'. All this Conybeare had written privately to Kuno Meyer, Professor of Celtic Philology at the

University of Berlin (1911–19), who was in the United States during the war. He had also told Meyer that he aired similar views 'very freely' in Oxford at meetings of university tutors and of the Fabian Society, and that he could 'not see any harm' resulting from his 'opinions being known'.[7] Meyer took this as permission to publish Conybeare's letters. At least two pamphlets under his name were widely distributed in the United States.[8] When news of this got back to Britain there was an immediate outcry. Sidney Ball, Fellow of St. John's College and an Oxford Fabian, wrote to *The Times* to dissociate himself from Conybeare, stressing that the meetings to which he had referred were private and unofficial.[9] Angry letters appeared in the *Morning Post* from other Oxford scholars, and an editorial in the paper called for the court-martialling of Conybeare as a traitor.[10] Walter Raleigh, one of the most belligerently anti-German dons, wrote gleefully to a friend that this response would be enough to make Conybeare 'willing to do anything short of crawling' in order to be left alone.[11]

Conybeare was no Bertrand Russell, but although he obviously regretted the publication of his letters, he did not retract the contents. Private discussion (and it *had* been a private letter) was quite in order. Perhaps his references to Grey had been 'intemperate'. Grey was less a knave than a fool — 'a weak man and given to vacillation'.[12] As Keith Robbins has noted, critics of the war 'wavered uneasily between the view that he was feeble and gullible, a mere tool of his permanent officials, and the conviction that he was devious and secretive'.[13] Conybeare had merely shifted the emphasis in his account. He now published an article in an American magazine on 'Responsibility for the War' in which he once again concluded that 'the future historian ... will blame Russia and Germany about equally'. Sazanof had 'provoked the poor Kaiser', and Germany had 'deliberately provoked' Britain. There was 'nothing for us now but to fight it out'.[14] Two years later Conybeare said his last public words on the subject in a letter to the *Cambridge Magazine*. Again he emphasised Grey's weakness:

> When I so intemperately attacked Sir Edward Grey on this score [the rejection of Lichnowsky's offer] I ignored the fact that — in spite of his declaring on August 1, 1914, that his hands were free — he was really bound hand and foot by commitments made (even before he assumed office) by King Edward and Lord Lansdowne in 1904. He inherited those obligations, and only lacked the insight into events, the foresight, courage, originality, and force of character needful in order to break away from them, and orientate our national policy afresh, while there was yet time to do so, say, prior to Agadir in 1911. It was, however, humanly speaking impossible that he should at the last moment, in August 1914, treat these commitments as scraps of paper; in my letter which gave so much offence to some of my friends, whose

judgement I respect, I assumed — it is true in deference to his denials of their existence — that he could and should have so treated them. He was indeed no more to be blamed for refusing the German offer of August 1, 1914, than a clock for striking the hour. If any were to blame, it was they who had fashioned, wound up, and set the clock going.[15]

Just who 'they' were Conybeare did not specify. No doubt the readers of the *Cambridge Magazine* did not require the identification of vested interests. But in Oxford Conybeare's name was still unpopular. He had after all held to his criticism of Grey, though now on the grounds of his being a mere cipher. His position in Oxford became so uncomfortable that in 1917 he sold his house and eventually moved to Folkestone. As he wrote to an American magazine from neutral Spain in 1916: 'Let any one in Berlin or London or Paris today raise his voice in favour of peace and the entire press will denounce him as a traitor'.[16] Conybeare continued to hold a similar view of the war up until his death in 1924.[17] In view of his treatment in Oxford it was perhaps not surprising that he left his valuable collection of Armenian books to the London Library, not the Bodleian. Perhaps if Meyer had not published the letters things would have been different. It was this which exposed Conybeare to violent criticism. His Oxford colleague, the philosopher F. C. S. Schiller, expressed similar views in letters to Bertrand Russell but had the good fortune not to see them in print.[18] The dangers of publicly questioning government policy were also demonstrated in the case of A. C. Pigou to which we now turn.

Pigou was Professor of Political Economy (1908–43) and Fellow of King's College, Cambridge. He had not been involved in public controversy before the war, apparently having no taste for the rough and tumble of debate — something which his Cambridge contemporary Russell often relished. As a former pupil noted, criticism of his views on the war:

> ... was responsible for transforming the gay joke-loving, sociable, hospitable bachelor of the Edwardian period into the eccentric recluse of more recent times. In the words of his colleague and life-long friend C. R. Fay, 'World War 1 was a shock to him, and he was never the same afterwards'.[19]

Like his Cambridge colleague, J. M. Keynes, Pigou worked for the Government during the war — in Pigou's case part-time at the Board of Trade. The fruits of this work appeared in numerous articles and in the book *The Economy and Finance of the War* (1916). Pigou also continued to lecture in Cambridge and did voluntary ambulance work at the Front in France, Belgium and later in Italy, where G. M. Trevelyan was doing similar work. But where Trevelyan undertook this work because of poor eyesight, Pigou did so as the result of a conscientious decision. His experiences at the Front sickened him, but even more unpleasant in some ways was the campaign against him by some of his Cambridge colleagues.

Pigou seems to have had doubts about the war from the beginning. In February 1915 he published in *The Nation* 'A Plea for the Statement of the Allies' Terms', which contained the following sentence: 'There are some of us who believe that Germany, like Britain, entered upon this war reluctantly, not as the result of a deep-laid plot, but from the mishandling of a diplomatic situation'. Pigou also stressed that the pursuit of 'victory for its own sake' and the imposition of a 'penal peace' could only be a mistake. Why did not the Allies state their war aims? Was it because they feared that Germany might accept them?[20] Not surprisingly this interpretation of events, so close to the writings of Lowes Dickinson, provoked an outcry led by the *Morning Post*. An editorial in this paper, entitled 'The Professor's Past', commented that 'we seem to remember that Professor Pigou has always been favourably inclined to Germany'.[21] In 1915 this was enough to prove guilt. Evidence for assertions about Pigou's political disloyalty was never produced, but two of his Cambridge colleagues sent in letters protesting at his views and calling for a penal peace settlement. Germany had 'committed crimes against God and man', wrote one of them. She was always 'ready to interpret any generosity as a sign of weakness on the part of the Allies and as a tribute to her own rectitude'.[22] Undeterred by this, Pigou again wrote to *The Nation* in May 1915 to warn against 'undiscriminating hatred' of Germans, especially those living in Britain, in the wake of the sinking of the *Lusitania* and the German use of poison gas on the Western Front. His argument was based on the distinction — common amongst British liberals — between the two Germanies:

> It is incumbent upon us to recollect that the direct responsibility for German methods of warfare lies upon the shoulders of a few men, by whom the Empire is controlled, and not upon those of the great mass of the German people.[23]

Six months later Pigou gave an address to the London Peace Society in which he returned again to the question of peace terms. Obviously influenced by U.D.C. ideas, Pigou saw three principles as essential for successful peacemaking: the right of national self-determination; negotiations 'with goodwill'; negotiation *initially* on the basis of the *status quo ante bellum*. Pigou's main concern was that 'none of the nations concerned' should be 'left suffering under a sense of outrage and wrong'. For this reason 'general war indemnities' were to be excluded, though not 'money compensation to Belgium', as Pigou put it, 'a concession to right and not to mere power'. As well as opposing plans to transfer the Kiel Canal to Denmark and to destroy the German fleet, Pigou rejected talk of 'deposition' of the Kaiser and any enforced change in the make-up of the

German Empire. This last revealed the deep gulf between Pigou and pro-war liberals, like Gilbert Murray, for whom the hope of forcing internal change in Germany was one reason for supporting the war effort. Yet Pigou's proposals were couched in very moderate terms. Peace negotiations were to be:

> ... started on *the general* basis of the territorial *status quo* before the war. That should be the *basis* of the negotiations. In certain cases, however, it would be necessary to depart from that basis, and I suggest that the departure should be made in this way. All the belligerents should recognise the *right* of others to territorial possessions as these existed before the war, and whenever any change was made it should be made by way of purchase. An arrangement of this sort might, I think, be so carried through as to leave no strong thirst for revenge or feeling of outrage and humiliation in any of the belligerent countries.[24]

Pigou again incurred the wrath of the *Morning Post* which returned to the attack with an editorial entitled 'Professorial Pedantry'.[25] In Cambridge R. H. MacLeod, Lecturer in Indian Law and former London organiser for the National Service League, attacked Pigou in the columns of the *Cambridge Daily News*. His angry and rather confused letter drew a reply from J. N. Keynes, the father of Maynard Keynes. While not in agreement with Pigou, Keynes senior felt obliged, as Chairman of the University Special Board for Economics and Politics, to rebut the charge that Pigou, by speaking at the Peace Society conference, was neglecting his job.[26] The existence of the diaries of John Neville Keynes enables us to see the full extent of the campaign of vituperation against Pigou in the University itself, since Keynes was also University Registrar and thus privy to most deliberations.[27] There were concerted attempts to remove Pigou from his chair of Political Economy, especially since he was having problems with the local conscientious objectors tribunal. On 8th May 1916 Neville Keynes recorded in his diary:

> A very trying meeting of the General Board [of Studies] to consider Pigou's claim not to serve in the army in consequence of the need of the University for his services.[28]

While Maynard Keynes could claim that he was engaged on work of national importance and get the Treasury to secure his exemption from military service, Pigou could only claim to work part-time at the Board of Trade and appeared to lack friends in high places. Where Maynard Keynes was extremely circumspect in his criticism of official policy, Pigou had dared to express his views in public. Both men were of 'military age', although Keynes (born 1883) was six years younger than Pigou (born 1877). However, Pigou's greatest disadvantage was to have an implacable enemy in H. S. Foxwell, Fellow of St. John's College, Cambridge, and Professor of Political Economy at University College, London (1881–1928).

Foxwell had been an unsuccessful candidate for the Cambridge chair of Political Economy when Pigou was elected in 1908. He also belonged to a rival school of economic thought, the 'historical school' which argued strongly in favour of protective tariffs. Pigou was a follower of Alfred Marshall in economics and a Liberal in politics. Both Foxwell and another of Pigou's enemies, Archdeacon William Cunningham (another 'historical economist'), were later connected to the extreme right-wing National Party.[29] For whatever reason — personal spite, professorial pique, or political enmity — Foxwell appealed against the tribunal's reluctant award of exemption from military service to Pigou. He offered 'if necessary [to] lecture in Pigou's place' if his university work was not deemed to be of national importance. Pigou would then be free to be drafted into the army. Not until poor Pigou had been before the tribunal *three* more times (as the result of repeated appeals against his exemption) was he finally left alone.[30] This result was due largely to the staunch support of some colleagues amongst the economics lecturers (especially J. H. Clapham) and the Vice-Chancellor T. C. Fitzpatrick. As Neville Keynes confided to his diary:

> We wonder how far MacLeod & Co. have been at work .... The other University men [ie. undergraduates] whose cases originally came up with Pigou's have apparently not been called to appear any more.[31]

The whole episode was rather disagreeable. Was this what a critic of military age could expect? The treatment of another young academic, G. D. H. Cole, suggests the subtler methods which could be used.

G. D. H. Cole had left Oxford with a first-class degree in 1912 to take up the post of Lecturer in Philosophy at Armstrong College, Newcastle. He found this 'highly uncongenial' — the transition from 'the high and rarified atmosphere of pre-war Oxford' to lecturing students in a technical college was not to Cole's liking. However, he was almost immediately elected to a prize Fellowship at Magdalen College, Oxford:

> ... which provided him for seven years with an annual income of several hundreds of pounds without any obligation to teach or to do anything else, with 'common room privileges', and a fine set of oriel-windowed rooms by the Deer Park.[32]

In these aristocratic surroundings Cole wrote *The World of Labour* (1913) which established his reputation as a student of trade union affairs. Already Cole was taking a separate if parallel path to the Webbs, as a guild socialist. He was an active member of the Oxford University Socialist Society, which had about 125 members by 1914. However, as one early member recalled, membership in no way dampened patriotic enthusiasm in August 1914, and 'as a result of the rush to join up, it was soon reduced to an unrepresentative group of fifteen or so'.[33] Early in 1915 the Society decided 'not to express an opinion on the war'. Hearing that the War Office contemplated action against this 'pacifist' society, R. W. Postgate (a pacifist) resigned his chairmanship and Cole got a motion passed by the Society disclaiming the charge that it had ever been 'pacifist'.[34] This too was the policy of the University Fabian Society from which the Socialist Society had split off before the war. In fact, the only group in Oxford at this time which did express critical opinions on the war was the University branch of the U.D.C. whose President was not a don (as at Cambridge), but an undergraduate at Queen's College, V. Gordon Childe (later to be Professor of Prehistoric Archaeology at Edinburgh).

According to R. Page Arnot, Cole was against the war but 'not utterly against it. He thought that Britain had been more justified in going to war, than had other Powers'.[35] A recent study, on the other hand, has stressed that for Cole the war itself 'was not the polar issue; class warfare was'.[36] How do we balance the contemporary judgement with that of the historian? The latter suggests similarities with Tawney — Cole 'was never a 'pure' pacifist, one who believed that there was nothing in the world worth fighting about'.[37] But where Tawney volunteered as an army private, Cole worked from 1915 onwards as an unpaid research officer for the Amalgamated Society of Engineers. A defence of trade union rights on the Home Front took priority for Cole, an attitude which annoyed others on the Left like Beatrice Webb. Some militant pacifists, like Clifford Allen of the No-Conscription Fellowship, also wondered if Cole was not simply avoiding the moral issues of the war by concentrating on trade union matters. Bertrand Russell, however, was more sympathetic, as Allen noted in his diary:

> Was G. D. H. Cole right in deciding his work for labour to be of greater value than standing out for A.E. [Absolute Exemption] as a C.O.? B.R. [Bertrand Russell] said yes since he did not make any bargain re. expression of opinion.[38]

And it could be argued that, given Cole's socialist beliefs with their emphasis on political pluralism (resisting the notion that the rights and powers of all other forms of association are derived from the state), he was simply following the logic of this position. Although, like Russell, a member of the No-Conscription Fellowship (they seem to have been the only academics who were), Cole was not active and spent most of his time on union affairs. This he was able to claim as being of 'national importance' (the A.S.E. was important in the munitions industry) and hence get exemption from military service.

This solution suited the members of the Oxford Conscientious Objectors Tribunal, most of whom were dons. Beatrice Webb commented rather acidly: 'It is said that the College authorities who dominate the tribunal, did not choose to see a Fellow of the College humiliated and made to look ridiculous'.[39] Cole was also lucky to have no academic enemies who might have appealed against his exemption (Pigou's fate), although at some point he seems to have feared that this might happen.[40] The Fellows of Magdalen may have had 'no formulated desire to punish' Cole.[41] They may even have had some idea of protecting free expression of opinion. But it may also have been the case that they hoped, by engineering Cole's exemption for trade union work, to avoid the name of the College being associated with pacifism or anti-war agitation. It was bad enough to have had Jim Larkin of the Irish Transport Workers' Union in College as Cole's guest during the Dublin lock-out (1913), without giving Cole the chance now to associate with anti-war agitators like E. D. Morel or Clifford Allen. But what the authorities were willing to do for Cole they were not willing to do for his 'followers' — undergraduate members of the University Socialist Society who came before the conscientious objectors tribunal. According to Beatrice Webb, even theological students preparing for the ministry had 'been turned down with contumely' — a sure sign that the Oxford tribunal was taking a hard line.[42] The previous year eighty 'members of the university' (unnamed but presumably mostly under-graduates) had written to the *Daily Chronicle* to protest at the call for the imposition of conscription published by the heads of Oxford colleges, and threatened that many of them were 'prepared to go to any lengths in resisting any form of conscription'. The fact that their names were not given was understandable, although 'patriotic' dons made much of this omission.[43]

Aldous Huxley, at this time an Oxford undergraduate, has left us a sketch of how the Oxford tribunal could go about its business. One of the members of the University Socialist Society, J. Alan Kaye, an under-graduate from St. John's College, had applied for exemption as a conscientious objector on the grounds of being an 'international socialist'. At this point in the proceedings the military representative:

> ... leapt up and made a Phillipic against him, bringing up the fact that he was the son of a naturalised German, that he was a Jew, that he had often been in Germany and finally ... tho' perhaps it was a little bathetic ... that he was a member of the Fabian Society. On the grounds of his being of alien extraction he declared that the army did not want him and that the tribunal had no powers to deal with him, a civil court meeting the case more adequately. The military man brandished a manifesto of the No-Conscription Fellowship, which Kaye had distributed and which was thought to do harm to recruiting.[44]

Kaye, 'a practitioner of the Pure Intrigue', now found himself tried under the Defence of the Realm Act and sentenced to two months' imprisonment for distributing material for the No-Conscription Fellowship. After appeal he was released on bail. Another member of the Society, Rajani Palme Dutt, a classical scholar at Balliol College, was also sent to prison in 1916 and sent down for socialist anti-war propaganda the following year.[45] V. Gordon Childe, a past President of the Society, had thrown up his research scholarship and returned to Australia to avoid trouble in Oxford over his views on the war. Unfortunately he found wartime hysteria there as well and was forced to resign from his post at St. Andrews College, University of Sydney.[46] The feeling against conscientious objectors in Oxford was so strong that the Warden of Wadham College, Joseph Wells, suggested that lists should be published,[47] presumably to make life as difficult as possible for them. It was a similar hostility to pacifism in Cambridge which led to Bertrand Russell's dismissal from his Trinity College lectureship.

At the outbreak of the First World War Russell was already inclined towards pacifism. Earlier, under the influence of the Webbs he had been a Liberal Imperialist and a supporter of the Boer War. However, early in 1901 he had become 'a pro-Boer and a Pacifist'. This was part of a sudden change in his conception of the world, a process which he later described as 'a sort of mystic illumination',[48] and which seems to have been akin to religious conversion in its completeness. In 1903 he resigned from the 'Coefficients' whom H. G. Wells described as a 'curious little talking and dining club' which met monthly between 1902 and 1908 to discuss imperial matters. It had been founded by Sidney Webb and, apart from politicians like Leo Amery and Lord Milner, it had a number of prominent academics among its members — W. A. S. Hewins and H. J. Mackinder, successive Directors of the London School of Economics (1895–1903 and 1903–08), and Michael Sadler, at that time Professor of Education at Manchester. Russell apparently left the club over the issue of tariff reform, saying that he 'would rather wreck the Empire than sacrifice freedom'. It was, Wells perceptively observed, 'a parting of the ways'.[49] Russell decided to stand as a candidate for Wimbledon at a by-election in 1907 on behalf of the National Union of Women's Suffrage Societies. This, together with his strong criticism of the foreign policy of Grey from 1910 onwards, marked him out as a Liberal radical. He joined one of the leading critics of British *rapprochement* with Russia, Professor E. G. Browne, in condemning Russian suppression of the liberal-nationalist movement in Persia. To Lady Ottoline Morrell he described the Anglo-Russian agreement on 'spheres of influence' in Persia in the harshest terms:

> We help in the perpetration of a crime, of a crime against liberty, justice & civilization .... *Motive*: fear of Germany — which nearly caused war last summer and is the ground for a vast naval expenditure. *Cure*: Friendship with Germany. *Means*: Assassination of Grey.[50]

It was to be expected therefore that Russell was one of the group of Liberal radicals who in July 1914 campaigned against British involvement in the threatened European war. He busied himself collecting the signatures of colleagues at Cambridge for the manifesto recommending British neutrality, which was published in the *Manchester Guardian*. However, Russell was one of the few British intellectuals who did not change his mind after the British declaration of war on the third of August. He could never understand why liberal intellectuals, like J. L. Hammond, 'who had been writing for years against participation in a European war, were swept off their feet by Belgium', and he broke with Hammond, G. M. Trevelyan and H. W. Massingham over this.[51] In part this stemmed from Russell's basic scepticism in the face of the flaccid moralising of liberal recantations. But there was also a gritty streak of realism in Russell's conception of foreign policy. This comes out in a letter to an American friend in the first month of the war:

> Germany is less guilty and we are less innocent, than the news from London would make you think. It is plain (though under the influence of war-fever people here deny it) that Germany and Austria thought they could punish Serbia without causing Russian intervention and that they desired a *diplomatic* humiliation of Russia. They did not expect war, but were hurried into it by Russian general mobilisation. As for Belgium, that was, for us merely a pretext. It has long been universally known that Belgian neutrality would be violated in the next Franco-German war. All the Great Powers except France are to blame, but not Germany only: it is the terror of Russia that has produced Germany's apparent madness .... And if we succeed, the only Power that will profit is Russia — the land of the knout.[52]

Apart from the reference to Russia (with which the Hammonds and Trevelyans would have agreed a few days earlier), this was a generally more level-headed view of the war than could be found amongst most critics of the British decision to intervene. Still, Russell was himself quite capable of using moral arguments — as he had done over Peria in 1911. This also comes through in his *Autobiography* written all those years later:

> I never had a moment's doubt as to what I should do. I have at times been paralyzed by scepticism, at times I have been cynical, at other times indifferent, but when the war came I felt as if I heard the voice of God. I knew that it was my business to protest, however futile the protest might be. My whole nature was involved .... I hardly supposed that much good would come of opposing the war, but I felt that for the honour of human nature those who were not swept off their feet should show they stood firm.[53]

From the first Russell was very close to the members of the executive of the U.D.C., and he was one of the main forces in the establishment of a branch in Cambridge. As we have seen, by mid-1915 many people formerly sympathetic to the idea of 'democratic control' had begun to turn against the U.D.C. Russell, as one of its best-known publicists, was singled out for special criticism. After the sinking of the *Lusitania* 'a fiercer spirit began to prevail. It seemed to be supposed that I was in some way responsible for the disaster', he wrote later.[54] 'I wonder where R[ussell] will end up', the philosopher Bernard Bosanquet remarked:

> His views about the war are not unreasonable I think, but the steps he has got involved in are undesirable. I all but gave my name to the Union of Democratic Control when it first started but felt an instinct that it would develop into things one could not approve.[55]

Russell's pamphlet *War The Offspring of Fear* (1915), published by the U.D.C., had earned the distinction of being probably the first work to be publicly burnt in a British university since Froude's *Nemesis of Faith* more than half a century earlier. Appropriately, the incendiaries were led by one of the Divinity professors.[56] However, it was the lectures given by Russell in Caxton Hall, London, between January and March 1916, which brought his name before an even wider public. These were published as *Principles of Social Reconstruction* (1916) on the recommendation of the philosopher J. H. Muirhead — someone who by no means shared Russell's views on the war. This book, published in the United States as *Why Men Fight* (1917), a title that Russell did not entirely like, gave Russell a following in North America as well. Other wartime essays were published in Chicago as *Justice in War-Time* (1916).[57] Some copies of *Principles of Social Reconstruction* reached soldiers at the Front, and at least one young officer was almost persuaded to declare a conscientious objection to the war after reading Russell. A. G. West had been studying for a degree in English Literature at Oxford when the war broke out, and he had joined the Public Schools Batallion. On leave he 'stayed up late and read B. Russell's 'Justice in War Time', and went to bed so impressed with its force' that he 'determined to stand out openly against re-entering the Army'. He did, however, return to France (promoted to officer) and was later killed.[58]

Not surprisingly Russell's name (and that of the U.D.C.) began to be linked with the anti-conscription campaign which was gathering strength from mid-1915 onwards. Nathaniel Wedd, Fellow of King's College, Cambridge, noted that:

> There is a general belief that our friends [Lowes Dickinson and Russell] when not making speeches or pamphlets against their country, spend their time persuading possible recruits not to enlist! I cannot quite believe that![59]

Others were convinced that Russell had indeed broken the law. A. E. Taylor, an Oxford philosopher then holding the chair of Moral Philosophy at St. Andrews, wrote to *The Times* to protest at the failure of the authorities to prosecute Russell: 'Is there one law for the working-class agitator and another for members of the Whig oligarchy who are also Fellows of Trinity College, Cambridge?' he asked.[60] But Russell was not deterred, and when the Military Service Bill passed through Parliament in January 1916 he began to work for the No-Conscription Fellowship. From June of that year until February 1918 Russell was a leading figure in the N.C.F., becoming its acting chairman when Clifford Allen and other leaders were imprisoned. In this capacity he wrote ten feature articles and forty-five editorials for its magazine *The Tribunal*, including one for which he was imprisoned for six months in 1918.[61] Even more than his work for the U.D.C., this put Russell quite beyond the academic pale. If, like Lowes Dickinson, he had involved himself in the league of nations movement when the U.D.C. appeared to have reached a dead end, Russell would have retained some academic respectability. But the N.C.F. was 'a much less 'intellectual' body than the U.D.C.'.[62] The only other academic who was a member was G. D. H. Cole and he was not a very active one. But for Russell this political activism injected new meaning into his life. As he wrote to Lady Ottoline Morrell:

> I look round my shelves at the books of mathematics and philosophy that used to seem so full of hope and interest, and now leave me utterly cold . . . . The work I have done seems so little, so irrelevant to this world in which we are living.[63]

Russell's isolation from the academic world was increased as Fellows of Trinity College who had belonged to the U.D.C. got commissions in the army and left Cambridge. J. E. Littlewood, for example, turned his mathematical skills to good effect, 'doing ballistics as a Second Lieutenant in the Royal Artillery'.[64] Russell was left as the only critic of the war still in college — or at least the only one who would speak out publicly. He began to find himself avoided at high table. His friend and one-time philosophical mentor John McTaggart Ellis McTaggart asked Russell to no longer visit him 'because he could not bear' his opinions on the war.[65] His close friend and collaborator on the *Principia Mathematica*, Alfred North Whitehead, who had a younger son killed in the war, disagreed strongly with Russell's views and a lasting coolness grew up between them. This, Russell later noted, was 'much more my fault than his',[66] and there was a sense in which he may have increased his own isolation by his uncompromising attitude. 'If I were Prince of Peace', one Fellow of Trinity remarked, 'I would choose a less provocative Ambassador.'[67] But it is important not to underestimate Russell's difficulties and the strain that he was under. He also had some very antagonistic colleagues, in particular

Henry Jackson, Regius Professor of Greek and Vice-Master of Trinity College. His wartime letters equal any examples from the German side of wartime hatred — directed against the enemy within as much as the foreign foe: 'What pigs the Germans are! It is a sacred duty to hate them'. 'When the country is in danger, I think that those who are not prepared to come to the rescue should lose their citizenship.' And finally, the armchair warrior:

> There was a time when I shrank from taking life, and *might perhaps* have become a conscientious objector. But in 1889 I learned to kill mosquitoes and I regret that I am now too old to kill a German or two.[68]

It was to be Jackson who led the campaign for Russell's removal from his lectureship, but well before this there were signs of difficulties over his position at Trinity. When the Lectureship in Logic and the Principles of Mathematics came up for renewal early in 1915, there was an attempt to get Russell a Fellowship which would have given him greater security. In the end the College Council renewed the lectureship for another five years. The reason for this, according to G. H. Hardy, was that Russell's intention of using his two terms' leave of absence for political activities had alarmed the Council. Electing him to a Fellowship, they had felt, might 'be interpreted as a public gesture of approbation, and might have had serious effects on the future of the College'. The fact that Russell was not a Fellow of Trinity College after the expiry of his prize fellowship (1895–1901) meant that his position was much more vulnerable, since a Fellow could only be deprived of his Fellowship in exceptional circumstances. Under the old statutes 'disgraceful conduct' or a criminal conviction could lead to expulsion by the College Council. A lecturer, on the other hand, merely held the post 'during the pleasure of the Council'; there need be no mention of disapproval in a case of dismissal.[69]

In June 1916 Russell appeared before the Lord Mayor at Mansion House in London on the charge of having made 'statements likely to prejudice the recruiting and discipline of His Majesty's forces' in a pamphlet he had written to protest against the imprisonment of a conscientious objector.[70] The charge does not seem to have been borne out by the evidence — perhaps the reason for the Government's suppression of the report of the proceedings. Russell's friends were able to attend, Lytton Strachey leaving us with a description:

> The Lord Mayor looked like a stuck pig. Counsel for the prosecution was an incredible Daumier caricature of a creature — and positively turned out to be Mr. Bodkin. I felt rather nervous in the Brigand's cave.[71]

Russell was convicted and order to pay a fine of £100. This was paid by anonymous friends when his valuable library was threatened with sale as the result of his non-payment. The Trinity College Council then decided that since Russell 'had been convicted under the Defence of the Realm Act, and the conviction . . . affirmed on appeal', he was to 'be removed from his Lectureship in the College'.[72] Technically the Council was within its rights: a lecturer could be dismissed without reference to the other College Fellows not on the Council (the majority). The real reason for dismissal was Russell's views on the war, something which G. H. Hardy's pamphlet (published for private circulation in 1942) conclusively shows.[73] No doubt the motives of those on the Council who voted for the resolution were mixed. McTaggart claimed that he was not voting on Russell's views but rather 'because of his conviction':

> I looked on the case as if it had been one of removal of a Fellow . . . . I do not blame Russell morally. I think he acted honourably [revealing himself as author of the anonymous pamphlet] . . . . But I do think that after such a conviction he ought not to be a lecturer of Trinity.[74]

This is unconvincing and it did not convince contemporaries either. Russell's dismissal aroused a good deal of adverse criticism among British philosophers who, while not agreeing with Russell's views, felt able to 'respect honest convictions' and had expected the College Council to do the same.[75] One of the older Fellows of Trinity, James Ward, a pioneer in the developing discipline of psychology, gives some idea of the feeling amongst the 'pacifically-minded' minority in the College in a letter to Russell:

> I am amazed and grieved to see how you are being badgered and hounded about. It is most outrageous, and what the motive for it all may be I am quite at a loss to surmise. Are they afraid that you will sneak off to America or is there some rabid fanatic trying to persuade us that you are what the McTaggarts call us — pro-Germans?[76]

There were also public protests from other Fellows and from former members of Trinity College, including one on active service.[77] There was a world of difference between the views of the handful of Fellows on the College Council (all older men) and the body of Trinity Fellows as a whole. The special conditions of wartime explained Russell's vulnerability. As the classicist F. M. Cornford told him:

> Something will have to be done when the younger ones come back. I am sure there would have been a majority of the whole body against the Council, if it had come to a full College meeting.[78]

But the difficulty was that under wartime conditions a general meeting was very difficult to arrange, many of the younger Fellows being on active service. Besides, such drastic action would have been deemed inappropriate by many. 'The Council, in fact, were for the time in an impregnable position; they had only to sit tight and say nothing.'[79] In the end there was an official protest to the Council from twenty-two (out of a total of over sixty) Fellows. 'Without implying concurrence in Mr. Russell's political views', the signatories 'deplored the fact of a reversal of University traditions.'[80] However, no action was proposed while the war lasted, and it was not until 1919 that Russell was offered another five-year lectureship as the result of a manifesto signed by twenty-eight Fellows calling for his reinstatement. This was signed by all Fellows who had served in the armed forces during the war, and contained the veiled threat that harmony within the College would not be maintained if it were rejected. Significantly the manifesto did not imply 'that the action taken during the war was not right in the circumstances then obtaining'.[81] Russell was to accept the offer of the lectureship, only to resign for personal reasons a year later in 1920.

The Russell case as it became known, surprisingly did not lead to a general discussion of the idea of academic freedom during or even after the war. It has been said that in Britain this idea rests 'much more on tradition, on atmosphere, and on public opinion than upon legally established rules'.[82] However, the lessons of the Russell case were that none of these supposed defences were effective. In the United States there were also examples of the dismissal of academics in 'loyalty cases', but here the stronger professionalisation of university teaching led to the establishment of guidelines on academic freedom in wartime. The newly-formed American Association of University Professors (1915) took the lead in this, but even so its guidelines left something to be desired. Arthur Lovejoy and John Dewey, both strong supporters of American entry to the war, produced a report which recognised four grounds for dismissal of faculty (three of them involving no prior government action): conviction for disobeying a law or wartime regulation, involvement in anti-conscription propaganda or opposition to military law, attempting to dissuade others from assisting the war effort, and 'hostile and offensive expressions concerning the United States or its government' (in public or in private) by professors of German origin. Not surprisingly, there were many cases of dismissals and forced resignations, of which those of W. A. Schaper (Professor of Political Science, Minnesota), J. McK. Cattell (Professor of Psychology, Columbia) and H. W. L. Dana (Professor of Comparative Literature, Columbia) are only the most celebrated.[83] Under A.A.U.P. rules Russell would have been no more secure, although in the United States the dismissal might have occurred in a glare of publicity.

In Germany where the idea of *lehrfreiheit* was first formulated, the fate of academic critics of the Government was a mixed one. While there was evidence that universities themselves had excluded Jews and Social Democrats from top teaching appointments, there was only one case of obvious government pressure to deprive an academic of his teaching post before 1914. In 1898 the Prussian Ministry of Education had asked the Philosophical Faculty of the University of Berlin to dismiss a mathematician, Leo Arons, on the grounds that he was a Social Democrat. This the Faculty refused to do, even after the Prussian Diet passed a special law empowering the government to step into the case:

> But when the authorities asserted that it was the mission of the university to prepare students for service to state and church and that an avowed socialist was by definition unfit for this task, the guardians of academic freedom quietly gave in.

During the war there was little evidence of academic criticism of official policy (perhaps even less than in Britain), and anyway 'the authorities were sensitive to the charge of interfering with academic freedom'.[84] Professors were technically civil servants, but universities could resist pressure from the state (under the code of *lehrfreiheit*). It was this, paradoxically, which led to the most celebrated academic freedom case in Germany immediately after the war. The individual involved, Georg Friedrich Nicolai, was very similar to Bertrand Russell in many respects — in his ability to attract female admirers as much as in his opposition to the war — although, unlike Russell, few now remember his name.

Nicolai was a leading cardiologist (he treated the German Empress) and Professor of Physiology at the University of Berlin (1909–20). On the outbreak of war he quickly aligned himself with the small remaining body of pacifists (only one other of whom was an academic, Professor F. W. Förster of Munich), and organised a counter-manifesto to the notorious manifesto of 'the ninety-three' which we examined earlier. This was drafted by Nicolai and signed by Förster (making amends for his signature on the manifesto of 'the ninety-three') and by Albert Einstein. Einstein was Swiss and, although opposed to the war, did not again speak out publicly, deeming such gestures useless and perhaps inappropriate from a foreign neutral. Nicolai sent 'the Appeal to Europeans' to members of the academic community in Berlin, all of whom refused to sign. It was not published until 1917, when it was appended to Nicolai's book *Die Biologie des Krieges*, although it came to the attention of the German authorities long before that. Nicolai had volunteered his services in a civilian medical capacity on the outbreak of war, but also gave anti-war lectures at the University of Berlin. Rather than intervene directly against this, the authorities transferred him away from Berlin to the little garrison town of Graudenz in Prussia, 'where he was assigned as a mere assistant to a unit

for contagious diseases, a field in which he had little experience'.[85] Here he
wrote his anti-war book, and was transferred again to a post at a prisoner-
of-war camp nearby for expressing 'anti-national' views. The authorities
clearly wished to restrict his movements, but when Nicolai had to return to
Berlin because of ill health, he again resumed his anti-war lectures. He was
transferred again to Danzig and drafted into the *Landsturm* (Home Guard)
as a medical orderly, subject to military discipline. This was a favoured
means of silencing critics, but even so Nicolai refused to take the military
oath and made no attempt to prevent the publication of his book in
Switzerland. When *Die Biologie des Krieges* appeared in Zürich in 1917,
Nicolai was court-martialled for violating military censorship and
insulting his superiors. He was fined and again transferred, this time to
Eilenburg, near Leipzig, as an infantry rifleman. However, he continued to
appeal his case through the military courts and refused to carry sidearms.
In 1918 he published another controversial work, *Sechs Tatsachen als
Grundlage der heutigen Machtpolitik*, in Switzerland and finally took
advantage of an opportunity to escape by air from Germany to neutral
Denmark.

Even allowing for the hardship which Nicolai endured, his treatment
seems to have been surprisingly lenient — perhaps the result of having
friends in high places, which Nicolai still did (in this too Russell was
similar). However, his troubles had only just begun. When he returned to
Berlin after the November Revolution which toppled the Kaiser, Nicolai
was soon marked out by the political right as one of the 'November
criminals' who had allegedly stabbed Germany in the back and brought
defeat by the Allies. His involvement in the leading pacifist organisation
Bund Neues Vaterland and his contacts with 'enemy' anti-war intellectuals,
like Romain Rolland, made him an easy target for the large number of
right-wing students at the University of Berlin. The resumption of his
medical lectures in 1920 led to disturbances and disruption, and finally a
petition to the University for Nicolai to be deprived of his post. The
University Senate, led by the conservative historian Eduard Meyer, finally
deprived him of teaching privileges for alleged treason and desertion from
the army. Again Nicolai pursued the matter through the courts, but not
even a sympathetic socialist Minister of Education could save him. In the
Arons case a conservative minister had overridden any university claim to
autonomy; in the Nicolai case the new republican government in Prussia
proved unwilling or unable to do the same, although in this case it would
have been intervening to protect *lehrfreiheit*. Meyer saw to it that Nicolai
was blacklisted in all German and Austrian universities. Having lost his
lawsuit and having no prospect of employment, Nicolai took up the offer of

a chair of Physiology at the University of Córdoba in Argentina. The remainder of his academic career (as a sociologist after 1928) was spent in universities in Argentina and Chile. Nicolai finally died in 1964.[86]

A handful of other German academics suffered after the war — a sign of the general political docility rather than of the protection afforded by the university environment. Nicolai's friend F. W. Förster was forced to resign from his chair in the University of Munich in May 1920. The prevailing political tone in German universities during the Weimar period (1919–33) continued to be very right-wing — socialists, let alone pacifists, were an embattled minority amongst staff and students. In part this was the consequence of defeat in war (what would the atmosphere in British universities have been if Britain had been on the losing side?), in part it was a reflection of the socially exclusive nature of the university. Like the civil service, it remained a bastion of imperial values in a republican age. It is ironical, therefore, that the defenders of Bertrand Russell during the war often charged the authorities at Trinity College with an act of 'shoddy Prussianism' — a combination of 'German abuse of authoritative power malignly compounded with English contempt for ideas'.[87] It may be that the record of British universities was no better than that of German ones. Both Lowes Dickinson and Gilbert Murray publicly protested at this clear case of political muzzling. If there was 'any place where opinions supposed to be pernicious' could 'be aired with comparative safety and exposed to the full blast of intelligent criticism', then surely that place was 'one of the great seats of learning'.[88] But the silence from the rest of the academic community in Britain was deafening.

Unlike Nicolai, Russell even spent six months in prison from May 1918, after being found guilty of 'having made certain statements likely to prejudice His Majesty's relations with America'. On the strength of a report of speeches in the United States Senate, Russell had alleged that American soldiers would be used as strike-breakers in Britain as they had been in their own country. Russell had in fact first made this charge five months earlier in August 1917,[89] and well before this had been the target of a campaign of government harassment. As someone who had been convicted under the Defence of the Realm Act, his movements within Britain were subject to restriction. Lloyd George claimed that Russell had to be prohibited from giving lectures in special security areas (including all coastal towns and cities) because they 'undoubtedly' interfered with 'the prosecution of the war in this country'.[90] But for Russell, now without means of support, perhaps the worst blow was the refusal of the Foreign Office to grant him a passport to travel to Harvard University to lecture on logic and ethics, ostensibly on the grounds of his conviction, but really because he was considered 'one of the most mischievous cranks in the country'.[91] Quite apart from the issue of civil liberty,[92] there was the simple question of financial support. Russell was lucky therefore to have friends prepared to rally round and support him when he came out of prison in September 1918. Gilbert Murray organised a campaign to raise money to support a lectureship with a salary of £150 to £200 a year for three years:

> ... in order to enable ... [Russell] to devote himself exclusively to philosophical work, in the form of teaching or research or both. It is to be feared, however, that he may find this impossible, since in the present state of public feeling no ordinary university institution is likely to be willing to employ him as a teacher after his expulsion from Trinity College, Cambridge.[93]

This was signed by many leading British philosophers, including A. E. Taylor, who in September 1915 had called for the prosecution of Russell. Taylor underlined the fact that universities, even if they felt reasonably well-disposed towards Russell, faced certain pressures: They had:

> ... to think very much of student fees, and ... any which appointed Bertrand Russell might have to face a real falling off from the illogical wrath of the British Parent in his present mood .... I certainly do not see what is going to become of *lehrfreiheit* if he can be victimised in this way without a very energetic protest.[94]

Despite all his difficulties, Russell was fortunate in being an eminent philosopher and a man with connections in high places. Unlike his fellow political prisoner, E. D. Morel, he was able to get into the first division at Brixton Prison on appeal. With more comfortable conditions he was able to read and write what he wanted, provided he did not indulge in political propaganda (this was Nicolai's position before being drafted into the army). Acting on the suggestion of Gilbert Murray, the Conservative elder statesman Lord Balfour had intervened with the Home Secretary on behalf of a fellow-philosopher to secure prison conditions which would not break Russell physically or mentally.[95] E. D. Morel, Clifford Allen and John Maclean were not so fortunate. Nor were the professors of German origin who were working in British universities in 1914. Their treatment aroused virtually no publicity, and, unlike the cases of Russell and Maclean, have been virtually forgotten.

On the outbreak of war university teachers who were German nationals could expect to be interned if they were males of military age. This was the fate of Julius Freund, Professor of German at Sheffield University (1906–15). At the end of 1916 his professorship was terminated by the University Council because it believed that 'there was little likelihood that students would want to be taught by one of his nationality'.[96] After his release at the end of the war, Freund became a professor at the University of Berlin in 1919. Others, like Max Freund, Professor of German at Queen's University, Belfast (1903–14), were in Germany in August 1914. All were quickly removed from chairs and lectureships by governing bodies. In Max Freund's case his claim for arrears of salary was not settled until 1927, by which time he was Professor of German at the Rice Institute (later University) in Texas.[97] There were similar cases with lecturers in German at Reading (K. Holl), St. Andrews (G. Schaafs), and Dundee (W. Stede). The Professor of Greek and Reader in Oriental History at Liverpool University (1911–14), C. F. F. Lehmann-Haupt, resigned soon after the outbreak of war. He was a well-known scholar, as was H. J. Eggeling, Professor of Sanskrit and Comparative Philology at Edinburgh University (1875–1914). Eggeling was in Germany in August 1914 and immediately resigned his chair. His high standing within the University (and perhaps the relief at his action) is shown in the long extract in the minutes of the Senate regretting his departure. His son, however, continued to teach German in the University.[98]

Wartime anti-German feeling was not very discriminating. People with German names were easy targets, even if they were British nationals, or were Germans who had lived in Britain for twenty or so years but who had never bothered with naturalisation. W. T. S. Sonnenschein, Vice-Principal of Brasenose College, Oxford (together with his father) assumed his paternal grandmother's name Stallybrass. This was one way of avoiding persecution by the 'good haters' of Germany. However, his uncle, E. A. Sonnenschein, Professor of Latin at Birmingham University, did not change his name, although his son did (to Somerset).[99] Sir Charles Waldstein, born in the United States of German parents, former Professor of Art at Cambridge, anglicised his surname to Walston.[100] In the same way the orientalist Arthur Schloss became Arthur Waley. Provincial universities and colleges were least able to withstand pressure because of the strong representation of local interests on their governing bodies. The exception was Manchester University in the midst of a city with a long-established community of German origin and many university teachers with German names. There was seemingly only one Manchester professor who had been born in Germany (or rather of German parents in Russian-ruled Livonia), Arvid Johannson. Educated at the universities of Dorpat, Tübingen and Berlin, he had been Professor of German at Manchester since 1895. There appeared to be no difficulty about his being appointed Dean of the Faculty of Arts in 1916. By August 1914 another naturalised Briton of German origin, Arthur Schuster, had moved from the chair of Physics at Manchester to the Secretaryship of the Royal Society.

Anti-German hysteria was present from almost the first days of the war, but it reached its height from 1915 onwards. In December 1914 the shelling of east-coast towns, in January 1915 the first Zeppelin raids, in April 1915 the sinking of the *Lusitania*, all fuelled the hysteria. In April 1915 there were anti-German riots in London's East End, and in May the Stock Exchange excluded brokers of German birth (even if naturalised). In October 1914 the First Sea Lord, Prince Louis of Battenberg, had been forced from office because of his German origins. In May 1915 the Tories secured the exclusion of Haldane from office, presumably because his Hegelianism rendered him suspect. Spy mania affected otherwise intelligent people, and, together with stories of Russian soldiers with snow on their boots passing through Britain, provide evidence of the disturbed state of the public mind. The Principal of the University of Birmingham blamed the shell-shortage on spies and *agents provocateurs*. The 'natural tendency of hard-worked and ignorant men to drink and idleness' was, he claimed, 'readily fostered by aliens', who were 'loathsome and filthy as well as horrible'.[101] An Oxford historian wrote of treason in high places: Britain had for many years 'been infested by spies, who were to be found in every grade of ... society and who regularly notified their views of the political situation to the German authorities'.[102]

In May 1915, the month of Haldane's exclusion from the new wartime coalition, the Government announced further alien internments. At this time a letter appeared in *The Times* from five professors of German origin but British nationality, who held chairs of German at Oxford, Cambridge, Birmingham, Leeds and London. They publicly declared their 'unswerving loyalty' to the country of their adoption.[103] There were many similar declarations in the newspapers at this time. Five days later another letter appeared in which the Professor of International Law at Cambridge — another British national of German origin — expressed his disgust at German 'atrocities' in Belgium. Lasa Oppenheim had been in Britain since 1895, had been naturalised since 1900, and had clearly left Germany for political reasons (like many other Anglo-Germans). However, he was still very sensitive about his identity, as is shown by his reaction to a colleague's jibe about the 'Anglo-German' appearance of his writing.[104] Subsequent events were to show that not even such declarations could save at least two of the signatories of the first letter from persecution by the communities in which they lived. The cases of Professors Karl Wichmann of Birmingham University and A. W. Schüddekopf of Leeds University were examples of men who were loyal British subjects being treated as enemy aliens.

Wichmann had been born in Germany and had taken a degree at Kiel University. He probably came to Britain for political reasons, and lectured at Birmingham before taking up the chair of German at Sheffield

University (1901–07). He returned to Birmingham as Professor of German in 1907. According to William Ashley, the eminent economic historian and Vice-Principal of Birmingham University, Wichmann was a great admirer of Britain:

> ... with a great admiration of English political institutions and a great detestation of Prussian methods of government and of Prussian militarism. While proud of the traditions of the great age of German philosophy and Literature and Music — the age of Kant, and Goethe and Beethoven — he greatly disliked the materialistic tendencies of modern Germany. I must confess that there always seems to me a strain of unpracticality in his ideas, but, in theory and temperament, he was poles asunder from the pan-German or militarist German type. His influence, I am convinced, among his students, was on the side of all that is high and noble in the best of the German literature of the past.

The occasion for Ashley's letter was the news that Wichmann was the subject of investigation by the 'Certificates of Naturalisation (Revocation) Committee' in London. Ashley was at pains to portray Wichmann as a 'good German'. In Wichmann's lectures on 'German institutions' he had pointed out to the students 'the lack of genuine self-government in the German constitution'. From Ashley's letter it is also clear that Wichmann had been forced to resign from his chair in 1916:

> ... due to the action of the City Council, which ... was not based upon any specific charge of any kind but on the broad principle that no German might hold a chair in an English university .... [Wichmann had resigned not for] any specific fault on his part, or any charge against him, but because, whether wisely or not, it was thought that his presence was undesirable in a munition area, and in a University where so much confidential work was being done for the Government.[105]

Ashley's reference was to research on explosives, poison gas, aircraft alloys and submarines.[106] His letter did not seem to help Wichmann who seems to have quietly disappeared from the scene (there is no official mention of his resignation in the Report to the University Council for 1916–17).[107] His chair remained vacant until 1918 when a Dr. Sandbach, formerly Special Lecturer in Commercial German, became Professor.

The fate of Wichmann's colleague at Leeds *is* known. It could be said that Albert-William Schüddekopf was killed by the mental anguish of seeing the two countries he loved best at war with each other, and by the shoddy treatment he received from the community in which he lived. He had been born in Germany and had graduated from Göttingen in 1885. He settled in Britain soon after and was Professor of German at Bedford College, London (1888–90), before going to the University of Leeds as a Lecturer in 1890. He was appointed Professor of German at Leeds in 1896. With the outbreak of war his difficulties were apparently compounded by his wife's habit of speaking her mind. Her comments on the truthfulness of the Bryce Report (which we examine in the next chapter) had led some local people to complain to the Vice-Chancellor, Sir Michael Sadler. In July 1915 a local M.P. (J. Butcher) asked the Home Secretary in parliament whether it was true that Schüddekopf had 'refused to allow his son [a Second Lieutenant in a Territorial Regiment] to fight against the Germans'. Apparently the Professor was quite 'willing that his son should serve for home defence, but did not wish him to fight Germans abroad'.[108] Schüddekopf was now expressly prohibited from associating with members of the armed forces 'without the permission of a competent military authority' — and this despite his being a naturalised British subject. In November 1915 the University was forced to grant him indefinite leave of absence because the City of Leeds Education Committee had threatened to withdraw its grant to the University.[109] In June 1916 Sadler advised Schüddekopf to resign, and three months later he died in a nursing home in Harrogate aged fifty-four.

One further case deserves mention. It involves not a Professor of German but an eminent German-born Orientalist. C. Hermann Ethé held a combined chair of German and Oriental Languages at University College, Aberystwyth from 1875. Like Wichmann and Schüddekopf, he was 'a political exile who was too liberal to live easily in Bismarck's new Germany'.[110] After four years as a lecturer in Oriental Languages at Munich University (1867–71), Ethé had come to Britain where he married an Englishwoman. He gained an international reputation amongst scholars for his catalogue of Persian, Turkish, Hindustani, Pushti and Arabic manuscripts in the Bodleian Library (published from 1872 onwards) and his catalogue of Persian manuscripts in the India Office Library. This was one reason for his appointment as public examiner for the Honours School of Oriental Studies at Oxford in 1887. As a former colleague noted in 1916, the only reason Ethé never got a chair in a German university was because of his political views:

> With the growth of his reputation attempts were made naturally to recall him. To many Oriental faculties in German universities it seemed anomalous that one of the first Persian scholars in Europe should be spending the prime of his life in teaching French and German at a little town on the coast of Wales, and he was repeatedly nominated for an Oriental chair. Very possibly he would have accepted the call. But all these attempts broke down before the resolute refusal of the Imperial Ministry to tolerate a scholar of his suspicious political opinions in a German university chair.[111]

When war broke out, Ethé and his wife were in Germany, but he was allowed back to Britain at the request of the College authorities. Back in Aberystwyth in October 1914, Ethé and one of his colleagues (an

Englishman with a German name and a German wife, G. A. Schott, Professor of Applied Mathematics) were threatened by a mob led by a local magistrate and a town councillor. Ethé took refuge with his wife's family, and, although in obvious financial difficulties, was asked to resign by the College Council. Even the small pension offered by the College was attacked by a member of the Town Council who asked 'why a member of the family of brutes who left our men to die and jeered when they saw their coffins pass' should receive £150. This reference to the alleged treatment of British prisoners of war at Wittenberg Camp in Germany was enough to persuade the Council to condemn the annuity.[112] Although Ethé (unlike Wichmann and Schüddekopf) had never taken British nationality, he had been in Britain for forty-two years. All the time he had worked in the India Office (for no remuneration since 1901) no one had ever suggested that he was 'concocting treasonable information for Berlin'.[113] This affair caused a good deal of ill-feeling between town and gown in Aberystwyth. Ethé died at Reading in 1917 without returning to the College that he had served so faithfully. 'Despite his age he was a casualty of the war just as certainly as any young soldier killed at the Front.'[114]

These seem to have been the only cases of actual persecution of German-born academics. However, at Cambridge some of the opposition to the idea of an English Tripos (put forward during the war) was probably due to anti-German feeling. Two of the leading reformers, Hermann Breul (Professor of German) and E. G. W. Braunholtz (Reader in Romance Languages), were German-born.[115] At Oxford Hermann Georg Fiedler, Taylorian Professor of German (1907–39), had his loyalty called into question by an undergraduate magazine early in 1915 — the title of the article, 'Can the Leopard Change his Spots', gives a fair indication of its contents. Although 144 undergraduates protested publicly against the 'innuendo and veiled threats', it was perhaps surprising that only two dons signed the letter.[116] Two months later Fiedler was taken to task by a Fellow of Jesus College (A. E. W. Hazel) for not being specific enough when he had written to *The Times* with other professors of German in May 1915. 'An ambiguous declaration of this kind', Hazel wrote, 'may save their windows, but will hardly save their reputations.' Fiedler must have taken this to heart, for a week later he sent a letter to the *Oxford Magazine* emphasising his revulsion at the sinking of the *Lusitania* and at the German use of poison gas.[117]

In this examination of the pressures on political dissent in universities during wartime it seems clear that academics themselves were willing accomplices in the general desire to stifle criticism — the 'peacefulness of being at war', L. P. Jacks had called it. Although the number of academics willing, for whatever motive, to persecute colleagues may not have been large, they were hardly outnumbered by those who publicly defended the right to criticise government policy. The attitude of the majority was one of either tacit acceptance of the war or of a desire not to get involved. Whether academic freedom was in fact being infringed depended on a definition of academic freedom (even more difficult in Britain than in Germany, it could be argued), but it would be hard to deny that the war revealed new limits to the kind of freedom of speech an academic could expect to enjoy.[118] On the evidence of this chapter alone, it is difficult to share the view of Lord Chorley (writing in 1963) when he claimed that there did not 'appear to have been any case where even a colourable argument has been advanced that a dismissal took place which involved a breach of academic freedom'.[119] And even where dismissals did not occur, life could be difficult for an academic who dared to question government policy. George Unwin, Professor of Economic History at Manchester University, was a member of the U.D.C. and of the Fellowship of Reconciliation, a Christian pacifist organisation. He admitted to organising lectures for 'that miscreant Russell' and to 'going about in a sneaking way insinuating the subversive principles of the Sermon on the Mount at Methodist Colleges and other unlikely places'. In general his views were not unlike those of Lowes Dickinson — 'no nation was guiltless, and, compared with the general responsibility, the relative criminality of the different combatants was a question of secondary importance'.[120] Although he kept his chair at Manchester, it is clear that 'Unwin was a victim of social ostracism for his pacifist views'.[121] It was in this atmosphere that the proposal was made in the House of Lords to bar conscientious objectors from the teaching profession in state schools in November 1917. It was rejected, much to the relief of H. A. L. Fisher, at this time President of the Board of Education (1916–22).[122] It is Fisher who provides a link to the next chapter because of his long friendship with the leading academic in politics, Lord Bryce, who was heavily involved in wartime propaganda.

CHAPTER 10

Academics and the Propaganda War

In the wars of to-day, which comprise entire peoples, thought is enlisted; thought kills as well as cannons; it kills the soul; it kills beyond the seas, it kills across centuries; it is the heavy artillery which works at a distance.

Romain Rolland, *Clerambault* (1920)

The dividing line between propaganda and history can be a fine one, and never more so than during wartime. The writings of British historians which we have examined were often little more than attempts to justify the Allied cause. They were propagandist. However, they were often very similar in their content to works published before the war which sought to explain German culture or Britain's role in Europe.

It is easy enough in the case of Gilbert Murray to distinguish propagandist and scholarly writings. But what of the historians whose business it was to write, in peacetime, on the history of Wilhelmine Germany or European diplomacy? In such cases a dividing line cannot be drawn through August 1914. Lord Acton had written that a 'knowledge of the past, the record of truths revealed by experience', was valuable not just for itself, but as 'an instrument of action' and a 'power' for 'the making of the future'.[1] And while some might have taken issue with Acton's injunction to the historian to make moral judgements, few historians dissented from his belief that modern history was characterised by unmistakable signs of 'forward movement'. It was hardly surprising therefore that historians were deeply involved in presenting 'Britain's case'. It was only a short step from this to involvement in official propaganda, the 'heavy artillery' in the war of ideas.

In August 1914 Britain was as unprepared to wage what would now be called propaganda warfare as it was to fight a long continental campaign. G. W. Prothero, editor of the *Quarterly Review* and previously Professor of History at Edinburgh (1894–99), was one of the first to realise this deficiency. Barely two weeks after the outbreak of war he wrote to *The Times* expressing grave concern at the 'evidence that in large and influential sections of the population' the war was 'not regarded with whole-hearted approval, or, indeed, approval at all'. The reason for this was that 'even if the demands of and the maintenance of treaties' made a 'widely-understood appeal', vital British interests did not appear to be involved. It was clear that it was with 'the vast masses of working people in the north and the centre of England' that Prothero was concerned.[2] His

167

fears might be dismissed as those of a Conservative with little knowledge of working-class opinion, except that one of the leading figures in the university extension and adult education movement confirmed them. There is ample evidence in the papers of A. L. Smith, History Tutor at Balliol, of his attempts to combat what he saw as the disturbing lack of enthusiasm for the war amongst members of his W.E.A. classes. One of his circular letters to branches mentions Prothero's letter in *The Times* but argues that it would be better for any campaign:

> ... to come less academically and more through their own working class organisations, and if possible through membership of their own (W.E.A.) class; so as to be above suspicion of being in any 'interest' (political, religious, academic or social).[3]

A year later Smith felt that there had in fact been a ''clarification' of working-class opinion', due largely to W.E.A. lectures.[4]

Before we put Smith's views down to the over-optimistic assessment which teachers often make when viewing the results of their work, it is useful to remember that one of the most widely-read books on the war originated in a series of lectures to W.E.A. Summer Schools in August 1914. The preface of *The War and Democracy* (1915) states that the book:

> ... originated in the experience of its five writers at the Summer Schools for working-class students held in connection with the Workers' Educational Association. In the early days of August, at the outbreak of the war, Summer Schools were in full swing at Oxford, Cambridge, Eton, Bangor, and Durham, and it at once became apparent, not merely that the word 'citizen' had suddenly acquired a new depth and significance for men and women of our generation, but also that for the individual citizen himself a large new field of study and discussion had been opened up on subjects and issues hitherto unfamiliar. This book was planned to meet the need there expressed ....

The authors clearly shared some of Smith's concerns:

> After four months of war we feel that, in spite of the splendid response of the nation at large, in spite of a unanimity which has no parallel in our previous history, there are still large sections of the community who fail to realise the vastness of the issues at stake, the formidable nature of the forces ranged against us, and the true inner significance of the struggle.[5]

Smith himself wrote privately of workers who greeted recruiting drives with the claim that they would not 'be any worse off under German rule'.[6] The message he attempted to put across in answer to this is suggested by the broadsheets advertising his lectures with titles like 'The People and the Duties of Empire', 'The Empire Fabric', 'What the War Really Means' and 'Never Again'.[7]

The Oxford University Extension Delegacy also had a well-organised network of lecturers. Its secretary, the historian J. A. R. Marriott, was another ardent imperialist (although a Tory rather than a Liberal) who sought to influence working-class opinion. 'Propaganda in the narrower sense was not within our proper province', he wrote later. 'But we substituted for our usual lecture subjects, courses which had a direct bearing on the war, its antecedents and issues.'[8] Revelations of German 'frightfulness' in Belgium from 1915 onwards provided welcome ammunition, while the task of influencing 'neutral' opinion overseas became more important. But even so, it was not completely true that the propaganda effort was 'directed, not towards the ignorant masses, but to educated doubters'.[9] It is possible to find published lectures aimed at quite unsophisticated audiences. At least two of the Oxford pamphlets were originally lectures delivered under W.E.A. or similar auspices,[10] and many of the others required little from their readers except an ability to read. The Oxford Delegacy and the W.E.A. were from September 1915 represented on a 'Central Committee of National Patriotic Organisations', together with the Victoria League, Cavendish League, Business Men's League and Social Service Bureau. The Committee, in Prothero's words, set out to 'unify and coordinate the work of the several leagues and associations already engaged in educating and arousing the country as to the reason, justice and necessity of the war'.[11] It was one of the many private initiatives in the field of propaganda in the first two years of the war, along with the 'Fight For Right' movement and the 'Oxford pamphlets on the war'.

The question of whether universities should become more directly involved in this patriotic activity arose at this point. E. A. Sonnenschein, Professor of Classics at Birmingham, thought that they should take 'a prominent part in the campaign of enlightenment' which was 'needed not only to stimulate recruiting, but also to clear away some cobwebs from the minds of certain sections' of the population. However, Alfred Marshall, the eminent Cambridge economist, was less happy about the proposal to recruit academics as travelling patriotic lecturers. Picking up one of Prothero's points — that there should be no need for 'bitter or inflammatory' addresses since the *truth* about German actions was bad enough — Marshall raised the spectre of jingoism. The need was to win over German opinion, not to alienate it:

> It is to be remembered that a great many Germans, especially among the working classes, are very averse to wars of exploitation, but, like similar classes at home, are exasperated by insults to the fatherland.[12]

Marshall made no secret of his belief in the 'good Germany'. As he had written earlier:

> ... those who know and love Germany, even while revolted by the hectoring
> militarism which is more common there than here, should insist that we have no
> cause to scorn them.[13]

These were brave words in August 1914, and Marshall was attacked from
all sides for 'professorial folly'. L. R. Farnell, Rector of Exeter College,
Oxford, and a pugnacious man at the best of times, felt that such 'moderate
and compromising speech' was 'unworthy of this moral doomsday of
Europe, and flatly inadequate as a criticism of Germany's guilt'.[14]
Marshall was in no doubt that Britain was fighting in 'the right cause',[15]
but his 'attempt ... to discriminate between the German Government and
the German people, between the policy of one and the culture of the other',
was what caused offence. To another, who like Marshall had seen German
Wissenschaft at first hand, this distinction was 'an otiose and dangerous
thing' — German professors were completely the creatures of the state
which appointed them. J. H. Morgan, Professor of Constitutional Law at
University College, London, and later to be a member of the Inter-Allied
Control Commission in postwar Germany, was in no doubt that the
German public were the accomplices of their government's policy:

> No one who has lived in Germany can fail to be impressed with the hypnotism
> exercised upon the German mind by the pomp and circumstance of war. It has acted
> like an opiate on all the finer feelings of the people.[16]

Morgan presented an argument for total war on Germany in terms
stronger than those employed by most academics. He had an important
wartime role as legal advisor to the British Expeditionary Force (1914–19)
and was involved in collecting evidence of German atrocities. After the war
he was a member of the official Committee of Enquiry into 'War Crimes',
and devoted his energies to documenting German avoidance of the
military provisions of the Treaty of Versailles. This was finally published
more than twenty years later as *Assize of Arms* (1945) at a time when
Morgan was involved in war-crime trials at the end of another world war.
As we shall see, Morgan had no great love for Germans and was impatient
with the notion of 'the two Germanies' in the writings of scholars like
James Bryce and H. A. L. Fisher — the distinction between militarist,
authoritarian Wilhelmine Germany and the gentler, more cosmopolitan
Germany of their youth. However, this distinction tended to lose its force
as the war went on, and as propaganda concentrated on the dangers of
premature peace and on the need for total victory. In the first two years of
the war there was a great flood of writing on the 'ideals of 1914' from
British universities and colleges. This began to peter out by 1916 — no
doubt the slaughter on the Western Front had something to do with this —

by which time the official government propaganda machine was openly revealed for the first time. But even before the creation of the War Propaganda Bureau in 1916 the Government was secretly organising the war of ideas.[17]

In the first month of the war C. F. G. Masterman, Chancellor of the Duchy of Lancaster in the Asquith government, was entrusted with the task of consulting with leading figures from the fields of journalism, literature and universities, with a view to speeding up the flow of privately organised propaganda. From 2nd September 1914 a series of meetings took place at Wellington House, headquarters of the National Insurance Commission. Present were Gilbert Murray, H. G. Wells, G. M. Trevelyan, John Masefield, Thomas Hardy, John Galsworthy, G. K. Chesterton, Robert Bridges, Arnold Bennett, F. M. Hueffer (later Ford) and other literary figures. Present also was Sir Arthur Conan Doyle, who had been knighted for his services in defending the British army from atrocity charges during the Boer War. Masterman may not have seemed an obvious choice for the job of organising propaganda, but he did have a background in Liberal journalism, and his membership of the Christian Social Union (to which A. L. Smith also belonged) had involved him in campaigning against the 'loss of values' in British life.[18] The first meeting he called had been concerned with organising a reply to the manifesto of the German theologians; later meetings organised the distribution and funding of 'privately-produced' pamphlets. By June 1915 'Wellington House', as it came to be known to a select few, had distributed some two and a half million copies of various titles. Civil servants who had been concerned with National Insurance in peacetime now found themselves part of a clandestine propaganda bureau. The Press Section of the Foreign Office dealt officially with foreign editors, but 'Wellington House' placed 'articles and interviews designed to influence opinion in the world's newspapers and magazines, especially in America'.[19]

One of Wellington House's most successful ventures was the distribution of the manifesto of the Oxford theologians *To The Christian Scholars of Europe and America* (1914), which most recipients did not recognise as having any connection with official propaganda. Just how this happened has been described by W. Macneile Dixon, Professor of English at Glasgow and head of the North American branch of Wellington House. With a list of all the principal American newspapers and of all the leading public men in the United States, Dixon was able to send them pamphlets and books as though they had come straight from the publishers themselves, and not from the propaganda bureau.[20] On the other hand, publications written by members of Wellington House, or commissioned by it, were issued by commercial publishers (including Oxford University Press) or by non-official propaganda bodies, like Prothero's Central Committee. Wellington House supplied them with literature, and they in turn 'interested in their scheme many well-known people' in Britain, who directed the literature 'to their distinguished friends abroad'. Thus a 'personal touch' was given 'to what was in essence propaganda'.[21] Apart from civil servants seconded from other departments, academics were probably as numerous as journalists on the staff at Wellington House.

Arnold Toynbee, then Fellow of Balliol College, was involved in propaganda for the United States market until his transfer to the Political Intelligence Department of the Foreign Office in April 1918. This was the beginning of a long familiarity with the corridors of power. Toynbee was to be a member of the British delegation to the Paris Peace Conference, and twenty years later in another world war he again headed a team of expert advisors at the Foreign Office, housed this time in Balliol College. From King's College, Cambridge, came J. W. Headlam (later Sir James Headlam-Morley) who had worked as Historical Advisor in the Foreign Office before the war, and would do so again after the war (1920–28). Lewis Namier, who advised on Polish and Austrian affairs, also divided his time between Wellington House and the Foreign Office. After the war he went on to a distinguished career as an academic historian. Edwyn Bevan, the classical scholar formerly of New College, Oxford, was assigned the job of studying the German press, and he soon became an authority on the Pan-German movement. Later he was joined by H. H. Joachim, philosophy tutor at Merton College, Oxford, whose major work ironically had been *The Nature of Truth* (1906). Joachim was the son of a Hungarian who had settled in Britain. He was, notes his biographer, 'most scrupulous in dealing with German documents . . . to avoid distorting the translation to a sense more favourable to the allied cause than it properly bore'.[22] Nevertheless, Joachim was part of a propaganda machine which was little concerned with such scruples. Three other members of the Wellington House staff were popular novelists — Gilbert Frankau, Anthony Hope (Sir Anthony Hope Hawkins, creator of *The Prisoner of Zenda*) and Sir Gilbert Parker (also a Tory M.P.). Their professional skills were arguably of as much use to the bureau as the American contacts provided by Norman Kemp Smith, Professor of Philosophy at Princeton University (1914–18).[23]

The United States was clearly the main object of attention, and several academics like Sir George Adam Smith (Vice-Principal of Aberdeen University) and G. G. G. Butler (History Fellow of Corpus Christi College, Cambridge) went there on speaking tours,[24] Wellington House having prepared the way. In the United States after April 1917 war propaganda (and academic involvement in it) was always more openly organised. The Committee on Public Information, an official body under the journalist George Creel, and the National Board of Historical Services, a group of historians under the chairmanship of Professor James Shotwell of Columbia University, divided the 'general' and 'educated' markets between them. The National Board was not a government body (its closest ties were with the American Historical Association). It claimed not 'to swerve in any way from historical impartiality' but still managed to produce material not dissimilar from the more obviously propagandist work of historians working for Creel's committee.[25] According to Lord Bryce, who admired the way American historians had organised themselves to support the war effort, a body like the National Board was not really possible in Britain where historians formed 'a very small class'.[26] However, British historians seemed to require no prompting to get on with the task of enlightening the public on the issues involved in the war, and their pamphlets and articles could be widely distributed on the clandestine Wellington House network. However, from 1916, when Wellington House was reorganised, propaganda increasingly became the province of the newspaperman rather than the scholar.

Harold Lasswell, father of research into techniques of propaganda, has remarked of journalists that:

> ... they are not hampered by what Dr. Johnson has termed 'needless scrupulosity'. They have a feeling for words and moods and they know that the public is not convinced by logic, but seduced by stories.[27]

When the two press lords Northcliffe and Beaverbrook took over the British propaganda machine in 1918 after two years of upheaval, there seemed to be a further relaxation of standards. The 'academics' at Wellington House (Headlam, Toynbee, Namier, Zimmern and Bevan) moved to the more exalted surroundings of the Foreign Office. Only R. W. Seton-Watson stayed to work on propaganda for Eastern Europe.[28] But, even before these changes, it was clear that Wellington House was unhampered by 'needless scrupulosity'. Masterman's first official report (June 1915) claimed that the bureau presented 'facts and general arguments based upon the facts', but also that the intention was always to make its audience 'take a right view of the actions of the British government'. Its most serious lapse from 'scrupulosity' was the 'Kadaver Factory' story, by which it was claimed that the Germans were melting down dead soldiers' bodies for glycerine to use in fertilisers and explosives. The idea had originated with Haig's Chief of Intelligence (General Charteris), and was 'repugnant to the more scrupulous men in Wellington

House, who already had some doubts as to the authenticity of the tale'. However, they still circulated bound volumes of Louis Raemaker's *Cartoon History of the War* (1916) in which there was a reference to the story.[29] This was a case of outside pressure on Wellington House; the same may not have been true of the 'Lusitania medal' which had (to say the least) an ambiguous basis in fact. The German medal was originally satirical in intention, but the British interpreted it as celebratory, and produced a large number of copies (all with a misspelt date) distributed by Wellington House.[30]

One person who referred to the 'Lusitania medal' as evidence of German 'frightfulness' — although not alluding to the use made of it in British propaganda — was the eminent scholar-politician Lord Bryce.[31] Bryce did not work for Wellington House but seems often to have acted as an advisor. He was also involved in the specialist area of atrocity propaganda, assisted by the young Arnold Toynbee. This was one form of persuasion where the printed word held its own against the newer medium of the motion picture, and in the context of growing shortages of paper. The Bryce Commission of Enquiry into alleged German atrocities in Belgium also represents another outstanding success for Wellington House. Not only was James Bryce (the commission's chairman) one of Britain's best-known scholars — an historian and political scientist with strong ties of affection and respect for German *Wissenschaft*[32] — but he had also been a very popular British ambassador in the United States (1907–13). He was every inch the public's (especially the American public's) image of a grey-bearded, dispassionate scholar, as well known in Cambridge Massachusetts as in Cambridge England. As an editorial in the *St. Louis Republican* put it: 'If there is one man in the entire British Empire whom the people of this nation [the United States] are prepared to believe implicitly, it is James Bryce'.[33] And this was the common reaction in that country when the sensational findings of the Bryce Commission were published.

The outbreak of the war had been a great shock to Bryce. H. A. L. Fisher, himself a member of the Bryce Commission, has left this description of Bryce's view of Germany in August 1914:

> From early youth he had drunk deeply from the well of German literature and historical science, counting as one of the happiest recollections of his life those student days in Heidelberg, in that delightful, old, idealistic Germany, which had been so easy and hospitable and so intent upon the things which minister to the higher needs of man. Then as a young man he had made his literary reputation by a treatise on German history [*The Holy Roman Empire*], which won for him a widening circle of friendship among German students, which he was careful and glad to preserve. Having been brought up in the strongly anti-Louis-Napoleonic atmosphere of his generation, and being somewhat defective on the side of French

humanities, he was perhaps inclined to overrate the specific contribution of the German genius to the literary culture of Europe. Moreover, although he was alive to the dangers of Prussian militarism, he had always hoped and believed that the forces of moderation and good sense which he knew to be widely spread among the German people would prevail against the mania for violence. He was never, therefore, in the company of alarmists.[34]

The German invasion of Belgium was decisive for Bryce's attitude to the war, as it was for many liberal intellectuals. But Bryce was closer to Germany, intellectually and emotionally, than most. Thus the distinction between 'good' and 'bad' Germans was very important for him. Writing in 1916 of the ideas of the necessity and desirability of war, and of the elevation of the state above morality, Bryce noted:

> I do not attribute to the German people an adherence to the former set of doctrines, for I do not know how far these doctrines are held outside the military and naval caste which has now unhappily gained control of German policy, and I cannot believe that the German people, as I have hitherto known them, ever since I studied at a German university more than fifty years ago, could possibly approve of the action of their Government if their Government suffered them to know the facts relating to the origin and conduct of the war as those facts are known to the rest of the world. We have no hatred of the German people .... Our quarrel is with the German Government.[35]

Once Bryce had made this distinction between government and people, he felt quite able to support the British war effort wholeheartedly. For him the war presented itself 'as a conflict of principles', and, since Britain's cause was 'righteous', there should be no half-measures. As he wrote to an American friend in 1917:

> At present we rejoice to believe that it is not going to be a war of half-measures and limited liability. War is one of those things that if done at all ought to be done with all one's might.[36]

This seems to have been Bryce's position throughout the war. Although he was a leading member of the movement for a postwar league of nations, he was never numbered among the Liberal critics of official policy. He published many pamphlets and articles for the American market to air, as he told Theodore Roosevelt, the 'supreme moral issues' of the conflict.[37] The Allied cause was 'a righteous cause' — *that* was the point to be 'constantly impressed' on the Americans. The Allied case was like that of the North in the American Civil War:

> Had the curse of slavery prevailed, all moral ideas would have been sadly set back, not to speak of political ideals. So now if Germany were to succeed, the sense of right and the sentiments of common humanity would receive a terrible blow .... [38]

This message, together with his success in blackening the reputation of the

German government, was Bryce's great contribution to British propaganda warfare. The investigation into alleged German atrocities in Belgium also served to strengthen Bryce's resolve to support the war effort and to dispel any lingering doubts he might have had about German 'frightfulness'. This too was the intended effect on neutral (especially American) readers of the Bryce Report.

Commissions of inquiry into alleged atrocities were a feature of the propaganda campaigns of most belligerent states, even of the smaller ones like Serbia and Belgium. 'One after the other established an inquiry, or an 'atrocity commission', always with the avowed purpose of getting at the 'truth', the 'real facts''.[39] The attitude of the soldiers at the Front, if Robert Graves is any guide, was one of extreme scepticism. As Graves wrote in his autobiography:

> Propaganda reports of atrocities were, it was agreed, ridiculous. We remembered that while the Germans *could* commit atrocities against enemy civilians, Germany itself, except for an early Russian cavalry raid, had never had the enemy on her soil. We no longer believed the highly-coloured accounts of German atrocities in Belgium; knowing the Belgians now at first-hand. By atrocities we meant, specifically rape, mutilation, and torture — not summary shooting of suspected spies, harbourers of spies, *francs-tireurs*, or disobedient local officials. If the atrocity-list had to include the accidental-on-purpose bombing or machine-gunning of civilians from the air, the Allies were now committing as many atrocities as the Germans. French and Belgian civilians had often tried to win our sympathy by exhibiting mutilations of children, stumps of hands and feet, for instance, representing them as deliberate, fiendish atrocities when, as likely as not, they were merely the result of shell-fire. We did not believe rape to be any more common on the German side of the line than on the Allied side.[40]

Graves was writing at the height of the reaction against the war in 1929, and no doubt this coloured his account. But of course atrocity propaganda was not intended for frontline soldiers but rather for the civilians at home and in neutral states. With this consideration in mind, the use of eminent jurists and academics by the Allies on their atrocity commissions showed a greater degree of sophistication in the approach to propaganda than the German use of government employees, usually from the Ministries of War and Foreign Affairs.[41]

In Britain there had at first been some talk of having the popular novelist Sir Henry Rider Haggard (author of *She* and *Ayesha*) as a member of the Bryce Commission because of his name and his experience as a chairman of Quarter Sessions. However, it was felt by the Government 'that a reputation for writing blood-curdling stories of a highly imaginative order' would not be appropriate preparation for a body with the task of conveying sober objectivity.[42] In the event the 'Commission on Alleged German

Outrages' consisted, besides Bryce, of four lawyers (all King's Counsels), the historian H. A. L. Fisher (at that time Vice-Chancellor of Sheffield University), and the economist, journalist and former Liberal M.P. Harold Cox. The lawyers were Sir Alfred Hopkinson (former Vice-Chancellor of Victoria University, Manchester), Sir Edward Clarke (former Tory Solicitor-General, 1886–92), Sir Kenelm Digby (formerly a permanent Under-Secretary at the Home Office and Vinerian Reader in Law at Oxford, 1868–74), and Sir Frederick Pollock (formerly Corpus Professor of Jurisprudence at Oxford, 1883–1903). The collection of evidence began in September 1914 and over 1,200 depositions were to be taken from Belgian witnesses under the supervision of the Director of Public Prosecutions, Sir Charles Matthews. Evidence from British soldiers at the Front was collected by Professor J. H. Morgan, acting as Home Office representative with the Expeditionary Force. Morgan also collected the diaries of dead German soldiers for use as evidence.[43]

In the 1930s historians, and especially American 'revisionist' historians, made much of the fact that a great deal of the evidence from witnesses outside London was collected by twenty barristers who had, in the words of the Bryce Report itself, 'no authority to administer an oath'.[44] The American historian H. C. Peterson, writing in 1939, concluded that the Bryce Report:

> ... was a collection and not an analysis .... Rumours and opinions were included uncritically. It is not impossible that many of the statements used were the products of leading questions. Incomplete versions of actual events were the basis of the report .... [It] dignified a great many old wives' tales and considerable barrack-room gossip.[45]

Another American historian, J. M. Read, writing two years later, distinguished between atrocity stories and the evidence of the execution of *francs-tireurs*, the latter being allowed in international law. There was, he concluded, 'not one clear-cut case of confessed 'atrociousness'' in any of the stories, although many told 'of the execution of alleged *francs-tireurs* and more of plunderings'.[46] This had been suggested as a possibility by Alfred Marshall, although before the publication of the Bryce Report. In August 1914 he had written to *The Times* to point out that tales of German troops 'shooting civilians in cold blood should never be repeated without inquiry whether the laws of war had been broken by hostile action on the part of the non-combatants'.[47] This was a courageous thing to say at a time when most people seemed to believe the worst of Germans. In another letter he pointed out that when Britain had been at war at other times (presumably a reference to the Boer War), other nations had accused British soldiers of 'cruelties of which we have been certain they are incapable'. If there had been German atrocities, then alcohol and a 'criminal' element might well be the root causes.[48]

Part of the problem was public ignorance about the finer points of international law. Marshall pressed for 'the dissemination of accurate information as to the conditions under which the civil population of a country' could 'oppose the violence of an invading army':

> The Belgian Government had no time to arrange this: and a few errors by Belgian civilians seem to have been to some extent the real occasion, and to a greater extent the pretended occasion, of violence that has horrified the world.[49]

Marshall's point was reinforced by the international lawyers. Sir Thomas Erskine Holland, former Chichele Professor of International Law at Oxford (1874–1910), pointed out that the Hague Convention (1907) had ruled decisively 'against the legality of resistance by individual civilians' to an invading army. 'Lawful belligerents' had to be 'responsibly commanded', to bear 'distinctive marks visible at a distance', to 'carry their arms openly', and to 'conform to the laws of war' — though the first two requirements could be dispensed with if there had not been time to organise properly. Despite its invasion of Belgium, under international law Germany had certain rights of 'self-defence' as the occupying power. It was just that these had been abused. 'No one . . . would have complained of her stern repression of civilian attacks on her troops, so long as it was confined to actual offenders', Holland concluded.[50] This was also the point made by the German-born Professor of International Law at Cambridge, Lasa Oppenheim. The inhabitants of a conquered country owed temporary allegiance to an occupying power, and were thus liable to the doctrine of 'war treason' for resistance. Britain had applied this in South Africa during the Boer War, but now in Belgium Germany had gone too far. The occupying power was 'justified in threatening and eventually carrying out, punishments for the purpose of deterrence' but 'by no means justified in pronouncing and carrying out brutal and inhuman sentences'. The execution of Nurse Cavell (October 1915) was thus 'outrageous':

> Natural justice, humanity, and the public conscience of the world demand that punishments . . . be in due proportion to the harm to his [the occupying power's] interests comprised in the criminal acts concerned. There is neither a need nor a right of the occupant to set up a reign of terror and frightfulness.[51]

Oppenheim, as we have seen, was not immune from attack on account of his German origins, so his attempts to maintain standards of disinterested inquiry are impressive. International lawyers themselves were sometime liable to be influenced by the passions of wartime as well,[52] and the investigations of the Bryce Commission were surrounded by rumours of the wildest kind. L. R. Farnell, the Rector of Exeter College, Oxford, later recounted the claims of a speaker on a recruiting drive near Newcastle that the Germans had buried alive Belgian civilians in a pit (he was speaking before an audience of miners). At this appeal to 'the miners' code of chivalry', 4,000 of them 'at once downed tools and marched to the recruiting office'. Farnell heard of this and had it 'corroborated' by a Belgian minister then working on his government's atrocity report.[53] This wartime atmosphere of rumour and hearsay was captured perfectly by the unknown Admiralty clerk who wrote:

> Absolute evidence have I none —
> But my Aunt's charwoman's sister's son,
> Heard the policeman in Downing Street,
> Say to a housemaid on his beat,
> That he has a brother, who has a friend,
> Who knows to a day when the War will end.[54]

However, amongst all the sensational evidence of the Bryce Commission there was a 'prevailing base of truthfulness'.[55] It could not simply be assumed that, since some of the allegations were unproven and sensational, all the others had been greatly exaggerated. Recent evidence shows, as another American historian has put it:

> ... that the behaviour of the German military authorities in occupied areas was extraordinarily severe, if not brutal, and that the Bryce Report was essentially correct in its major indictment, namely that the German army used terror as a weapon of intimidation.[56]

This too is the conclusion of a recent work on the history of the international law of war. Firstly, the Belgians suffered unprovoked invasion by a powerful neighbour, and then blockade of its coast by two other powerful neighbours. Neither Germany, France nor Britain would take responsibility for seeing that the Belgians were fed, and only the humanitarianism of American citizens (under a scheme organised by Herbert Hoover) 'brought Belgium enough food in the winter of 1914–15 to save it from starvation, then and thereafter'. Secondly, the Germans (perhaps with the war of 1870–1 against France in mind) consistently magnified the problem of *francs-tireurs*. No doubt some Belgian citizens, egged on by 'irresponsible patriotic pamphleteers', ignored the express instruction of their government *not* to engage in private resistance to the German invasion, but they seem to have been the exception. The Germans, keyed up to expect a *Franktireurkrieg*, overreacted — but then, so had the British in South Africa.[57]

German behaviour was bad, but not in the sense of widespread and systematic atrocities alleged in the Bryce Report. In this there were stories of the mutilation of corpses (Uhlans were apparently the worst offenders), the bayonetting of babies, the burning alive of innocent civilians (400 at Andenne), the general rape and pillage and desecration (especially by defaecation, supposedly a German trait), the cutting off of women's breasts (as at Malines and Hofstade). And, even with this mound of evidence of Hunnish bestiality, the Commission claimed to 'have rejected hearsay evidence except in cases where hearsay furnished an undesigned confirmation of facts' for which there was already 'direct testimony from some other source', or where hearsay 'explained in a natural way facts imperfectly narrated or otherwise perplexing'.[58] Such exceptions no doubt explained the inclusion of the sensational evidence, and this proved to be the rock on which the reputation of the Bryce Report foundered in the 1930s. The Commissioners would have done well to study the sober account of the same events by the exiled Belgian historian F. van Langenhove.[59]

The Bryce and Fisher papers give little information on the way in which the Commission went about its work, and the private discussions which must have taken place. However, one letter from Sir Frederick Pollock to Lord Bryce is an interesting comment on the matter of the reliability of evidence. Apparently Harold Cox wanted the Commission itself to examine witnesses. Pollock was provoked by this into amazement at:

> . . . Cox's state of mind in dealing with the testimony. He seems to require a far higher degree of probability than a court of justice ever gets, and to think that every statement of fact must be absolutely true or absolutely false.[60]

But this, unfortunately for the Report's later reputation, was just what many of its readers thought. Pollock, from other evidence, seems to have been rather a 'fire-eater', and was no doubt ready to read the evidence in a manner most damaging to the reputation of the German army.[61] However, his former colleague at Oxford, Sir Thomas Erskine Holland, as an international lawyer of some repute, was generally more sceptical of atrocity stories. In letters to Bryce he pointed out the current view of international lawyers: an invader could 'shoot civilians' who fired on his troops, and could even take hostages 'for the fulfilment of agreements or carrying out of requisitions'. He wrote that there was 'nothing in black and white about punishment for civilian resistance', adding 'not that Germany would care if there were'.[62] It may have been this legal uncertainty which made the Commissioners more ready to clutch at what seemed more damning evidence.

The hand of Lord Bryce is obvious when reading the Commission's report. It opened with the admission that the Commissioners had begun 'the inquiry with doubts whether a positive result could be attained'. But the further they went, the more evidence they examined, the more their 'scepticism' was reduced.[63] This tallies with Fisher's observations of Bryce during the Commission's deliberations.[64] The general conclusion, as to where responsibility for the atrocities should lie, also reflected Bryce's analysis of the situation in Germany. The individual German soldier was absolved from much of the blame. True, some 'outrages' were the result of individual excess — what else could be expected when 'intoxication was extremely prevalent among the German Army in Belgium and France'? But there had been more of this kind of excess than 'would be expected in warfare between civilised Powers'. The breaches differed 'rather in extent than in kind from what has happened in previous though not recent wars'. More serious was the 'deliberate plan' by which non-combatants were 'systematically killed' in large numbers during the first weeks of the invasion of Belgium. The purpose of these killings was 'to strike terror into the civilian population and dishearten the Belgian troops, so as to crush down resistance and extinguish the very spirit of self-defence'. The Germans used the pretext of civilians allegedly firing on their troops 'to justify not merely the shooting of individual *francs-tireurs*, but the murder of large numbers of innocent civilians, an act absolutely forbidden by the rules of civilised warfare'. The Report clearly claimed 'deliberate and systematically organised massacres of the civilian population, accompanied by many isolated murders and other outrages'. Men and women were 'murdered in large numbers', and women and children raped during the general 'conduct of war'. 'Looting, house-burning, and the wanton destruction of property were organised and countenanced', even planned, by German officers, not because of 'military necessity', but simply to create general terror. And finally:

> ... the rules and usages of war were frequently broken, particularly by the using of civilians, including women and children, as a shield for advancing forces exposed to fire, to a less degree by killing the wounded and prisoners, and in the frequent abuse of the Red Cross and the White Flag.[65]

Stories of Belgian *francs-tireurs* were rejected because either the Germans did not recognise 'legitimate military operations', or because they fired upon each other by mistake, or because they were part of dubious claims about atrocities by Belgian civilians (especially the gouging out of German soldiers' eyes).

The Report was thus a blend of fact and fiction. For example, a recent study of one of the most notorious 'excesses' of the German army in Belgium — the burning of Louvain and the shooting of many of its citizens — reaches a similar conclusion to the Bryce Report. There were no *francs-tireurs*, and German fear of them led to their troops firing on each other. The Germans also seem to have interpreted 'military necessity' in the broadest possible terms. But then Germany was the only belligerent state on the Western Front to meet 'anything like guerilla resistance and to reveal its feelings so nakedly'.[66] On the other hand, the Bryce Report was perhaps too ready to absolve the individual soldier. It talked of a specifically military doctrine as an explanation for the treatment of Belgium:

> ... [It] cannot be supposed to be a national doctrine for it neither springs from nor reflects the mind and feelings of the German people as they have heretofore been known to other nations .... [It is] the outcome of a theory held by a ruling caste who have brooded and thought, written and talked and dreamed about war until they have fallen under its obsession and been hynotised by its spirit .... Whoever has travelled among the German peasantry knows that they are as kind and good-natured as any people in Europe.[67]

As we shall see later, the belief in innocent peasant conscripts led astray by their 'ruling caste' hardly faltered even when Bryce was faced with the terrible evidence of massacres of Armenians by the Turkish army. But for the moment we can note that the Bryce Report had an immediate bearing on the whole question of Allied reprisals for German 'frightfulness'.

Bryce was to repeat many times his belief that the German people were not responsible for the actions of their rulers, and he could claim quite correctly in support of this the autocratic nature of the German government. In a review of J. H. Morgan's popularisation of the Bryce Report, *German Atrocities: An Official Investigation* (1916), Bryce denied the suggestion that all Germans shared 'in all the guilt of their Government'. The strictness of official censorship, and the German habit of unquestioning obedience to authority, both argued against this. And Bryce hoped that after the war, when 'the facts hitherto concealed from the people' became known and were 'reflected on with calmness', there would be a 'condemnation' of the outrages, and that the Central Powers would join in efforts 'to regulate and mitigate the conduct of war'. This review was appended to Morgan's book,[68] but Bryce had refused to contribute a preface to it on the grounds that Morgan advocated a policy of reprisals against Germany. Bryce's view was that such a policy would *not* in fact 'lead the enemy Government to desist from breaches of the usages of war'. This was because:

> ... every cruelty tends to call forth another, and in a competition of cruelty the Government against which we are fighting would always win. There is no reason to think any recourse to inhuman practices shocking to philosophy and morality, such as the enemy have adopted, would have the slightest effect on him or promote in any

way our military success. We should not gain: indeed we should certainly lose, because there is nothing which has more won for us the approval of all that is best in neutral nations than that we have championed the cause of justice and humanity .... We stand for the interests of mankind as a whole. We acknowledge a moral law; and we acknowledge it as a State no less than as individuals. From that position we must never depart.'[69]

In other words, it would be difficult to claim to fight for 'Right' against 'Might' if German methods were copied.

However, apart from this disagreement over reprisals, Bryce swallowed whole the conclusions of Morgan's book, even more lurid than those of the Bryce Report itself. These included a belief in the innate sexual perversion of Germans, especially sodomy and child rape. Then there was what Morgan termed 'deliberate defilement' and 'bestial pollution' of billets. Official German statistics showed the 'moral distemper' of the German people, but Morgan also cited the French historian Fustel de Coulanges (1830–89) on the unusually high incidence of homosexuality in Berlin. Since the Germans appeared to show all the atavistic characteristics of the original Huns, there might even 'be force in the contention of those who believe that the Prussian is not a member of the Teutonic family at all, but a 'throw-back' to some Tartar stock', Morgan concluded. Germany was a 'hybrid nation' with the acquired 'idiom' of Europe and the 'instincts ... of some pre-Asiatic horde'. Like 'the intellectual savage', Germany nurtured 'dark atavisms and murderous impulses' beneath a civilised veneer.[70] Much of this was stock-in-trade for the Germanophobe, in much the same way that the more extreme Cold War warriors of our own era have claimed to see Russia as an 'Asiatic' power on the eastern borders of Europe. Over one and a half million copies of Morgan's book were printed, and no doubt the use of Bryce's name not only helped sales but also lent weight to Morgan's wilder claims.

Bryce's name was also used to sell Morgan's 1915 translation of the *Kriegsbrauch im Landkriege* (1902), a semi-official handbook for German officers on 'The Usages of Land warfare'. Morgan claimed that this was an accurate reflection of official German 'military ideas and methods', a 'Handbook of the Hun', and the views expressed in it (especially the attitude to civilians) were harsh indeed. There is some debate over whether it did reflect the views of the General Staff or merely of 'Young Turks' in the officer corps,[71] but for Morgan it constituted the final argument for a policy of reprisals:

It is the fondest of delusions to imagine that all this blood-guiltiness is confined to the German Government and the General Staff .... The whole people is stained with it. The innumerable diaries of common soldiers in the ranks which I have read betray a common sentiment of hate, rapine and ferocious credulity. Again and again English soldiers have told me how their German captors delighted to offer them food in their famished state and then to snatch it away again.

It was 'useless to discriminate between the people and their rulers'. The Germans were 'rotten to the core'. One could 'extirpate a dogma', but one could 'not alter a temperament'.[72] The roots of 'Vansittartism' were well and truly established during the First World War. Even people who could in no sense of the word be described as Germanophobe reluctantly conceded that Germans seemed to have 'a comparatively less strong inner revulsion from atrocious actions performed by authorized agents of their Government'.[73] Edwyn Bevan, who had close ties with German scholars but who was now working in Wellington House, wrote that, since German soldiers had shown 'a singular degree of callousness', there must be 'some want of sensibility' among the German population as a whole — excepting of course the Germany represented by Meinecke and Troeltsch, Naumann and Harnack.[74]

It was clearly easier to consider reprisals against Germany if it could be separated off from the rest of Europe. Morgan had talked of 'Tartar' origins and he was not alone in this. Walter Raleigh, predictably enough, remarked that in 'a portrait of eight German generals with the Kaiser' only two 'have European faces — the others are Kalmucks'.[75] Historians tended to be a little more cautious and talked merely of Prussians (the 'real' enemy) as 'German in little save language'.[76] Even the 'very word 'Prussia'' was not German, another wrote. The Prussians, 'in whom Treitschke managed to see the quintessence of the Germanic race', were 'at bottom either Germanized Slavs or at the most the result of a mixture between Slavs and Germans'.[77] And as in Lord Vansittart's *Black Record: Germans Past and Present* (1941), Tacitus was cited as evidence of the long tradition of German obedience to authority.[78] In an age when the same value was not attached to human life if skins were not white, the use of the term 'Hun' was significant. J. P. Mahaffy, Provost of Trinity College, Dublin, may have had this in mind when he advised a meeting of Church of Ireland clergymen in July 1918 that as long as the Germans openly repudiated 'all the limitations of justice and humanity', and made 'brutality and cruelty the attributes of victory', then so long were the Allies 'bound to regard them as poisonous reptiles, or as vermin, which the most Christian man does not feel it any violation of his duty to exterminate'.[79]

Mahaffy was unusual amongst academics in his call for reprisals, with tortuous justifications to reconcile the Sermon on the Mount with the 'universal law among sentient creatures' of retaliation.[80] Leading academic theologians, in so far as they expressed themselves publicly, were opposed to such a policy,[81] as were the members of the Bryce Commission with the exception of Morgan (who was not officially a 'member'). H. A. L. Fisher, for example, stressed that whatever the Germans might do, it was for the British 'to show the world how a nation of gentlemen conducts the most arduous and terrible business of life'. Unlike the Germans, British soldiers were 'chivalrous, temperate and disciplined'.[82] At about the same time (September 1914), two other leading figures — Sir Frederick Pollock and Sir Thomas Erskine Holland — also warned publicly against the adoption of a policy of reprisals. Holland especially showed considerable restraint in his public utterances when dealing with the case of Nurse Cavell and with German air raids and submarine warfare.[83] However, once it became clear that British, and not just Belgian or French, civilians were going to bear the brunt of German 'frightfulness' (in the form of Zeppelin raids and coastal bombardments), then more public figures began to call for retaliation.[84] In the *Cambridge Magazine* for May 1915 a letter on 'Asphyxiating Gases and their Use in Wartime' argued that there seemed 'to be no valid objection against the use of every scientific contrivance possible' against an 'unscrupulous foe' like Germany.[85] Perhaps the distinction, which Bryce and other liberal academics had made, between German people and German government, was under threat. One way around this was to insist on a War Crimes Tribunal after Germany had been defeated. As A. F. Pollard argued, retaliation simply punished 'the innocent and let the guilty go free'.[86] As it happened, this was at a time (June 1917) when Lord Curzon was putting to the Cabinet the idea of bombing German cities. Then there was opposition to resorting to methods very close to those of German 'frightfulness', although, when Curzon again raised the matter in September 1917, those objections had disappeared.[87] War had a way of grinding down liberal scruples.

For his part Bryce — whether he realised it or not — was caught up in the atrocity propaganda machine which fed the very desire for revenge which he was so at pains to oppose. The Bryce Report was translated into thirty languages, and in Britain its low publication price (sixpence) ensured wide circulation. In addition, there were various 'popular accounts' based on the Report (Morgan's was just one of many), and newspapers published long verbatim extracts. Bryce also wrote introductory sections to many atrocity pamphlets, notably those of Arnold Toynbee of Wellington House. For example, there was Toynbee's *Belgian Deportations* (1916) which was concerned to expose the forced shipment of Belgian workers to Germany. Bryce saw this as 'virtual slavery', worse than anything in the Thirty Years War and little better than 'those Arab slave-raiders in Africa who carried off negroes to the coast to sell'. But, as always, Bryce returned to the ordinary German soldier: "Hans' . . . a good, simple, kindly sort of fellow' in peacetime, but 'in the Army . . . merely the passive instrument of his officers'. It was the latter who were clearly to blame.[88] Toynbee, on the other hand, was less restrained since his job was simply to whip up feeling against Germany:

> In 1914 the Belgians were attacked, ruined, and massacred. In 1915 they were stripped of their manufactures and raw materials, their capital and their plant. In 1916 they are being exploited like their own cattle and machines by the State which has inflicted all these outrages upon them. They are being deported forcibly to Germany and compelled by violence to labour there that their labour may assist Germany to secure the fruits of her crimes and to evade a just retribution for them, at the hands of Belgium and her Allies.[89]

The evidence against the Germans *was* damaging, as recent historians have noted,[90] and Toynbee made the most of this with his rising crescendo of accusation. His lasting contribution to British propaganda was to coin the phrase 'vampire-state' to describe the way in which Germany sucked 'the life blood of any nation' which fell into her clutches. This was the logical end-product of the 'German organisational genius', Toynbee wrote in another atrocity pamphlet.[91]

Toynbee produced further compilations of German 'frightfulness' for Wellington House: *The Destruction of Poland* (1916) was written especially for the Polish-American market to counter German claims that the sufferings of the Poles were due to the Allied blockade; *The German Terror in Belgium* (1917) and the *German Terror in France* (1917) were based on French and Belgian atrocity reports as well as the Bryce Report.[92] But it was his investigation of the massacre of Armenians by Turkish 'irregulars' in 1915 which is the best illustration of Toynbee's involvement in the shady world of atrocity propaganda. Although there was even less doubt than in the case of Belgium that atrocities had in fact been perpetrated, the motives of the Allies in publicising the fate of the Armenian people surpassed even the normal level of governmental cynicism. There was of course a long and honourable history of concern for the fate of this nationality at the hands of the Ottoman Empire. In the 1894–6 period the Armenians had been massacred by the Kurdish irregular cavalry of the Ottoman army, after an abortive uprising. Then the protest in Britain had been led by liberal intellectuals, many of whom had been active in the Bulgarian Atrocities agitation of 1876.[93] James Bryce had in fact cut his teeth as a campaigner against Turkish policy in this first agitation after some 15,000 Bulgarians had been killed. By 1896 the death toll, this time amongst Armenians, was of the order of at least 120,000. Another 21,000 were massacred in 1909 after the 'Young Turk' revolution. There were further massacres in Macedonia and Albania between 1910 and 1912, but these paled into insignificance beside the wartime massacres of Armenians. But, as we shall see, these last occurred at an opportune time for the Allies.

News of the massacres reached the Allies in October 1915. As in 1896, the Armenians were the scapegoats for Turkish military reverses — this time in the Caucasus at the hands of the Russians. Armenians in the Ottoman army were deserting in droves, and exiled Armenian nationalists were trying to secure Allied assistance. The Turkish response was to deport Armenian men, women and children from their homeland. Those who did not die from exhaustion or starvation in the mountains of central Anatolia or the deserts of Eastern Turkey were often massacred in large numbers. The death toll was certainly one million, possibly as high as one and a half million.[94] However, at the same time evidence of pogroms in the Jewish Pale carried out by the retreating Russian army had come to light. The German General Staff had invited American journalists to view the results of these smaller-scale, but no less horrible, atrocities. It was quickly realised in London that publicity for the Turkish massacres of Armenians, and, if possible, evidence of German complicity, would be an excellent counter to the news of the pogroms. Again, opinion in the United States — this time that of the Jewish-American community — was an important consideration.[95] Over fifty years later Toynbee wrote of his (and Bryce's) innocence in the affair:

> At the time, I was unaware of the politics that lay behind this move of H.M.G's [His Majesty's Government], and I believe Lord Bryce was as innocent as I was. Perhaps this was fortunate. For, if our eyes had been opened, I hardly think that either Lord Bryce or I would have been able to do the job that H.M.G. had assigned to us in the complete good faith in which we did, in fact, carry it out. Lord Bryce's concern, and mine, was to establish the facts and to make them public, in the hope that eventually some action might be taken ... .[96]

It is interesting that in this context Toynbee does not mention his work at Wellington House.

The result of the labours of Bryce, assisted by Toynbee, was a government Blue Book, *The Treatment of Armenians in the Ottoman Empire* (1916). This was republished by Hodder and Stoughton, thus achieving a wide circulation. It was prefaced by supporting letters from leading British academics. Gilbert Murray, for example, gave his unqualified approval to the sifting of evidence 'from regions so far removed from the eyes of civilised Europe':

> I realize that in times of persecution passions run high, that oriental races tend to use hyperbolical language, and that victims of oppression cannot be expected to speak with strict fairness of their oppressors .... But the evidence of these letters and reports will bear any scrutiny and overpower any scepticism.[97]

H. A. L. Fisher also had no doubt that the Blue Book bore 'all the marks of credibility'. Then he turned to what was to become the most important issue — that the evidence tended to suggest that the Central Powers 'were, in a general way, favourable to the policy of deportation' which led to the massive death toll.[98] Bryce had actually been careful not to charge them with complicity in his preface:

> I have not so far been able to obtain any authentic information regarding the part said to have been taken by German officials in directing or encouraging these massacres, and therefore it would not be right to express any opinion on the subject.[99]

Toynbee, who had compiled the evidence and written the report, was also careful to say that the 'active participation of German officials' was 'not sufficiently proven', and that it was 'on the whole unlikely that the German authorities initiated the crime'. The Turks, he noted, had no need of 'tempters'. However, the Germans had made no effort to stop the massacres, although they had the power to do so. They 'had but to pronounce the veto, and it would have been obeyed'. The German Government had been 'criminally apathetic', Toynbee concluded, and added for good measure that it had sought to profit from the destruction of Armenian economic power in the Ottoman Empire.[100] No mention, of course, was made of Tsarist massacres of Armenians in 1905. Only after the February Revolution in Russia did Toynbee refer to forced deportations of Armenians by the Tsarist authorities (including those during the war) to make room for Russian settlers.[101]

Later in the war Bryce was ready to label German policy over the Armenians as one of 'tacit acquiescence'. The Germans, he noted, had made 'themselves accessories, whether before the crime or after the crime, to the most awful catastrophe that has even befallen a Christian nation'. Some German consuls seemed even to have encouraged the slaughter, while their government had deceived the German people with false tales of Armenian insurrection, and had imposed strict censorship on the revelations of German missionaries, like Dr. Johannes Lepsius.[102] Toynbee, too, in a pamphlet designed for the United States market, charged the Germans with doing a deal on the massacres: in return for German 'moral and military support', the Turks provided "cannonen futter" for the war effort. But, more than this, the policy of "Ottomanisation" of minority groups, which had in Armenia been carried to the bloody extreme of mass killings, had been inspired by the "Prussianisation" of the Poles and the "Magyarisation" of Roumanian, Slovak and Southern Slav minorities in the Dual Monarchy.[103] These were extremely serious charges to make and they have been repeated at least once more recently.[104] But the most authoritative study of Ottoman-German relations during the war, while stressing that the massacres were part of a 'deliberate' Turkish policy, concludes that it 'was neither instigated or welcomed by the German Government'. At the most, Berlin and Vienna (and some of their representatives in Constantinople) 'were guilty of extremely poor judgement, a considerable degree of moral callousness, and an altogether excessive concern with what was or seemed to be politically expedient':

> Despite mounting indications to the contrary, they accepted far too long the spurious claims of the Porte that its anti-Armenian policies were necessitated by widespread sedition in the eastern provinces. More importantly, even after it became apparent that the Ottoman 'security measures', including the ruthless evacuation of entire provinces, were part of a deliberate effort to decimate and disperse the Armenian population in Asia Minor, the German and Austro-Hungarian governments steadfastly refused to do anything drastic about the matter. While they abhorred and were acutely embarrassed by the brutal policies of the Turks and directed numerous admonitions and protests to the Porte, the statesmen in both Berlin and Vienna were too much concerned with keeping the Turks in the war to risk alienating the Porte by really strong pressures. But it should be added that there were numerous German and Austro-Hungarian officials, particularly diplomatic and consular, who did not condone such a policy of expediency and whose efforts to stop or to mitigate the brutal measures against the Armenians were a great deal more emphatic than has hitherto been assumed.[105]

Germany had no more control over its Turkish ally than Britain had over its Russian ally. And perhaps it was fortunate that Britain was not placed in a similar position (in terms of the magnitude of atrocity), since the calculation of political advantage commonly outweighs humanitarian considerations, especially in wartime. It was also just as well that Bryce was not aware that the British Government was quite willing to pursue separate peace negotiations with Turkey. If these had succeeded, they would very probably have involved dropping the British demand for an autonomous Armenia.[106] Perhaps this also makes the efforts of Bryce on behalf of the Armenians of little real importance, even though they did form part of a more general campaign to dismember the Ottoman Empire. The Turk 'as a Governing Power', noted the veteran of the 1876 campaign, was 'irreclaimable', but the common soldier was not. As with German 'outrages' in Belgium, Bryce continued to believe the best of the Turkish peasant who was honest and kindly 'when not roused by fanaticism'.[107] It was the Turkish Government which aroused widespread 'ideological hostility' even within the Foreign Office.[108]

Hence the story of James Bryce and the Armenian atrocities is not one of successful lobbying on behalf of a small nationality — as could be said of the wartime activities of R. W. Seton-Watson and Harold Temperley (the

South Slavs) or of Ronald Burrows (the Greeks)[109] — but rather of the uses to which a scholar's reputation and a liberal's conscience can be put. It might be said that, as principal advocate of Armenian independence (Bryce was founder and first president of the Anglo-Armenian Society) from the 1870s, Bryce was as much using propaganda for his own purposes as being used by the British Government. It seems on the face of it unlikely, and of course the Armenians never won independence. Under the Treaty of Sèvres (August 1920) Turkey was to agree to a free and independent Armenia. However, by December 1920 the Turks were to win back this region, exacting the usual revenge on the hapless Armenians in the process. By the Treaty of Lausanne (October 1922) the new powerful Turkish Republic was to be recognised by the states of Europe. Dying in 1921, Bryce was spared knowledge of new massacres (including those of Greeks at the hands of the Turks at Smyrna in 1922) and the reconquest of the Straits by Mustafa Kemal. Ironically, Toynbee lost himself the new Koraïs chair of Byzantine and Modern Greek Studies in the University of London because of his reports for the *Manchester Guardian* of Greek atrocities against Turks in the Smyrna area in 1919.[110] There is another irony as well. Toynbee, who had done so much work for the propaganda war against Germany, became during the 1930s one of the leading apologists for a policy of 'appeasing' Germany. He also, as Director of Studies at the Royal Institute of International Affairs (from 1925), worked for the formal readmission of German scholars to international conferences and meetings. In pursuit of this objective, he was joined by his father-in-law Gilbert Murray, after the death of Bryce, perhaps the academic best known to the general public. Murray, as a member of the executive of the Committee on Intellectual Cooperation (a League of Nations body based in Geneva), was intimately involved in the machinations of institutionalised international scholarship,[111] an area to which we now turn.

CHAPTER 11

Postwar Reconciliation?

Before 1914, if any of us had been questioned as to the position of scholars in the event of a war between nations, I think our answer would in substance have been that scholars, as men, would take such part in the defence and assistance of their country, as circumstances qualified them to take, but that as scholars they would have no share in the hostilities and would be ready, when the war was over, if not before, to take up in common that pursuit of truth which is the scholar's function. It has been recalled that at the height of the Napoleonic Wars Sir Humphrey Davy was invited to Paris and received with great honour; and I think most of us would have felt that on scholars, more perhaps than on any other class of men the duty would lie of keeping alive the spirit of sane human relationships, which war tends to interrupt so forcibly. The facts have turned out otherwise.

Sir Frederick Kenyon, *International Scholarship* (1920)

Early in 1915 Bertrand Russell had described Europe as 'a house on fire, where the inmates instead of trying to extinguish the flames' were 'engaged in accusing each other of having caused the conflagration'.[1] When peace came at least half of the house was in ruins and the inmates were no longer on speaking terms. Russell was anxious that there should be no condemnation of intellectuals for their 'wartime transgressions', so that reconciliation could proceed smoothly.[2] But, although individual British scholars were in touch again with German colleagues as soon as peace was declared,[3] the institutional framework of international scholarship seemed — as Russell had predicted — to have been broken permanently. This can clearly be seen in the controversy which surrounded the question of Germany's participation in postwar scholarly congresses and conferences. Before the outbreak of the war these had been increasing both in scale and in number.[4] The war had put a virtual end to them. Now with peace came the question of whether the wartime activities of German professors had put them quite outside the international community of scholars — the same question never arose about the activities of academics in the Allied states. Bernard Bosanquet, who had been elected President of the projected Fifth International Congress of Philosophy to be held in London in 1915, hoped to be able to offer 'cordiality to all philosophers after peace'. However, this aroused opposition amongst other members of the General Organising Committee, and Bosanquet had to be content with the more cautious statement expressing 'an earnest hope that the confederacy of the entire philosophical world' would not 'be set aside for a longer time' than 'outward circumstances' rendered 'absolutely imperative':

We are confident that the common interest in philosophy which has expressed itself
so effectively in the past meetings of the Congress will prove to be an enduring bond.[5]

But German and Austrian philosophers were not invited to the
Philosophical Congress in Oxford in 1920, nor to the Fifth International
Congress which was held, not in London, but in Naples in 1924. Only in
1926, at the Sixth Congress held at Harvard University, were German and
Austrian philosophers officially represented.[6]

The story of the International Historical Congress is very much the
same. Last held in London in 1913, planned for St. Petersburg in 1918,
postponed by war, revolution and civil war, it was finally abandoned.
Austrian scholars attended the 1924 Brussels congress in an unofficial
capacity, and not until 1926 were German, Austrian and Bulgarian
delegates officially invited to join the new *Comité des Sciences Historiques*.[7]
The war also put an end to plans for congresses of Orientalists at Oxford in
1916, and of Anthropology and Prehistoric Archaeology at Madrid in
1915. However, the International Congress of Americanists did go ahead
as planned in Washington D.C. in December 1915. The list of participants
for the latter included two from the Central Powers, and one German
scholar gave a paper. But even so neutral a gathering could not escape
entirely from the politics of European war, and there were official
representatives from 'Bohemia' and 'Russian Poland' in attendance.[8] This
must have been one of the few important scholarly congresses held during
wartime. Otherwise the picture was bleak. Many years' work was lost when
the International Association of Universities (established in 1901) and the
International Association of Academies (established in 1899) broke up
during the first months of the war. But of greater importance was the
disruption of international cooperation of scholars on projects like the
Anglo-German edition of the *Mahābhārata*.[9] Doubtless there were many
other lesser-known examples.

Yet, even during the war, some eminent British scholars talked of the
time when links with German and Austrian colleagues could be renewed.
Considering the hysteria and the hatreds of the time, the few who did speak
their minds deserve our admiration. That crusty old individualist James
Bryce was one such. In 1916 he informed members of the British Academy
that it was for 'learned bodies to try to link up the bonds of personal regard
and intellectual cooperation' then 'unhappily severed' — but only after
'bitterness of feeling' had subsided.[10] Obviously the Academy would find
it difficult to be too much out of step with public opinion, but at a time
when many people were calling for enemy nationals to be struck off the
rolls of learned societies, both the British Academy and its sister institution
the Royal Society successfully resisted this demand. The wartime

behaviour of German professors (especially the manifesto of 'the ninety-three') was difficult to explain away, and even Bryce felt that the distinction between willing and unwilling participation in expressions of anti-British feeling was not always clear. In May 1918 the British Academy heard an address on 'International Scholarship After The War' by the Oxford theologian William Sanday, when the same issue came up again. As the most prestigious body of British scholars in the humanities, the Academy was the natural place for discussion of future relations with German and Austrian scholars. Even so, Bryce's successor as President, Sir Frederick Kenyon, was careful to affirm the belief of the Academy in the rightness of the war. As *The Times* reported:

> The President . . . stated that the discussion of the subject was not to be taken as a sign of any weakening on the part of British scholars with regard to the war. On behalf of the Academy he could affirm that they believed as firmly as ever in the righteousness of the war, and in the necessity of fighting until an honourable peace was secured. It would be impossible to resume intercourse with German scholars until they had renounced the crimes against civilisation which Germany had committed. But if such a change of mind should take place when Germans discover the truth, British scholars might assist the process of conversion by which alone Germany could win readmission to the fellowship of civilised nations. This would be done, not by condoning crimes, but by making the truth known, without unnecessary acts of unfriendliness such as the expulsion of enemy members of learned societies.

There was the usual amount of self-righteousness, as well as some good sense, in such sentiments. Bryce and others referred to Germany as a sinner in the world community — her 'absolution' would depend on 'repentance'. Sanday gravely asked his audience just how 'a gentleman' would behave after 'a serious quarrel . . . in which one of the disputants had right on his side and in which he had great cause to be aggrieved'. The revelations of Prince Lichnowsky, the former German ambassador in London, should cause 'a complete revulsion and revolution in public feeling in Germany'. But would they? Here was a 'great opportunity' for those theologians, like Loofs, Troeltsch and Harnack, who had signed anti-British manifestoes, to assist in the process of 'repentance'. As for Britain:

> There was probably no country whose population was, on the whole more chivalrous, sportsmanlike and fair than our own, but the provocation we had received was so deep and so deadly that it was not surprising that Germany was regarded by many as having made itself an outlaw among the nations.[11]

Obviously for scholars like Sanday German re-entry to the world of international scholarship was conditional upon a renunciation of statements made during wartime in the heat of the moment, just as German participation in the League of Nations was later to be seen as conditional upon far-reaching internal political changes.[12] But even this carefully qualified expectation of future normalisation of relations between scholars was bitterly attacked by those whose sole concern was to 'get on with the war and win it'.[13] Where Sanday and Bryce saw apostacy on the part of German professors, other British academics saw the professors as 'agents of the German Government', and German universities as bastions of 'the political and military power of the German nation'. Perhaps Britain should learn from the 'German academic offensive' during the war and plan for the postwar struggle with Germany? British universities could be marshalled to meet the threat of *Wissenschaft*:

> Subsidies to universities, careful study of the needs of foreign students, help towards the expenses of research, cheap production of good literary and scientific books, especially for export, immediate translation ... of noteworthy treatises in other languages ....[14]

There were implications here for the relationship between state and university, as well as for the role of national scholarship as an adjunct of foreign policy, some of which were worked out after the war.[15] However, the general impression gained from reading the discussion on postwar developments is of a desire to simply take up the contacts again where they had been broken off in 1914, but not to fundamentally alter the basis of that contact. This was assisted by developments on the German side. Even before the war had ended some signatories of the manifesto of 'the ninety-three' were having second thoughts. The great Lujo Brentano, pioneer historian of British labour and economic history, claimed as early as 1916 that he had not read the manifesto before signing.[16] This was reported in the British press in November 1918, together with similar explanations by other German scholars.[17] However, other equally eminent scholars, like the classicist Ulrich von Wilamowitz-Moellendorff, never recanted their wartime views,[18] but they seem to have been a smaller group. By 1919 over half of the signatories who were still alive had publicly acknowledged that they had been mistaken in accepting the assertions in the manifesto, or that they had not read it before signing.[19] In November 1919 Brentano was in London as a German delegate at a meeting of the 'Fight the Famine Council' in Caxton Hall, London. Here he met Keynes, Hobhouse and Leonard Woolf.[20] Brentano's visit seems to have gone largely unnoticed, unlike the visit two years later of Albert Einstein. Einstein had never signed the manifesto of 'the ninety-three', and, as we have seen, was one of the few signatories of Nicolai's counter 'Manifesto to Europeans'. Even so, Ernest Barker, who as Principal had brought Einstein to King's College, London, to lecture, feared that there might be a public outcry. Although

Einstein had renounced his German nationality in 1896 and become a Swiss citizen in 1906, he had worked at the Kaiser Wilhelm Institute for Physics in Berlin since 1914. Barker's fears proved groundless and Einstein was elected a member of the Royal Society and went on to receive an honorary D.Sc. from Manchester University.[21] On his return to Berlin Einstein spoke of the desire 'among English savants and statesmen' for a resumption of 'friendly relations with Germany'.[22] The theologian Ernst Troeltsch, one of 'the ninety-three', was invited to give a series of lectures in Oxford and London in March 1923, but died before leaving Germany.[23]

Perhaps understandably, it was British scientists who made the first moves towards reconciliation. Although they had placed their knowledge at the disposal of the war effort, they had on the whole not been involved in the bitter war of words between Britain and Germany. Possibly they could also claim in one sense to have a less subjective attitude towards their work than, say, historians. Could one talk of *British* physics in quite the way that one would of British history? There were some British scientists who did call for a boycott of German scientists and scientific publications. Lord Walsingham of Trinity College, Cambridge, proposed to ignore scientific papers in German in future.[24] But few were as extreme as Sir George Hampson of the Natural History Museum in London who alleged in the journal *Science* that:

> German is, without doubt, a barbarous language only just emerging from the stage of primitive Gothic character, and I venture to suggest that it would be to the advantage of science to treat it as such.[25]

More usually the debate amongst scientists in the correspondence columns of *Nature* and *The Times* proceeded on the assumption that reconciliation would come about — the only question was how. The learned societies of former neutral states were calling for the inclusion of German scholars in international meetings. In *Nature* one of the elder statesmen of British science recommended his colleagues to oppose this move (Sir Edwin Ray Lankester), while Professor D'Arcy Thompson of St. Andrews advised that German overtures be 'freely reciprocated':

> I cannot say that I have always been on the side of tolerance and reconciliation but already we have had some little time to think.[26]

However, it took another year before any formal overture was made to German scientists. The lead was taken by Oxford scholars, many of whom had been in the forefront of the wartime propaganda battle. According to the organiser Robert Bridges, the Poet Laureate, a manifesto was sent to one hundred and twenty members of the University 'whose names were picked on the register solely for their position and eminence'. Significantly, slightly more than half of those approached had refused to sign, and the resulting list, though impressive enough, was criticised as not really being representative.[27] One of the signatories (D. G. Hogarth) also pointed out that as late as November 1918 Bridges had still been putting his poetic skills at the service of the 'haters of Germany'.[28] Still, the manifesto is worth quoting at length since it made no demand for a public confession of national guilt from German professors — a point commented on unfavourably by a leader in *The Times*:

> ... justice demands that there shall be no pardon, to say nothing of 'amicable reunion' and the restoration of former 'friendliness' until the offenders publicly confess their guilt, exhibit heartfelt sorrow for their crimes, and make the utmost satisfaction in their power. Then, and only then, will it be time to readmit them upon equal terms either into the fellowship of learning or into 'the honourable comity of European states'.[29]

The manifesto, which *The Times* regarded with such disfavour, was addressed to 'the Professors of Arts and Sciences and to the members of the Universities and Learned Societies in Germany and Austria':

> Since there will be many of you who fully share our heartfelt sorrow and regret for the breach that the war has occasioned in our friendly intercourse, and since you cannot doubt the sincerity of the feeling which engendered and cherished that old friendliness, you must we believe, be sharing our hope for its speedy re-establishment.
>
> We, therefore, the undersigned doctors, heads of houses, professors, and other teachers and officers in the University of Oxford, now personally approach you with the desire to dispel the embitterment of animosities that under the impulse of loyal patriotism may have passed between us.
>
> In the field where our aims are one, our enthusiasms, our rivalry and ambition generous, we can surely look to be reconciled, and the fellowship of learning offers a road which may — and if our spiritual ideals be alive, must — lead to wider sympathy and better understanding between our kindred nations.
>
> While political dissensions are threatening to extinguish the honourable comity of the great European states, we pray that we may help to hasten that amicable reunion which civilization demands. *Impetret ratio quod dies impretratura est.*[30]

Some eminent scholars were still uneasy 'about the temper still prevailing in German universities' or were doubtful whether this was really the best way to go about normalising relations.[31] The case for greater caution had been put by Sir Frederick Kenyon in July 1920 as President of the British Academy. The 'notorious' manifesto of 'the ninety-three' was 'a gross crime against scholarship' and 'an offence against good manners and the common decencies of life' — the latter being regarded as equally important amongst the British. But, Kenyon noted, even though 'the pressure of official authority' had been removed from German scholars, there was still no official disavowal. British scholars had 'legitimate grounds for resentment', especially now that Germany and Austria were appealing for help to maintain their 'intellectual life'. Throughout Kenyon's presidential address the tone was that of the injured party:

> We do not ... ask for express withdrawal or apology. We do not want to make reconciliation difficult. But I think English scholars are entitled to some indication that German scholars desire the resumption of relations; that they recognize that an obstacle stands in the way of any cordiality in such relations; that they regret the obstacle, for the existence of which there may be excuses, though not justification; that they do not, in short, hold such opinions of England as must make sincere and genuine relations impossible.

There were, of course, no such difficulties with scholars in former allied or neutral states, but restoration of links with Germany would be 'a matter of years'.[32]

In the end it seems that Kenyon's views prevailed over the more open-handed Oxford approach. Although individual scholars continued to extend the hand of friendship to German and Austrian colleagues, there was a fairly effective boycott at the level of organised international scholarship. Sometimes there were serious differences of opinion between supporters and opponents of normalising relations, as in the Royal Asiatic Society in 1921. The proposal to invite Germans to attend centenary celebrations was defeated on the governing council, and the Persian scholar E. G. Browne who voted with the minority 'came very near to resigning from the Society'.[33] At an international level American and especially Scandinavian scholars exerted pressure on their British and French colleagues for the invitation to congresses, like those of the historians at Brussels in 1924 and Oslo in 1928, to be extended to Germany and Austria. The Belgians were very reluctant to agree and invited only historians from countries which were members of the League of Nations (by 1924 these included Bulgaria, Hungary and Austria, but not Germany). The Belgian historian Henri Pirenne, who had been imprisoned during the war by the Germans (first in Belgium and then in Germany itself), 'explained that they did not want to exclude private German historians', but that they could not bring themselves 'to address official invitations to German universities and academies'. Danish and Swedish historians then refused to accept invitations, and the Norwegians (supported by the Americans) moved 'to assure a complete international organisation of the following congress by moving it over to neutral ground'. Thus, Oslo rather than Warsaw was chosen for 1928, and the Germans were invited to attend.[34]

By the end of the 1920s German and Austrian scholars were again participating in international congresses, although sometimes in an unofficial capacity. However, membership of the *Union Académique Internationale* and the International Council of Scientific Unions remained closed to them. These two bodies had been established after the war to replace the old International Association of Academies, and their refusal to admit the former Central Powers to membership in the 1920s aroused a certain amount of hostile comment among British scholars. Finally, in 1935 Austria and Germany were invited to join the U.A.I. by a unanimous vote, 'though not without some lively previous discussions'.[35] These countries, together with Turkey, Bulgaria and Hungary, were invited to join the I.C.S.U. in 1926 on the proposal of Britain (with Sweden and Holland). Several previous attempts had been defeated, and by 1928 only Hungary and Bulgaria had joined.[36]

In one field there was a re-establishment of prewar ties. In 1926 the formation of the Anglo-German Academic Board, acting in association with the *Akademischer Austauschdienst* of Berlin, helped to encourage more British students to travel to Germany for study and research.[37] However, it is unlikely that the number of British students attending German universities reached prewar levels. Generally since 1900 there had been a falling-off in numbers — the war had simply underlined an existing trend. But, quite apart from the estrangement caused by the war, German universities were in a difficult financial position after the war and may thus have been less attractive centres for research. In addition, the establishment of the Ph.D. as a research degree in British universities from 1917 onwards had the effect of encouraging British students to continue their studies in British universities, although the new degree had originally been intended to attract 'colonial' and American students away from German universities.[38] The spell of German *Wissenschaft* had been broken by the war, and any chance of re-establishing close links with German universities was ended by the decline of German universities after 1933. The invitation to British universities to participate in the 550th anniversary celebrations of the University of Heidelberg in June 1936 was declined, first by Oxford and Birmingham, and then by all the British universities.[39]

Postscript

This study has been concerned with the way in which British academics responded to war with Germany. It is clear that, as in other belligerent states, their wartime role was very often that of apologist for government policy. To an age which might expect this group to undertake a more critical stance, this may seem surprising. Often in conversations I learned that people assumed that Bertrand Russell had been only one amongst many other less well-known wartime dissenters. In fact Russell in Britain and Nicolai in Germany were highly unusual. However, even to a perceptive observer in the 1920s the reasons for this state of affairs were obvious. J. A. Hobson, an economist who never held an academic post, took up Julien Benda's theme of intellectual betrayal in his book *Free Thought in the Social Sciences* (1926). He was the only person, to my knowledge, who did this in Britain, and perhaps it is significant that he developed his ideas in a series of lectures at the Brookings Institute in Washington D.C. Like Benda, Hobson concluded that:

> The graver perils to free-thought and scientific progress lie in ... timid conservatism of ... professors and their genuine class sympathies and reverences. They are not so much the intellectual mercenaries of the vested interests as their volunteers.

The 'definite fear of losing a teaching post' played 'but a small part', compared with 'the more constant and insidious breathing' of the 'conservative atmosphere' of the university.[1]

Hobson also suggested that the lack of importance attached to intellectual activity in Britain might also play its part. In a section which shows the influence of Thorstein Veblen he noted:

> The 'intellectual' is terribly sensitive to the approval and disapproval of rulers and other authorities in the outside world. His strong personal sympathies are engaged in keeping the good opinion of successful practical men. The knowledge that he and his fellows and the intellectual life they conduct are not directly productive of economic values, and are in this sense 'parasitic' on the practical life, feeds the sentiment of deference. His feeling for the dignity and importance of his intellectual function no doubt stands out more clearly in his 'consciousness', but underneath, in the hidden recesses of his mind, the sense of weakness and inferiority rankles. Man is primarily a doer, not a thinker.[2]

It had been this feeling that Jane Harrison had detected during the war, which explained the eagerness with which academics 'positively welcomed' the conflict.[3]

The 'war-spirit' amongst intellectuals in 1914 is by now well-documented,[4] although it still seems difficult to comprehend in the wake of two world wars and in the shadow of nuclear weapons. Yet there are similarities between the period before the First World War and the present, as the book by Geoffrey Barraclough, *From Agadir to Armageddon* (1982), shows. The 'garrison intellectual' too is alive and well. From the 'Congress for Cultural Freedom' in the 1950s[5] to the 'Academic Council for Peace and Freedom' in the 1980s, academics have been queuing up to fight in the Cold War. The 'Open Letter to the Academic Community' of the A.C.P.F.[6] appeared in the British press as a declaration of 'opposition to the arguments' of the Campaign for Nuclear Disarmament 'and its allies ... in British institutions of higher education'. With its roll-call of academics and institutions it looks strikingly like the 'Manifesto of the Intellectuals of Germany' — the manifesto of 'the ninety-three' — of October 1914. It is true that the German manifesto was addressed 'to the civilised world' and the British manifesto is of more modest proportions, but then Britain could hardly now be said to occupy a position in the world of scholarship like that of Germany before 1914.

Bibliography

MANUSCRIPT SOURCES

(Items of most value marked*)

C. R. Ashbee Journal (King's College, Cambridge) contains letters from Dickinson.

W. J. Ashley (British Museum Add. Mss. 42242–56) on war work for the Government.

A. C. Benson (British Museum Add. Mss. 51290) correspondence with C. E. Sayle.

**J. Bryce* (Bodleian Library) correspondence with Murray & Toynbee; material relating to investigation of atrocities committed in Belgium & Armenia.

Cambridge University Fabian Socialist and Socialist Societies (Cambridge University Library Add. Mss. 7451–3) various minute books 1911–20.

E. Canaan (British Library of Political and Economic Science) letters from Dickinson and Morel.

F. C. Conybeare (New College, Oxford) comments by E. F. Carritt on Conybeare.

W. H. Dawson (Birmingham University Library) letters.

**G. L. Dickinson* (King's College, Cambridge) letters.

W. McN. Dixon (Mitchell Library, Glasgow) letters from W. Raleigh.

H. G. Fiedler-C. Harding (Birmingham University Library) letters.

**H. A. L. Fisher* (Bodleian Library) correspondence with Murray and concerning the Bryce Commission.

H. W. Garrod (Merton College, Oxford) 'Three Years in Whitehall' (wartime experiences in the Ministry of Munitions).

D. Grant (British Museum Add. Mss.) Letters from J. M. Keynes.

**J. L. and B. Hammond* (Bodleian Library) correspondence with Murray.

F. J. C. Hearnshaw (Professor L. S. Hearnshaw) unpublished autobiography (typescript), chapter XI (on the war).

F. von Hügel (St. Andrews University Library) letter from J. Ward (Ms. 3126).

P. Kerr (Lord Lothian) (Scottish Record Office) correspondence with B. Pares & J. Y. Simpson (GD.40/17).

J. M. Keynes (King's College, Cambridge) correspondence with Pigou, Fay, Dickinson; material relating to Russell.

**J. N. Keynes* (Cambridge University Library) diary for 1914–17.

E. D. Morel (British Library of Political & Economic Science) letter from C. R. Beazley.

**G. Murray* (Bodleian Library) correspondence with A. C. Bradley, Cole, Fisher, Rissell; material on conscientious objectors and the League movement.

A. F. Pollard (Institute of Historical Research, London) letters to his father during the war.

R. Poole (Bodleian Library Ms. Top. Oxon. d. 563) 'Oxford in Wartime' (unpublished typescript).

G. W. Prothero (Royal Historical Society, London) correspondence with W. Raleigh; material relating to wartime propaganda.

C. P. Scott (British Museum Add. Mss. 50908) letters from Dickinson and A. Marshall.

**A. L. Smith* (Balliol College, Oxford) correspondence with Morel; material on wartime propaganda through the W.E.A.

T. F. Tout (John Rylands University Library, Manchester) letters from former students at the Front.

G. Wallas (British Library of Political and Economic Science) material relating to neutrality manifestos July 1914.

C. Walston (Waldstein) (King's College, Cambridge).

B. Webb (Passfield) diary v. 33–34.
C. Webster (British Library of Political and Economic Science) material on work for the Foreign Office during the war.
N. Wedd (King's College, Cambridge) memoir of Dickinson; correspondence (typescript) with E. F. Bulmer.
L. S. Woolf (Sussex University Library) letters from Dickinson.
A. Zimmern (Bodleian Library) letters from various correspondents.
War Cabinet Minutes (Public Record Office CAB 24/24).

Letters to the author from:
Mr. A. Allen (University of Liverpool Library), 24 May 1973.
Mr. A. W. Chapman (former Registrar of the University of Sheffield) 25 July 1973.
Sir Keith Feiling, 21 Mar. 1973.
Professor L. S. Hearnshaw, 15 Dec. 1975.
Mr. J. G. Thomas (Registrar of the University of Wales), 6 June 1976.

PUBLISHED SOURCE MATERIAL: PERIODICALS
(for 1914–19 period unless stated)
Anglo-German Courier (Jan.–Oct. 1906).
The Cambridge Daily News.
The Cambridge Magazine: Edited by Members of Cambridge University (1912–23).
The Cambridge Review: A Journal of University Life and Thought (1899–).
The English Historical Review.
Goodwill: A Journal of International Friendship.
The Hibbert Journal: A Quarterly Review of Religion, Theology and Philosophy.
History: The Quarterly Journal of the Historical Association.
Mind: A Quarterly Review of Psychology and Philosophy.
The Nation (1910–).
Nature: A Weekly Illustrated Journal of Science.
The Oxford Magazine (1899–).
The Peace Yearbook (1910–).
Proceedings of the Aristotelian Society.
Proceedings of the British Academy.
Students' Handbook to the Universities and Colleges of Cambridge (1902–).
The Times (1899–).
The Times Educational Supplement.
The Times Literary Supplement.
Transactions of the Royal Historical Society.
The Varsity: A Social View of Oxford Life.
War and Peace: A Norman Angell Monthly (1913–).
The Yearbook of Universities of the British Empire.

Calendars for the following universities and university colleges:
Aberdeen, Belfast, Birmingham, Bristol, Cambridge, Dublin, Durham, Edinburgh, Glasgow, National University of Ireland, Leeds, Liverpool, London, Manchester, Oxford, St. Andrews, Sheffield, Wales, Nottingham, Reading.

PUBLISHED SOURCE MATERIAL: BOOKS AND ARTICLES
(place of publication is London, unless otherwise stated)

Acton, J. E. E. *Historical Essays and Studies*, 1907.
Lectures on Modern History, 1906.
The War of 1870: A Lecture Delivered at the Bridgnorth Literary and Scientific Institution on the 25th of April, 1871.

Adams, W. G. S., 'The Basis of Constructive Internationalism', *Annals of the American Academy of Political and Social Science*, LXI (Sept. 1915), 217–29.
International Control (Papers for Wartime, Ser. 2/no.22), Oxford 1915.
The Responsibility for the War (Oxford Pamphlets no. 3), Oxford 1914.

Allen, J. W. *The Danger of Peace: Being the Substance of a Lecture Delivered at King's College, London, on May 19, 1915*, 1915.
Germany and Europe, 1914.
The Place of History in Education, Edinburgh, 1909.

Anglo-German Understanding Conference, British Joint Committee. *Report of the Proceedings of the Anglo-German Understanding Conference, 1912.*

Aristotelian Society, 'Symposium: Ethical Principles of Social Reconstruction', *Proceedings of the Aristotelian Society* N.S. XVII (1916–17), 256–300.
'Symposium: The Nature of the State in View of its External Relations', *Proceedings of the Aristotelian Society*, NS. XVI (1915–16), 290–325.

Arnold, E. V. 'The Ferment of Revolution', *The Times*, 25 Sept.–28 Sept. 1917.
'Germany's Peace Offer', *New Age*, XX, 4 (23 Nov. 1916), 80–1.
'The New Orientation', *Cambridge Magazine*, VI, 24 (9 June 1917), 689–91.
'Reckless Propaganda', *New Age*, XX, 5 (30 Nov. 1916), 103–4.
War-Time Lectures, 1916.

Ashley, W. J., 'The Present Position of Political Economy in England', in *Die Entwicklung der deutschen Volkswirtschaftslehre im neunzehnten Jahrhundert: Gustav Schmoller zur siebenzigsten Wiederlehr seines Geburtstages 24 Juni 1908*, Bd. I, Leipzig, 1908.
The War and Its Economic Aspects (Oxford Pamphlets no. 44) Oxford, 1914.

Baillie, J. B. *Studies in Human Nature*, 1921.

Barker, E. A. *Confederation of Nations: Its Powers and Constitution*, Oxford 1918.
'The Constitution of a League of Nations', *New Europe*, X, 125 (6 Mar. 1919), 180–4; 126 (13 Mar. 1919), 196–203; 127 (20 Mar. 1919), 220–6.
'The Discredited State: Thoughts on Politics Before the War', *Political Quarterly*, 5 (Feb. 1915), 101–21.
Great Britain's Reasons for Going to War, 1915.
Ireland in the Last Fifty Years (1866–1916), 2nd rev. ed., Oxford, 1919.
Linguistic Oppression in the German Empire, 1918.
Mothers and Sons in War Time and Other Pieces (Reprinted from The Times), rev.ed., 1918.
Nietzsche and Treitschke: The Worship of Power in Modern Germany (Oxford Pamphlets no. 20), Oxford, 1914.
Political Thought in England, 1848–1914, 2nd rev.ed., 1947.
The Relations of England and Holland, 1915.
The Submerged Nationalities of the German Empire, 1915.
'The Superstition of the State', *Times Literary Supplement*, XVII, 861 (18 July 1918), 329–30.

Baynes, A. H. 'German Student Life', *Fraser's Magazine*, N.S. XXIV (Nov. 1881), 630–45.

Beavan, M. *Austrian Policy Since 1867* (Oxford Pamphlets no. 9), Oxford, 1914.
'The Pact of Bjorko', *New Europe*, IV, 52 (11 Oct. 1917), 389–99.
Beazley, R. N. Forbes and G. A. Birkett, *Russia From the Varangians to the Bolsheviks*, Oxford, 1918.
Beesly, E. S. 'The Russian Alliance', *Positivist Review*, XX, 261 (1 Sept. 1914), 198–9.
Belgium, *Reports on the Violation of the Rights of Nations and of the Laws and Customs of War in Belgium*, 2v., 1915.
Benians, E. A. *The British Empire and The War*, 1915.
Bennett, A. *The Journals of Arnold Bennett*, v.3 (1911–21), 1932.
The Letters of Arnold Bennett, v.2 & 3, 1967.
Benson, A. C. 'An Impression of the War', *Atlantic Monthly*, CXVIII, I (July 1916), 125–30.
The Happy Warrior: A Sight of General Smuts at Cambridge, May 1917, Cambridge, 1917.
Bosanquet, B. *Bernard Bosanquet and His Friends: Letters Illustrating the Sources and Development of his Philosophical Opinions*, 1935.
'The History of Philosophy', in *Germany in the Nineteenth Century* (ed. C. H. Herford), Ser. 2, Manchester, 1915.
'A Note on Mr. Cole's Paper', *Proceedings of the Aristotelian Society*, NS. XV (1914–15), 160–3.
'The Notion of a General Will', *Mind*, NS. XXIX, 113 (Jan. 1920), 77–81.
The Philosophical Theory of the State, 4th ed. 1923.
Review of Russell's *Principles of Social Reconstruction*, *Mind*, NS. XXVI, 102 (July 1917), 233–4.
Review of Vaughan's edition of *The Political Writings of Rousseau*, *Mind*, NS, XXV, 99 (July 1916), 399–404.
Social and International Ideals: Being Studies in Patriotism, 1917.
Some Suggestions in Ethics, 1918.
'The State and The Individual', *Mind*, NS. XXVIII, 109 (Jan. 1919), 75–7.
Boswell, A. B. *Poland and The Poles*, 1919.
'The Polish Question', *Scientia*, XXIII (Oct. 1917), 294–302.
Bradley, F. H. 'The Limits of Individual and National Self-Sacrifice', in *Collected Essays*, Oxford, 1935.
Britain, Home Office, *Report of the Committee on Alleged German Outrages*, 2 v., 1915.
British Universities and The War: A Record and Its Meaning, 1917.
Broad, C. D., *Ethics and The History of Philosophy*, 1952.
'The Prevention of War', *International Journal of Ethics*, XXVI, 2 (Jan. 1916), 241–57.
'The Notion of a General Will', *Mind*, NS. XXVIII, 112 (Oct. 1919), 502–4.
Review of *Proceedings of the Aristotelian Society* (1916–17), *Mind*, NS. XXVII, 107 (July 1918), 366–70.
'War Thoughts in Peace Time', in *Religion, Philosophy and Psychical Research*, 1953.
'The Broken Fellowship', *Times Literary Supplement*, 720 (4 Nov. 1915, 385–6.
Brooke, R. *The Letters of Rupert Brooke Chosen and Edited by Geoffrey Keynes*, 1968.
Brooke, T. and H. S. Canby, *War Aims and Peace Ideals: Selections in Prose and Verse Illustrating the Aspirations of the Modern World*, New Haven, 1919.
Browne, E. G. *A Brief Narrative of Recent Events in Persia Followed by An Appendix on the Persian Constitution*, 1909.
The Persian Constitutionalists: An Address, 1909.

The Persian Crisis of December 1911: How it Arose and Whither It May Lead Us Compiled for the Use of the Persia Committee, Cambridge 1912.

The Persian Revolution of 1905–1909, Cambridge, 1910.

'The Persian Oil Concession', *War and Peace*, I, 11 (Aug. 1914), 315–6.

The Reign of Terror at Tabriz: England's Responsibility . . . Compiled for the Use of the Persia Committee, Manchester, 1912.

Bryce, J. *The Attitude of Great Britain in the Present War*, 1916.

Essays and Addresses in War Time, 1918.

'The Future of Armenia', *Contemporary Review*, CXIV, 6 (Dec. 1918), 604–11.

The Last Phase in Belgium: Statement by Viscount Bryce on the Belgian Deportations Made in Reply to a Letter from the Representative of the New York 'Tribune', 1916.

Race Sentiment As a Factor in History: A Lecture Delivered Before the University of London on February 22, 1915, 1915.

'War and Human Progress', *Atlantic Monthly*, CXVIII, 3 (Sept. 1916), 301–15.

University and Historical Addresses Delivered During a Residence in the United States as Ambassador of Great Britain, 1913.

Burns, C. 'The Balance of Power', *War and Peace* (Supplement to *Nation*), 51 (Dec. 1917), 147–9.

'Diplomatic Despotism', *Cambridge Magazine*, IV, 11 (30 Jan. 1915), 221–2.

'The Idea of the State', *Mind*, NS. XXVII (1918), 188–97.

'The Ideal of Peace', *Times Literary Supplement*, 731 (20 Jan. 1916), 26.

'Moral Effects of War and Peace', *International Journal of Ethics*, XXV, 3 (April 1915), 317–27.

'When Peace Breaks Out', *International Journal of Ethics*, XXVI, 1 (Oct. 1915), 82–91.

Burgh, W. G. de. 'The Peril of Hubris', *Edinburgh Review*, CCV, 460 (April 1917), 2288–302.

Burnet, J. *Higher Education and The War*, 1917.

Burrows, R. M. *The Abdication of King Constantine: Being a Reprint of Articles* (Anglo-Hellenic League Pamphlet no. 34), 1917.

'Albania and Greece', *New Europe*, IX, 105 (19 Dec. 1918), 227–31.

The Crisis in Greece (Anglo-Hellenic League Pamphlet no. 19), 1915.

Greece in 1917 (Anglo-Hellenic League Pamphlet no. 33), 1917.

'Greece and the Balkan Settlement', *Quarterly Review*, CCIX, 455 (April 1918), 576–84.

'The Greek White Book', *Contemporary Review*, CXIII, 1 (Jan. 1918), 129–34.

'The Korakas Forgery', *New Europe*, V, 57 (15 Nov. 1917), 133–40.

'The Need for Self-Renunciation', *New Europe*, VI, 69 (7 Feb. 1918), 99–103.

'Philhellenism in England and France', *Contemporary Review*, CIX, (Feb. 1916), 161–4.

The New Greece (Anglo-Hellenic League Pamphlet no. 14), 1914.

The Present Position in the Balkans (Anglo-Hellenic League Pamphlet no. 27), 1916.

'Venizelos and the Greek Crisis', *Contemporary Review*, CVII, 5 (May 1916), 545–52.

Bury, J. B. 'Freedom of Speech and The Censorship', *R.P.A. Annual and Ethical Review*, 1919, 16–19.

Germany and Slavonic Civilisation, 1914.

Selected Essays, Cambridge, 1930.

Butler, G. G. *International Law and Autocracy: A Public Lecture Delivered Before the University of Pennsylvania*, 1917.

Cairns, D. S. *An Answer to Bernhardi* (Papers for Wartime no. 12), Oxford, 1914.

Carpenter, J. E. 'The Development of Liberal Theology in England', in *Religion and the*

Future and Other Essays, 1911.

The Promotion of International Peace through Universities (National Peace Council Pamphlet, Educational Series), 1912.

(ed.) *Ethical and Religious Problems of the War: Fourteen Addresses*, 1916.

Carritt, E F. ' 'Shall We Serve God for Nought?' Treitschke & Hegel', *Hibbert Journal*, XIII, 3 (1915), 558–72.

Childs, W. M. *Universities and Their Freedom*, 1921.

Clapham, J. H. 'J'Accuse', *Cambridge Magazine*, IV, 24 (5 June 1915), 466–8.

Cole, G. D. H. 'Conflicting Social Obligations', *Proceedings of the Aristotelian Society*, NS, XV (1914–15), 140–59.

Labour in War Time, 1915.

Social Theory, 1920.

Conrad, J. *The German Universities for the Last Fifty Years*, Glasgow, 1885.

Conybeare, F. C. *The Awakening of Public Opinion in England: A Letter by Dr. F. C. Conybeare of Oxford University, England*, N.Y., 1915.

'A Message from Aristophanes', *Open Court*, XXX, 1 (Jan. 1916), 41–59.

'New Light on the Causes of the War', *England on the Witness Stand: The Anglo-German Case Tried by a Jury of Englishmen*, N.Y., 1915.

'Responsibility for the War', *Open Court*, XXIX, 7 (July 1915), 394–403.

'The Spanish Press and Public Opinion in Spain,' *Cambridge Magazine*, V, 17 (11 Mar. 1915), 387–8.

Correspondence of Robert Bridges and Henry Bradley, 1900–1923, Oxford, 1940.

Coulton, G. G. *The Case for Compulsory Military Service*, 1917.

Compulsory Military Service, Should the Working Class Support It?, Glasgow, 1912.

'Continental Democracies and Compulsory Military Service', *Fortnightly Review*, NS. C, 595 (1 July 1916), 55–65.

Debate Between Mr. G. C. Coulton . . . and Mr. Fred Maddison . . . Held at the Memorial Hall George Lane, Woodford on . . . Friday, January 31, Cambridge, 1913.

Debate on Compulsory Service at Northampton Town Hall on Tuesday . . ., December 17th 1912, Between Mr. Fred Maddison and Mr. G. C. Coulton, Cambridge, 1912.

'Democracy and Compulsory Service', *Hibbert Journal*, XV, 2 (Jan. 1916), 204–16.

'Do Warlike Nations Inherit the Earth?', *War and Peace*, III, 25 (Oct. 1915), 14.

'Editorial Note' to J. Jaures, *Democracy and Military Service: An Abbreviated Translation of the 'Armée Novelle' . . .*, 1916.

'A Liberal's Plea for Compulsory Service', *Nineteenth Century*, LX, 357 (Nov. 1906), 719–27.

The Main Illusions of Pacificism: A Criticism of Mr. Norman Angell and of The Union of Democratic Control, Cambridge, 1916.

Our National Army: A Question for the People, 1900.

'Our Conscripts at Crécy', *Nineteenth Century*, LXV, 384 (Feb. 1909), 251–7.

'Pacifism, Truth and Commonsense', *Nineteenth Century*, LXXVI, 452 (Oct. 1914), 908–17.

Pacifist Illusions: A Criticism of the Union of Democratic Control, Cambridge, 1915.

A Strong Army in a Free State: A Study of the Old English and Modern Swiss Militias, 1900.

True Liberalism and Compulsory Service: An Appeal to the British Working Man, 1914.

'Voluntary or Compulsory Service? (3) The Volunteer Spirit'', *Nineteenth Century*, LXXVII, 455 (Jan. 1915), 19–29.

Workers and The War, Cambridge, 1914.

Cunningham, W. *British Citizens and Their Responsibility to God: Six Sermons, in Preparation for the National Mission, 1916, Preached in Great St. Mary's, Cambridge,* 1916.

The Commonweal: Six Lectures on Political Philosophy, Cambridge, 1917.

'Impartiality in History', *Rivista di Scienza,* I (1907).

'The Economic Basis of Universal Peace', *Economic Review,* XXIII, I (Jan. 1913), 7–13.

'Prospects of Universal Peace', *Atlantic Monthly,* LXXXIV, 502 (Aug. 1899), 236–41.

'Why had Roscher so Little Influence in England?', *Annals of the American Academy of Political and Social Science,* V, 3 (Nov. 1894), 317–34.

Davis, H. W. C. *The Battle of Ypres-Armentieres* (Oxford Pamphlet no. 46), Oxford, 1915.

The Battles of Marne and Aisne (Oxford Pamphlets no. 28), Oxford, 1914.

History of the Blockade Emergency Departments, 1921.

The Political Thought of Heinrich Von Treitschke, 1914.

The Retreat From Mons (Oxford Pamphlet no. 27), Oxford, 1914.

What Europe Owes to Belgium (Oxford Pamphlet no. 36), Oxford, 1914.

Dewey, J. 'The Mind of Germany', in *Characters and Events: Popular Essays in Social and Political Philosophy,* v. I, 1929.

Dicey, A. V. 'Burke on Bolshevism', *Nineteenth Century,* LXXXIV, 498 (Aug. 1918), 274–87.

'The Conscientious Objector', *Nineteenth Century,* LXXXIII, 492 (Feb. 1918), 357–73.

How We Ought to Feel About the War (Oxford Pamphlet no. 55), Oxford, 1914.

'Wordsworth and The War', *Nineteenth Century,* LXXVII, 459 (May 1915), 1041–60.

Dickinson, G. L. 'The Abyss', *Nation,* XLVIII, 6 (8 Nov. 1930), 211–2.

After the War, 1915.

'After the War', *Atlantic Monthly,* CXV, I (Jan. 1915), 111–6.

'The Allied Note', *Cambridge Magazine,* VI, 10 (27 Jan. 1917), 244.

'The American League to Enforce Peace', *War and Peace,* III, 33 (June 1916), 134–5.

'The Basis of Permanent Peace', in *Towards a Lasting Settlement* (ed. C. R. Buxton), 1915.

Causes of International War, 1920.

The Choice Before Us, 1917.

'The Choice Before Us', *Cambridge Magazine,* VI, 14 (24 Feb. 1917), 357–8.

'The Choice Before Us', *Covenant,* I, 2 (Jan. 1920), 182–95.

'The Conditions of a Durable Peace', *Cambridge Magazine,* VI, 5 (11 Nov. 1916), 103–4; 6 (18 Nov. 1916), 130; 7 (25 Nov. 1916), 158–9; 8 (2 Dec. 1916), 201.

'Democratic Control of Foreign Policy', *Atlantic Monthly,* CXVIII, 2 (Aug. 1916), 145–52.

'Economic Policy After the War', *War and Peace,* III, 35 (Aug. 1916), 167–8.

Economic War After the War, 1916.

The European Anarchy, 1916.

'The Freedom of the Seas", *War and Peace,* III, 28 (Jan. 1916), 56–9.

'The Future of British Liberalism', *Atlantic Monthly,* CXXV, 4 (April 1920), 550–5.

The Future of the Covenant, 1920.

'A German on the War', *Hibbert Journal,* XIV, 1 (Oct. 1915), 30–6.

'The German Socialists and The War', *War and Peace,* II, 23 (Aug. 1915), 168–9.

'The Holy War', *Nation,* XV, 19 (8 Aug. 1914), 699–700.

'How Can America Best Contribute to the Maintenance of the World's Peace', *Annals of the American Academy of Political and Social Science,* LXI (Sept. 1915), 235–8.

'The Illusion of War', *Nation*, XI, 19 (10 Aug. 1912), 702.

The International Anarchy, 1904-1914, new ed. 1937.

Introduction to C. R. Ashbee, *The American League to Enforce Peace: An English Interpretation*, 1917.

Introduction to *Documents and Statements Relating to Peace Proposals and War Aims* (December 1916–November 1918), 1919.

Introduction to National Peace Council, *Problems of the International Settlement*, 1918.

Introduction to R. Rolland, *Above the Battlefield*, Cambridge, 1914.

'Is War Inevitable?', *War and Peace*, I, 8 (May 1914), 221-3; I, 9, (June 1914), 252-3.

'The League of Nations', *Common Sense*, V (2 Nov. 1918), 665-8.

'A League of Nations Now? A Symposium', *War and Peace* (supplement to *Nation*), 60 (Sept. 1918), 327-8.

'On 'Punishing Germany' ', *War and Peace*, II, 20 (May 1915), 121-2.

'Peace Or War?', *Albany Review*, II, 8 (Nov. 1907), 130-9.

'The Pilgramage of Peace', *Athenaeum*, 4696 (30 April 1920), 586-7.

'President Wilson's Speech to the Senate', *Cambridge Magazine*, VI, 11 (3 Feb. 1917), 271.

'The Problem of Armaments and A League of Nations', *Friends' Quarterly Examiner*, LI, 202 (April 1917), 193-7.

'Quo Vadis?', *Independent Review*, VIII, 2 (Feb. 1906), 148-57.

'Rival Imperialisms', *Cambridge Magazine*, VI, 13 (17 Feb. 1917), 326-7.

'The Significance of the American Note', *Cambridge Magazine*, VI, 9 (20 Jan. 1917), 213-4.

'The Social Ideal', *Working Men's College Journal*, X, 182 (May 1908), 334-9.

'The Social Ideal of Democracy', *Working Men's College Journal*, XI, 209 (Dec. 1910), 430-3; XII, 210 (Jan. 1911), 18-19.

'War and Peace', *Independent Review*, X, 34 (July 1906), 113-20.

The War and The Way Out, 1914.

'The War and The Way Out', *Atlantic Monthly*, CXIV, 6 (Dec. 1914), 820-37.

'The War and The Way Out: A Further Consideration', *Atlantic Monthly*, CXV, 4 (April 1915), 516-24.

'The War and The Way Out: A Positive Plan', *Atlantic Monthly*, CXV, 5 (May 1915), 691-700.

War Its Nature, Cause and Cure, 1923.

Dixon, W. McN. *The British Navy at War*, 1917.

The Fleet Behind the Fleet: The Work of the Merchant Seamen and Fishermen in the War, 1917.

Egerton, H. E. *British Foreign Policy in Europe to the End of the 19th Century: A Rough Outline*, 1918.

Is the British Empire the Result of Wholesale Robbery? (Oxford Pamphlet no. 23), Oxford, 1914.

The War and The British Dominions (Oxford Pamphlet no. 21), Oxford, 1914.

Feiling, K. *Italian Policy Since 1870* (Oxford Pamphlet no. 10), Oxford, 1914.

Figgis, J. M. *The Will to Freedom or the Gospel of Nietzsche and the Gospel of Christ: Being the Bross Lectures (1915) Delivered in Lake Forest College*, 1917.

Fight for Right Movement, *For The Right: Essays and Addresses by Members of the 'Fight for the Right Movement'*, 1916.

Firth, C. H. *A Plea for the Historical Teaching of History*, Oxford, 1904.

Then and Now or a Comparison Between the War with Napoleon and The Present War: Being the Creigton Lecture for 1917 Delivered at King's College, London, on October 7th, 1917.

Fisher, H. A. L. *The British Share in the War*, 1915.

'German 'Kultur' ', *Quarterly Review*, CCIII, 443 (April 1915), 313–52.

An International Experiment: The Earl Grey Memorial Lecture Delivered Feb. 26, 1921 at Armstrong College, Newcastle-on-Tyne, Oxford, 1921.

'The Remapping of Europe', *Nation*, XVII, 3 (17 April 1915), 87–8.

Studies in History and Politics, Oxford, 1920.

The Value of Small States (Oxford Pamphlet no. 17), Oxford, 1914.

The War and Its Causes: Three Addresses Given in Sheffield on Aug. 31, Sept 1 and Sept. 2, 1914, 1914.

Fletcher, C. R. L. *The Germans (I) Their Empire How They Made It* (Oxford Pamphlet no. 6), Oxford, 1914.

The Germans (II) What They Covet . . . A Sequel . . . (Oxford Pamphlet no. 7), Oxford, 1914.

Forbes, N. *The Southern Slavs* (Oxford Pamphlet no. 58), Oxford, 1915.

(ed.) *The Balkans: A History of Bulgaria, Serbia, Greece, Roumania, Turkey*, Oxford, 1915.

France, Ministère des Affaires Etrangères. *Germany's Violations of the Laws of War 1914–15 Compiled Under the Auspices of the French Ministry of Foreign Affairs*, 1915.

Frazer, J. G. 'The Cursing of Venizelos', *New Europe*, II, 19 (22 Feb. 1917), 174–9.

'The Future of International Congresses', *Geographical Journal*, LXI, 6 (June 1923), 440–3.

Gardner, P. *Oxford at the Crossroads: A Criticism of the Course of Literae Humaniores in the University*, 1903.

and A. W. F. Blunt, 'Two Studies of German Kultur', *Hibbert Journal*, XIII, 3 (1915), 511–32.

Geddes, P. 'Wardom and Peacedom: Suggestions Towards an Interpretation', *Sociological Review*, VIII, I (Jan. 1915), 15–25.

and G. Slater, *Ideas at War*, 1917.

'The German Professor', *Saturday Review*, 58 (12 July 1884), 47–8; (23 Aug. 1884), 246–7.

Gill, C. *National Power and Prosperity: A Study of the Economic Causes of Modern Warfare*, 1916.

Ginsburg, B. W. (ed.), *War Speeches, 1914–1917*, Oxford, 1917.

Goodrick, A. T. S. 'The Decline of the German University System', *Macmillan's Magazine*, XLII (July 1880), 180–8.

Goudy, H. 'Introduction' to *Transactions of the Grotius Society*, I (1915), 1–7.

'The Neutrality of Belgium', *Juridical Review*, XXIX, 2 (1917), 119–23.

Grant, A. J. 'France and Alsace-Lorraine', *Political Quarterly*, 6 (May 1915), 17–36.

et al, *An Introduction to the Study of International Relations*, 1916.

Green, T. H. *Lectures on the Principles of Political Obligation*, 1941.

Gwatkin, H. M. *Britain's Case Against Germany: A Letter to a Neutral*, 1917.

Harrison, J. *Peace with Patriotism*, Cambridge, 1915.

Hart, B. *The Psychology of Insanity*, 2nd. ed., Cambridge, 1928.

Harte, W. J. 'Fifty Years of British Foreign Policy', *History*, NS. I, (July 1916), 97–107.

Hassall, A. '*Just for a Scrap of Paper*' (Oxford Pamphlet no. 5), Oxford, 1914.

Headlam, J. W. *Belgium and Greece*, 1917.

Hearnshaw, F. J. C. 'The Balance of Power', *Fortnightly Review*, NS. CII, 6 (Dec. 1917), 917–27.

'The Baltic and The Sequel to a Premature Peace', *Nineteenth Century*, LXXIX, 470 (April 1916), 791–9.

'Compulsory Military Service in England', *Quarterly Review*, CCXXV, 447 (April 1916), 416–37.

'Democracy and Discipline', *New Europe*, V, 62 (20 Dec. 1917), 305–9.

Democracy and the British Empire, 1921.

Democracy at the Crossways: A Study in Politics and History with Special Reference to Great Britain, 1918.

'Democratic Control', *National Review*, LXVI, 6 (Feb. 1916), 876–85.

Freedom in Service: Six Essays on Matters Concerning Britain's Safety and Good Government, 1916.

'History as a Means of Propaganda', *Fortnightly Review*, NS. CXIV, 2 (1 Aug. 1923), 321–31.

Main Currents of European History, 1815–1915, 1917.

'The Problem of the Baltic', *New Europe*, I, 12 (4 Jan. 1917), 363–8.

'The Questions of the East as they have been transformed by the Russian Revolution', *Scientia*, XXIV (1918), 445–54.

'Russia and The Lessons of 1848', *New Europe*, II, 25 (5 April 1917), 362–7.

Heidelberg and The Universities of America, N.Y., 1936.

Heitland, W. E. *'Democratic': A Discursive Study*, Cambridge, 1915.

If We Win – A Search for a Path to Stable Peace, With Some Remarks on the So-Called Union of Democratic Control, Cambridge, 1915.

Herford, C. H. 'The Intellectual and Literary History', in *Germany in the 19th Century: Five Lectures*, Manchester, 1912.

'The Problem of German Kultur', *Positivist Review*, XXIII, 273 (Sept, 1915), 193–8.

Hicks, G. D. 'German Philosophy and The Present Crisis', *Hibbert Journal*, XIII, 1 (Sept. 1915), 89–101.

Higgins, A. P. *The Binding Force of International Law*, Cambridge, 1910.

Defensively-Armed Merchant Ships and Submarine Warfare, 1917.

The Law of Nations and The War (Oxford Pamphlet no. 24), Oxford, 1914.

Hobhouse, L. T. *Democracy and Reaction*, 1904.

'The Ideas of Treitschke', *Nation*, XIX, 13 (24 June 1916), 382, 384.

The Metaphysical Theory of the State, 1918.

Questions of War and Peace, 1916.

'Science and Philosophy as Unifying Forces', in *The Unity of Western Civilization* (ed. F. S. Marvin), 1915.

'The Social Effects of the War', *Atlantic Monthly*, CXV, 4 (April 1915), 544–50.

'The Soul of Civilization', *Contemporary Review*, CVIII, 2 (Aug. 1915), 158–65.

The World in Conflict, 1915.

Holland, T. E. *Letters to 'The Times' Upon War and Neutrality (1881-1920) With Some Commentary*, 3rd. ed., 1921.

Housman, A. E. 'Housman's Cambridge Inaugural', *Times Literary Supplement*, 3454 (9 May 1968), 476–7.

Housman, L. (ed.) *War Letters of Fallen Englishmen*, 1930.

Howe, M. De W.(ed.) *The Pollock-Holmes Letters: Correspondence of Sir Frederick Pollock and Mr. Justice Holmes 1874-1932*, 2 v., Cambridge, 1942.

Holmes-Laski Letters: The Correspondence of Mr. Justice Holmes and Harold J. Laski, 2 v., 1953.

Hulme, T. E. *Further Speculations*, Minneapolis, 1965.

Speculations, 1924.

'War Notes by North Staffs', *New Age*, XVIII, 2 (11 Nov. 1915) — XVIII, 18 (2 Mar. 1916).

Huxley, A. *Letters of Aldous Huxley*, 1969.

Imperial Studies Committee of the University of London and The Royal Colonial Institute. *The Empire and the Future: A Series of Imperial Studies Lectures*, 1916.

The International Crisis in its Ethical and Psychological Aspects, 1915.

The International Crisis: The Theory of the State, 1916.

Jacks, L. P. 'The Changing Mind of a Nation at War', *Atlantic Monthly*, CXV, 4 (April 1915), 334-44.

'The Clearing Aim of the War', *Atlantic Monthly*, CXX, 1 (July 1917), 31-8.

'The Common Foe', *Atlantic Monthly*, CXXII, 2 (Aug. 1918), 145-56.

'The Insane Root', *Atlantic Monthly*, CXIX, 1 (Jan. 1917), 12-22.

'Loyalty Once More', *Atlantic Monthly*, CXXI, 2 (Feb. 1918), 212-7.

'A Theological Holiday — and After', *Hibbert Journal*, XIV, 1 (Oct. 1915), 1-14.

James, W. 'The Moral Equivalent of War', in *War: Studies From Psychology, Sociology, Anthropology* (eds. L. Bramson and G. W. Goethals), N.Y. 1968

Jones, E. 'War and Sublimation', *International Review* (Zürich), I, 10-11 (24 Dec. 1915), 453-61.

Jones, H. *Form the League of Peace Now: An Appeal to my Fellow-Citizens* (League of Free Nations Association Pamphlet Ser. 2 No. 5), 1918.

'Why We Are Fighting', *Hibbert Journal*, XIII, I (Oct. 1914), 50-67.

Kelly, H. 'German Idealism', *Church Quarterly Review*, LXXXIII, 1 (April 1916), 1-20.

Kenyon, F. *International Scholarship: Presidential Address*, 1920.

Kettle, T. M. *The Ways of War*, 1917.

Keynes, J. M. *The Collected Writings of J. M. Keynes*, v. X (Essays in Biography) and v. XVI (Activities 1914-1919: The Treasury and Versailles), 1971-2.

The Economic Consequences of the Peace, 1919.

'The Economics of War in Germany', *Economic Journal*, XXV, 3 (Sept. 1915), 443-52.

Kirkpatrick, J. *Origins of the Great War or the British Case*, 1914.

'This Realm This England' Born Again: Short National Studies, Edinburgh, 1916.

Laffan, R. G. D. *The Guardians of the Gate: Historical Lectures on the Serbs*, Oxford, 1918.

Laski, H. J. 'The Sovereignty of the State', in *Studies in the Problem of Sovereignty*, New Haven, 1917.

Lawrence, T. J. 'The Effect of the War on International Law', *Transactions of the Grotius Society*, II (1916), 105-15.

International Problems and The Hague Conferences, 1908.

'The Inviolability of Private Property at Sea in Time of War', *Peace Yearbook*, 1913, 6-9.

Lectures on the League of Nations, Bristol, 1919.

'Present Policy', *Peace Yearbook*, 1914, 14-17.

The Society of Nations: Its Past, Present and Possible Future, 1919.

The Third Hague Conference and Innocent Commerce in Time of War, 1912.

'The Tsar's Rescript', *International Journal of Ethics*, IX, 2 (Jan. 1899), 137-52.

and M. Carter, 'Neutrality and War Zones', *Transactions of the Grotius Society*, I (1915), 33–45.

Lindsay, A. D. 'Political Theory', in *Recent Development in European Thought* (ed. F. S. Marvin), 1920.

'The Political Theory of Mr. Norman Angell', *Political Quarterly*, 4 (Dec. 1914), 127–45.

'The State Against the Commonwealth', *Atlantic Monthly*, CXVI, 2 (Aug. 1915), 275–84.

'The State in Recent Political Theory', *Political Quarterly*, I (Feb. 1914), 128–45.

War Against War (Oxford Pamphlet no. 16), Oxford, 1914.

Lodge, O. *The Function of a League of Nations* (League of Nations Union Publication no. 15/ser. 2), 1918.

The War and After: Short Chapters on Subjects of Serious Practical Import for the Average Citizen in A.D. 1915 Onwards, 1916.

'The War From a British Point of View', *Scientia*, XVII (1915), 190–7.

Macdonell, J. *The Growth of the Pacific Spirit* (National Peace Council Pamphlet), 1913.

'The New Blockade', *Nation*, XVI, 25 (20 Mar. 1915), 793–4.

'Our Relations with the United States (I) An Anglo-American Tribunal', *Nineteenth Century*, LXXVIII, 463 (Sept. 1915), 495–9.

'The Outlook for Neutrals', *Contemporary Review*, CVII, 4 (April 1915), 448–56.

'Seven Postulates of International Law', *Contemporary Review*, CIX, 1 (Jan. 1916), 35–48.

'Silent Neutrals', *Contemporary Review*, CVII, 1 (Jan. 1915), 67–75.

'Some Notes on the Blockade', *Transactions of the Grotius Society*, I (1915), 97–111.

Some Plain Reasons for Immunity From Capture of Private Property at Sea, 1910.

'The Third Hague Conference', *Peace Yearbook*, 1913, 5–6.

'The True Freedom of the Sea', *Nineteenth Century*, LXXXIII, 489 (Nov. 1917), 1007–21.

MacDougall, E. *Germany and The Germans* (Papers for War Time, ser 2. no. 16), 1916.

McDougall, W. *The Group Mind: A Sketch of the Principles of Collective Psychology with some Attempt to Apply Them to the Interpretation of National Life and Character*, Cambridge, 1920.

Introduction to Social Psychology, 1908.

Janus; The Conquest of War; A Psychological Enquiry, 1927.

MacIver, R. M. *Community: A Sociological Study: Being An Attempt to Set Out the Nature and Fundamental Laws of Social Life*, 1917.

The Modern State, Oxford, 1926.

'War and Civilization', *International Journal of Ethics*, XXII 2 (Jan. 1912), 127–45.

Mahaffy, J. P. 'The Ethics of Retaliation', in *Ad Clerum* (eds. A. J. Johnston, A. L. Ford and J. G. F. Day). Dublin, 1918.

Maitland, F. W. *The Letters of Frederic William Maitland*, 1965.

Marett, R. R. 'Presidential Address: Primitive Values', *Folk-Lore*, XXVII, I (May 1915), 12–30.

'Presidential Address: War and Savagery', *Folk-Lore*, XXI, I (Mar. 1915), 10–27.

Medley, D. J. *The Educational Value of a Study of History: An Inaugural Lecture Delivered on Monday October 23rd, 1899*, Glasgow, 1899.

'The War and The Races of Europe', *Proceedings of the Royal Philosophical Society*, Glasgow, XLVI (1914–15), 1–15.

Why Britain Fights: A Popular Account, Glasgow, 1914.

A Miscellany Presented to John Macdonald Mackay L.L.D. July 1914, Liverpool, 1914.

Montmorency, J. E. G. de. 'The Barbary States in International Law', *Transactions of the Grotius Society*, IV (1918), 87–94.

'Contraband and Continuous Transport', *Contemporary Review*, CVII, 2 (Feb. 1915), 177–85.

'International Law After the War', *Scientia*, XXI (1917), 54–66.

'The Principles Underlying Contraband and Blockade', *Transactions of the Grotius Society*, II (1916), 21–30.

Morgan, F. and H. W. C. Davis, *French Policy Since 1871* (Oxford Pamphlet no. 11), Oxford, 1914.

Morgan, J. H. *German Atrocities: an Official Investigation*, 1916.

'The War and The Empire', *Law Quarterly Review*, XXXIII, 131 (July 1917), 214–35.

(ed.) *The German War Book: Being 'The Usages of War On Land' Issued by the Great General Staff of the German Army*, 1915.

and R. S. Nolan, 'Dishonoured Army: German Atrocities in France', *Nineteenth Century*, LXXVII, 460 (June 1915), 1213–48.

Moulton, J. H. *British and German Scholarship* (Papers for Wartime ser. 3 no. 31), 1915.

Muir, R. 'The Antipathy Between Germany and England', *Scientia*, XVIII (1915), 257–66.

Britain's Case Against Germany: An Examination of the Historical Background of the German Action in 1914, Manchester, 1914.

The Character of the British Empire, 1917.

'The Difficulties of a League of Peace', *New Europe*, II, 16 (1 Feb. 1917), 65–77.

Introduction to E. Rignano, *The War and The Settlement: An Italian View*, 1916.

Mare Liberum: The Freedom of the Seas, 1917.

The National Principle and The War (Oxford Pamphlet no. 19), Oxford, 1914.

National Self-Government: Its Growth and Principles The Culmination of Modern History, 1918.

Muirhead, J. H. *German Philosophy and The War* (Oxford Pamphlet no. 62), Oxford, 1915.

German Philosophy in Relation to the War, 1915.

Murray, G. 'Address', in *General Meeting of the Anglo-Hellenic League, Thursday July 11 1918 ...* (Anglo-Hellenic League Pamphlet no. 37), 1918.

'Conclusions Without Premises', *Nation*, XVIII, 13 (Dec. 1915), 480–2.

A Conversation with Bryce, The James Bryce Memorial Lecture, Somerville College, Oxford, Friday 12 November 1943, 1944.

The Cult of Violence: Being an Inaugural Address Given at the Opening of the Session 1933–34 at Aberystwyth, 1934.

'Democratic Control of Foreign Policy', *Contemporary Review*, CIX, 2 (Feb. 1916), 180–92.

'The Diplomacy of Lord Grey', *Nation*, XXV, 25 (20 Sept. 1919), 734.

Essays and Addresses, 1921.

'The Exploitation of Inferior Races in Ancient and Modern Times: An Imperial Labour Question with a Historical Parallel', in *Liberalism and The Empire: Three Essays by Francis W. Hirst, Gilbert Murray and J. L. Hammond*, 1900.

Faith, War and Policy: Lectures and Essays, 1918.

The Foreign Policy of Sir Edward Grey, 1906–1915, Oxford, 1915.

'German 'Kultur' — (III) German Scholarship', *Quarterly Review*, CCIII, 443 (April 1915), 330–9.

Great Britain's Sea Policy: A Reply to an American Critic, 1917.

Impressions of Scandinavia in Wartime, 1916.

Introduction to Mrs. H. Hobhouse, '*I Appeal Unto Ceasar': The Case of the Conscientious Objector*, 1918.

'Is An Estimate of Our Own Age Possible?', *Contemporary Review*, CXVI, 2 (Aug. 1919), 131–43.

The League of Nations and The Democratic Idea, 1918.

'A League of Nations Now? A Symposium', *War and Peace* (supplement to Nation) 59 (Aug. 1913), 305.

Liberality and Civilization: Lectures Given at the Invitation of the Hibbert Trustees in the Universities of Bristol, Glasgow and Birmingham in October and November 1937, 1938.

'Medicine-Man or Regular Practitioner?', *Nation*, XVII, 4 (24 April 1915), 118–9.

The Ordeal of This Generation: The War, the League and the Future, Halley Stewart Lectures 1928, 1929.

'*The Pale Shade*', 1917.

Preface to K. M. Fürst von Lichnowsky, *My Mission to London, 1912–1914*, 1918.

The Problem of Foreign Policy: A Consideration of the Present Dangers and The Best Methods for Meeting Them, 1921.

'The Old Critics of War', *R.P.A. Annual and Ethical Review*, 1919, 11–15.

The Way Forward: Three Articles on Liberal Policy, 1917.

Namier, L. B. 'Danzig: Poland's Outlet to the Sea', *Nineteenth Century*, LXXXI, 480 (Feb. 1917), 300–5.

'The Old House and The German Future', *Nineteenth Century*, LXXX, 472 (July 1916), 169–90.

Nicolai, G. F. *The Biology of War*, 1919.

'Why I Left Germany', *The Times*, 30 Sept. 1918–7 Oct. 1918.

Nicholson, J. S. *The Neutrality of the United States in Relation to the British and German Empires*, 1915.

Oakeley, H. 'German Thought: The Real Conflict', *Church Quarterly Review*, LXXIX, 3 (Oct. 1914), 95–118.

Official Book of the German Atrocities Told by Victims and Eye-Witnesses: The Complete Verbatim Reports of the Belgian, French and Russian Commissions of Enquiry, 1915.

Oman, C. *The Outbreak of the War of 1914–18: A Narrative Based Mainly On British Official Documents*, 1919.

Oman, J. *The War and Its Issues: An Attempt at a Christian Judgement*, Cambridge, 1915.

Oppenheim, L. 'The Legal Relations Between An Occupying Power and The Inhabitants', *Law Quarterly Review*, XXXIII, 132 (Oct. 1917), 363–70.

The League of Nations and Its Problems: Three Lectures, 1919.

'On War Treason', *Law Quarterly Review*, XXXIII, 131 (July 1917) 266–86.

O'Sullivan, J.M. 'The Problem of Poland', *Studies*, VI, I (Mar. 1917), 80–94.

Oxford University. *To The Christian Scholars of Europe and America: A Reply From Oxford to the German Address to Evangelical Christians* (Oxford Pamphlet no. 2), Oxford, 1914. (Members of the Faculty of Modern History). *Why We Are at War: Great Britain's Case*, 2nd rev. ed., Oxford, 1914.

Pares, B., 'The Black Spot in Europe', *New Europe*, IX, 3 (28 Nov. 1918), 147–51.

Day By Day With the Russian Army, 1914–15, 1915.

The League of Nations and Other Questions of Peace, 1919.

'Russias's Hopes and Aims', *Edinburgh Review*, CCIV, 457 (July 1916), 99–113.

Paterson, W. P. (ed.), *German Culture: The Contribution of Germans to Knowledge, Literature, Life and Art*, 1915.

Peake, A. S. *Prisoners of Hope: The Problem of the Conscientious Objector*, 1918.

Pearson, K. *National Life From the Standpoint of Science*, 1905.

'The Proposed University of London', *Academy*, XXVI, 660 (27 Dec. 1884), 430-1.

Review in *Academy*, XXV, 619 (15 Mar. 1884), 177.

Perry, R. B. 'Non-Resistance and The Present War: A Reply to Mr. Russell', *International Journal of Ethics*, XXV, 3 (April 1915), 307-16.

Our Side is Right, Cambridge, Mass., 1944.

Puritanism and Liberty, N.Y., 1944.

'What is Worth Fighting For', *Atlantic Monthly*, CXVI, 6 (Dec. 1915), 822-31.

Perry, W. C. 'German Universities', *Macmillan's Magazine*, XXXVII (Dec. 1877), 148-60.

Phillips, W. A. 'The Balance of Power', *New Europe*, V, 55 (1 Nov. 1917), 65-75.

'British Imperialism and The Ultimate Problems of the Peace', *Edinburgh Review*, CCII, 453 (July 1915), 41-59.

'The Ethics of Prussian Statecraft', *Quarterly Review*, CCXXX, 457 (Oct. 1918), 280-302.

'Europe and The Problem of Nationality', *Edinburgh Review*, CCI, 451 (Jan. 1915), 25-43.

'National Federations and World Federation', *Edinburgh Review*, CCXXVI, 461, (July 1917), 1-27.

'President Wilson's Peace Programme and The British Empire', *Edinburgh Review*, CCV, 460 (April 1917), 227-48.

'The Price of 'The Society of Nations' ', *New Europe*, IX, 112 (5 Dec. 1918), 173-6.

Pigou, A. C. 'The Conditions of a Permanent Peace', *War and Peace*, III, 28 (Jan 1916), 54-5.

Pollard, A. F. *The Commonwealth at War*, 1917.

Factors in Modern History, rev. ed., 1932.

The League of Nations an Historical Argument, Oxford, 1918.

The League of Nations in History, 1918.

'The Use and Abuse of Diplomacy', *Contemporary Review*, CXIII, 4 (April 1918), 406-12.

A Short History of the Great War, 1920.

The War: Its History and Morals: A Lecture, 1915.

Pollock, F. *The League of Nations and The Coming Rule of Law*, 1919.

Power, E. 'The Teacher of History and World Peace', in *The Evolution of World Peace* (ed. F. S. Marvin), 1921.

Powicke, F. M. *Bismarck and The Origin of Modern Germany*, 1914.

Proceedings of the 19th International Congress of Americanists, Washington, 1915.

Prothero, G. W. *German Policy Before the War*, 1916.

Rait, R. S. 'Dual Alliance and Triple Entente', *Proceedings of the Royal Philosophical Society*, Glasgow, XLVI (1914-15), 58-73.

Why Are We Fighting Germany: A Village Lecture, n.p., 1914.

Raleigh, W. 'The Anatomy of the Pro-Boer', *National Review*, XXXVIII, 223, (Sept. 1901), 52-60.

England and The War: Being Sundry Addresses Delivered During the War and Now First Collected, Oxford, 1918.

The Faith of England: An Address to the Union Society of University College, London,

Oxford, 1917.

The Letters of Walter Raleigh (1879–1922), v. 2, rev. ed., 1928.

Might Is Right (Oxford Pamphlet no. 8), Oxford, 1914.

Some Gains of the War: An Address to the Royal Colonial Institute, Oxford, 1918.

The War and The Press, Oxford, 1918.

The War of Ideas: An Address to the Royal Colonial Institute, Oxford, 1917.

Ramsay, W. M. 'Confessions of a Peacemaker', *Nineteenth Century*, LXXXIII, 493 (Mar. 1918), 637–54.

The Imperial Peace: An Ideal in European History, Oxford, 1913.

Rashdall, H. *Conscience and Christ: Six Lectures on Christian Ethics*, 1916.

Reichel H. R. *Why a League of Free Nations?* (League of Nations Union Publication Ser. 2 no. 21), 1918.

Report of the Commissioners Appointed to Inquire into the Property and Income of Oxford and Cambridge . . ., 1874.

Resolutions of Protest, Official Correspondence and Other Data Relating to the Destruction of Historic Monuments During the War, Westerham, 1915.

Richards, H. E. *Does International Law Still Exist?* (Oxford Pamphlet no. 70), Oxford, 1915.

International Law: Some Problems of the War, Oxford, 1915.

'The Issues at Stake in this War', *Scientia*, XXII (1917), 200–3.

The Progress of International Law and Arbitration, Oxford, 1913.

Ridgeway, W. F. 'Presidential Address', *Proceedings of the Classical Association*, XII (Jan. 1915), 19–31.

'The Problem of our Racial and National Safety', *Eugenics Review*, VIII, 2 (1915), 123–30.

Ritchie, D. G. 'A Further Reply to Mr. J. M. Robertson', *International Journal of Ethics*, XII, 1 (Oct. 1901), 113–4.

'The Moral Problems of War: A Reply to Mr. J. M. Robertson'. *International Journal of Ethics*, XI, 4 (July 1901), 493–505.

'War and Peace', *International Journal of Ethics*, XI, 2 (Jan. 1901), 137–58.

Rivers, W. H. R. 'Psychology and The War', in *Instinct and The Unconscious: A Contribution to the Biological Theory of the Psycho-Neuroses*, Cambridge, 1922.

Rose, J. H. 'British and German Foreign Policy', *Fortnightly Review*, NS. XCVII, 579 (Mar. 1915), 371–81.

'Count Reventlow on War and Politics', *Cambridge Review*, XXXVI, 906 (19 May 1915), 324–5.

'1815 and 1915', *Contemporary Review*, CVII, 1 (Jan. 1915), 12–18.

'The Encircling Myth Once More', *New Europe*, VI, 69 (7 Feb. 1918), 104–8.

'The Folly of Early Offers of Peace', *Fortnightly Review*, NS. XCVII, 580 (1 April 1915), 693–704.

'France and The Rhine Frontier', *Nineteenth Century*, LXXXI, 480 (Feb. 1917), 289–99.

'The Future of Europe', *Scientia*, XIX (1916), 290–8.

German Misrepresentations, 1915.

How the War Came About Explained to the Young of all English-Speaking Countries, 1914.

'The Imitation of Napoleon I By the Germans', *Contemporary Review*, CXIII, 4 (Oct. 1915), 471–80.

'The National Idea', *Contemporary Review*, CIX, 3 (Mar. 1916), 331–7.

Nationality as a Factor in Modern History, 1916.

The Origins of the War: Lectures Delivered in the Michaelmas Term, Cambridge, 1914.

' 'Peace Without Victory': What Is the Verdict of History?', *New Europe*, II, 18 (15 Feb. 1917), 129–36.

'The Polish Problem Past and Present', *Contemporary Review*, CX, 6 (Dec. 1916), 715–23.

'The Political History', in *Germany in the 19th Century: Five Lectures*, Manchester, 1912.

'The War and Nationality', *Scientia*, XVIII (1915), 25–34.

Why Are We at War?, Cambridge, 1914.

Why We Carry On, 1918.

Royal Commission on the University of Oxford: Part I. Minutes of Evidence ..., 1881.

Russell, B. 'Can England and Germany be Reconciled After the War?', *Cambridge Review*, XXXVI, 898 (10 Feb. 1915), 185–6; 900 (24 Feb. 1915), 218–9; 902 (10 Mar. 1915), 250–1.

'The Ethics of War', *International Journal of Ethics*, XXV, 2 (Jan. 1915), 127–42.

Free Thought and Official Propaganda, 1922.

'Idealism On The Defensive', *Nation*, XXI, 23 (8 Sept. 1917), 588–90.

'Individual Liberty and Public Control', *Atlantic Monthly*, CXX, I (July 1917), 112–20.

Justice in War-Time, Chicago, 1916.

'National Independence and Internationalism', *Atlantic Monthly*, CXIX, 5 (May 1917), 622–8.

'New Powers and Old Frontiers', *Nation*, XXV, 10 (7 June 1919), 293–5.

'A Personal Statement', *Open Court*, XXX, 3 (Dec. 1916), 766–7.

'Philosophy and Virtue', *Athenaeum*, 4644 (2 May 1919), 270.

'The Philosophy of Pacifism', in *Towards Ultimate Harmony: Report of Conference on Pacifist Philosophy of Life, Caxton Hall, London, July 8th and 9th, 1915*, 1915.

The Policy of the Entente, 1904–14: A Reply to Professor Gilbert Murray, Manchester, 1915.

Political Ideals, 1st English ed., 1963.

Principles of Social Reconstruction, 1916.

Rex v. Bertrand Russell: Report of the Proceedings Before the Lord Mayor at the Mansion House Justice Room ..., 1916.

Roads to Freedom: Socialism, Anarchism and Syndicalism, 1918.

'Some Psychological Difficulties of Pacifism in War Time', in *We Did Not Fight* (ed. J. Bell), 1935.

Contributions to *The Tribunal*, Aug. 1916–Jan. 1918.

'The War and Non-Resistance: A Rejoinder to Professor Perry', *International Journal of Ethics*, XXVI, 1 (Oct. 1915), 23–30.

War The Offspring of Fear, 1915.

Which Way to Peace, 1936.

Sadler, M. E. 'The History of Education', in *Germany in the 19th Century: Five Lectures*, Manchester, 1912.

'Need We Imitate German Education', *Times Supplement on War and Education*, 14 Jan. 1916.

Preface to F. Paulsen, *The German Universities and University Study*, 1906.

Modern Germany and The Modern World, 1914.

Sanday, W. *The Deeper Causes of the War* (Oxford Pamphlet no. 1), Oxford, 1914.

'International Scholarship After the War', *Times*, 10 May 1918.

In View of the End: A Retrospect and A Prospect, Oxford, 1916.

The Meaning of the War for Germany and Great Britain: An Attempt at Synthesis, Oxford, 1915.

Schiller, F. C. S. 'Examination versus Research', *Nature*, LXXVII, 1997 (6 Feb. 1908), 322–4.

'The Philosophy of Friedrich Nietzsche', *Quarterly Review*, CCXVIII, 1 (Jan. 1913), 148–67.

Review of G. Santayana, *Egotism in German Philosophy*, *Mind*, NS. XXVI, 102 (April 1917), 222–6.

Review of J. Dewey, *German Philosophy and Politics*, *Mind*, NS. XXV, 98 (April 1916), 250–5.

Scott, W. R. *Economic Problems of Peace After the War: The W. Stanley Jevons Lectures at University College, London, in 1917*, 2 v., Cambridge 1917–18.

'Economics of Peace in Time of War', *Report of the 38th Meeting of the British Association for the Advancement of Science, 1916*, pp. 495–503.

'Nationality and Cosmopolitanism', *Scientia*, XXIII (1918), 360–7.

Selbie, W. B. *Christian Nationalism*, 1917.

The War and Theology (Oxford Pamphlet no. 53), Oxford, 1915.

Seth, J., *Universities and The Peace Movement* (National Peace Council Pamphlet Education Ser. 4), 1911.

Seton-Watson, R. W. *The Balkans, Italy and The Adriatic*, 1915.

German, Slav and Magyar, 1916.

'The Pan-German Plan and Its Antidote', *Contemporary Review*, CIX, 4 (April 1916), 422–8.

Roumania and The Great War, 1915.

'Serbia's Need and Britain's Danger', *Contemporary Review*, CVIII, 5 (Nov. 1915), 576–81.

Europe in the Melting Pot, 1919.

What Is at Stake (Papers for War Time, Ser. 3 no. 35), Oxford, 1915.

and J. D. Wilson, A. E. Zimmern & A. Greenwood, *The War and Democracy*, 1914.

Shakespeare Centenary Committee, *Book of Homage to Shakespeare* (ed. I. Gollancz), Oxford, 1916.

Shipley, A. E. *The Minor Horrors of War*, 1915.

Sidgwick, H. 'The Morality of Strife', *International Journal of Ethics*, I, 1 (Oct. 1890), 1–15.

Practical Ethics: A Collection of Addresses and Essays, 1898.

Simpson, J. Y. 'After 'The Great Days' of the Revolution: Impressions From a Recent Visit to Russia', *Nineteenth Century*, LXXXII, 485 (July 1917), 136–48.

'The Present-Day Significance of Siberia', *Nineteenth Century*, LXXXIV, 499 (Sept. 1918), 569–81.

'The Russian Revolution in Retrospect and Forecast', *Nineteenth Century*, LXXXIII, 494 (April 1918), 715–33.

'Russia's Self-Realisation', *Nineteenth Century*, LXXXI, 482 (April 1917), 773–84.

The Self-Discovery of Russia, 1916.

'Transcaucasia Before and After the Revolution', *Contemporary Review*, CXIV, 1 (July 1918), 41–7.

Slater, G. *Peace and War in Europe*, 1915.

Smith, A. L. *The Christian Attitude to War* (Oxford Pamphlet no. 52), Oxford 1915.

Church and State in the Middle Ages: The Ford Lectures Delivered at Oxford in 1905, Oxford, 1913.

'History and Citizenship: A Forecast', *Cornhill Magazine*, NS. XXVI, 5 (May 1909), 603–18.

The War and Our Social Duty (Christian Social Union Pamphlet no. 47), 1915.

Smith, G. A. *Our Common Conscience: Addresses Delivered in America During the Great War*, 1918.

Smith, J. A. 'Progress As An Ideal of Action', in *Progress and History: Essays Edited and Arranged by F. S. Marvin*, 1916.

Sonnenschein, E. A. 'The German Professors', *Nineteenth Century*, LXXXVI, 510 (Aug. 1919), 321–33.

Idols of Peace and War (Oxford Pamphlet no. 61a), Oxford, 1915.

Through German Eyes (Oxford Pamphlet no. 61), Oxford, 1915.

Sorley, W. R. 'Can England and Germany be Reconciled After the War?' *Cambridge Review*, XXXVI, 899 (17 Feb. 1915), 201.

'The Morality of Nations', *International Journal of Ethics*, I, 4 (July 1891), 427–46.

Spooner, W. A. 'Two Permanent Causes of Industrial Unrest', *Church Quarterly Review*, CXXXV, 3 (Oct. 1917), 121–34.

Stallybrass, W. T. S. *A Society of States or Sovereignty, Independence and Equality in a League of Nations*, 1918.

Stein, L. (ed.) *England and Germany by Leaders of Public Opinion in Both Empires*, 1912.

Tawney, R. H. *The Acquisitive Society*, 1921.

The Attack and Other Papers, 1953.

'The Personnel of the New Armies', *Nation*, XVI, 22 (27 Feb. 1915), 676–8.

'The Philosophy of Power', *Athenaeum*, 4614–7 (April–May 1917), 168–72, 213–8.

R. H. Tawney's Commonplace Book, Cambridge, 1972.

The Sword of the Spirit, 1917.

Taylor, A. E. Critical Notice in *Mind*, NS. XXIX, 113 (Jan. 1920), 91–105.

Temperley, H. V. W. *Emperor Frederic and Kaiser Joseph*, 1915.

History of Serbia, 1917.

(ed.) *A History of the Paris Peace Conference*, v. 1, 1920.

Terry, C. S. *German Sea Power* (Oxford Pamphlet no. 35), Oxford, 1914.

'British Diplomacy 1902–14', *Aberdeen University Review*, III, 7 (Jan./Mar. 1915), 36–47; 8 (Feb. 1916), 142–54.

'Germany and Her Neighbours', *History*, IV (Jan./Mar. 1915), 21–36.

Persia and The Anglo-Russian Agreement of 1907, n.p., n.d.

Treitschke, Bernhardi and Some Theologians, Glasgow, 1915.

(ed.) *Battle of Jutland Bank: The Dispatches of Sir J. Jellicoe and Sir D. Beatty*, 1916.

(ed.) *Ostend and Zeebrugge: April 23: May 20 1918: The Dispatches of Sir Roger Keyes*, 1919.

Tillyard, E. M. W. *The Athenian Empire and The Great Illusion*, Cambridge, 1914.

Tönnies, F. *Warlike England as Seen by Herself*, N.Y. 1915.

Tout, T. F. 'National and International Co-Operation in Historical Scholarship', *Transactions of the Royal Historical Society*, Ser. 4, X (1927), 1–20.

Toynbee, A. J. 'Armenia, Its Past and Future', *Ararat*, IV, 48 (June 1917), 545–50.

Armenian Atrocities: The Murder of a Nation, rev. ed., 1915.

The Belgian Deportations, 1916.

The Destruction of Poland: A Study in German Efficiency, 1916.

The German Terror in Belgium, 1917.

The German Terror in France, 1917.

Greek Policy Since 1882 (Oxford Pamphlet no. 39), Oxford, 1914.

'*The Murderous Tyranny of the Turks*', N.Y. 1918.

Nationality and The War, 1915.

'The Position of Armenia', *New Europe*, IV, 50 (27 Sept. 1917), 329–35.

Turkey: A Past and A Future, N.Y., 1917.

(ed.) *The Treatment of Armenians in the Ottoman Empire: Documents Presented to Viscount Grey of Falloden*, 1916.

Trotter, W. *Instincts of the Herd in Peace and War, 1916–1919*, definitive ed., 1953.

Ure, P. N. *Venizelos and His Fellow-Countrymen: A Paper Read to the Classical Association January 6, 1917* (Anglo-Hellenic League Pamphlet no. 30), 1917.

Urquart, F. F. *The Eastern Question* (Oxford Pamphlet no. 15), Oxford, 1914.

'A Plea for International Law', *Dublin Review*, CLVI, 312 (April, 1915), 312–25.

Vaughan, C. E. 'Epilogue' to *The Political Writings of Jean Jacques Rousseau Edited From the Original Manuscripts and Authentic Editions With Introduction and Notes*, v. 2, Cambridge 1915.

Introduction to Rousseau, *A Lasting Peace Through the Federation of Europe and The State of War*, 1917.

Vinogradoff, P. ' 'The Bolsheviks': A Protest', *New Europe*, VII, 81 (2 May 1918), 71–2.

'The Causes of the War', *Scientia*, XVII (1915), 426–36.

'Intellectual Intercourse With Russia', *New Europe*, III, 37 (28 June 1917), 328–32.

'The Manner of Intervention in Russia', *New Europe*, VII, 86 (6 June 1918), 176–8.

'Oxford and Cambridge Through Foreign Spectacles', in *Collected Papers*, v. 1, Oxford, 1928.

Russia: The Psychology of a Nation (Oxford Pamphlet no. 12), Oxford, 1914.

The Russian Problem, 1914.

'The Russian Revolution: Its Religious Aspect', *Land and Water*, LXI, 2882 (2 Aug. 1917), 43–4.

Self-Government in Russia, 1915.

The Slavophil Creed', *Hibbert Journal*, XIII, 2 (1915), 243–60.

'Some Elements of the Russian Revolution', *Quarterly Review*, CCXXVIII, 452 (July 1917), 184–200.

'Some Impressions of the Russian Revolution', *Contemporary Review*, CXI, 5 (May 1917), 553–61.

'Visit to Russia', *Quarterly Review*, CCXXIII, 443 (April 1915), 544–54.

Wallas, G. 'Ante-War Ideals', *Nation*, XVIII, 1 (2 Oct. 1915), 23.

The Great Society: a Psychological Analysis, 1914.

Human Nature in Politics, 1908.

Men and Ideas, 1940.

'Mobilizing the Administration', *New Republic*, v. 53 (6 Nov. 1915), 12–14.

Our Social Heritage, 1921.

'Oxford and English Political Thought', *Nation*, XVII, 7 (15 May 1915), 227–8.

Review of A. E. Christensen, *Politics and Crowd Morality*, in *Hibbert Journal*, XIV (Oct. 1915), 224–8.

'Veblen's Imperial Germany and The Industrial Revolution', *Quarterly Journal of Economics*, XXX, 1 (Nov. 1915), 179–87.

Ward, A. W. *Founders' Day in War Time: An Address Delivered on 23rd March 1917, at a Memorial Service for Members of Manchester University Who Have Fallen in the War*, Manchester, 1917.

Germany 1815–1890, 3 v. Cambridge, 1916–18.

'Goethe and The French Revolution', *Transactions of the English Goethe Society*, XIV (1912).

Securities of Peace a Retrospect (1848–1914), 1919.

Waugh, W. T. *Germany*, 1915.

Germany, 1916.

Webster, C. K. *The Study of 19th Century Diplomacy: An Inaugural Lecture Delivered Before the University of Liverpool*, 1915.

Wehburg, H. *Wider den Anruf der 93! Das Ergebnis einen Rundfrage an die 93 Intellektuellen über die Kriegsschuld*, Charlottenburg, 1920.

Wells, H. G. *Mr. Brittling Sees It Through*, 1916.

West, A. G. *Diary of a Dead Officer*, Oxford, 1919.

Westlake, J. *The Transvaal War: A Lecture Delivered in the University of Cambridge on 9th November, 1899*, 1899.

Wolf, A. *The Philosophy of Nietzsche*, 1915.

BIOGRAPHICAL MATERIAL
(I) AUTOBIOGRAPHIES AND MEMOIRS

Arnot, R. P. Contribution to *Historical Bulletin of the Society for the Study of Labour History*, 13 (Autumn 1966).

Barker, E. *Age and Youth: Memoirs of Three Universities and Father of the Man*, 1953.

Bowra, M. *Memories 1898–1939*, 1966.

Broad, C. D. 'Autobiography', in *The Philosophy of C. D. Broad* (ed. P. A. Schilpp), N.Y., 1959.

Browning, O. *Memories of Later Years*, 1923.

Cole, M. *Growing Up Into Revolution*, 1949.

Collingwood, R. G. *An Autobiography*, Oxford, 1939.

Coulton, G. G. *Four Score Years: An Autobiography*, Cambridge, 1943.

Court, W. H. B. 'Growing Up in the Age of Anxiety', in *Scarcity and Choice in History*, 1970.

Dickinson, G. L. *The Autobiography of G. Lowes Dickinson and Other Unpublished Writings*, 1973.

Farnell, L. R. *An Oxonian Looks Back*, 1934.

Fiedler, H. G. *Memories of 50 Years of the English Goethe Society*, Cambridge, 1936.

Fisher, H. A. L. *An Unfinished Autobiography*, 1940.

Gardner, P. *Autobiographica*, Oxford, 1933.

Gooch, G. P. *Under Six Reigns*, 1958.

Graves, R. *Goodbye to All That*, Harmondsworth, 1960 (first published 1929).

Grundy, G. B. *Fifty-Five Years at Oxford: An Unconventional Biography*, 1945.

Haldane, R. B. *An Autobiography*, 1929.

Heitland, W. E. *After Many Years: A Tale of Experiences and Impressions Gathered in the Course of an Obscure Life*, Cambridge, 1926.

Hirst, F. W. *In the Golden Days*, 1947.

Hobson, J. A. *Confessions of an Economic Heretic*, 1938.

Joad, C. E. M. *Under the Fifth Rib: A Belligerent Autobiography*, 1932.

Jones, T. *Whitehall Diary*, vol. I, 1969.

Lodge, O. *Past Years: An Autobiography*, 1931.

Lowndes, M. B. *Diaries and Letters of Marie Belloc Lowndes, 1911–1947*, 1971.

McDougall, W. M. Contribution to *A History of Psychology in Autobiography*, vol. I, Worcester, Mass., 1930.

MacIver, R. M. *As a Tale That is Told: The Autobiography of R. M. MacIver*, Chicago, 1968.

Marett, R. R. *A Jerseyman at Oxford*, 1941.

Marriott, J. A. R. *Memories of Four Score Years: The Autobiography of the Late Sir John Marriott . . .*, 1946.

Martin, K. *Father Figures: A First Volume of Autobiography, 1897–1931*, 1966.

Masterman, J. C. *On the Chariot Wheel: An Autobiography*, 1975.

Mitchell, P. C. *My Fill of Days*, 1937.

Muir, R. *An Autobiography and Some Essays*, 1943.

Muirhead, J. H. *Reflections by a Journeyman in Philosophy on the Movements of Thought and Practice in His Time*, 1942.

Murray, G. *The League of Nations Movement: Some Recollections of the Early Days*, 1955.

——. *An Unfinished Autobiography With Contributions by his Friends*, 1960.

Oman, C. *Memories of Victorian Oxford and Of Some Early Years*, 1941.

——. *Things I Have Seen*, 1933.

Pares, B. *My Russian Memories*, 1931.

Petrie, C. *A Historian Looks at His World*, 1972.

——. *Scenes of Edwardian Life*, 1965.

Pinto, V. de S. *The City That Shone: An Autobiography (1895–1922)*, 1969.

Price, M. P. *My Three Revolutions*, 1969.

Reilly, C. *Scaffolding in the Sky: A Semi-Architectural Autobiography*, 1935.

Rothenstein, W. *Men and Memories*, vol. 2, 1932.

Rowse, A. L. *A Cornishman at Oxford*, 1965.

Russell, B. *Autobiography*, 3 vols., 1967–9.

——. *Portraits From Memory and Other Essays*, 1956.

Sassoon, S. *The Complete Memoirs of George Sherston*, 1932.

——. *Siegfried's Journey, 1916–1920*, 1945.

Sayce, A. H. *Reminiscences*, 1923.

Schmitt, B. E. *The Fashion and Future of History: Historical Studies and Addresses*, Cleveland, Ohio, 1960 (autobiographical chapters).

Schuster, A. *Biographical Fragments*, 1932.

Seton-Watson, R. W. 'The Origins of the School of Slavonic Studies', *Slavonic and East European Review*, XVII, 50 (Jan. 1939), 360–71.

R. W. Seton-Watson and the Yugoslavs: Correspondence 1906–41 (eds. H. Seton-Watson *et al*), 2 vols., London and Zagreb, 1976.

Shanks, E. *The Old Indispensables: A Romance of Whitehall*, 1919 (a fictional memoir).

Sully, J. *My Life and Friends: A Psychologist's Memories*, 1918.

Thomson, J. J. *Recollections and Reflections*, 1936.

Todd, J. E. 'The Apprenticeship of a Professor of History, 1903–1919', *History*, XLIV (1959), 124–33.

Toynbee, A. J. *Acquaintances*, 1967.

——. *Experiences*, 1969.

Trevelyan, G. M. *An Autobiography and Other Essays*, 1949.

Wells, H. G. *Experiment in Autobiography: Discoveries and Conclusions of a Very Ordinary Brain (Since 1866)*, 2 vols., 1934.

Westermarck, E. *Memories of My Life*, 1929.
Widgery, A. *A Philosopher's Pilgrimage*, 1961.
Wilamowitz-Moellendorff, U. von *My Recollections, 1848-1914*, 1930.
Willey, B. *Spots of Time: A Retrospect of the Years 1897-1920*, 1965.
Woodward, E. L. *Short Journey*, 1942.
Woolf, L. *Sowing: An Autobiography of the Years 1880-1904*, 1960.
_____. *Beginning Again: An Autobiography of the Years 1911-1918*, 1964.

(2) *BIOGRAPHIES*
Dictionary of National Biography (and Supplements).
Kurschners Deutscher Gelehrten-Kalandar.
Minerva: Jahrbuch der Gelehrten Welt.
Who Was Who, vols. 1-4.

Adams, H. P. 'Sir Raymond Beazley, 1868-1955: His Work as a Scholar and Teacher', *University of Birmingham Historical Journal*, V (1955-6), 103-7.
Addision, W. G. *J. R. Green*, 1946.
Ashley, A. *William James Ashley: A Life*, 1932.
Ausubel, H. J., B. Brebner and E. M. Hunt (eds.) *Some Modern Historians of Britain: Essays in Honour of R. L. Schuyler*, N.Y., 1951.
Ball, O. H. (ed.), *Sidney Ball: Memories and Impressions of an 'Ideal Don'*, Oxford, 1933.
Barbour, G. F. 'Memoir', in J. Y. Simpson, *The Garment of the Living God*, 1934.
_____. 'Memoir', in A. Seth Pringle-Pattison, *The Balfour Lectures on Realism Delivered in the University of Edinburgh*, 1933.
Baynes, N. H. 'Memoir', in *A Bibliography of the Works of J. B. Bury ...*, Cambridge, 1929.
Blunt, W. *Cockerell: Sidney Carlisle Cockerell, Friend of Ruskin and William Morris and Director of the Fitzwilliam Museum*, Cambridge, 1964.
Bolsover, G. H. *Robert William Seton-Watson, 1879-1951*, 1951.
Bosanquet, H. *Bernard Bosanquet: A Short Account of his Life*, 1924.
Brittain, F. *Bernard Lord Manning: A Memoir*, Cambridge, 1942.
Butler, J. R. M. *Henry Montagu Butler: Master of Trinity College Cambridge, 1886-1918*, 1925.
Cam, H. *Zachary Nugent Brooke, 1883-1946*, 1946.
Campbell, O. 'Memoir', in J. Ward, *Essays in Philosophy*, Cambridge, 1927.
Carpenter, L. *C. G. D. H. Cole: An Intellectual Biography*, 1973.
Chaudhuri, N. C. *Scholar Extraordinary: The Life of Professor the Rt. Hon. Friedrich Max Muller P.C.*, 1974.
Clapham, J. H. 'Eileen Power, 1889-1940', *Economica*, NS. VII, 27 (Aug. 1940), 351-9.
Clark, G. N. *Sir John Harold Clapham, 1873-1946*, 1946.
Clark, R. W. *The Life of Bertrand Russell*, 1975.
Cole, M. *The Life of G. D. H. Cole*, 1971.
Conway, R. S. *Sir William Ridgeway, 1853-1926*, 1928.
Coon, R. H. *William Warde Fowler: An Oxford Humanist*, Oxford, 1934.
Court, W. H. B. 'Two Economic Historians', in *Scarcity and Choice in History*, 1970.
Crawford, R. M. *'A Bit of a Rebel': The Life and Work of George Arnold Wood*, Sydney, 1975.
Crawley, C. W. 'Sir George Prothero and his Circle', *Transactions of the Royal Historical Society*, Ser. 5 XX (1970), 101-27.

Croone, H. A. 'Edward Augustus Freeman, 1823–1892', *History*, XXVIII, 107 (Mar. 1943), 78–92.

Cunningham, A. *William Cunningham: Teacher and Priest*, 1950.

Darroch, S. J. *Ottoline: The Life of Lady Ottoline Morrell*, 1976.

Dickinson, G. L. *J. McT. E. McTaggart with Chapters by Basil Williams and S. V. Keeling*, Cambridge, 1931.

Elton, O. *Frederick York Powell: A Life and a Selection from his Letters and Occasional Writings*, 2 vols., Oxford, 1906.

Eyck, F. *G. P. Gooch: A Study in History and Politics*, 1982.

Fayle, C. E. (ed.) *Harold Wright: A Memoir*, 1934.

Fisher, H. A. L. *James Bryce (Viscount Bryce of Dechmont O.M.)*, 2 vols., 1927.

———. 'Memoir', in *The Collected Papers of Paul Vinogradoff*, vol. I, Oxford, 1928.

Forster, E. M. *Goldsworthy Lowes Dickinson and Related Writings* (Abinger edition of the Works of E. M. Forster), 1973.

Gaselee, S. 'Prefatory Note' to G. W. Prothero, *Select Analytical List of Books Concerning the Great War*, 1923.

Gilbert, E. W. *Sir Halford Mackinder, 1861–1947: An Appreciation of his Life and Work*, 1961.

Glasgow, G. *Ronald Burrows: A Memoir*, 1924.

Gooch, G. P. *Harold Temperley, 1879–1939*, 1939.

Gordon, M. C. *The Life of George S. Gordon, 1881–1942*, 1945.

Gow, A. S. F. *A. E. Housman: A Sketch Together with a List of his Writings and Indexes to his Classical Papers*, Cambridge, 1936.

———. *Sir Stephen Gaselee K.C.M.G.*, 1944.

Guillebaud, C. W. 'Some Personal Reminiscences of Alfred Marshall', *History of Political Economy*, III (1971), 1–8.

Halperin, S. W. (ed.) *Some 20th Century Historians: Essays on Eminent Europeans*, Chicago, 1961.

Hammond, J. L. *C. P. Scott of the Manchester Guardian*, 1934.

Harrod, R. F. *The Life of John Maynard Keynes*, 1951.

Haverfield, F. J. 'Biographical Note' in *Essays by Henry Francis Pelham*, Oxford, 1911.

Havighurst, A. F. *Radical Journalist: H. W. Massingham (1860–1924)*, Cambridge, 1974.

Hazeltine, H. D. *Sir Frederick Pollock, 1845–1937*, 1949.

Headlam-Morley, A. 'Introduction' to J. W. Headlam-Morley, *A Memoir of the Paris Peace Conference, 1919*, 1972.

Herford, C. H. (ed.) *Joseph Estlin Carpenter: A Memorial Volume*, Oxford, 1929.

Hetherington, H. J. *The Life and Letters of Sir Henry Jones, Professor of Moral Philosophy in the University of Glasgow*, 1924.

Hirsch, F. E. 'Biographical Article: George Peabody Gooch', *Journal of Modern History*, XXVI, 3 (Sept. 1954), 260–71.

Hobson, J. A. and M. Ginsburg *L. T. Hobhouse: His Life and Work . . . With Selected Essays and Articles*, 1931.

Holroyd, M. *Lytton Strachey: A Critical Biography*, 2 vols., 1968.

Johnson, H. G. 'Arthur Cecil Pigou, 1877–1959', *Canadian Journal of Economics and Political Science*, XXVI, I (Feb. 1960), 150–5.

Johnston, W. M. *The Formative Years of R. G. Collingwood*, The Hague, 1967.

Jones, A. R. *The Life and Opinions of T. E. Hulme*, 1960.

Jones, H. and J. H. Muirhead, *The Life and Philosophy of Edward Caird*, Glasgow, 1921.

Ker, N. 'A. S. Napier, 1853–1916', in *Philological Essays* (ed. J. L. Rosier), The Hague, 1970.

Keynes, M. (ed.) *Essays on John Maynard Keynes*, Cambridge, 1975.

Laird, J. 'Memoir', in S. Alexander, *Philosophical and Literary Pieces*, 1939.

Laski, H. J. 'Lowes Dickinson and Graham Wallas', *Political Quarterly*, III, 4 (Oct.–Dec. 1932), 416–8.

Little, A. G. 'Memoir', in C. E. Vaughan, *Studies in the History of Political Philosophy Before and After Rousseau*, vol. I, Manchester, 1923.

Lloyd, J. E. (ed.) *Sir Harry Reichel, 1856–1931: A Memorial Volume*, Cardiff, 1934.

Lockhart, J. G. and C. M. Woodhouse, *Rhodes*, 1963.

Lyon, B. *Henri Pirenne: A Biographical and Intellectual Study*, Ghent, 1974.

Mackail, J. W. *James Leigh Strachan-Davidson, Master of Balliol*, Oxford, 1925.

NcNair, A. D. *Alexander Pierce Higgins, 1865–1935*, 1935.

Marett, R. R. *Ferdinand Canning Scott Schiller, 1864–1937*, 1937.

Martin, K. *Harold Laski, 1893–1950: A Biographical Memoir*, 1953.

Matheson, P. E. *The Life of Hastings Rashdall D.D., Dean of Carlisle, Fellow of the British Academy, Honorary Fellow of New College*, 1928.

Moulton, W. F. *James Hope Moulton by his Brother*, 1919.

Muirhead, J. H. 'Bernard Bosanquet', *Mind*, NS. XXXII, 128 (Oct. 1923), 393–407.

Murray, G. *Edwyn Robert Bevan, 1870–1943*, 1944.

———. *Francis MacDonald Cornford, 1874–1943*, 1944.

Myers, C. S. 'The Influence of the Late W. H. R. Rivers', in W. H. R. Rivers, *Psychology and Politics*, 1923.

Namier, J. *Lewis Namier: A Biography*, 1971.

Newton, A. P. *Lord Lansdowne: A Biography*, 1929.

Ogg, D. *Herbert Fisher, 1865–1940: A Short Biography*, 1947.

Pares, R. 'Introduction' to B. Pares, *A History of Russia*, 1955.

Parry, R. St. J. *Henry Jackson O.M., Vice-Master and Regius Professor of Greek in the University of Cambridge: A Memoir*, Cambridge, 1926.

Peake, L. S. *Arthur Samuel Peake: A Memoir*, 1930.

Pigou, A. C. (ed.) *Memorials of Alfred Marshall*, 1925.

Powicke, F. M. 'Memoir', in *Collected Papers of Thomas Frederick Tout*, vol. I, Manchester, 1932.

Rait, R. S. (ed.) *Memorials of Albert Venn Dicey: Being Chiefly Letters and Diaries*, 1925.

Richards, I. A. 'Some Recollections of C. K. Ogden', *Encounter*, IX, 3 (Sept. 1957), 10–12.

Robbins, K. *Sir Edward Grey: A Biography of Lord Grey of Falloden*, 1971.

Roberts, W. R. 'The Late Dr. E. V. Arnold', *North Wales Chronicle*, 1 Oct. 1926.

Robertson, C. G. *Sir Charles Oman, 1860–1946*, 1947.

Robertson, J. G. *Charles Harold Herford, 1853–1931*, 1933.

Robinson, A. L. *William McDougall M.B. D.Sc. F.R.S: A Bibliography Together with a Brief Outline of His Life*, Durham, N. Carolina, 1943.

Ross, E. D. 'Edward Glanville Brown: A Memoir', in E. G. Brown, *A Year Amongst the Persians: Impressions As To the Life, Character and Thought of the People of Persia Received during Twelve Months' Residence in that Country in the Years 1887–1888*, 3rd. ed., 1950.

Russell, L. M. *John Adam Cramb: Patriot, Historian, Mystic*, 1950.

Sadleir, M. *Michael Ernest Sadler (Sir Michael Sadler K.C.S.I.), 1861–1943: A Memoir by Son*, 1949.

Schmitt, B. E. (ed.) *Some Historians of Modern Europe: Essays in Historiography by Former Students of the Department of History of the University of Chicago*, Chicago, 1942.

Scott, D. *A. D. Lindsay: A Biography*, Oxford, 1971.

Sidgwick, A. and E. M. Sidgwick *Henry Sidgwick*, 1906.

Sidgwick, E. *Mrs Henry Sidgwick: A Memoir by her Niece*, 1938.

Smith, M. F. *Arthur Lionel Smith, Master of Balliol (1916-1924): A Biography and Some Reminiscences by his Wife*, 1928.

Snow, C. P. 'Foreword' to G. H. Hardy, *A Mathematician's Apology*, new ed., Cambridge, 1967.

Stephens, W. R. W. *The Life and Letters of Edward A. Freeman*, 2 vols., 1895.

Stewart, H. F. *Francis Jenkinson, Fellow of Trinity College, Cambridge and University Librarian: A Memoir*, Cambridge, 1926.

Stewart, J. *Jane Ellen Harrison: A Portrait from Letters*, 1959.

Tawney, R. H. 'Introductory Memoir', in *Studies in Economic History: The Collected Papers of George Unwin*, 1927.

Terrill, R. *R. H. Tawney and His Times: Socialism as Fellowship*, 1974.

Tout, T. F. 'Memoir', in A. T. Bartholomew, *A Bibliography of Sir Adolphus William Ward, 1837-1924 . . .*, Cambridge, 1926.

_____ . 'Mark Hovell (1888-1916)', in *The Chartist Movement by the Late Mark Hovell, M.A.*, Manchester, 1918.

'Tributes to R. W. Seton-Watson: A Symposium', *Slavonic and East European Review*, XXX, 75 (June 1952), 331-63.

Tucker, M. G. *John Neville Figgis: A Study*, 1950.

Walker-Smith, D. and E. Clarke *The Life of Sir Edward Clarke*, 1939.

Weaver, J. R. H. 'Memoir', in Weaver and A. L. Poole, *Henry William Carless Davis, 1874-1928: A Memoir . . . and a Selection of his Historical Papers*, 1933.

Webb, C. C. J. *Reginald Lane Poole, 1857-1939*, 1939.

Wedd, N. 'Goldie Dickinson: The Latest Cambridge Platonist', *Criterion*, XII, 47 (Jan. 1933), 175-83.

Whittuck, E. A. 'Professor Oppenheim', *British Yearbook of International Law*, I (1920-1), 1-9.

Wiener, M. J. *Between Two Worlds: The Political Thought of Graham Wallas*, Oxford, 1971.

Willey, B. 'Eustace Mandeville Wetenhall Tillyard', *Proceedings of the British Academy*, LXIX (1963), 387-405.

Williams, J. R., R. M. Titmuss, F. J. Fisher, *R. H. Tawney: A Portrait by Several Hands*, 1960.

Winkler, H. R. 'J. L. Hammond', in *Historians of Modern Europe* (ed. H. A. Schmitt), Baton Rouge, 1971.

Wollheim, R. *F. H. Bradley*, Harmondsworth, 1959.

Wood, A. *Bertrand Russell The Passionate Sceptic*, 1957.

Wood, H. G. *Terrot Reaveley Glover: A Biography*, Cambridge, 1953.

Other secondary material is listed in the notes to each chapter.

Appendix 1: German Education of British Scholars

J. B. Acton	Munich	Historian
F. E. Adcock	Berlin, Munich	Ancient Historian
E. V. Arnold	Tübingen	Classicist/Sanskrit Scholar
W. J. Ashley	Göttingen (1880)	Economic Historian
J. B. Baillie	Halle, Strassburg, Paris	Philosopher
J. S. Blackie	Göttingen, Berlin	Philologist
J. Bryce	Heidelberg	Lawyer/Historian
C. Burt	Würzburg	Psychologist
J. B. Bury	Göttingen (1880), Leipzig (1883)	Historian
I. Bywater	Bonn (1868) Heidelberg	Classicist
H. M. Chadwick	Berlin (1895)	Philologist
J. H. Clapham	Göttingen, Paris	Economic Historian
G. G. Coulton	Heidelberg	Historian
W. Cunningham	Tübingen	Economic Historian
H. W. C. Davis	Dresden	Historian
L. R. Farnell	Berlin, Munich	Classical Scholar
H. A. L. Fisher	Berlin (1890), Paris (1889)	Historian
G. D. Hicks	Leipzig (1896) Ph.D.	Philosopher
C. H. Herford	Vienna, Berlin (1881–2)	Comparative Literature Scholar
M. Hovell	Leipzig	Historian
L. P. Jacks	Göttingen	Theologian
A. G. Little	Dresden, Göttingen (1886–8)	Historian
J. S. McKenzie	Berlin	Philosopher
J. S. Mackinnon	Heidelberg (1890) D.Phil	Church Historian
W. McDougall	Göttingen (1901)	Psychologist
R. W. Macan	Jena, Zürich	Ancient Historian
R. R. Marett	Berlin	Anthropologist
R. Muir	Marburg (1914)	Historian
A. S. Napier	Berlin, Göttingen	Philologist
H. Nettleship	Berlin	Classical Scholar
J. W. Oman	Erlangen, Heidelberg	Theologian
W. P. Paterson	Leipzig, Erlangen, Berlin (1883–85)	Theologian
J. Peile	Göttingen (1866)	Philologist
L. R. Phelps	Göttingen, Leipzig (1876–7)	Provost of Oriel
R. L. Poole	Leipzig (1882) Ph.D.	Historian
W. M. Ramsay	Göttingen	Classical Archaeologist
J. Rhys	Leipzig	Philologist
W. H. R. Rivers	Jena (1892) Heidelberg (1893)	Psychologist/ Anthropologist
J. G. Robertson	Leipzig (1892) D.Phil.	German Scholar
A. Seth Pringle-Pattison	Berlin, Jena, Göttingen (1878–80)	Philosopher
R. W. Seton-Watson	Berlin, Vienna, Paris (1903–6)	Historian

227

H. Sidgwick	Dresden	Philosopher
C. E. Spearman	Leipzig, Ph.D. Würzburg, Göttingen (1900, 1902–7)	Psychologist
G. A. Smith	Tübingen (1876), Leipzig (1878), Berlin	Theologian
N. Kemp Smith	Zürich, Berlin, Paris (1895–6)	Philosopher
W. R. Sorley	Tübingen	Philosopher
J. Sully	Göttingen, Berlin	Psychologist
H. Sweet	Heidelberg	Philologist
G. H. Thomson	Strassburg (1906) Ph.D.	Psychologist
G. Unwin	Berlin (1898)	Economic Historian
J. Ward	Leipzig, Göttingen (1870)	Psychologist
J. C. Wilson	Göttingen (1873–4)	Philosopher
E. L. Woodward	Darmstadt (1912)	Historian
J. Wright	Heidelberg, Leipzig	Philologist
H. C. K. Wyld	Bonn, Heidelberg (1890)	Philologist
H. J. Watt	Berlin, Würzburg, Leipzig	Psychologist

Appendix 2: British International Lawyers and the First World War

At the outbreak of war in 1914 international law as a university discipline in Britain was still at a relatively undeveloped stage — even, as one lawyer noted, in an 'unsatisfactory condition'. With few teachers and poorly endowed chairs (even in the three great universities), there was also little public interest in the subject. One effect — and perhaps a contributory cause — of this neglect was that there was no British journal devoted to the study of international law. 'Indeed', the same observer noted, 'in the scientific study of the subject less interest is shown in this country than in almost any other leading State.'[1] Yet, British entry to the war was ostensibly, as Asquith put it, in 'the first place to vindicate the sanctity of treaty obligations'.[2] The German invasion of Belgium was portrayed by British international lawyers (and by historians) as a challenge to 'the existence of any code of law at all between nations'. 'Any system of international law must be based on the equality of States', the Chichele Professor of International Law at Oxford told the readers of the Italian review *Scientia*. Every state had to have 'the same rights and the same duties irrespective of its power or of its resources naval and military'.[3] In reality, of course, international law simply provided 'a valuable cloak of respectability to justify a decision taken on other grounds' — national interest, specifically, strategic interest in the Belgian coast and in the European 'balance of power'. Not even the 1839 treaty of guarantee of Belgian neutrality obliged Britain 'to take unilateral action if the other guarantor powers did not join in'.[4]

Nevertheless, the German invasion of Belgium in August 1914 was widely believed to be the *casus belli*, and it seemed to deliver a body blow to international law. Before 1914 international lawyers had sometimes cautioned against over-optimistic assessments of the 'binding force' of international law. A. P. Higgins, for example, in 1910 noted that:

> Hague Conferences, Inter-Parliamentary Unions, Federations, Unions of Workers, and such-like gatherings all conduce to a growing feeling of solidarity among the nations of the world, and tend to create an atmosphere in which the observance of International Law will be increasingly easy to be realised. But as yet I see no prospect of perpetual peace. International Law is developing, but has not yet reached the fullness of the development of national laws.[5]

With the outbreak of war it did not take long for hopes to be expressed of some future improvement in its 'binding force', *after* an Allied victory. As Sir H. Erle Richards told a W.E.A. meeting in Birmingham, the picture was, at first sight, gloomy. Britain was at war because 'her enemy ... declined to be bound by International Law'. Even so, since public opinion was 'some check even in the darkest days', it was possible to believe that international law still did exist and that at the end of the war would 'stand on a more secure footing than before'.[6] This confidence was reflected in the decision to investigate the conduct of the German army in occupied Belgium (although this was also part of propaganda warfare), in the plans (which never came to anything) for a general commission to investigate German violations of the laws of war, and in some of the planning of a postwar league to enforce settlement of future disputes.

Confidence in the future of international law was perhaps reflected also in the founding of the Grotius Society in 1915. This filled the gap caused by the cessation (for the duration of the war) of the activities of the International Law Association. Membership of the Grotius Society was restricted to British subjects, although foreign nationals (invariably from allied or neutral states) were allowed to become honorary or corresponding members. This was to avoid the embarrassing situation in which the I.L.A. found itself on the outbreak of the war.[7] However, the first President of the Society, Henry Goudy (Regius Professor of Civil Law at Oxford), was at pains to disclaim any intention to 'discuss international questions from a purely British standpoint, or to support dogmas because they might be thought advantageous to the British interest'. Discussion would be from a 'cosmopolitan point of view'; suggestions for the reform of international law were to be 'based on humanity and justice wherever possible'. This was a brave standard to nail to the mast in wartime, and a few sentences later Goudy showed clear signs of partiality in his interpretation of recent events in the light of international law. Mention was made of the dynastic autocracy of the Greek monarchy, at that time proving a little too independent for the liking of the British Government, but nothing was said of the autocratic system of Tsarist Russia.[8]

The greatest test for the scholarly standards of British international lawyers came over the question of the law of the sea — a matter of the utmost importance for a maritime nation like Britain. Before the outbreak of the war the whole question of the rules of naval warfare had been raised at a conference in London, which had taken place as the result of an initiative by the British Government in December 1908. The resulting 'Declaration of London' of 1909 was accepted by the British Government, the Foreign Office and Admiralty apparently finding it a distinct improvement on the existing situation.[9] But influential sections of political and naval opinion, plus a 'club-land army ... of no fewer than 122 retired admirals', campaigned against the Liberal Government's bill embodying the provisions of the Declaration. Although it passed through the House of Commons, it was thrown out by the Lords in December 1911.[10] There was a similar division of opinion between 'doves' and 'hawks' amongst British international lawyers — especially on the merits of the central proposal in the Declaration, the immunity from capture of private property at sea in time of war. Throughout the nineteenth century there had been pressure for some limitation of the forms of naval warfare (blockade, seizure of contraband, stoppage of enemy trade) which affected commerce. Equally, throughout the nineteenth century British Governments had resisted this pressure, until in the first decade of the twentieth century there had been agreement for an international conference. However, this was not simply a concession to American pressure (important though that was), but also a realisation that Britain, like other trading nations, had 'the need to calculate, from time to time, whether a state of law that would suit them when neutral would suit them also when belligerent'.[11] The process of calculation was reflected in the work of British international lawyers.

The former Chichele Professor of International Law at Oxford, T. E. Holland, was strongly opposed to the proposals embodied in the Declaration of London, and, echoing what had been official government policy up until 1908, he also argued against any restraints on the British right of blockading enemy ports and capturing enemy ships.[12] However, his successor in the Chichele chair, Sir H. Erle Richards, seems to have come down on the other side. As late as 1915 he was arguing for some compromise, on the question of contraband, between complete abandonment of belligerent right of search, and on the other hand including all conditional contraband in the category of absolute contraband. Richards did not discuss blockade specifically, but he did propose the establishment of an International Prize Court, a favourite idea of the 'liberal' school of international lawyers.[13] Two other leading international lawyers, Sir John Macdonell (University College, London) and the Rev. T. J. Lawrence (Bristol University), campaigned strongly for the Declaration of London. Both men were involved in attempts to foster better Anglo-German relations before 1914 (no coincidence one would imagine), and

Lawrence's *Principles of International Law* (1895) was one of the major works on the subject.[14] Macdonell's contribution to the 'Anglo-German Understanding Conference', held in London in 1912, was a sustained critique of opponents of the Declaration: those who argued that 'liability to capture' was really a 'deterrent from war' since people who would otherwise be 'untouched' by war felt its effects, and those who argued that 'every concession to the cause of peace' was an admission of weakness. This argument, which Macdonell labelled 'Mahanism', could only lead to an erosion of all rules of war (not just those concerned with contraband). It was, he argued, little better than the arguments of Social Darwinists, representatives of that:

> ... upthrust of barbarism; a secret admiration of force unrestricted; impatience at every limitation of the area of warfare; an unavowed belief in war as something divine, or as the true field for manly virtue.[15]

Clearly, the arguments of international lawyers were bound up with a wider debate about war and peace. Macdonell was speaking the same language as the social scientists like MacIver and Wallas, whom we touched on in the first chapter. The question in 1912 was whether the persistence of certain attitudes would lead to war at a time when nations were becoming increasingly interdependent in economic and financial terms. As Lawrence noted in the *Peace Yearbook* for 1914:

> The increasing community of interests among nations, the reciprocity of services rendered by international commerce, becomes every year a greater obstacle to the free use of the right of capture.

The inviolability of private property in wartime was thus an issue upon which 'the pacifist, the politician and the trader' could 'heartily agree'.[16] Agreement on this would also 'limit the destructiveness of war', and perhaps even the peacetime arms race which so exercised the minds of delegates at the Anglo-German Understanding Conference.[17] Macdonell even argued that capture and blockade were not the potent weapons against an enemy that they once had been. It was 'highly probable' that their use would cause 'much trouble with neutral States', and besides it was 'ridiculous to suppose' that the ' 'bottling-up' to any extent of the German merchant marine could appreciably influence the issue of hostilities'.[18]

Events only a few years later were to prove Macdonell very wrong on the last point. Lawrence seems to have been more realistic in his assessment of what could be achieved. As he observed in 1908, the claim that the abolition of the right to make war on innocuous seaborne commerce would enable 'navies ... to conform to the standard of humanity already reached in military operations', showed little knowledge of the barbarity of war on land, even allowing for the Geneva Convention of 1906. One could not argue in moral terms: 'The capture of an enemy's merchantman is an operation as regular as the levy of a requisition for beef on a country village'. Barbarous as war was:

> ... it would be still more barbarous if disciplined forces were deprived of the power of striking hard blows at the warlike resources of their enemies. There would be in it no more of mercy and humanity than at present, and it would last longer.

The formula for advance was thus to 'protect scrupulously persons and things not immediately useful for warlike purposes, and seize or destroy all who are'.[19] In other words, Lawrence did not feel that *complete* abandonment of belligerent right of search at sea was desirable. Advance in international law he argued for in terms of a practical step-by-step approach rather than by reference to abstract principles. And when the war did break out, and the Declaration of London came increasingly to be ignored by the belligerent states, Lawrence's reaction was a perceptive one:

> ... the ill-starred Declaration of London, whose misfortune was that it either came too late or too soon — too late for the regulation of a sea-order about to perish owing to the advances of science and retrogressions of morality, and too soon for the regulation of a new order whose outlines are yet in the making.[20]

On the outbreak of war the Central Powers promised to observe the Declaration of London if the Allies did likewise. The latter, however, only agreed to this 'subject to certain modifications and additions' which they deemed 'indispensible to the efficient conduct of naval operations'. Such piecemeal ratification violated Article 65 of the Declaration (which Britain had not ratified anyway). More importantly, it was a first step in a retreat from the spirit as well as the letter of all rules of naval warfare, including the Declaration of Paris (1856) on blockade and capture. Both sides were to blame for the subsequent measures and counter-measures (maritime zones, mining, long-distance blockade, unrestricted submarine warfare, armed merchantmen).[21] Both sides claimed the necessities of war in justification — in this respect the 'war-making traditions' of the Royal Navy 'were tough ones; every bit as tough, *mutatis mutandis*, as those of the Prusso-German general staff'.[22] And both sides could call on the services of international lawyers to provide a defence of departures from international law, whether the invasion of Belgium or the scrapping of the Declaration of Paris. In this respect, too, Professor J. H. Morgan distinguished himself, as he had over the investigation of German 'frightfulness' in Belgium. Now, however, the shoe was on the other foot, and Morgan had to defend British 'law-breaking' at sea. His Rhodes lecture of November 1915 has more than a whiff of *Realpolitik* about it:

> I believe that our departures from the orthodoxy of international law have been thoroughly justified. If I have any criticism to make of them, it is not that they were made too soon, but that they were not made soon enough. But their justification is to be found less in law than in morality. If we have 'scrapped' the Declaration of London and laid a profane hand on the Declaration of Paris, it is because the Germans have broken nearly every one of the Hague Regulations governing the conduct of the war on land, and have sunk neutral merchantmen by way of vindicating what they are pleased to call the freedom of the seas. We were justified and more than fully justified. But let us realise no less resolutely than sadly that international conventions never counted for so little as they do now. We must, I think, take a long farewell of the American contention that peace, and with it the commerce of neutrals, should govern the rules of war. This is an age of iron, and it has little room for such academic conceptions.[23]

There was little to choose between this conception of war at sea and German 'frightfulness' on land. ' 'Military necessity' was just as well lodged in Portsmouth as in Potsdam.'[24] In his introduction to *The German War Book* Morgan had written that its 'peculiar logic' consisted 'for the most part in ostentatiously laying down unimpeachable rules and then quietly destroying them by debilitating exceptions'.[25] Was not this exactly what the British were doing at sea, in effect using the notorious justification of *Notwendigkeit* which had been used to justify the German invasion of Belgium? This was exactly the question dealt with by J. E. G. de Montmorency, Lecturer in International Law at Cambridge, and after the war (1920) Macdonell's successor in the chair of Comparative Law in London. Writing in February 1915, Montmorency noted that there were 'two points of view' on international law during wartime:

There is the purely legal view, difficult and complex, often involving the clash of nations, statesmen and jurists, a legal view that is ultimately based upon economic necessity, and one therefore that varies from nation to nation. The other point of view, the non-juridical and common-sense point of view, is the view that is too little considered, though it is the view that has ultimately determined and must always ultimately determine the minds of statesmen and the policy of nations. War is a form of reality that will not have its dread purpose thwarted by unrealities. If a legal doctrine has ceased to be a reality, if it is a mere echo of realities once all important under conditions that have passed away, then such a doctrine, though it may persist on record in times of peace, is necessarily swept away when a new economic position is forced by war.

If there was a hint of 'blood and iron' in Morgan's ideas, was there not a touch of von Treitschke in Montmorency's words? This of course he denied. He was not advocating on the law of the sea:

... the monstrous German doctrine of *Kriegsverrath*. Necessity whether in war or peace, has no claim to interfere with fundamental principles of righteousness. Neither might nor necessity justifies the overturning of right .... But a legal doctrine is not necessarily a principle of righteousness, and, indeed, has often proved a perverse and evil thing, that has been handed on from one set of economic conditions that justified it, to later sets of economic conditions that abhorred it. The continual adjustment of the doctrines and practices of law to changing economic conditions is one of the explanations of the growth of English Common Law .... [26]

A recent 'neutral' international lawyer has criticised exactly this kind of justification of British policy during the First World War:

As the existing law must be observed until it is repealed or amended in a regular manner, *changed conditions* may not be invoked as a ground for establishing war zones ... the British observed that obsolete rules of warfare were simply being adapted to suit new conditions better, and that there was no intention of deviating from the general rules of international law concerning blockade. But this explanation too is unsatisfactory. [27]

At the time there were a few British voices expressing misgivings along the same lines. Macdonell, for example, was particularly worried by British departure from previously accepted rules of blockade. An Order in Council of March 1915 'empowering British cruisers to detain all vessels attempting to enter or leave German ports' prompted his comment that international law of the sea now consisted of little more than 'polite fictions'. It was just 'an imposing name for opportunism'.[28] And in a reference to the kind of arguments put forward by Morgan and Montmorency, he attacked those people in positions to 'influence our actual policy' who now suggested 'either let there be no rules, or rules drawn in terms so elastic and vague that they be interpreted to meet any new or unexpected circumstances'. Such talk meant 'the abrogation of all law'. It was 'the familiar doctrine of necessity, to be reprobated on land, but, it would seem, to be approved at sea'. The 'actual working creed of some Governments' — and here he meant his own in particular — could be summed up in the following way:

By all means let there be rules and let them be observed when they are not seriously inconvenient. But when they prove to be very much in the way, let us break free of them, paying damages, to be awarded by an international tribunal. Compensation to neutrals is, and must be, no small part of the normal cost of a modern naval war.[29]

Macdonell's judgement is echoed by more recent assessments of British policy at sea. Britain sought a blockade of the Central Powers 'as nearly absolute and total — ie. as prohibitive of anything whatsoever by whatever route — as political considerations would permit'.[30] Additions were made to lists of contraband, both 'conditional' and 'absolute', and from April 1916 'contraband' (now all considered absolute) was intercepted even if it were bound for neutral ports. The idea of 'continuous voyage' assumed that goods were eventually destined for official government use in Germany and could thus be intercepted at any stage of the journey. Neutrals were thus kept from trading, not only with Germany, but also with each other — something which the state of international law had not led them to expect in 1914. While Holland and the Scandinavian countries were continually protesting at Britain's interference with 'the freedom of the seas' (at least of non-contraband trade), it was American opinion which the British had to keep in mind. And here they were assisted by German policy which 'repeatedly played into British hands by revealing Germany as no more careful of neutral rights and interests than Britain was'. Not only the invasion of Belgium, which the British, of course, never failed to mention, but also Germany's response to the Allied naval stranglehold — submarine warfare — prevented Germany being able to fully score propaganda points. The difference in newness and intensity between blockade (a traditional weapon) and submarine warfare (very new) 'worked to Britain's psychological advantage':

> The blockade of Germany directly killed no neutrals, though the threat that they might get killed if they didn't obey the Anglo-French (and later American) rules was certainly there in the background. Ultimately, no doubt, the Allied blockade tended towards the killing of German civilians, if German soldiers were given first claim on food; but this was a very long delayed conclusion, which could be easily avoided by any government desirous to avoid it. Submarine warfare, by contrast, could not only not avoid killing British civilians; at its most intensive, it killed neutrals too.[31]

Time and again neutral opinion, unhappy with British policy, was swung back to viewing it more favourably by German use of submarine warfare. Unrestricted U-boat warfare after January 1917 left neutrals more or less giving the Allies (after April 1917 joined by the most powerful neutral, the United States) the benefit of the doubt. This was very much the case too with British critics of official policy. For Macdonell the entry of the Americans into the war invited new historical parallels:

> ... three times have the United States interposed with armed force in the affairs of the Old World .... First in 1805; next in 1815; and lastly in 1917, and all three times with the like object — in 1805 and 1815 to put down the unrestricted invasion of the freedom of the seas by the Barbary pirates, and in 1917 to stop unrestricted U-boat warfare. The American troops and sailors are now doing much the same work as did Admiral Decatur's ships against the Bey of Algiers.[32]

This invitation to view German policy as 'barbaric' in a new, literal sense effectively diverted attention from the equally dubious British policy of arming merchantmen, especially the notorious 'Q-ships' (merchantmen pretending to be defenceless but actually armed).[33] The newness — in 1908 Lawrence had called submarines a 'monstrous race of maritime hermaphrodites'[34] — and the spectacular nature of submarine warfare meant that it tended to arouse repugnance sooner than blockade, a weapon hallowed by long use (though not in its present all-encompassing form). It was perhaps inevitable that international lawyers would be influenced by 'patriotic' considerations during wartime — neither philosophers nor historians had been able to resist. We have only to compare T. J. Lawrence writing in 1908, where he criticises equally the categorising of food as absolute contraband and arming merchantmen (the British wartime policy), and the mining of the high seas and the use of submarines (the German wartime policy), with Lawrence writing in 1919, to see the great changes wrought by the pressures of war.[35] Perhaps, too, the international lawyer, standing closer than the philosopher or the historian to the realities of power, had less room for manoeuvre. As J. E. G. de Montmorency noted in February 1915:

> No doubt, from a juridical point of view, it is important to see if possible the processes of growth by which legal doctrines are expanded to meet new conditions; but from the point of view of the businessman and statesmen the practical question of the moment is the thing that must be faced, it is the business of the jurist later to show that this new attitude was in fact an inevitable growth.[36]

Appendix 3: Academic Membership of the Anglo/British-German Friendship Society

W. R. Anson (Warden of All Souls)
Sir Thomas Barlow (Professor of Medicine, London)
C. R. Beazley (Professor of History, Birmingham)
K. Breul (Professor of German, Cambridge)
A. J. Butler (Professor of Italian, London)
E. Caird (Master of Balliol College, Oxford)
Sir William M. Conway (Professor of Art, Cambridge)
T. W. Rhys Davies (Professor of Camparative Religion, London)
Sir Herbert von Herkhomer (Professor of Art, Oxford)
Sir John Macdonell (Professor of Comparative Law, London)
Alfred Marshall (Professor of Economics, Cambridge)
J. H. Muirhead (Professor of Philosophy, Birmingham)
W. P. Paterson (Professor of Theology, Edinburgh)
Sir William Ramsay (Professor of Old Philology, Aberdeen)
J. G. Robertson (Professor of German, London)
M. E. Sadler (Vice-Chancellor, Leeds University)
A. W. Ward (Master of Peterhouse, Cambridge)

Appendix 4: Academic Membership of the National Peace Congress

J. Bryce
E. G. Brown (Professor of Arabic, Cambridge)
J. E. Carpenter (Principal of Manchester College, Oxford)
T. J. Lawrence (Reader in International Law, Bristol)
Sir John Macdonell (Professor of Comparative Law, London)
W. J. Roberts (Professor of Economics, Cardiff)
A. Schuster (Professor of Physics, Manchester)
F. E. Weiss (Vice-Chancellor, Manchester University)

Appendix 5: Academics in Wartime Whitehall

The involvement of British academics in government service during the Second World War
— subject of many an autobiographical or fictional account of the corridors of power[1] —
had been foreshadowed during the 1914–1918 war. The Civil Service is an environment not
unlike that which academics normally inhabit, and, when the war broke out in 1914,
university men too old for active service searched out old school or college friends in the
hope of finding anything which appeared to provide useful employment. Sir Charles
Oman, Professor of History at Oxford, found a job on the Neutral Press Committee
through his old school chum Sir John Simon, the Home Secretary.[2] Almost anything, it
seemed, was better than lecturing to half-empty classrooms. Some, like the Oxford
philosopher and ancient historian R. G. Collingwood, found jobs which required certain of
their professional skills. Collingwood found a job in Admiralty Intelligence from 1915
onwards. Here he 'employed his knowledge of French, German, Spanish and Italian, as
well as his skill in sifting evidence which he had developed as an archaeologist'.[3] In his
Autobiography (1939) Collingwood tells of how he worked on a philosophical treatise, *Truth
and Contradiction*, during this time, and Admiralty Intelligence seems to have become
rather a haven for philosophers. Besides the usual clutch of classicists, Collingwood's
colleagues included the Kantian scholar Norman Kemp Smith (who had also worked for
Wellington House) and two Oxford moral philosophers, H. J. Paton and Hastings
Rashdall.[4] Working closely with the Admiralty, as well as with the Board of Trade, was a
small group of academics who organised the Trade Intelligence Section of Postal
Censorship. This 'Trade Clearing House' was formally recognised as a branch of the War
Trade Department in February 1915, with the job of licensing exports. A few months later
it was again transformed into the War Trade Intelligence Department, with two Oxford
historians as chairman and vice-chairman — T. H. Penson (Pembroke College) and H. W.
C. Davis (Balliol College).

So successful was Davis in his job of drafting daily minutes for the Cabinet on the
progress of the commercial blockade of the Central Powers that he was chosen to represent
the Department on the British delegation at Versailles in 1919. This in turn led to a C.B.E.
in the New Year's Honours List, and offers of Vice-Chancellorships from the universities
of Liverpool and Sheffield. The Chancellor of the Exchequer was apparently also
considering Davis for an 'important position', and all this made Davis hesitate before
returning to academic life. But, apart from taking over the direction of the Department of
Overseas Trade for six weeks (March–April 1919) while his superiors were absent, Davis
did not rise in the civil service.[5] However, his wartime experience seems to have had a
profound effect on his scholarly activities. The editor of Stubbs' *Select Charters* and the
author of *England Under the Normans and Angevins* now turned his attention to the
antecedents of the war. Contributions to Harold Temperley's *History of the Peace
Conference of Paris* (1920–24) and articles on pre-war diplomacy in the *English Historical
Review* testify to his new concern with contemporary history.[6]

Lloyd George did not have Asquith's intimate links with Oxford, and he is better known
for recruiting businessmen than academics to government service during wartime.
However, he was not averse to advisors or even ministers (H. A. L. Fisher) from the
universities. One member of his secretariat — 'the garden suburb' — was W. G. S. Adams,
Gladstone Professor of Political Theory and Institutions at Oxford (1912–33) and founder
of *Political Quarterly* (1914). Adams had joined the Ministry of Munitions, which was
well-stocked with Oxford dons, in 1915. A year later he joined Lloyd George's staff, where

he remained until 1919, editing the War Cabinet Reports (1917–18) and working on labour matters. Adams was also a member of the commission which examined the Civil Service (1918), and he acted as liaison officer between Lloyd George and Sir Horace Plunkett, chairman of the Irish Convention. However, he was probably closer to Lord Milner than to Lloyd George, which may account for Beatrice Webb's description of Adams as 'a high-browed idealist' who wanted to 'change the 'world spirit' rather than alter social machinery'.[7] The other academic member of Lloyd George's secretariat was Arthur Greenwood, until just before the war Lecturer in Economics at Leeds. In 1914 he had been appointed General Secretary of the Council for the Study of International Relations. In 1916 he became a member of the secretariat, and between 1917 and 1919 worked in the Ministry of Reconstruction under Christopher Addison. Later still he became one of the leading members of the Labour Party until his death in 1954.[8]

Lloyd George's other notable academic appointment was of H. A. L. Fisher as President of the Board of Education (December 1916) with the task of introducing major educational reforms.[9] Fisher was sensitive to criticism from fellow liberal academics over his decision to work for the politician who had so recently deposed Asquith as Premier. In the eyes of people like Gilbert Murray, Lloyd George seemed as dangerous and ambitious as Gladstone had to an earlier generation of academic liberals during the Home Rule controversy.[10] 'All my sympathies are with Asquith and Grey. The press campaign against them has been hateful', Fisher wrote to Murray. But his decision to accept Lloyd George's offer of political office had not been 'as a politician but as an educationist'. And in another letter to Murray, Fisher defended his choice as one which allowed him to do 'a big piece of national work'.[11] Fisher's doubts about Lloyd George were shared, in more extreme form, by the leading academic liberal of the next generation, John Maynard Keynes, who from January 1915 worked full-time at the Treasury. With many of his friends conscientious objectors, Keynes found the moves towards the introduction of conscription made his position difficult. However, a letter to his mother of January 1916 shows a genuine liking for life in the corridors of power, mixed with a dislike of some of the men he found there:

> Things drift on, and I shall stay now, I expect, until they begin to torture one of my friends. I believe a real split now and a taste of trouble would bring peace nearer, not postpone it; otherwise I'd swallow a great deal. I've been very busy and with occasional excursions into high life — met the P.M. at dinner on Saturday, refused to dine with the old scoundrel on Sunday, banqueted with the Lord Mayor yesterday.[12]

A year later he vented his feeling about Lloyd George to Duncan Grant: 'Did you read his last speech? 'The war is a road paved with gold and cemented with blood.' God curse him'. And again to Grant: 'I work for a Government I despise for ends I think horrid'.[13] In the event, he did not break from Lloyd George until the Peace Conference in 1919.

A fuller list of academics employed in government departments and secretariats follows.

1. *Admiralty Intelligence*:
F. E. Adcock (King's College, Cambridge; later Professor of Ancient History, Cambridge)
C. Bailey (Balliol College, Oxford; classics)
J. Baillie (Professor of Moral Philosophy, Aberdeen), O.B.E. 1918
W. M. Calder (Professor of Greek, Manchester)
R. G. Collingwood (Pembroke College, Oxford; classics and philosophy)
H. N. Dickson (Professor of Geography, Reading)

G. B. Grundy (Corpus Christi College, Oxford; ancient history)

L. G. Wickham Legg (New College, Oxford; history)

R. B. Mowat (Corpus Christi College, Oxford; later Professor of History, Bristol)

J. Orr (Lecturer in French, Queen Mary College, London; from 1919 Professor of French at Manchester)

H. J. Paton (Queen's College, Oxford; philosophy)

H. Rashdall (New College, Oxford; philosophy)

N. Kemp Smith (Professor of Philosophy, Princeton; from 1919 Professor of Philosophy, Edinburgh)

W. B. Stevenson (Professor of Hebrew, Glasgow)

2. *War Office Intelligence*:

S. Alexander (Professor of Philosophy, Manchester)

C. F. Crutwell (Hertford College, Oxford; history)

J. D. Denniston (Hertford College, Oxford; classics)

G. Gordon (Professor of English, Leeds and later Oxford)

G. B. Grundy

R. Hackforth (Sidney Sussex College, Cambridge; classics)

R. G. D. Laffan (Queen's College, Cambridge; history)

W. Lorimer (Lecturer in Greek, St. Andrews)

K. W. M. Pickthorn (Corpus Christi College, Cambridge; history)

J. T. Sheppard (King's College, Cambridge; classics)

H. Sumner (All Souls College, Oxford, from 1919)

H. Temperley (Peterhouse, Cambridge; history tutor and later Regius Professor)

C. K. Webster (Professor of Modern History, Liverpool and later Professor of International History at Aberystwyth and London)

3. *War Trade Intelligence Department*:

H. W. C. Davis (Balliol College, Oxford; history tutor and later Regius Professor)

T. H. Penson (Pembroke College, Oxford; economics)

F. M. Powicke (Professor of History, Belfast and later at Manchester and Oxford)

R. B. Rait (Professor of Scottish History, Glasgow)

C. E. Vaughan (Professor of English at Leeds until 1913)

W. T. Waugh (Lecturer in History, Manchester)

4. *Ministry of Munitions*:

W. G. S. Adams (Professor of Political Theory and Institutions, Oxford)

C. Bailey

J. B. Baillie

F. M. Cornford (Trinity College, Cambridge; classics tutor and later Professor of Ancient Philosophy)

H. W. Garrod (Merton College, Oxford; classics tutor and later Professor of Poetry)

A. E. W. Hazel (Jesus College, Oxford; law)

A. J. Jenkinson (Brasenose College, Oxford; classics)

W. T. S. Stallybrass (Vice-Principal of Brasenose College), O.B.E. 1918

5. *Other*:

W. G. S. Adams: Lloyd George's Secretariat

E. Barker (New College, Oxford; philosophy) Ministry of Labour

Z. N. Brooke (Gonville and Caius College, Cambridge; history) Ministry of Food

G. G. G. Butler (Corpus Christi College, Cambridge; history) News Department of the Foreign Office, then Department of Information

J. H. Clapham (King's College, Cambridge; economics tutor and later Professor of Economic History) Board of Trade and Cabinet Committee on Priorities

A. Greenwood (former Lecturer in Economics, Leeds) Lloyd George's Secretariat

A. P. Higgins (Lecturer and later Professor of International Law, Cambridge) Treasury and the Trade Division of the Admiralty

H. S. Jones (Trinity College, Cambridge; classics) Foreign Office

J. M. Keynes (King's College, Cambridge; economics) Treasury

A. D. Lindsay (Balliol College, Oxford; politics) Deputy Controller of Labour in France

R. McKenzie (St. John's College, Cambridge; classics) Foreign Office

C. W. C. Oman (Chichele Professor of History, Oxford) Neutral Press Committee of the Home Office and from 1916 attached to the Foreign Office, C.B.E. 1918 and K.B.E. 1920

L. Oppenheim (Professor of International Law, Cambridge) Foreign Office

A. C. Pigou (Professor of Economics, Cambridge) Board of Trade

6. *Paris Peace Conference, 1918–1919*:

W. M. Calder: Foreign Office advisor

H. W. C. Davis: Foreign Office 'Intelligence Clearing House'

C. Guillebaud (St. John's College, Cambridge; economics) Supreme Economic Council advisor

A. P. Higgins: Advisor to the Admiralty

J. M. Keynes: Treasury

R. B. Mowat: War Cabinet Secretariat under Smuts

H. J. Paton: Foreign Office advisor

T. H. Penson: Foreign Office 'Intelligence Clearing House'

H. Sumner: Military Intelligence Section (Assistant Secretary)

C. K. Webster: Military Intelligence Section (Secretary)

N.B. For academics working in propaganda agencies, see Chapter 10.

Appendix 6: List of Signatories of the October 1920 Oxford Manifesto

W. G. S. Adams, E. Barker, A. D. Lindsay, G. Murray, R. Bridges, H. W. C. Davis and
    E. Armstrong (Pro-Provost Queen's)
J. D. Beazley (Christ Church)
H. Boyd (Principal of Hertford)
G. C. Bourne (Professor of Zoology)
J. E. Carpenter
E. F. Carritt (University, Hertford)
R. W. Chapman (Secretary to the Delegates of the University Press)
A. C. Clark (Professor of Latin)
G. A. Cooke (Professor of Hebrew)
Sir Arthur Evans (Professor of Prehistoric Archaeology)
P. Gardner (Professor of Classical Archaeology)
E. E. Genner (Jesus)
H. Goudy (Emeritus Professor of Civil Law)
B. P. Grenfell (Professor of Papyrology)
J. S. Haldane (New)
G. H. Hardy (Professor of Geometry)
A. C. Headlam (Professor of Divinity)
C. B. Heberden (former Principal of Brasenose)
D. G. Hogarth (Keeper of the Ashmolean Museum)
L. P. Jacks (Principal of Manchester)
H. A. James (President of St. John's)
H. H. Joachim (Professor of Logic)
H. W. B. Joseph (New)
S. Langdon (Professor of Assyriology)
T. E. Lawrence (All Souls)
W. Lock (Professor of Divinity)
F. J. Lys (Provost of Worcester)
J. C. Masterman (Christ Church)
J. Murray (Christ Church)
J. L. Myres (Professor of Ancient History)
C. S. Orwin (Research Officer in Agricultural Economics)
R. L. Ottley (Professor of Pastoral Theology)
L. R. Phelps (Provost of Oriel)
Judge Radcliffe (All Souls)
C. G. Robertson (All Souls)
W. R. Ross (Oriel)
A. S. Russell (Lee's Reader)
C. H. Sampson (Principal of Brasenose)
W. Sanday (Emeritus Professor of Divinity)
F. C. S. Schiller (Corpus Christi)
W. B. Selbie (Mansfield)
J. A. Smith (Professor of Moral and Metaphysical Philosophy)
W. A. Spooner (New)

G. H. Stevenson (University, Balliol)
J. L. Stocks (St. John's)
T. B. Strong (former Dean of Christ Church)
T. H. Tizard (Oriel)
M. N. Tod (Oriel)
J. Wells (Warden of Wadham)
H. H. Williams
***

C. M. M. Adye (St. Hugh's)
M. P. Appleby (St. John's)
C. Bailey (Balliol)
J. V. Bartlett (Exeter)
J. Bell (Queen's)
K. N. Bell (Balliol)
K. Bourdillon (University)
F. H. Brabant (Wadham)
A. M. Bruce (Vice-Principal, Somerville)
J. McL. Campbell (Hertford)
A. J. Carlyle (University)
E. I. Carlyle (Lincoln)
D. L. Chapman (Jesus)
M. V. Clarke (Somerville)
N. Cunliffe (Forestry School)
H. C. Deneke (Lady Margaret Hall)
J. D. Denniston (Hertford)
C. H. Dodd (University)
P. W. Dodd (Jesus)
G. Elton (Queen's)
H. J. George (Jesus)
T. W. Grundy (Christ Church)
H. L. Henderson (New)
W. E. Hiley (Queen's)
C. N. Hinshelwood (Balliol)
R. H. Hodgkin (Queen's)
M. Holroyd (Brasenose)
J. S. Huxley (New)
M. L. Jacks (Wadham)
K. E. Kirk (Magdalen)
R. Lennard (Wadham)
A. E. Levett (Vice-Principal, St. Hilda's)
K. K. M. Leys (University)
E. C. Lodge (Vice-Principal, Lady Margaret Hall)
H. L. Lorimer (Somerville)
E. W. Lummis (Worcester)
K. H. McCutcheon (Lady Margaret Hall)
D. G. McGregor (Balliol)
I. Macrae (Manchester)
N. Micklem (New)

W. H. Moberley (Lincoln)
W. H. Moberley (Principal, St. Hilda's)
A. W. Pickard-Cambridge (Balliol)
E. G. C. Poole (New)
M. K. Pope (Somerville)
H. J. Pybus (St. Hilda's)
H. R. Raikes (Exeter)
A. E. J. Rawlinson (Christ Church)
A. M. H. Rogers (St. Hugh's)
E. W. Rooke (St. Hilda's)
J. W. Russell (Balliol)
N. V. Sidgwick (Lincoln)
M. G. Skipworth (Lady Margaret Hall)
A. H. Smith (New)
E. M. Spearing (St. Hugh's)
J. Spens (Lady Margaret Hall)
C. G. Stone (Balliol)
B. H. Streeter (Queen's)
H. T. Wade-Geny (Wadham)
A. F. Walden (New)
E. Walker (Balliol)
C. R. Young (Somerville)

NOTES

Introduction

1. A. H. Halsey, 'British Universities', *European J. of Sociology*, III (1962), 97.

2. H. Perkin, *The Key Profession*, 1969, pp. 26–7.

3. J. Ben-David, *Centers of Learning*, N.Y., 1977, p. 21.

4. V. H. H. Green, *The Universities*, Harmondsworth, 1969, p. 73.

5. T. W. Bamford, 'Public school masters: a 19th-century profession', in *Education and the Professions* (ed. T. G. Cook), 1973, p. 40.

6. Perkin, *op. cit.*, p. 39.

7. J. Ben-David and A. Zloczower, 'Universities and Academic Systems in Modern Societies', *European J. of Sociology*, III (1962), 69.

8. F. K. Ringer, *The Decline of the German Mandarins*, Cambridge, Mass., 1969, p. 3.

9. S. Rothblatt, *The Revolution of the Dons*, 1968; A. Engel, *From Clergyman to Don*, Oxford, 1983 — respectively on Cambridge and Oxford.

10. Veblen's *The Higher Learning in America* (1918) was written well before the war. Paulsen's *The German Universities and University Study* (1902) appeared in English translation in 1906.

11. See: Ringer, *op. cit.*; K. Schwabe, *Wissenschaft u. Kriegsmoral*, Göttingen, 1969; C. F. McClelland, *State, Society and University in Germany 1700–1914*, Cambridge, 1980.

12. R. Hofstadter and W. Metzger, *The Development of Academic Freedom in the United States*, N.Y., 1955.

13. C. S. Gruber, *Mars and Minerva*, Baton Rouge, 1975. Cf. G. T. Blakey, *Historians on the Homefront*, Lexington, Kentucky, 1973, for a much less imaginative approach to the First World War.

14. F. Mulhearn, 'Introduction' to R. Debray, *Teachers, Writers, Celebrities*, 1981, pp. xviii–xix.

15. 'The Intellectual Aristocracy', in *Studies in Social History* (ed. J. H. Plumb), 1955, pp. 244, 285.

16. A. H. Halsey and M. Trow, *The British Academics*, 1971, p. 139. There were about 500 teachers each in provincial 'redbrick' and in Scottish universities, with under 250 in London. There were more than twice the number of professors alone (c. 4,000) in German universities at the same time.

17. For the way in which Scottish universities were 'anglicised' before 1914, see the differing interpretations in G. E. Davie, *The Democratic Intellect*, 2nd. ed., Edinburgh, 1964 and R. D. Anderson, *Education and Opportunity in Victorian Scotland*, Oxford, 1983.

18. P. Anderson, 'Components of the National Culture', in *Student Power* (eds. A. Cockburn and R. Blackburn), Harmondsworth, 1969, p. 228.

19. F. Mulhearn, *The Moment of 'Scrutiny'*, 1979, pp. 9–10 and n. 20; Halsey and Trow, pp. 144–5.

20. Ben-David, p. 22.

21. S. Rothblatt, *Tradition and Change in English Liberal Education*, 1976, p. 164. For France, see T. W. Clark, *Prophets and Patrons*, Cambridge, Mass., 1973, pp. 28, 181–2. On the United States, see J. Herbst, *The German Historical School in America*, Ithaca, N.Y., 1965, *passim*.

22. G. Haines, *Essays on German Influence upon English Education and Science, 1850–1919*, Hamden, Conn., 1969, p. 4. Cf. W. Schirmer, 'German Literature, Historiography and Theology in 19th-Century England', *German Life and Letters*, N.S. I, 3 (April 1948),

168. Generally speaking the private scholar gave way increasingly to the university-based scholar.

23. Hofstadter and Metzger, p. 373. Literally 'scholarship', 'learning', 'science'.

24. See M. Richter, *The Politics of Conscience*, 1964.

25. Rothblatt, *Tradition and Change*, p. 165.

26. See J. Sparrow, *Mark Pattison and the Idea of a University*, pp. 110–25. For similar plans for the University of London, see K. Pearson, 'The Proposed University for London', *Academy*, 26, 660 (27 Dec. 1884), 430.

27. See the table in G. Hollenberg, *Englische Interesse am Kaiserreich*, Wiesbaden, 1974, p. 294 and in J. Conrad, *The German Universities for the Last Fifty Years*, Glasgow, 1885, p. 41. The numbers of British students rose from 26 (1835) to 42 (1860) to 71 (1880), but always remained 5% or 6% of the total number of foreign students. There seem to have been temporary drops in their numbers in the early 1870s, 1880s and 1900s. U.S. students rose sharply in number and percentage from 1835 (4 or 1%) to 1880 (173 or 15.5%). But the largest group (apart from Swiss and Austrians) was Russian: 18% of foreign students in 1880. By the 1900s foreign students, according to McClelland (*State, Society and Universtiy*, p. 250) made up nearly 9% of the total, double the percentage of the 1860s. Restrictions on the entry of foreign students were introduced in 1913.

28. *Times Educational Supplement*, 10 (16 June 1911), 91. Carlyle was addressing the 'Albert Committee' which sought to promote the study of German in British schools and universities. For a list of British students at German universities before 1914, see Appendix I.

29. H. A. L. Fisher, *James Bryce*, 1927, I, 58–9 and J. Bryce, 'The Mission of the State Universities' (June 1908), reprinted in his *University and Historical Addresses*, 1913, pp. 156–7. Cf. his 'Presidential Address' to the *International Congress of Historical Studies*, 1913.

30. *German Universities and University Study*, 1906, pp. vi–vii.

31. 'German Schools of History', reprinted in Acton, *Historical Essays and Studies*, 1907, p. 370.

32. McClelland, *State, Society and University*, p. 274. For an early critical voice, see 'Housman's Cambridge Inaugural', *TLS*, 67 (9 May 1968), 476 (its first publication).

33. S. Rothblatt, 'The Diversification of Higher Education in England', in K. Jarausch (ed.), *The Transformation of Higher Learning, 1860-1930*, Chicago, 1983, pp. 146–8. Until the 1880s provincial universities and colleges relied on private sources of finance (or, in the case of Nottingham College, municipal funds). Between 1882 and 1884 grants were given successively to the new Welsh colleges. From 1889 government money was provided for 11 institutions, 14 by 1904, but never on a generous scale — in 1904 £54,000, in 1905 £100,000, in 1912 £150,000. This was still far short of the £500,000 Sidney Webb considered necessary for proper financial support. R. O. Berdahl, *British Universities and the State*, 1959, pp. 48–57.

34. 'Preface' to Paulsen, *op. cit.*, p. vii. At this time Sadler was Professor of the History and Administration of Education at Manchester (1903-11). He had contributed to special reports on German education for the Board of Education.

35. Bryce, 'Mission of the State Universities', *loc. cit.* For contemporary German criticism of discrimination, see M. Weber articles from the *Frankfurter Zeitung* (Sept. 1908) reprinted as 'The Power of the State and the Dignity of the Academic Calling in Imperial Germany …', *Minerva*, XII, 4 (1973), 17. Cf. McClelland, *op. cit.*, pp. 289–30 and Ringer, pp. 136–7, 141–3.

36. See the comments of M. E. Grant Duff, member of the Royal Commission on Oxford in the 1850s and friend of the 'reformers' Benjamin Jowett and Mark Pattison, *cit*. Haines, *Essays*, p. 102.

37. 'The Future of the 19th-Century Idea of a University', *Minerva*, VI, i (Autumn 1967), 4–5.

38. Ben-David and Zloczower, 49–50; Ben-David, pp. 22–3, 103–6. Birmingham (1900), Liverpool (1903), Leeds (1904), Sheffield (1905), Bristol (1909) received university charters. Southampton (1902) and Nottingham (1903) became university colleges and remained so before the war. If anything, these new institutions came to resemble the older universities, or at least sought to.

39. Ben-David and Zloczower, 48.

40. *Cit*. V. H. H. Green, p. 72. Cf. the following accounts by participants in the debate: J. C. Masterman, *On the Chariot Wheel*, Oxford, 1976, pp. 148–9; C. H. Firth, *A Plea for the Historical Teaching of History*, Oxford, 1904; O. H. Ball (ed.), *Sidney Ball*, Oxford, 1923, pp. 189–201; L. R. Farnell, *An Oxonian Looks Back*, 1934, pp. 105, 272; P. Gardner, *Oxford at the Crossroads*, 1903; F. J. Haverfield, 'Biographical Note' to *Essays by Henry Francis Pelham*, Oxford, 1911, pp. x–xi.

41. Engel, *From Clergyman to Don*, p. 284.

42. Rothblatt, 'The Diversification of Higher Education . . .', p. 136.

43. Engel, *op. cit*., p. 255. The value of fellowships dropped to between £80 and £250 p. a. depending on the (Oxford) college. Green, p. 180.

44. See R. M. Crawford, '*A Bit of a Rebel*', Sydney, 1975, pp. 108–10; J. E. Todd, 'Apprenticeship of a Professor of History, 1903–1919', *History*, XLIV (1959), 124–33; R. M. MacIver, *As A Tale is Told*, Chicago, 1968, pp. 74–5.

45. Halsey and Trow, p. 149; Perkin, *Key Profession*, pp. 23, 39 and 'Manchester and the Origins of the A.U.T.', *British University Annual*, 1964, 88. On the 'Corporation of Junior Faculty' in Germany, see Ringer, p. 55.

46. A. W. Coats, 'John Elliotson Symes, Henry George and Academic Freedom in Nottingham during the 1880s', *Renaissance and Modern Studies*, VII (1963), 113–37. Professors received, on average, £300 p. a. plus 2/3 student fees in the 1890s, and £600 without fees by 1910. But at Leeds, for example, professors could earn £1,000 p. a. — not far short of the most remunerative Oxbridge chairs (theology, divinity and related subjects). Lecturers and assistant lecturers got £70–£150 without fees in the 1890s, and an average of £200 p. a. by 1918 — although some earned as little as £30 p. a. See Halsey and Trow, p. 173; Perkin, 'Manchester . . .', 88–91; P. H. J. H. Gosden and A. J. Taylor, *Studies in the History of a University, 1874–1974*, Leeds, 1975, p. 8; E. J. Somerset, *The Birth of a University*, Oxford, 1934, pp. 23–4; T. Kelly, *For the Advancement of Learning*, Liverpool, 1981, pp. 91–2.

47. G. J. Stigler, 'Alfred Marshall's Lectures on *Progress and Poverty*', *J. of Law and Economics*, XII, I (April 1969), 217–26; J. Whitaker, 'Alfred Marshall, the Years 1877–1885', *History of Political Economy*, IV (1972), 25.

48. VIII, 5 (29 Oct. 1910), 196–7.

49. J. Beveridge, *An Epic of Clare Market*, 1960, p. 66. See the letters of support from two former Principals (W. A. S. Hewins and H. J. Mackinder), *The Times*, 22 Oct. 1910, p. 10b and 24 Oct. p. 14c.

50. *Free Thought in the Social Sciences*, 1926, p. 54. On Hobson's failure to obtain academic employment, see his *Confessions of an Economic Heretic*, 1938, pp. 30–1. On the situation in the United States, see Hofstadter and Metzger, chapter IX.

51. *Cit.* A. N. Shimmin, *The University of Leeds*, Cambridge, 1954, p. 40. Cf. Gosden and Taylor, pp. 239–40.

52. See eg. Coats, 'John Elliotson Symes . . .', 112.

53. E. Barker, *Age and Youth*, 1953, p. 334.

54. L. Woolf, *Beginning Again*, 1964, p. 185.

55. MacIver, *As a Tale that is Told*, pp. 61–2.

56. C. Petrie, *A Historian Looks at his World*, 1972, p. 80. After the Second World War the 'cut-off date' was moved to 1914. At Cambridge the situation was the same: increased emphasis on European history after changes in the Tripos in 1897, but still (despite a paper on International Law) focused on the period before 1870. See *The Students' Handbook to . . . Cambridge, 1914–15*, pp. 407–18 and G. Kitson Clark, 'A Hundred Years of Teaching History at Cambridge, 1873–1973', *Historical J.*, XVI, 3 (1973), 548–50.

57. *Short Journey*, 1942, p. 38. At Oxford there was the occasional undergraduate, like Lewis Bernstein (later Namier) or his cousin Ludwig Ehrlich, or, less frequently, a college fellow, like Arthur Zimmern (New College, 1904–9), with some knowledge of central and eastern Europe. Generally their talk of the danger of war was greeted with amusement. See A. Toynbee, *Acquaintances*, 1967, pp. 50, 64–5, 74.

58. R. T. Shannon, *Gladstone and the Bulgarian Agitation, 1876*, 1963, p. 202. The comparison is made, not merely because of 'the brilliance of patronage and the opposition which it evoked among the greatest names in literature, art, science and philosophy', but also because the critics of the agitation were 'men of the emerging era of idealism, imperialism, power, of challenge to the assumptions of mid-century Liberalism'. There were, in other words, clear similarities between British Liberal Imperialism and French radical nationalism.

59. A. and E. M. Sidgwick, *Henry Sidgwick*, 1906, pp. 581–2, 576–7; J. Sully, *My Life and Friends*, 1918, pp. 286–7; F. W. Maitland, *Letters*, 1965, pp. 249, 258–9.

60. 'The Morality of Strife', *IJE*, I, 1 (Oct. 1890), 14. In reprinting this in his *Practical Ethics* (1898) Sidgwick omitted the phrase beginning 'doubtless right . . .' (p. 106).

61. *The Transvaal War*, 1899, pp. 4–7. Cf. the critical notice in the *Cambridge Rev.*, XXI (23 Nov. 1899), 102–3.

62. *Cambridge Rev.*, XXI (19 and 26 Oct. 1899; 22 Feb. 1900; 1 and 3 Mar. 1900; 3, 17 and 31 May 1900), 27–8, 43–4, 227–8, 244, 292, 353–4. Cf. O. Browning, *Memories of Later Years*, 1923, p. 60.

63. C. Mallet, *History of the University of Oxford*, 1927, III, 476; J. G. Lockhart and C. M. Woodhouse, *Rhodes*, 1963, p. 404; *The Times*, 20 June 1899, p. 10c (for the protest letter) and *Oxford Mag.*, XX (21 June 1899), 6–7 (for the Vice-Chancellor's refusal to print the letter in the official gazette).

64. H. Jones and J. H. Muirhead, *The Life and Philosophy of Edward Caird*, Glasgow, 1921, pp. 153–4; F. W. Hirst, *In the Golden Days*, 1947, p. 199. Caird was a supporter of radical causes like the Russian Strikers' Relief Fund of 1905. See B. Hollingsworth, 'The Society of Friends of Russian Freedom: English Liberals and Russian Socialists', *Oxford Slavonic Papers*, N.S. III (1970), 61.

65. *Oxford Mag.*, XIX, 16 (13 Mar. 1901), 269–70 and XX, 11–14 (5–26 Feb. 1902), 153, 186–7, 208, 224–5, 227, 244. Cf. Farnell, pp. 148–57, 327.

66. Eg. at Bangor and Aberystwyth. See J. E. Lloyd (ed.), *Sir Harry Reichel, 1856–1931*, Cardiff, 1934, p. 87; E. L. Ellis, *The University College of Wales Aberystwyth, 1872–1972*, Cardiff, 1972, p. 174. Cf. *Cambridge Rev.*, XXI, 527 (25 Jan. 1900), 160.

67. See the letter of E. A. Sonnenschein (Professor of Classics, Birmingham) to H. G.

Fiedler (Professor of German, Oxford), 21 Jan. 1902, Fiedler-Harding Mss. F.H. 33. Cf. the letter to *The Times*, 21 June 1902, p. 11c.

68. Walter Raleigh (then Professor of English at Glasgow), 'The Anatomy of the Pro-Boer', *National Rev.*, XXXVIII (Sept. 1901), 55–7. The war was a 'struggle for existence'.

69. See Appendix III.

70. *Anglo-German Courier*, I, 2 (13 Jan. 1906), 15–17. This answered a manifesto from 14 German intellectuals.

71. *Ibid.*, I, 23 (8 June 1906), 240–1. Cf. L. Stein (ed.), *England and Germany*, 1912, pp. 28–34. Breul had come to Cambridge first as a Lecturer in 1884. He became Reader (1899) and then Professor (1910) of German.

72. H. A. L. Fisher, *An Unfinished Autobiography*, 1940, p. 82 and *The War: Its Causes and Issues*, 1914, p. 11; T. F. Tout, 'Mark Hovell (1888–1916)' in Hovell, *The Chartist Movement*, Manchester, 1916, p. xxi.

73. C. F. McClelland, *German Historians and England*, Cambridge, 1971, pp. 168–90, 201–13.

74. Woolf, *Beginning Again*, p. 185.

75. A. J. P. Taylor, *The Troublemakers*, 1969, p. 94; H. Weinroth, 'Norman Angell and 'The Great Illusion': An Episode in pre-1914 Pacifism', *Historical J.*, XVII, 3 (1974), 560; M. Ceadal, *Pacifism in Britain, 1914–45*, Oxford, 1980, chapter 4; J. C. Masterman, p. 96. See membership lists in the Angellite journal *War and Peace*.

76. Green, *Lectures on the Principles of Political Obligation*, new ed. 1941, p. 178 ('as the trade between members of the different states becomes freer and more full, the sense of common interests between them, which war would infringe, becomes stronger'); Taylor, *op. cit.*, p. 93.

77. Tillyard, esp. pp. 17, 29–33 ('the fall of Athens was her economic salvation, and for her it was lucky that it came when it did'). On the resolution in the Union, see C. E. Fayle (ed.), *Harold Wright*, Cambridge, 1934, pp. 41–2 and *War and Peace*, I, 6 (Mar. 1914), n.p. Two young economics lecturers (later holders of the chairs at Cambridge and Oxford), D. H. Robertson and D. H. Henderson, were both fervent Angellites.

78. Pp. 275–6. *The Great Illusion* is cited on p. 425. Cf. MacIver, *The Modern State*, 1926, pp. 246–8.

79. *Community*, pp. 423–4, 336. MacIver repeated much of this 30 years later in *Towards an Abiding Peace* (1944).

80. Green, *op. cit.*, p. 176 ('Till all the methods have been exhausted by which nature can be brought into the service of man, till society is so organised that everyone's capacities have free scope for their development, there is no need to resort to war for a field in which patriotism may display itself').

81. Reprinted in *War* (eds. L. Bramson and G. W. Goethals), N.Y., 1968, p. 23. The essay had originally been given as a lecture at Stanford University (Oct. 1909) and had been widely published in U.S. periodicals.

82. J. E. Carpenter, *The Promotion of International Peace Through Universities*, 1912, p. 4. Cf. T. J. Lawrence, 'The Tsar's Prescript', *IJE*, IX, 2 (Jan. 1899), 145.

83. *Principles of Social Reconstruction*, 1916, p. 95. See also his review of 'The Moral Equivalent of War', in *Cambridge Rev.*, XXXIII, 817 (16 Nov. 1911), 118. Russell wrongly dated James's essay to the time of the Spanish-American War (1898) which James had opposed.

84. 'Moral Equivalent', p. 27. James cited *Justice and Liberty* (1909), one of Dickinson's

then much-admired political dialogues, as exhibiting these faults. On Dickinson, see N. Wedd, 'Goldie Dickinson: The Latest Cambridge Platonist', *Criterion*, XII, 47 (Jan. 1933), 178 and E. M. Forster, *Goldsworthy Lowes Dickinson*, new ed. 1973, pp. 95–6.

85. 'War and Peace', *Independent Rev.*, X, 34 (July 1906), 115. This was a review of F. W. Hirst's anonymous *Arbiter in Council* (1906). Dickinson, Hirst, G. M. Trevelyan and C. F. G. Masterman had founded the *Independent Review* in October 1903, a journal of radical Liberalism.

86. 'The Illusion of War', *The Nation*, XI, 19 (10 Aug. 1912), 702. This was a review of the Quaker J. W. Graham's *Evolution and Empire* (1912).

87. 'Peace or War', *Albany Rev.*, II, 8 (Nov. 1907), 138 and 'War and Peace', 119. Dickinson had spent some time demolishing Social Darwinist theories (see 'Peace or War?', 133–4).

88. Dickinson, 'Is War Inevitable?', *War and Peace*, I, 8 (May 1914), 221–3 and 9 (June 1914), 252–3; Green, *op. cit.*, p. 171 (although first published in 1882 after Green's death, the book had been finished in 1879).

89. 'Is War Inevitable?', 252–3; 'War and Peace', 113, 115.

90. 'Peace or War?', 137–8.

91. Dickinson, *ibid.*, 130–1; Wallas, *Human Nature in Politics*, 4th ed. 1948, p. 285. Dickinson lectured on political theory at the L.S.E. (as well as teaching history and economics at King's College, Cambridge); Wallas lectured on public administration.

92. M. J. Wiener, *Between Two Worlds*, Oxford, 1971, p. 89.

93. Dickinson, *cit. ibid.*, p. 124 and H. J. Laski, 'Lowes Dickinson and Graham Wallas', *Political Quly.*, III, 4 (Oct./Dec. 1932), 461.

94. *The Great Society*, 1914, pp. 173–9. There was, in fact, a 'clear biological disadvantage' in war, but it could not be simply legislated out of existence. Change, like the development of law within states, would be based on 'custom arising from thousands of free decisions'. Wallas briefly mentions James's essay on p. 66 n.1.

95. *Ibid.*, pp. 171–2, 179, 181–3. Cf. Wiener, pp. 157–9.

96. Pp. 46, 15, 68. Cf. R. N. Soffer, 'The Revolution in English Social Thought, 1880–1914', *AHR*, LXXXV, 7 (Dec. 1970), 1962.

97. *The Great Society*, p. 176 (and pp. 39–40). Nevertheless, Wallas leaned heavily on McDougall's work.

98. Pp. 279, 281. James's *Principles of Psychology* is cited at various points in the book.

99. Wiener, pp. 56–7.

100. *Introduction to Social Psychology*, p. 295.

101. *Janus: The Conquest of War*, 1927, p. 13. But, in the foreword McDougall listed horrible cases of 'war madness' from his experience as a wartime major in the R.A.M.C. and he admitted that 'even before the Great War the argument against war was already strong, the need for its restriction or abolition already urgent' (pp. 7–12, 15).

102. See R. N. Soffer, 'New Elitism: Social Psychology in Prewar England', *J. of British Studies*, VIII, 2 (May 1969), 111–40, which seems to overestimate the influence of McDougall in Oxford (pp. 115–6 n.10). Cf. L. S. Hearnshaw, *A Short History of British Psychology, 1840–1940*, 1964, p. 185 (and pp. 168–84 on the late development of psychology as an academic discipline in Britain); McDougall, in *A History of Psychology in Autobiography*, Worcester, Mass., 1930, p. 207.

103. *The Great Society*, p. 171.

104. See P. Burroughs, 'John Robert Seeley and British Imperial History', *J. of Imperial and Commonwealth History*, I, 2 (Jan. 1973), 191–211. For Pearson's Social Darwinism, see

his *National Life from the Standpoint of Science*, 1905, pp. 26–7 ('a time when the sword shall be turned into the ploughshare' would mean that 'mankind will no longer progress').

105. Wallas had rejected Idealism (and orthodox religious beliefs) after his first year at Oxford in 1877 (See Wiener, pp. 5–9, 67–8). He was never as thoroughgoing a critic of Idealism as, say, Russell (see Wallas, 'Oxford and English Political Thought', *The Nation*, XVII, 7 (15 May 1915), 227, but he never got the chair at Oxford he wanted (the Gladstone chair of Political Theory and Institutions).

106. Reprinted in Bradley, *Collected Essays*, Oxford, 1935, I, 168, 176. The article had been written as early as 1878 or 1879.

107. *Ibid.*, 170–3, 175–6.

108. 'The Morality of Nations', *IJE*, I, 4 (July 1891), 442–6. Sorley was father of the war poet Charles Hamilton Sorley.

109. Bradley rejected Social Darwinist arguments for war. See *Collected Essays*, I, 174 ('how can we consistently set up tribal morality and a mere struggle between states as ultimate, when within tribal morality the principle of selfishness is not paramount').

110. 'War and Peace', *IJE*, XI, 2 (Jan. 1901), 148–51. Ritchie also had his doubts about 'crude applications of biological conceptions to social evolution'. The nation was obviously not an organism in the biological sense and human evolution did not 'take place only by war' (154).

111. *Ibid.*, 137–8.

112. 'The Moral Problems of War — In Reply to Mr. J. M. Robertson', *IJE*, XI, 4 (July 1901), 494.

113. 'War and Peace', 149.

114. See Wallas's notes and minutes, Wallas Mss. Box 39. Cf. letters from J. Estlin Carpenter (13 Sept. 1914) suggesting a national conference of peace organisations, to L. T. Hobhouse (8 Aug. 1914) and Lowes Dickinson (n.d.) in Wallas Mss. Box 5.

115. See M. Swartz, 'A Study in Futility: the British Radicals at the Outbreak of the First World War', in A. J. A. Morris (ed.), *Edwardian Radicalism, 1900–1914*, 1974, pp. 246–61.

116. E. G. Browne (Professor of Arabic), F. C. Burkitt (Professor of Divinity), J. E. Carpenter, F. J. Foakes-Jackson (Jesus College), K. Lake (Professor of Theology at Leiden University), W. M. Ramsay (Professor of Humanity, Aberdeen), J. J. Thomson, W. B. Selbie (Principal of Mansfield College, Oxford). Carpenter and Selbie as heads of Nonconformist colleges were not representative of Oxford theologians. *The Times*, 1 Aug. 1914, p. 6d. Taylor mentions 81 Cambridge signatories of the letter (*Troublemakers*, p. 117), but for the reactions of one Cambridge don who refused to sign, see W. E. Heitland, *After Many Years*, Cambridge, 1926, p. 209.

117. Both cuttings in the Wallas Mss. Box 39. The second letter was signed by Wallas, Murray, Hobhouse, Hirst, Hobson, Hammond, Trevelyan, A. G. Gardiner and Ramsay MacDonald.

118. *Loc. cit.*

119. *Guardian*, 1 Aug. 1914, p. 10b. Cf. letters from S. Alexander (Professor of Philosophy), A. S. Peake (Professor of Biblical Exegesis), R. S. Conway (Professor of Latin), all of Manchester University, and W. M. Geldart (Vinerian Professor of Law, Oxford) in the same issue. Later letters appeared from T. N. Toller (Emeritus Professor), G. Unwin (Professor of Economic History), A. E. Boycott (Professor of Pathology), all of Manchester; E. de Selincourt (Professor of English, Birmingham), C. H. Reilly (Professor of Architecture, Liverpool), L. T. Hobhouse. *Guardian*, 3 Aug., 1914 (p. 9a), 4 Aug. 1914 (p. 14c), 5 Aug. 1914 (p. 3c). Cf. C. H. Reilly, *Scaffolding in the Sky*, 1938, p. 182.

120. *Guardian*, 3 Aug. 1914, p. 6d/e (Trevelyan); Beesly, 'The Russian Alliance', *Positivist Rev.*, 22, cclxi (1 Sept. 1914), 198–9. A. V. Dicey, Beesly's contemporary, shared his view of the Russians. See F. Pollock to J. Bryce, 26 Dec. 1914, Bryce Mss UB. 57.

121. *The Times*, 1 Aug. 1914, p. 6d (Marriott) and 4 Aug. 1914, p. 5d (Jones). Cf. A. Quiller-Couch (Professor of English, Cambridge), *Morning Post*, 4 Aug. 1914, p. 4g.

122. *The Times*, 5 Aug. 1914, p. 9b (Rose) and 15 Aug. 1914, p. 7d (Ramsay). Cf. Ramsay, 'Confessions of a Peacemaker', *19th Century*, LXXXIII (Mar. 1918), 637.

123. *Autobiography of Bertrand Russell*, 1968, II, 16; Weinroth, 'Norman Angell and 'The Great Illusion' . . .', 570. A good example of the transition is the Persian scholar E. G. Browne (Professor of Arabic, Cambridge) and supporter of Irish Home Rule, Welsh language rights, Boer independence and most notably Persian independence. See his 'Persia' in the *Peace Yearbook 1913*, pp. 21–4, letters to *The Nation*, V, 13 (25 June 1910), 456 and VI, 25 (21 Sept. 1912), 900–1, and the material cited in n. 14 of chapter 6 of this work.

124. 8 Aug. 1914, *cit.* H. Smith, 'World War I and British Left-Wing Intellectuals: The Case of Leonard Hobhouse', *Albion*, V, iv (Winter 1973), 265 and a letter from Hobhouse to *The Nation*, XVII, 5 (31 Oct. 1914), 142–3 calling for a manifesto from 'anti-militarists of long standing'. Emily Hobhouse was a leading anti-war campaigner.

125. *The World in Conflict*, 1915, p. 17. The Triple Entente had translated Germany's geographical vulnerability into 'positive political fact'. This, plus the vagueness of its terms, gave it 'an appearance of hostility and barely concealed . . . menace' in German eyes. Hence the decision for war — it was not worth Germany's while 'to forfeit any immediate advantage' in the hope of securing British neutrality.

126. Letters to Emily Hobhouse, *op. cit.* and Graham Wallas, 8 Aug. 1914, Wallas Mss. V.

127. See R. Chickering, *Imperial Germany and a World Without War*, Princeton, 1975, pp. 135–48; T. Starr, *Romain Rolland and a World at War*, Evanston, Illinois, 1956, p. 63; S. Lukes, *Emile Durkheim*, 1973, pp. 549–54; J.-J. Becker, *The Great War and the French People*, 1985, chapter 10.

128. The phrase 'sorrowful acceptance' is that of J. A. Hobson, who was very reluctant to accept official explanations for British entry to the war. See Hobson and M. Ginsburg, *L. T. Hobhouse*, 1931, p. 50.

Chapter 1

1. Letter to W. H. Dawson, 24 Mar. 1915, Dawson Mss. 269. Dawson himself had married twice into German families.

2. Pp. 3–4. Cf. W. J. Ashley, *Progress of the German Working Classes* (1904).

3. T. F. Tout, 'Memoir', in A. T. Bartholomew, *A Bibliography of Sir Adolphus William Ward 1837–1924*, Cambridge, 1926, p. xxvii. Ward was the son of the British Consul-General at Leipzig and Hamburg, Minister-Resident to the Hanse towns. Ward had a Prussian knighthood (1911) and an honorary degree from the University of Leipzig.

4. 'Goethe and the French Revolution' (Presidential Address), *Publ. of the English Goethe Soc.*, XIV (1912), 2.

5. A. W. Ward, *Founders' Day in War Time*, Manchester, 1917, p. 2; A. W. Ward to C. P. Scott, 26 Mar. 1915, *cit.* J. L. Hammond, *C. P. Scott*, 1934, p. 184; review in *EHR*, XXXIII, 2 (April 1918), 284.

6. 'The Problem of German Kultur', *Positivist Rev.*, 23 (Sept. 1915), 193.

7. To J. Harvey, 9 Aug. 1914, *cit.* M. Sadleir, *Michael Ernest Sadler*, 1949, p. 270. Sadler had visited Germany in 1897 to gather material for a report on German secondary education (1902).

8. J. Bryce 'Preface' to A. Toynbee, *The Belgian Deportations*, 1916, p. 8; Bryce to H. A. L. Fisher, 15 Oct. 1914, Fisher Mss., Box 3/1.

9. *The War: Its Causes and Issues*, 1914, p. 8; Fisher to Bryce, 19 Oct. 1914, Bryce Mss., UB 23. Joseph von Görres had been Professor of History at Munich.

10. Herford, 'Problem of German Kultur', 194.

11. 'Manifesto of the Intellectuals of Germany', in W. W. Coole and M. F. Potter (eds.), *Thus Spake Germany*, 1941, p. 45.

12. *To the Christian Scholars of Europe*, Oxford, 1914, pp. 3–4, 8.

13. W. B. Selbie, *The War and Theology*, 1915, p. 8.

14. *To the Christian Scholars . . .*, pp. 6–7.

15. *Ibid.*, pp. 9–10.

16. *Germany's Aims in the First World War*, 1967, p. 156, n.1.

17. 'Manifesto of the Intellectuals . . .', *cit.* Coole and Potter, pp. 44–5. Cf. the less emotional response from some signatories in *The Times*, 5 June 1916, p. 6d.

18. Selbie, *The War and Theology*, p. 8; W. Sanday, *The Meaning of the War*, 1915, pp. 68–9; J. Herbst, *The German Historical School in American Scholarship*, Ithaca, N.Y., 1965, p. 169.

19. P. Gardner, *Autobiographica*, Oxford, 1933, p. 44; A. V. Dicey, *How We Ought To Feel About the War*, Oxford, 1914, pp. 7–8; Sanday, *Meaning of the War*, p. 109. On the latter, see *Correspondence of Robert Bridges and Henry Bradley*, Oxford, 1940, pp. 145–6.

20. J. Kirkpatrick, *Origins of the Great War*, 1914, p. 25.

21. 'Problem of German Kultur', 194–7.

22. Herford, *loc. cit*; Ashley, *The War and Its Economic Aspects*, pp. 4–5.

23. 'Presidential Address', *Proc. of the Classical Assoc.*, XII (1915), 19–20.

24. Comments of another delegate (T. E. Page), *ibid.*, 31.

25. Sonnenschein, *Idols of Peace and War*, Oxford, 1915, p. 17; Walter Raleigh to Emile Legouis, 19 Aug. 1914, in *The Letters of Sir Walter Raleigh*, rev. ed., 1928, II, 404. Sonnenschein had been born in London (1851) of an Austrian father.

26. 'The Changing Mind of a Nation at War', *Atlantic Monthly*, CXV (4 April 1915), 344; 'A Theological Holiday — And After', *Hibbert J.*, XIV (1915), 6.

27. J. Oman, *The War and Its Issues*, Cambridge, 1915, p. 91. Cf. J. H. Moulton, *British and German Scholarship*, 1915, p. 6.

28. *War and Theology*, pp. 3, 7, 9. Cf. the comments of L. Elliott-Binns, *English Thought, 1860–1900*, 1956, p. 339.

29. 'Science and Philosophy as Unifying Forces', in *The Unity of Western Civilization*, 1915, pp. 171–2.

30. 'German 'Kultur' — III German Scholarship', *Quarterly Rev.*, 223 (April 1915), 333, 336.

31. *Germany and Europe*, 1914, pp. 45–6.

32. Hobhouse, 'Science and Philosophy . . .', pp. 170, 172–3.

33. *The Times*, 22 Dec. 1914, p. 6c. For the correspondence which followed, see *The Times*, 24 Dec. (p. 9d), 28 Dec. (p. 7d), 30 Dec. 1914 (p. 9d) and 2 Jan. 1915 (p. 9e).

34. *The Times*, 28 Dec. 1914, p. 7d and 23 Dec. 1914, p. 9c; G. de Beer, *The Sciences Were Never At War*, 1960, *passim.*

35. *The Times*, 26 Dec. 1914, p. 7d.

36. *The German Universities*, p. vii; Sadler, 'The History of Education', in *Germany in the 19th Century*, Manchester, 1912, *passim*; Sadler, 'The Strengths and Weaknesses of German Education', *German Culture* (ed. W. P. Paterson), 1915, p. 301.

37. *TLS*, XV, 748 (18 May 1916), 237 and 754 (29 June 1916), 309; U. von Wilamowitz-Moellendorff, *My Recollections*, 1930, pp. 382–3; F. Kenyon, *The British Academy: the First Fifty Years*, 1952, pp. 21–2. The wartime publications of the Aristotelian Society, British Association for the Advancement of Science, Royal Asiatic Society, Royal Anthropological Institute, Royal Historical Society, Royal Economic Society, and Royal Society of Edinburgh all still list German and Austrian names amongst their 'corresponding fellows'.

38. *Morning Post*, 21 June 1916, p. 1f and 19 June 1916, p. 4c; L. Housman (ed.), *War Letters of Fallen Englishmen*, 1930, p. 128.

39. Letters of Mr. A. Allan (Liverpool University Archives), 24 May 1973 and Mr. J. G. Thomas (Registrar of the University of Wales), 8 June 1976 to the writer; *The Times*, 2 Jan. 1915, p. 9e and 28 Dec. 1914, p. 3e. See also the correspondence in *The Times*, 8 Mar. and 9 Mar. 1915, p. 9e in both cases, 7 Jan. 1915, p. 9e.

40. *PBA*, 1915–16, 3–6.

41. W. T. Starr, *Romain Rolland and a World at War*, Evanston, Illinois, 1956, p. 118.

42. 'Presidential Address', 19.

43. Ridgeway, 'The Problem of Racial and National Safety', *Eugenics Rev.*, VII (1915), 123–30 and his letter to *The Times*, 23 April 1915, p. 9d.

44. P. N. Ure, *Venizelos and his Fellow-Countrymen*, 1917, p. 2.

Chapter 2

1. J. H. Muirhead, 'God and the World', in J. E. Carpenter (ed.), *Ethical and Religious Problems of the War*, 1916, p. 98.

2. Bosanquet to Muirhead, 25 April 1915, *cit. Bernard Bosanquet and His Friends*, 1935, pp. 167–8, 171–2; H. Bosanquet, *Bernard Bosanquet*, 1924, p. 131.

3. *Hibbert J.*, XIII, i (Oct. 1914), 52. Cf. R. Metz, *A Hundred Years of British Philosophy*, 1938, p. 302.

4. 'Autobiography', in *The Philosophy of C. D. Broad*, N.Y., 1959, p. 53. Cf. Broad, 'The Prevention of War', *IJE*, XXVI, 2 (Jan. 1916), 241; Metz, pp. 663–4.

5. *The International Crisis in its Ethical and Psychological Aspects*, 1915, pp. 123–5.

6. R. R. Marett, 'Presidential Address: War and Savagery', *Folk-Lore*, XXI, 1 (Mar. 1915), 26–7. Cf. an opponent of retaliation Dicey, *How We Ought To Feel . . .*, pp. 8–9, and a supporter of retaliation J. P. Mahaffy, 'The Ethics of Retaliation', in *Ad Clerum*, Dublin, 1918, pp. 180–2.

7. *The International Crisis . . .*, pp. 123–4.

8. *The Policy of the Entente, 1904–14*, Manchester, [1916], pp. 3, v–vi.

9. Russell to Lady Ottoline Morrell, 11 June 1915, *cit.* Russell, *Autobiography*, II, 52.

10. 'The War and Non-Resistance: a Rejoinder to Professor Perry', *IJE*, XXVI, 1 (Oct. 1915), 24–5. Cf. R. B. Perry, 'Non-Resistance and the Present War: A Reply to Mr. Russell', *IJE*, XXV, 3 (April 1915), 316.

11. Reprinted in Russell, *Justice in War-Time*, Chicago, 1916, pp. 1, 4, 11, 14–15.

12. 'When two dogs fight in the street, no one supposes that anything but instinct prompts them, or that they are inspired by high and noble ends . . . . And what is true of dogs in the street is equally true of nations in the pre‿ ‿nt war.' *Ibid.*, pp. 13–14.

13. *Mind*, N.S. XXV, 98 (April 1916), 254. Schiller, who was a Fellow of Corpus Christi

College, Oxford, had been born in Germany but brought up and educated in Britain.

14. Editorial, 'Why We Are At War', *Philosophy*, XIV, 56 (Oct. 1939).

15. *The World in Conflict*, 1915, pp. 29, 33-4, 38-40, 42, 51.

16. Letter to Emily Hobhouse, 8 Aug. 1914, *cit.* S. Collini, 'Hobhouse, Bosanquet and the State', *Past and Present*, 72 (Aug. 1976), 89 n.13.

17. J. H. Muirhead, *German Philosophy in Relation to the War*, 1915, p. 46; H. D. Oakeley, *Church Quarterly Review*, LXXIX, 3 (Oct. 1914), 97; L. P. Jacks. 'An Interim Religion', in Fight for the Right Movement, *For the Right*, 1916, p. 64.

18. *Questions of War and Peace*, 1916, p. 26; *The Metaphysical, Theory of the State*, 1918, p. 6 (part of a prefatory dedication to Lt. R. O. Hobhouse, R.A.F.).

19. J. Bryce, 'Opening Address', *The International Crisis: The Theory of the State*, 1916, p. 2. See the different treatment accorded to Hegel and Nietzsche in A. D. Lindsay, 'German Philosophy', *German Culture* (W. P. Paterson ed.), pp. 59, 62-3. However, during the Second World War Hegel was still under fire, as the debate between E. F. Carritt and T. M. Knox in *Philosophy*, XV (1940), shows. See pp. 51-63, 190-6, 313-7.

20. *Questions of War and Peace*, pp. 19, 180; *World in Conflict*, pp. 56, 99.

21. E.g. G. W. Prothero, *German Policy Before the War*, 1916, pp. 5-14.

22. A. Wolf, *The Philosophy of Nietzsche*, 1915, p. 10. Although he could see dangers in a 'system of ethics . . . characterized by naturalism and evolutionism', Wolf felt Nietzsche's political views were more reminiscent 'of the peace societies and of the Society of Friends rather than Bernhardi and Treitschke' (pp. 17-18, 22-3).

23. C. R. L. Fletcher, p. 5. Cf. E. Barker, *Neitzsche and Treitschke*, Oxford, 1914, pp. 4-5.

24. Wolf, p. 10; C. Bell, *Civilization*, 1928, p. 4.

25. H. J. Paton, *cit.* G. J. Warnock, *English Philosophy Since 1900*, 1958, pp. 2-3.

26. Oakeley, 113. Muirhead was considered one of the most Hegelian of English Idealists, compared to, say, Bosanquet whose Idealism was more eclectic.

27. Cf. W. R. Sorley, 'The State and Morality', *International Crisis: The Theory of the State*, pp. 36-42 (a critical view) with Bosanquet, *Social and International Ideals*, 1917, pp. 318-9 which sought to demonstrate that Fichte's reputation as the philosopher of racist imperialism was 'a perversion' of his ideas on 'a primary life-force'.

28. *German Philosophy in Relation to the War*, pp. vi, 51, 57, 60-1.

29. *Questions of War and Peace*, pp. 19-20.

30. *German Philosophy In Relation to the War*, pp. 35-7.

31. L. P. Jacks, contribution to 'Symposium: Ethical Principles of Social Reconstruction', *PAS*, N.S. XVI (1916-17), 258.

32. 'Some Personal Impressions of Russell as a Philosopher', *Bertrand Russell: Philosopher of the Century*, 1967, pp. 101-2. Bradley had been born in 1846, Bosanquet in 1848, Muirhead in 1855, Hobhouse in 1864, Russell in 1872, Moore in 1873, Broad in 1887.

33. *Ibid.*, p. 101. James Ward and J. McE. McTaggart exemplify mainstream Cambridge Idealism; Henry Sidgwick who died in 1900 provides the link between Utilitarianism and the generation of Russell and Moore.

34. D. Bell, 'Philosophy', in C. B. Cox and A. E. Dyson (eds.), *The 20th-Century Mind*, 1972, I, 174.

35. 'Oxford and Philosophy', *Philosophy*, XII, 47 (June 1937), 298. The first reference to Bradley comes in the 1891 Logic paper, but cf. R. G. Collingwood, *An Autobiography*, Oxford, 1939, pp. 17-19 and A. Wood, *Bertrand Russell*, 1957, p. 72.

36. Bell, pp. 223-4. Cf. A. M. Quinton, 'Social Thought in Britain', *ibid.*, p. 131.

37. Metz, p. 318 and 'Prefatory Note' to Baillie, *Studies in Human Nature*, 1921, p. vii; Schiller in *Mind*, N.S. XXV, 98 (April 1916), 250.

38. *Metaphysical Theory of the State*, pp. 17–18.

39. R. Wollheim, *F. H. Bradley*, Harmondsworth, Middlesex, 1959, p. 14.

40. *Metaphysical Theory . . .*, pp. 23–5.

41. B. Bosanquet, 'The Function of the State in Promoting the Unity of Mankind', *Social and International Ideals*, pp. 300–1.

42. J. A. Smith, 'Progress as an Ideal of Action', *Progress and History*, 1916, pp. 311–3.

43. A. C. Bradley, 'International Morality: The United States of Europe', *International Crisis . . . Ethical and Psychological Aspects*, pp. 64–5.

44. Schiller, *op. cit.*

45. Muirhead in *Bernard Bosanquet and His Friends*, p. 190.

46. *PAS*, N.S. XVI (1915–16), 312–5, 318. Cf. H. J. Laski, *Studies in the Problem of Sovereignty*, New Haven, 1917, pp. 6, 8, 12, 19, 20–1.

47. *Ibid.*, pp. 290–301. Burns castigated Bosanquet for confusing 'two quite distinct problems — (i) the relation of a citizen to the State, and (ii) the relation of the human being to society' (p. 294). But this conflation was basic to the whole Idealist approach.

48. *Ibid.*, p. 306.

49. On Russell, see Chapter 8; M. Cole, *Growing Up In Revolution*, 1949, p. 69.

50. Russell *op. cit.*, pp. 306–7.

51. 'There is a curious inversion of emphasis in Mr. Russell's article. It is not impossible that a distrust of vulgar opinion should lead a nicely analytical mind to exaggerate whatever is contrary to the general prejudice'. Perry, 'Non-Resistance and the Present War . . .', 316.

52. Russell, *Principles of Social Reconstruction*, 1916, pp. 12, 49 and *PAS*, N.S. XVI (1915–16), 302–3; Bosanquet review of Russell's *Principles . . .* in *Mind* N.S. XXVI (1917), 233.

53. Interest in Rousseau, for example, had been stimulated by C. E. Vaughan's definitive edition of *The Political Writings* (1915): see his 'Epilogue' to volume 2 for an unfavourable comparison of Fichte with Rousseau. Cole had produced a smaller edition of the *Social Contract* in 1913. For conservatives, of course, Rousseau was the source of trouble in the modern world. See A. E. Taylor's review of *The Metaphysical Theory of the State* in *Mind* N.S. XXIX, 113 (Jan. 1920), 92–3.

54. Russell was a not very active member of the National Guilds League. S. T. Glass, *The Responsible Society*, 1966, p. 39.

55. A. D. Lindsay, 'The State in Recent Political Theory', *Political Q.*, I (1914), 136.

56. Russell, *Autobiography*, II, 17, also 38–9; Barker, *Political Thought in England, 1848 to 1914*, 2nd rev. ed. 1947, p. 221.

Chapter 3

1. 'Closing Remarks' at the International Congress for Historical Study, London 1913, appended to J. Bryce, *Presidential Address*, Oxford, 1913, p. 28.

2. J. W. Allen, *Germany and Europe*, p. 4. But he went on to attempt this task as one might have expected of the author of the standard *English Political Thought, 1603–60* (1938).

3. H. Flaig, 'The Historian as Pedagogue of the Nation', *History*, 59, 195 (Feb. 1974), 18.

4. *Cit.* K. Robbins, '*History*, the Historical Association and the 'National Past' ', *History*, 66, 218 (Oct. 1981), 421.

5. F. J. C. Hearnshaw, 'History as a Means of Propaganda', *Fortnightly Rev.*, N.S. CXIV (1 Aug. 1923), 330. Hearnshaw believed that 'war-history' had failed to mislead public opinion.

6. J. F. C. Masterman, *On the Chariot Wheel*, 1975, pp. 146–7; G. Kitson Clark, 'A Hundred Years of Teaching History at Cambridge', *Historical J.*, 537–8.

7. E. A. Freeman (1823–92), William Stubbs (1825–1901), S. R. Gardiner (1829–1902), J. E. E. D. Acton (1834–1902), F. York Powell (1850–1904), J. R. Seeley (1834–95).

8. H. W. C. Davis, *A History of Balliol College*, rev. ed. Oxford, 1963, p. 241.

9. J. B. Bury, 'The Science of History' (1904), reprinted in *Collected Essays*, Cambridge, 1930, p. 17; J. W. Allen, *The Place of History in Education*, 1909, p. 61.

10. Trevelyan's plea for History as an art ('Clio A Muse' 1903) did not really raise the issue of relativism. However, see the criticisms in W. Cunningham, 'Impartiality in History', *Scientia*, I (1907), 121–3 and in C. H. Firth, 'A Plea for the Historical Teaching of History' (1904), in C. H. Williams (ed.), *The Modern Historian*, 1938, pp. 44–9.

11. D. J. Medley, *The Educational Value of a Study of History*, Glasgow, 1899, p. 11. Cf. B. E. Schmitt, *The Fashion and Future of History*, Cleveland, Ohio, 1960, p. 7. Schmitt had been a Rhodes Scholar at Oxford, 1905–8; Medley was Professor of History at Glasgow.

12. E.g. C. H. Firth in *TRHS*, Ser. 3 IX (1915), 20 and Ser. 3 X (1916), 15–24. Cf. H. Butterfield, 'Some Trends in Scholarship 1868–1968, In the Field of Modern History', *TRHS*, Ser. 5 XIX (1969), 264–5.

13. 'Oxford and the War', *TLS*, XX, 997 (24 Feb. 1921), 114. The Professor of English at Oxford claimed credit for the idea (see *Letters of Walter Raleigh*, II, 411). But in a letter to this writer (21 Mar. 1973) Sir Keith Feiling wrote: 'My clear recollection is that the moving force in the matter was H. W. C. Davis'.

14. *Why We Are At War*, 2nd rev. ed., Oxford, 1914, pp. 5–6. Overemphasis on official sources meant, for example, ignoring the informal Anglo-French military 'conversations' from January 1906 onwards.

15. Pp. vii, 41, 45. For a recent assessment of the treatment of Louvain, see P. Schöller, *Das Fall Löwen und das deutsche Weissbuch*, Köln, 1958.

16. C. Hazlehurst, *Politicians at War*, 1917, p. 103 (but see p. 14 for qualifications to the idea of Belgium as the deciding factor).

17. See Hammond's letters to Gilbert Murray (Murray Mss.) and Muir's 'Introduction' to E. Rignano, *The War and the Settlement*, 1916, pp. 9–10, where it is used to explain German anger with Britain.

18. *Why We Are At War*, pp. 27–8.

19. P. 5. Cf. H. M. Gwatkin, *Britain's Case Against Germany*, 1917, p. 7.

20. Pp. 5, 8–9. Rait was Professor of Scottish History at Glasgow.

21. Pp. 115–6.

22. H. E. Egerton, *The War and the British Dominions*, Oxford, 1914, p. 13. On the actual place of Belgium in Allied military planning, see S. R. Williamson, *The Politics of Grand Strategy*, Cambridge, Mass., 1969, esp. p. 178.

23. K. Feiling, *Italian Policy Since 1870*, Oxford, 1914, p. 3.

24. J. Dewey, 'The Mind of Germany' (Feb. 1916), in *Characters and Events*, 1929, I, 133–5.

25. Pp. 3–4, 10–12. For a recent assessment, see G. B. Leon, *Greece and the Great Powers, 1914–1917*, Thessalonika, 1974.

26. Sir H. E. Richards, 'The Issues at Stake in this War', *Scientia*, XII (1917), 202–3. Richards was Chichele Professor of International Law at Oxford.

27. W. R. Scott, 'The Economic Problems of Peace in Time of War', *Report of the 38th Meeting of the British Assoc. for the Advancement of Science* (1916), 501–2. The same point was made with characteristic force by Lloyd George (19 Sept. 1914) *Cit.* B. W. Ginsburg (ed.), *War Speeches, 1914–1917*, Oxford, 1917, pp. 43–5.

28. *Why We Are At War*, p. 56; J. B. Bury, *Germany and Slavonic Civilization*, 1915, p. 13.

29. Allen, *Germany and Europe*, pp. 110–12. Cf. the writings by the Professor of Natural Science at New College, Edinburgh, J. Y. Simpson, esp. his *The Self-Discovery of Russia* (1916) and J. H. Rose, 'The War and Nationality', *Scientia*, XVIII (1915), 27.

30. *Why We Are At War*, p. 79; Allen, *Germany and Europe*, pp. 75–6.

31. M. Beaven, *Austrian Policy Since 1867*, Oxford, 1914, pp. 3, 27–8; W. G. S. Adams, *The Responsibility for the War*, Oxford, 1914, pp. 6–7; Allen, *Germany and Europe*, p. 58; A. F. Pollard, *The War: Its History and Morals*, 1915, pp. 5–6. There was some disagreement as to the degree of Vienna's responsibility.

32. R. Muir, *Britain's Case Against Germany*, Manchester, 1914, p. 163.

33. *Ibid.*, pp. 15–20; D. J. Medley, 'The War and the Races of Europe', *Proc. of the Royal Philosophical Soc. Glasgow*, XLVI (1914–15), 15. On the other hand, Medley was able to see that German naval-building and its large army were partly the result of fear of 'encirclement'. See Medley, *Why Britain Fights*, Glasgow, 1914, p. 6.

34. F. J. C. Hearnshaw, *Main Currents of European History, 1815–1915*, 1917, pp. 303–4.

35. *German Policy Before the War*, p. 32. Cf. Hearnshaw, *op. cit.*, pp. 301–5; M. Sadler, *Modern Germany and the Modern World*, 1914, pp. 11–12; Pollard, *The War: Its History and Morals*, p. 20.

36. Ward wrote virtually all the chapters on German history in the *Cambridge Modern History* (1902–), apart from those written by continental scholars (notably Oncken and Meinecke).

37. *The Origins of the War*, Cambridge, 1914, p. 157.

38. *Germany*, 1914, p. 60. Cf. Muir, *Britain's Case*, pp. 126–7; A. D. Lindsay, *War Against War*, Oxford, 1914, p. 11; Fisher, *The War and Its Causes*, p. 10.

39. J. A. R. Marriott and C. G. Robertson, *The Evolution of Prussia*, Oxford, 1915, pp. 425–6. This book stayed in print until after the Second World War.

40. *The Political Thought of Treitschke*, 1914, esp. pp. 163–4, 173.

41. 'Modern German Historians' (April 1915), in *Studies in History and Politics*, Oxford, 1920, p. 125. Cf. *Why We Are At War*, pp. 109–12.

42. A. Dorpalen, *Heinrich von Treitschke*, N. Haven, 1957, p. 298.

43. *Germany and Europe*, p. 4.

44. J. A. Moses, *The Politics of Illusion*, 1975, chapter 1; McClelland, *The German Historians and England*, pp. 207–24.

45. Friedrich von Bernhardi, retired general of cavalry, had written the bestseller *Germany and the Next War* in 1912 (translated into English 1914) and *Britain As Germany's Vassal* (1913).

46. The only source for Cramb's life is an adulatory portrait by an ex-pupil, L. M. Russell, *John Adam Cramb* (1950), which also reproduces some of his lectures.

47. C. E. Playne, *The Pre-War Mind in Britain*, 1928, pp. 199–200.

48. P. 137. And on war in general: '... man values the power which it affords to life of rising above life, the power which the spirit of man possesses to pursue the Ideal' (p. 60).

49. Pollard, 'The War and British Realism', in T. Brooke and H. S. Canby (eds.), *War Aims and Peace Ideals*, New Haven, 1919, p. 117; *Why We Are At War*, p. 117; Muirhead, *German Philosophy ...*, pp. 83–4; R. W. Seton-Watson *et al*, *The War and Democracy*, 1914, pp. 120 and 250; W. P. Paterson (ed.), *German Culture*, p. 317; C. S. Terry, *Treitschke, Bernhardi and Some Theologians*, Glasgow, 1915, p. 9; W. A. Phillips, 'Europe and the Problem of Nationality', *Edinburgh Rev.*, 221 (1915), 40–1.

50. *Op. cit.*, p. 15.

51. C. S. Terry, 'British Diplomacy, 1902–14', *Aberdeen University Rev.*, III, 8 (Feb. 1916) 153–4. Cf. Rose, 'Origins of the War', pp. 183–4 and Allen, *Germany and Europe*, pp. 98–102.

52. H. A. L. Fisher, *The War and Its Causes*, p. 18.

53. A. P. Higgins, *The Law of Nations and the War*, Oxford, 1914, p. 21. Higgins lectured in international law at the L.S.E. and the Royal Naval War College.

54. J. H. Rose, *German Misrepresentations*, 1915, pp. 18–19; A. Hassall, '*Just for a Scrap of Paper*', Oxford, 1914, p. 6; *Why We Are At War*, p. 17.

55. J. H. Rose, *How The War Came About*, 1915, p. 12. Cf. C. R. L. Fletcher, *The Germans: What They Covet*, Oxford, 1914, p. 14.

56. *Warlike England*, N.Y., 1915, p. 22.

57. H. E. Egerton, *Is The British Empire The Result of Wholesale Robbery?*, Oxford, 1914, p. 27; F. Morgan and H. W. C. Davis, *French Policy Since 1871*, Oxford, 1914, p. 12.

58. E. A. Sonnenschein, *Through German Eyes*, Oxford, 1915, pp. 14–15.

59. Moses, p. 22.

60. Adams, *Responsibility for the War*, pp. 19–20; Egerton, *War and the British Dominions*, pp. 13, 17–18; Fisher, *The Value of Small States*, p. 22.

61. *Warlike England*, p. 12.

62. *The Submerged Nationalities of the German Empire*, 1915, pp. 19–20. Cf. his *Ireland in the Last Fifty Years (1866–1916)*, Oxford, 1917, pp. 107–8.

63. From 1929 they edited successive volumes of the *Cambridge History of the British Empire*; vol. 2 (1940) contains similiar justifications for empire to those of 1914.

64. Benians, pp. 3–4, 16; O. Lodge, 'The War From a British Point of View', *Scientia*, XVII (1915), 191.

65. *The War and the British Dominions*, p. 22.

66. *How We Ought To Feel About The War*, p. 5 (a lecture to the Working Men's College, London, Nov. 1914). Cf. R. S. Rait (ed.), *Memorials of Albert Venn Dicey*, 1925, p. 231.

Chapter 4

1. Letter to Lady Ottoline Morrell, 19 Mar. 1916, *cit.* Russell, *Autobiography*, I, 61.

2. Raleigh to Mrs W. Crum, 8 Aug. 1914, in Raleigh, *Letters*, II, 404; Rupert Brooke to R. Loines, Dec. 1914, *The Letters of Rupert Brooke*, 1968, p. 644.

3. From a letter to L. Gielgud, 30 Sept. 1917, *The Letters of Aldous Huxley*, 1969, p. 135.

4. 'Some Reflections of a Soldier' (Oct. 1916), reprinted in *The Attack and Other Papers*, 1953, pp. 24–6.

5. Ernest Barker, *Mothers and Sons in Wartime*, rev. ed. 1918, pp. 14, 67–9. These were articles reprinted from *The Times*, highly popular to judge by the number of reprintings.

6. 'The Antipathy Between Germany and England', *Scientia*, XVIII (1915), 266. H. A. L. Fisher was making the same point when he noted that young Englishmen read articles on golf or cricket, while young Germans read books on war. *The War and Its Causes*, p. 9.

7. *The Danger of Peace*, 1915, p. 8.

8. See letters from A. L. Prince and R. Bedford in the Tout Mss.

9. W. R. Scott in the W. S. Jevons Lecture for 1917. See Scott, *Economic Problems of Peace After The War*, Cambridge, 1917, Ser. I, 8.

10. The German theologian Ernst Troeltsch had coined the phrase 'die Ideen von 1914' in his *Deutsche Geist und Westeuropa* (1916).

11. *Peace With Patriotism*, Cambridge, 1915, pp. 10–14.

12. J. Boardman in *The Dictionary of National Biography, 1951–60*, p. 763.

13. Harrison, *op. cit.*

14. 'The People and the Duties of Empire', in *The Empire and the Future* (Imperial Studies Committee, University of London), 1916, pp. 43–4.

15. Letter to W. P. Ker, 15 Nov. 1914, *cit.* Rait, *Memorial of Albert Venn Dicey*, p. 231. Dicey was later able to use Burke against the Russian Revolution. See his 'Burke on Bolshevism', *Nineteenth Century*, LXXXIV, 498 (Aug. 1918), 274–87.

16. Pp. 4–6, 16. Smith also provided arguments against Christian pacifism.

17. John Oman, *The War and Its Issues*, pp. 23–35. Cf. the report of the lecture by the Professor of Divinity (F. C. Burkitt) in *Cambridge Rev.*, XXXI, 895 (20 Jan. 1915), 143.

18. 'A Parable of the War', reprinted in *The Commonwealth At War*, p. 254.

19. *The War and Our Social Duty*, 1915, p. 3.

20. See generally D. Newsome, 'The Assault on Mammon: Charles Gore and John Neville Figgis', *J. of Ecclesiastical History*, XVII, 2 (Oct. 1966), 227–41.

21. 'History and Citizenship: A Forecast', *Cornhill Mag.*, N.S. XXVI, 5 (May 1909), 607 ff. See also his Ford Lectures at Oxford for 1905: *Church and State in the Middle Ages*, Oxford, 1913; p. 134.

22. B. M. G. Reardon, *Religious Thought in the Victorian Age*, 1980, p. 472. Cf. P. d'A. Jones, *The Christian Socialist Revival, 1877–1914*, Princeton, 1968, chapter VI.

23. L. P. Jacks, 'The Changing Mind of a Nation at War', 342.

24. 'The Peacefulness of Being at War' (1915), reprinted in G. Wallas, *Men and Ideas*, 1940, pp. 99–102.

25. 'Comment on Dr Jack's Article 'The Peacefulness of Being At War' ', *ibid.*, pp. 95–8.

26. 'Veblen's Imperial Germany and the Industrial Revolution', *Quarterly J. of Economics*, XXX, i (Nov. 1915), 182.

27. 'Comment on Dr Jack's Article ...', p. 98.

28. Social Darwinism might have 'lessened rather than increased the possibility of world cooperation', but by 1921 Wallas claimed to sense 'a change in the problem-attitude of biologists' which might 'make biology one of the main sources of hope for a world cooperation founded on conscious purpose instead of blind struggle'. *Our Social Heritage*, 1921, p. 204.

29. *World in Conflict*, pp. 28, 48–52.

30. H. Smith, 267–72; Wallas to Lord Bryce, 17 Mar. 1916, Bryce Mss. UB. 23.

31. 'Comment on Dr Jack's Article ...', p. 98.

32. Farnell, pp. 148–57; R. R. Marett, *A Jerseyman at Oxford*, 1941, pp. 154–5; A. Summers, 'Militarism in Great Britain Before The Great War', *History Workshop*, 2 (Autumn 1976), 104–23.

33. Letter from Professor L. S. Hearnshaw to the writer, 15 Dec. 1975; Coulton, *Fourscore Years*, Cambridge, 1943, p. 270.

34. E. Fiddes, *Chapters in the History of Owens College and of Manchester University, 1851–1914*, Manchester, 1937, p. 143.

35. *The Case For Compulsory Service*, 1917, p. 3; 'Democracy and Compulsory Service', *Hibbert J.*, XV, 2 (Jan. 1916), 204; *A Strong Army In A Free State*, 1900, p. 37; 'A Liberal's Plea for Compulsory Service', *Nineteenth Century*, LX (Nov. 1906), 721.

36. *The Case For Compulsory Service*, pp. 202, 258, 278.

37. 'A Liberal's Plea for Compulsory Service', 724.

38. Hearnshaw, 'Compulsory Service in England', *Quarterly Rev.*, CCXXV, 447 (April

1916), 417; Coulton, 'Our Conscripts At Crecy', *Nineteenth Century*, LXV (Feb. 1909), 251-7.

39. Sonnenschein, *Idols of Peace and War*, p. 9 and his letter to *The Times*, 5 June 1915, p. 9d; Smith, *Christian Attitude to War*, p. 13.

40. J. Kirkpatrick, *War Studies*, 1914, pp. 26-32.

41. Hearnshaw, 'Compulsory Military Service in England', 417 and *Freedom in Service*, 1916, pp. 38-9 (articles reprinted from the *Morning Post*); J. H. Rose letter to *The Nation*, XVIII, 16 (15 Jan. 1916), 576.

42. See the correspondence in *The Nation*, XVIII, 18 (29 Jan. 1916), 640 (C. D. Burns, Lytton Strachey); 19 (5 Feb. 1916), 672-3 (Herford); XVII, 21 (19 Aug. 1915), 633 (Grant). Also the letters of Coulton: XVII, 9 (29 Jan. 1915), 12 (19 June 1915), 14 (3 July 1915), 17 (24 July 1915), 19 (7 Aug. 1915); XIX, 11 (10 June 1916), 14 (1 July 1916), 17 (22 July 1916), 20 (12 Aug. 1916); Oman, *The War and Its Issues*, pp. 84-5.

43. *The Commonweal*, Cambridge, 1917, p. 108.

44. 2 June 1915, p. 7e. Those who did not sign were F. W. Pember (All Souls), C. B. Heberden (Brasenose), T. B. Strong (Christ Church), T. Case (Corpus Christi), L. R. Phelps (Oriel), W. A. Spooner (New), W. Lock (Keble), Sir John Rhys (Jesus).

45. H. Smith, 267-72; *The Nation*, XVII, 25 (18 Sept. 1915), 803. Cf. Scott, *Economic Problems of Peace After War*, Ser. I, 11.

46. *The Nation*, XIX, 8 (20 May 1916), 209-10 (C. H. Herford), 22 (26 Aug. 1916), 644 and 24 (9 Sept. 1916), 729 (Dickinson); Smith, *Christian Attitude to War*, pp. 8, 14, 18. One of the few defences of 'absolutists' came from V. Gordon Childe, *Nation*, XIX, 25 (16 Sept. 1916), 760.

47. *Tribunal*, 30 (12 Oct. 1916), 3 (Dickinson, Fisher, Grant, Herford, Wallas, W. E. Johnson of King's College Cambridge, J. O. F. Murray Master of Selwyn College Cambridge, James Ward Professor of Mental Philosophy Cambridge, G. Unwin Professor of Economic History Manchester). For the efforts of Murray, Fisher and Keynes, see J. Rae, *Conscience and Politics*, 1970, *passim*.; D. Boulton, *Objection Overruled*, 1967, pp. 165-6, 191-2; Keynes, *Collected Writings*, XVI, 160-1, 177-9; A. S. Peake, *Prisoners of Hope*, *passim*; Murray, 'Introduction' to M. Hobhouse, *'I Appeal Unto Ceasar'*, 1918. This last had been written by Bertrand Russell, although not even Murray knew this.

48. Dicey, 'The Conscientious Objector', *Nineteenth Century*, LXXXIII (Feb. 1918), 371.

49. Letter by John Hughes, *Sunday Times*, 19 Oct. 1975.

50. Hearnshaw, *Freedom in Service*, pp. 45-6, 95-6 and *Democracy At the Crossways*, 1918, pp. 375-6. Cf. E. V. Arnold, *War-Time Lectures*, 1916, p. 132.

51. Hearnshaw, *Freedom in Service*, p. 46 and *Democracy at the Crossways*, p. 274.

52. *Westminster Gazette*, 13 Jan. 1915, p. 2c. One of their number, J. H. Moulton (Professor of Philosophy, Manchester) had been a strong Quaker and Vice-President of the Peace Society before 1914. His support for the war and for compulsion caused much headshaking in the latter body. He died in 1917 after his ship was torpedoed in the Mediterranean. W. F. Moulton, *James Hope Moulton*, 1919, pp. 111-2.

53. J. M. Winter, *Socialism and the Challenge of War*, 1974, chapter 6 deals comprehensively with Tawney's war experiences and the effect of the war upon him.

54. T. Jones, *Whitehall Diary*, 1969, I, 3-5.

55. Laski, *Studies in the Problem of Sovereignty*, pp. 19-21; *Holmes-Laski Letters*, 1953, I, 10, 43, 103, 148; Cole, *Labour in Wartime*, 1915, chapter 1.

56. 'Some Reflections of a Soldier', p. 23: '. . . to kill in hatred is murder, and we are not murderers, but executioners' (p. 27).

57. Tawney to A. L. Smith, 27 Dec. 1917, *cit.* Winter, p. 170.

58. 'The Philosophy of War', *Athenaeum*, 46616 (April 1917), 169. Only adherence to a set of 'moral principles' could justify war. Tawney, *The Sword of the Spirit*, 1917, pp. 3–4.

59. *Sword of the Spirit*, p. 10.

60. Tawney, *cit.* Winter, p. 158; Smith, *Christian Attitude to War*, pp. 3–4.

61. *R. H. Tawney's Commonplace Book*, Cambridge 1972, pp. 82–3 (28 Dec. 1914) and *The Attack*, pp. 33–4.

62. *Cit.* Winter, p. 157.

63. Tawney had joined the Fabian Society in 1906 and the Independent Labour Party in 1909.

64. Tawney to Smith, 27 Dec. 1917, *cit.* Winter, p. 170.

Chapter 5

1. Later author of *Basic English* (1930) and joint-author of *The Meaning of Meaning* (1923).

2. For the role of literary figures during the war, see D. G. Wright, 'The Great War, Government Propaganda and English 'Men of Letters' 1914–1916', *Literature and History*, 7 (Spring 1978), 70–100.

3. T. C. Fitzpatrick, *Morning Post*, 27 Feb. 1917, p. 4f; W. Ridgeway, 24 Feb. 1917, p. 6e and R. H. MacLeod (Lecturer in Indian Law), 1 Mar. 1917, p. 4.

4. *Cambridge Mag.*, VI, 15 (3 Mar. 1917), 382–3; 17 (17 Mar. 1917); 18 (24 Mar. 1917); 20 (19 May 1917), all n.p. (Dickinson, Wallas, Murray, E. V. Arnold, J. B. Bury, Quiller-Couch, C. H. Herford). For the Armistice Week Riot, see I. A. Richards, 'Some Recollections of C. K. Ogden', *Encounter*, IX, 3 (Sept. 1957), 10–11.

5. Including G. H. Hardy, G. E. Moore, A. S. Eddington (Professor of Astronomy), D. A. Winstanley, E. W. Barnes, F. G. Hopkins. See G. H. Hardy, *Bertrand Russell and Trinity*, Cambridge, 1970, p. 22 and *Cambridge Mag.*, IV, 13 (13 Feb. 1915), 260; II (30 Jan. 1915), 223; V, 21 (20 May 1916), 470–1.

6. G. H. Hardy, p. 11. See also M. Swartz, *The Union of Democratic Control In British Politics During The First World War*, Oxford, 1971, *passim*.

7. *PBA*, 1915–16, pp. 9–10. See also p. 24.

8. R. W. Seton-Watson, *What Is At Stake*, Oxford, 1915, pp. 4–5; Pollard, *The Commonwealth At War*, p. 122. Cf. A. L. Smith to E. D. Morel, 5 Sept. 1914, Smith Mss.

9. H. Hanak, *Great Britain and Austria-Hungary During The First World War*, 1962, p. 178.

10. *Main Currents of European History*, pp. 6, 352–3; *Democracy At the Crossways*, p. 470.

11. W. E. Heitland, *If We Win*, Cambridge, 1915, p. 13.

12. Hardy, p. 13.

13. W. E. Heitland, '*Democratic*', Cambridge, 1915, p. 39; Hearnshaw, *Democracy At The Crossways*, p. 479 and 'Democratic Control', *National Rev.*, LXVI, 6 (Feb. 1916), 880.

14. Characteristically, Coulton did not pull his punches when dealing with Angell, whom he accused of emigrating 'to make money and popularity by lecturing in America, as an American against the country of his birth' (p. 82).

15. Heitland, '*Democratic*', p. 39 and *If We Win*, pp. 12–13. Cf. Coulton, *op. cit.*, p. 217. Hardy, p. 12.

16. *The Danger of Peace*, pp. 8–9, 17, 30, 33. Cf. letters to *The Times*, 3 Feb. 1915, p. 9e (Oliver Lodge) and 13 Feb. 1915, p. 9d (Professor E. C. Clark).

17. *The Commonwealth At War*, pp. 181, 185–6.

18. J. H. Rose, '1815 and 1915', *Contemporary Rev.*, CVII, 1 (Jan. 1915), 12–18; ''Peace Without Victory': What Is The Verdict of History?', *New Europe*, II, 18 (15 Feb. 1917), 129–36; 'The Folly of Early Offers of Peace', *Fortnightly Rev.*, N.S. XCVII, 580 (April 1915), 693–704. Cf. A. V. Dicey, 'Wordsworth and the War', *Nineteenth Century*, LXXVII (May 1915), 1041–60.

19. E.g. letters to *The Times*, 17 Aug. 1917, p. 5e (M.J. Haverfield, Professor of Ancient History, Cambridge); 21 Aug. 1917, p. 4c (J. P. Mahaffy, Provost, Trinity College, Dublin). See also Hearnshaw, *Main Currents of European History*, p. 342 and A. F. Pollard, *The Commonwealth At War*, p. 193.

20. *Sword of The Spirit*, p. 10.

21. *War-Time Lectures*, 1916, p. 76; 'Germany's Peace Offer', *New Age*, XX, 4 (23 Nov. 1916), 80–1. Arnold felt that British ridicule of *Kultur* was 'misplaced'. It was in fact 'the maintenance of law and the upraising of industry'. 'To cross the border from German-Austria to the East' was 'to pass to the conditions of the Middle Ages when neither life nor property had any security' (*War-Time Lectures* p. 76).

22. 'Reckless Propaganda', *New Age*, XX, 5 (30 Nov. 1916), 103–4.

23. *War-Time Lectures*, pp. 86, 75.

24. *Ibid.*, p. 137. Arnold felt that a rejection of German peace-feelers could only strengthen the military party, already flushed with success on the battlefront. 'Germany's Peace Offer', 80–1.

25. 28 Sept., 1917, p. 9b.

26. War Cabinet Minutes, CAB. 24/24, pp. 160–3. Beatrice Webb's version (from Tom Jones) was rather inaccurate. See her diary for 5 Oct. 1917, pp. 96–7, B. Webb Mss. Cf. letters of N. Wedd to F. P. Bulmer, 27 June 1915 and 19 Jan. 1916, Wedd Mss.

27. *Democracy and The British Empire*, 1921, pp. 188–9.

28. *Democracy At The Crossways*, pp. 208 n.3, 280, 381.

29. *Ibid.*, pp. 193, 200. See also J. O. Stubbs, 'Lord Milner and Patriotic Labour', *EHR*, LXXXVII, 344 (July 1972), 717–54.

30. Wallas contributed articles to the *New Republic* and later in Feb. 1918 was consulted by Wilson's 'Special Commissioner', Ray Stannard Baker (together with G. D. H. Cole, Murray and A. E. Zimmern), on the question of war aims. See Wiener, pp. 168–74; A. J. Mayer, *Politics and Diplomacy of Peacemaking*, 1968, p. 35.

31. Bryce to T. Marburg, 7 Dec. 1916, *cit*. R. J. Bartlett, *The League To Enforce Peace*, Chapel Hill, N. Carolina, 1944, p. 66.

32. *The Danger of Peace*, pp. 27–9. Cf. W. H. D. Rouse, *cit*. C. E. M. Joad, *Under The Fifth Rib*, 1932, p. 75.

33. Bosanquet, *Social and International Ideals*, pp. 300–1; Jones, 'Morality and the War', in J. E. Carpenter (ed.), *Ethical and Religious Problems of the War*, p. 41.

34. *The Autobiography of G. Lowes Dickinson*, 1973, p. 191. The L.F.N.A. Council included W. G. S. Adams (Professor of Politics, Oxford), Ernest Barker, R. M. Burrows (Principal of King's College, London), W. G. Geldert (Professor of English Law, Oxford), L. P. Jacks, Sir Henry Jones, Gilbert Murray, C. W. C. Oman, Sir William Osler (Professor of Medicine, Oxford), Sir Frederick Pollock, Sir H. R. Reichel (Principal of University College, Bangor), W. Sanday, Sir Paul Vinogradoff, and E. de Selincourt (Professor of English, Birmingham).

35. Gilbert Murray, *cit*. H. R. Winkler, *The League of Nations Movement in Great Britain, 1914-1918*, N. Brunswick, N. Jersey, 1952, p. 70.

36. *Ibid.*, pp. 50-4; G. Murray and G. L. Dickinson, 'A League of Nations Now? A Symposium', *War and Peace*, 59 (Aug. 1918), 305 and 60 (Sept. 1918), 327-8 (published as a supplement to *The Nation*).

37. Sir Henry Jones, *Form The League Of Peace Now*, 1918, pp. 3-4. But cf. the views of another member: E. Barker in *The Times*, 28 June 1918, p. 5c.

38. 'The Paradox Of The British Empire' (June 1917), repr. in *The Commonwealth At War*, p. 228.

39. *The League Of Nations: An Historical Argument*, pp. 62-3, 66-7.

40. E.g. E. Barker, *A Confederation Of Nations*, Oxford, 1918; R. Muir, *Nationalism and Internationalism*, 1916; F. Pollock, *The League of Nations*, 1919; L. Oppenheim, *The League of Nations*, 1919; T. J. Lawrence, *Lectures On The League Of Nations*, 1919; W. T. S. Stallybrass, *A Society Of States*, 1918; W. A. Phillips, 'The Balance of Power', *New Europe*, V, 55 (1 Nov. 1917), 65-75 and 'The Price of 'The Society of Nations' ', *New Europe*, IX, 112 (5 Dec. 1918), 173-6; Phillips. 'National Federations and World Federation', *Edinburgh Rev.*, CCXXVI, 461 (July 1917), 1-27 and 'President Wilson's Peace Programme and the British Empire', *Edinburgh Rev.*, CCV, 460 (April 1917), 227-48.

41. Pollard, *op. cit.*, p. 51; Heitland, *'Democratic'*, p. 24.

42. Winkler, pp. 76-7.

43. See the Dickinson-Woolf letters for this period, Leonard Woolf Mss.

Chapter 6

1. Broadcast talk, 5 Jan. 1956. *cit.* A. Toynbee, 'The Unity of Gilbert Murray's Life and Work', in Murray, *An Unfinished Autobiography*, 1960, p. 212.

2. I. Henderson, 'The Teacher of Greek', *ibid.*, pp. 146-7.

3. A. Toynbee, *ibid.*, p. 215; J. A. K. Thomson, 'Foreword' to Murray, *Myths and Ethics*, 1944, pp. viii-ix.

4. Arthur Sidgwick was a Fellow of Corpus Christi College which had a reputation for political liberalism (other Fellows were F. C. S. Schiller and, for short periods, L. T. Hobhouse and Graham Wallas). L. R. Phelps (Oriel) was another of the small group of 'Home Rulers' among the dons.

5. M. P. Ashley and C. T. Saunders, *Red Oxford*, 2nd ed. 1933, p. 20.

6. 'National Ideals: Conscious and Unconscious', *IJE* (Oct. 1900) reprinted in Murray, *Essays and Addresses*, 1921, p. 160 (but cf. his second thoughts on this in 1921, p. 8).

7. *Foreign Policy of Sir Edward Grey, 1906-1915*, Oxford, 1915, pp. 9-10.

8. *Ibid.*, p. 10; Murray, 'Ethical Problems of the War', in J. E. Carpenter (ed.), *Ethical and Religious Problems of the War*, pp. 7-8, 2.

9. *Foreign Policy . . .*, pp. 10-11. Not everyone found the documents so convincing: cf. MacIver, *As A Tale Is Told*, p. 75.

10. *The League of Nations Movement*, 1955, p. 3.

11. *Foreign Policy . . .*, p. 123.

12. *Ibid.*, pp. 124, 127.

13. *Ibid.*, p. 11.

14. E.g. E. G. Browne, *A Brief Account of Recent Events in Persia* (1909), *The Persian Constitutionalists* (1909), *The Persian Revolution of 1905-1909* (1910), *The Persian Crisis of December 1911* (1912), 'The Persian Oil Concession', *War and Peace*, I, 11 (Aug. 1914), 315-6. Browne was Professor of Arabic at Cambridge and a leading Persian scholar. He was a leading Radical critic of Grey's failure to restrain Russian policy in Persia.

K

15. *Foreign Policy* . . ., p. 84; *The Way Forward*, 1917, p. 22.

16. *Foreign Policy* . . ., p. 9. 'Conclusions Without Premises', *The Nation*, XVIII, 13 (24 Dec. 1915), 480, 482, made similar criticisms of Lowes Dickinson.

17. *Foreign Policy* . . ., pp. 5–8. During the Boer War Murray had written that those who were called this were 'at least friends of almost all humanity and in practice . . . often the best friends of their own country'. 'National Ideals . . .', p. 181.

18. Russell, *Policy of the Entente*, pp. 2, 145; letter to Murray, 28 Dec. 1915, *cit.* *Autobiography*, II, 49–50; letter to L. Donnelly, 14 Dec. 1914, *cit.* R. W. Clark, *Life of Bertrand Russell*, 1975, p. 248.

19. 'America and England' (November 1916), reprinted in Murray, *Faith, War and Policy*, 1918, p. 181.

20. Reprinted *ibid.*, p. 20.

21. 'National Ideals . . .', p. 163.

22. 'How Can War Ever Be Right?', pp. 25, 30, 32, 39–40, 41–2.

23. 'First Thoughts On The War' (Aug. 1914) reprinted in *Faith, War and Policy*, p. 7. The names were those of two former students of Murray at Oxford.

24. *The Problem of Foreign Policy*, 1917, pp. 9–10. Elsewhere Murray insisted that 'No human being in Germany need starve' because she was 'completely self-supporting'. *Great Britain's Sea Policy*, 1917, p. 24.

25. 'First Thoughts On The War', p. 18.

26. See above, Introduction, n.117.

27. Members included Ramsay Muir, James Bryce, L. P. Jacks, Sir Frederick Pollock.

28. See letters of H. A. L. Fisher to Lady Mary Murray, Fisher Mss. Box 7.

29. 'Ethical Problems of the War', p. 20.

30. 'The Turmoil Of War' (Mar. 1917), reprinted in *Faith, War and Policy*, p. 254.

31. *War Against War*, Oxford, 1914, p. 3.

32. *The Way Forward*, p. 24.

33. 20 May 1915, Hammond Mss., vol. 30.

34. 'How We Stand Now' in Fight For the Right Movement, *For The Right*, 1916, pp. 88–91, 94–5.

35. 'First Thoughts On The War', p. 17.

36. *The Way Forward*, p. 16.

37. 'The Turmoil Of War', p. 254.

38. 1 Jan. 1918, *cit.* I. C. Willis, *England's Holy War*, N.Y., 1928, p. 247, n.8. Together with G. P. Gooch, Dean Inge, Stanley Unwin and Noel Buxton, Murray had signed an address to Lansdowne commending him for his initiative. M. Holroyd, *Lytton Strachey*, Harmondsworth, Middlesex, 1971, p. 756, n.15.

39. Murray to H. A. L. Fisher, 10 Aug. 1914 (typescript), Murray Mss. Box 19; 'Preface' to *Faith, War and Policy*, pp. ix, xiv, xi–xii; letters to J. L. Hammond from 1916 onwards, Hammond Mss. vol. 30.

40. H. A. L. Fisher, *An International Experiment*, Oxford, 1921, p. 11. B. Webb, Diary, 4 Nov. 1918; letters to A. E. Zimmern from J. Bryce (13 Feb. 1919) and J. Headlam-Morley (18 Feb. 1919), Zimmern Mss. Box I; Murray to Morel, 23 Aug. 1919, Morel Mss.

41. 'Ethical Problems of the War', p. 5; 'Preface' to *Faith, War and Policy*, p. iv.

42. Murray, 'The Democratic Control of Foreign Policy', *Contemporary Rev.*, CIX, 2 (Feb. 1916), 180–91 (a review of Arthur Ponsonby's *Democracy and Diplomacy*).

43. On Murray's visits to Asquith to prevent death sentences being carried out in France, see Murray to J. W. Graham, 28 Dec. 1920, Murray Mss. Box 57.

44. 'The Turmoil Of War', pp. 240–1.

45. *'The Pale Shade'*, 1917, p. 35.

46. 'Is An Estimate Of Our Own Age Possible?', *Contemporary Rev.*, CXVI, 2 (Aug. 1919), 133.

47. Taylor, *Troublemakers*, p. 156.

48. *The Cult of Violence*, 1934, p. 18.

49. 'Gilbert Murray and the League', in Murray, *Unfinished Autobiography*, pp. 186–7.

50. *Problems of Foreign Policy*, pp. 5–6; *The Ordeal of This Generation*, 1929, pp. 173–9. Like Hobhouse, Murray held the erosion of a synthetic world view (especially in science) as largely responsible for the existing intellectual 'chaos'.

51. On Hobhouse, see P. Weiler, 'The New Liberalism of L. T. Hobhouse', *Victorian Studies*, XVI, 2 (Dec. 1972), 160, n.61.

52. Letter to E. Lyttleton, 11 Jan. 1937, *cit.* J. Smith, '1889–1957: Some Personal and Chronological Notes From the Correspondence', in Murray, *Unfinished Autobiography*, p. 115.

Chapter 7

1. D. Proctor, 'Introduction' to *The Autobiography of G. Lowes Dickinson*, p. 2. Also p. 144; see *The Nation*, VI, 23 (5 Mar. 1910), 881; VII, 6 (7 May 1910), 205–6, 8 (21 May 1910), 277–8, 9 (28 May 1910), 312 and 10 (4 June 1910), 348–9 for the Budget controversy.

2. N. Wedd, 'Goldie Dickinson: The Latest Cambridge Platonist', *Criterion*, XII, 47 (Jan. 1933), 178.

3. *Loc. cit*; E. M. Forster, *Goldsworthy Lowes Dickinson*, 1973 edition, p. 72.

4. Forster, pp. 32–42.

5. *Ibid.*, pp. 72–3.

6. Dickinson, 'Is War Inevitable?', 222.

7. 'Quo Vadis?', *Independent Rev.*, VIII, 2 (Feb. 1906), 156.

8. E.g. 'The Social Ideal of Democracy', *Working Men's College J.*, XI, 209 (Dec. 1910), 430–3 and XII, 210 (Jan. 1911), 18–19 (lectures at the College).

9. 'Peace or War?', 132.

10. 'The Holy War', *The Nation*, XV, 19 (8 Aug. 1914), 700.

11. Letter to Janet Ashbee, 4 Nov. 1914 in C. R. Ashbee Journal, vol. 17.

12. K. G. Robbins, *The Abolition of War*, Cardiff, 1976, p. 49; G. W. Egerton, *Great Britain and The Creation Of The League of Nations*, 1979, pp. 7–8.

13. *Autobiography*, pp. 195–6. See Proctor's comments, p. 24.

14. Letter to N. Wedd, 4 Nov. 1916, Wedd Mss.

15. 'Some of my Contemporaries at Cambridge', *Portraits From Memory*, 1956, pp. 67–8.

16. Vernon Lee, *cit.* Forster, p. 133. Cf. K. Martin, *Father Figures*, 1966, pp. 117–27 and L. Woolf, *Beginning Again*, 1964, pp. 190–1.

17. Forster, p. 136.

18. Letter to J. Ashbee, 4 Nov. 1914, C. R. Ashbee Journal.

19. 9 Jan. 1918, cutting in Dickinson Mss. See also Dickinson's reply, ibid., 15 Jan. 1918, p. 6.

20. Letter to E. Canaan, 11 Sept. 1914, Canaan Mss. 1022. Canaan himself was rather sceptical of the practicability of 'democratic control'. See his letters to E. D. Morel, 12 Sept. 1914 and C. R. Buxton, 13 April 1916, Canaan Mss. 1023.

21. 'The War and The Way Out', *Atlantic Mthly.*, CXIV, 6 (Dec. 1914), 820; *The War and The Way Out*, 1914, p. 10.

22. 'Democratic Control of Foreign Policy', *Atlantic Mthly.*, CXVIII, 2 (Aug. 1916), 145, 148.

23. *The War and The Way Out*, p. 7.

24. Pp. 22, 126.

25. C. E. Playne, *Britain Holds On, 1917, 1918*, 1933, p. 59.

26. *After The War*, 1915, pp. 13, 7.

27. E.g. 'The war between these two ideals [atavistic nationalism and temporarily submerged nationalism] is the greater war that lies behind the present conflict ... What we are fighting, in fighting Germany, is the national spirit carried to a height of cynical unscrupulousness which shocks even the nationalists of other countries.' Introduction to R. Rolland, *Above The Battlefield*, Cambridge, 1914, p. 4.

28. Letters to F. P. Bulmer, 21 Feb. 1915 and 10 Sept. 1917 (both typescripts), Wedd Mss.

29. 2 Nov. 1918, Woolf Mss.

30. *European Anarchy*, pp. 134–5; *After The War*, p. 7.

31. 'The War and The Way Out: A Further Consideration', *Atlantic Mthly.*, CXV, 4 (April 1915), 518; *The Choice Before Us*, 1917, p. v.

32. 7 Dec. 1918, Woolf Mss.

33. 'The Basis of Permanent Peace', in *Towards A Lasting Settlement*, 1915, p. 15: 'The War and The Way Out: A Further Consideration', 518.

34. *European Anarchy*, p. 11.

35. Taylor, *The Troublemakers*, pp. 16, 162–3.

36. M. Swartz, *The Union of Democratic Control*, Oxford, 1971, p. 132.

37. M. D. Dubin, 'Towards the Concept of Collective Security: The Bryce Group's Proposals for the Avoidance of War, 1914–1917', *International Organization*, XXIV, 2 (Spring 1970), 289. See also Egerton, pp. 7–8; L. Martin, *Peace Without Victory*, New Haven, 1958, p. 62; Dickinson, *Autobiography*, pp. 190–1.

38. *Autobiography*, pp. 145–6.

39. E.g. by the international lawyer T. E. Holland in *The Times*, 18 Oct. 1915, p. 4d. See also M. Z. Doty, *The Central Organisation For A Durable Peace (1915–1919)*, Geneva, 1945, *passim*.

40. *Autobiography*, pp. 193–4.

41. *The War and The Way Out*, p. 41; *After The War*, p. 21.

42. P. vii.

43. Letter to C. R. Ashbee, 26 Mar. 1915, Ashbee Journal.

44. *The Choice Before Us*, p. 88.

45. 'On 'Punishing Germany' ', *War and Peace*, II, 20 (May 1915), 121–2. See also his articles 'The German Socialists and the War', *ibid.*, II, 23 (Aug. 1915), 168–9; 'A German On The War', *Hibbert J.*, XIV, I (Oct. 1915), 30–6 (but see L. P. Jacks's editorial note p. 33n.); letters to *The Nation*, XVIII, 9 (27 Nov. 1915), 326 and XIX, 25 (16 Sept. 1916), 757–8 and 27 (30 Sept. 1916), 324.

46. 10 June 1916, Scott Mss. B.M. Add. 50908. See also Dickinson, *Economic War After The War* (1916) and 'Economic Policy After The War', *War and Peace*, III, 35 (Aug. 1916), 167–8.

47. 'The Conditions of a Durable Peace', *Cambridge Mag.*, VI, 5 (11 Nov. 1916), 103–4, 6 (18 Nov. 1916), 130, 7 (25 Nov. 1916), 158–9 and 8 (2 Dec. 1916), 201.

48. 3 May 1918, Murray Mss. Box 81.

49. 'Face The Facts', *War and Peace* (Aug. 1916) reprinted in Keynes, *Collected Writings*, XVI, 183, 180.

50. *Ibid.*, p. 179.

51. 'The Economics Of War in Germany', *Economic J.*, XXV, 3 (Sept. 1915), 452.

52. 'The Choice Before Us', *Covenant*, I 2 (Jan. 1920), 186–90 (this was the journal of the League of Nations Union); 'The Plight of Germany', *The Nation*, XXVII, 11 (11 Dec. 1920), 381.

53. See Dickinson to Wilson, 20 May 1919, cit. Mayer, *Politics and Diplomacy of Peacemaking*, p. 877.

54. 'The Choice Before Us', 186.

55. Forster, p. 95; *The Causes Of International War*, pp. 103, 82.

56. *Causes Of International War*, pp. 83–4. Trotter denied that the mass of voters exercised rational choice. The 'herd instinct' encouraged conformity and fear of deviance. Any consensus was thus basically irrational, conservative and acquiescent to authority.

57. *Ibid.*, pp. 103–4; 'The Future of British Liberalism', *Atlatnic Mthly.*, CXXV, 4 (April 1920), 550, 553–4; 'The Plight of Germany', 381; 'Bolshevism', *International Rev.*, N.S. II, 7 (July 1919), 544–8; *The International Anarchy*, p. 45; Forster, p. 86.

58. *Causes Of International War*, p. 85.

59. *Autobiography*, pp. 198–9.

60. *The International Anarchy*, p. 492 (the last words in the book).

61. 'The Abyss', *The Nation*, XLVIII, 6 (8 Nov. 1930), 212.

62. E.g. his last article on the subject: 'Would You Fight For the League?', *Clarion*, III, 6 (June 1931), 107–8. Cf. Dickinson, *The Future of The Covenant*, 1920, pp. 5–11, 13; 'The League Under Fire', *Foreign Affairs*, VI, 2 (May 1925), 262–3. Dickinson had argued the case for an international armed force in 'The Problem of Armaments and A League Of Nations', *Friend's Quly. Examiner*, LI, 202 (April 1917), 193–7.

Chapter 8

1. *Policy of the Entente*, p. 3.

2. 'The Morality of Strife', 14.

3. *Justice in War-Time*, pp. 10–12.

4. *Policy of the Entente*, pp. vi–vii.

5. *Foreign Policy of Sir Edward Grey*, p. 8.

6. *Policy of the Entente*, pp. 4–5. Cf. C. Hazelhurst, *Politicians at War*, p. 14.

7. 'The Ethics of War', *IJE*, XXV, 2 (Jan. 1915), 127–9.

8. *Principles of Social Reconstruction*, pp. 85–6, 84. This chapter, 'War as an Institution', had originally been published in the *Atlantic Monthly* in May 1916.

9. In 1941 he still felt that 'the arguments for the policy of conciliation were very strong' up to the time of Munich. Letter to the *N.Y. Times*, 11 Feb. 1941, cit. V. J. McGill, 'Russell's Political and Economic Philosophy', in P. A. Schilpp (ed.), *The Philosophy of Bertrand Russell*, Evanston and Chicago, 1944, p. 585, n.13. However, as late as April 1939 he supported Roosevelt's mediation attempt. See Clark, pp. 465–6.

10. *Policy of the Entente*, p. 35; 'The War and Non-Resistance', *Atlantic Monthly* (Aug. 1915), reprinted in *Justice in War-Time*, p. 53.

11. 'The Philosophy of Pacifism', in *Towards Ultimate Harmony*, 1915, p. 8. This was a lecture at a conference on 'Pacifist Philosophy'.

12. A. F. Pollard, 'The Temptation of Peace' (1916), reprinted in *Commonwealth at War*, pp. 177–8.

13. E.g. 'But, of course, all that I have been saying is fantastic, degrading, and out of

touch with reality. I have been assuming that men are to some extent guided by reason, that their actions are directed to ends such as 'life, liberty, and the pursuit of happiness'.' *Justice in War-Time*, p. 52.

14. *Ibid.*, pp. 25, 27.

15. E.g. G. F. A. Best, *Humanity in Warfare*, 1980, pp. 255–7.

16. *Justice in War-Time*, pp. 127–9.

17. 'The Danger to Civilization', *Justice in War-Time*, p. 122.

18. Pp. 246–7. Coulton argued that neutrality imposed obligations as well as privileges.

19. Perry, 'Non-Resistance and the Present War ...', 312–3.

20. *Main Illusions of Pacificism*, p. 247.

21. *Autobiography*, II, 17. Cf. his letter to Ottoline Morrell (29 Oct. 1915) on hearing that D. H. Lawrence was leaving England (p. 55).

22. *Policy of the Entente*, pp. vi–vii.

23. *Main Illusions ...*, pp. 247–8.

24. *Policy of the Entente*, *loc. cit.*

25. *Justice in War-Time*, pp. 50–2.

26. Sonnenschein, *Idols of War and Peace*, p. 13.

27. *Justice in War-Time*, pp. 40–1.

28. P. 127. Cf. L. W. Aitken, *Bertrand Russell's Philosophy of Morals*, N.Y., 1963, pp. 63–5; D. H. Monro, 'Russell's Moral Theories', in D. F. Pears (ed.), *Bertrand Russell*, N.Y., 1972, pp. 328–30; R. Jager, *The Development of Bertrand Russell's Philosophy*, 1972, pp. 463–84.

29. A. Wood, *Bertrand Russell*, 1957, pp. 84–5; Monro, *loc. cit.*

30. 'War Notes by North Staffs', *New Age*, XVIII, 18 (2 Mar. 1916), 413 and 17 (24 Feb. 1916), 390. Hulme had dealt roughly with Russell's definition of 'scientific philosophy', separated off from traditional philosophical problems, in an unpublished essay. See Hulme's posthumously published *Speculations*, 1924, pp. 28–9, 43. He was killed in action in 1917.

31. 'War Notes by North Staffs', *New Age*, XVII, 218 (13 Jan. 1916), 246.

32. Reprinted from *Cambridge Mag.*, 5 Feb. 1916, in Hulme, *Further Speculations*, Minneapolis, 1955, p. 180. Russell replied that he was 'concerned to represent *both* sides as moved by impulse', and that difference of 'ethical valuation' was on the surface only. Ethical agreement could 'only arise through similarity of desires and impulses'. The claim which Hulme and others made for the 'universality' of their ethical judgements merely embodied 'the impulse to persecution or tyranny'. Reply reprinted in *Further Speculations*, pp. 209–13.

33. *Principles of Social Reconstruction*, p. 67.

34. Contribution to 'Symposium: The Nature of the State in View of its External Relations', p. 302.

35. *Justice in War-Time*, pp. 13–14, p. 26.

36. 'The Philosophy of Pacifism', p. 8. This had been seen by the 19th-century American pacifist Adin Ballou. See R. Wasserstrom, 'On the Morality of War: A Preliminary Enquiry', in Wasserstrom (ed.), *War and Morality*, Belmont, Calif., 1970, pp. 90–4.

37. 'The Economics of War in Germany', 449.

38. 'The Philosophy of Pacifism', pp. 8–9.

39. 'The Ethics of War', 130–7.

40. 'The Morality of Strife', 12.

41. 'The Philosophy of Pacifism', p. 9.

42. E.g. in *Political Ideals*, 1963, pp. 25–35 (first published 1917).

43. 'The Philosophy of Pacifism', *loc. cit.*

44. *Loc. cit.* and 'The War and Non-Resistance', pp. 44–8. Russell was much influenced by the syndicalist idea of the general strike and had (ironically, in view of his controversy with its translator) read Sorel's *Reflections on Violence*. See Russell, *Roads to Freedom*, 1918, pp. 70–95, 138.

45. 'The War and Non-Resistance', *loc. cit.* and 'The Philosophy of Pacifism', pp. 10–11.

46. *Autobiography*, II, 192.

47. *Which Way to Peace?*, 1936, pp. 142–3. Cf. pp. 136–41.

48. Perry, 'Non-Resistance and the Present War . . .', 310–11. Perry was, like many American academics, pro-British. See his 'What is Worth Fighting For?', *Atlantic Mthly.*, CXVI, 6 (Dec. 1915), 822–31.

49. 'The Philosophy of Pacifism', pp. 10–11, 14 and *Justice in War-Time*, pp. 44–8. No country, Russell felt, was likely to adopt non-resistance unilaterally.

50. In J. Bell (ed.), *We Did Not Fight 1914–18*, 1935, p. 330.

51. XV, 20 (15 Aug. 1914), 738. The 'incitements' of politicians, journalists, financiers and arms manufacturers Russell considered 'exactly analogous to those of men who distribute indecent pictures or produce lascivious plays'. *Justice in War-Time*, p. 58.

52. See Hart's preface, pp. v–vii (Russell cites it in *Principles of Social Reconstruction*, p. 15n).

53. *Principles of Social Reconstruction*, p. 90. Jones's article appeared in *International Rev.*, I, 10/11 (24 Dec. 1915), 443–61.

54. 'Is Permanent Peace Possible?', *Atlantic Mthly.* (Mar. 1915), reprinted in *Justice in War-Time*, pp. 87–8.

55. 'Why Nations Love War', *War and Peace* (Nov. 1914), reprinted in *ibid.*, pp. 61–4.

56. *Principles of Social Reconstruction*, pp. 95ff.

57. *Justice in War-Time*, p. 85.

58. *Principles of Social Reconstruction*, p. 43.

59. *Justice in War-Time*, p. 64.

60. *Ibid.*, pp. 92–3.

61. *Ibid.*, p. 58.

62. *Cit.* A. J. Ayer, *Russell*, 1972, p. 150.

63. *Cit.* A. Wood, p. 83.

64. *Justice in War-Time*, pp. 110–11, 117, 120. To William Rothenstein, Russell wrote on New Year's Day 1916: 'I wonder whether this year will see the end of the madness, and what will be left of Europe when peace returns. We who knew life before the war will come to seem like odd survivals of a softer age, like the Romans who lingered on after the barbarian invasion'. *Cit.* Rothenstein, *Men and Memories*, 1932, II, 316.

65. *Autobiography*, I, 68, 144.

Chapter 9

1. W. Blunt, *Cockerell*, 1964, p. 163.

2. Hardy, p. 10.

3. *Cambridge Mag.*, VI, 8 (17 Feb. 1917), 322–3 and 14 (24 Feb. 1917), 367. See also J. Stewart, *Jane Ellen Harrison*, 1959, p. 151.

4. 'New Light on the Causes of the War', in *England on the Witness Stand*, N.Y., 1915, p. 99. See also the clipping in Conybeare Mss. with E. F. Carritt's comments.

5. Murray, *The Foreign Policy of Sir Edward Grey*, p. 12. Cf. Murray to J. L. Hammond, 21 June 1915, Hammond Mss., vol. 30. Price was a founder-member of the U.D.C. and soon to be correspondent for the *Manchester Guardian* in Russia. See M. P. Price, *My Three Revolutions*, 1969, chapter 1.

6. Conybeare *op. cit.*, pp. 99–100. Count Stephen Tisza was Hungarian Prime Minister, 1913–17.

7. *Ibid.*, pp. 100–6. Serge Sazonov (Sazanof) was Russian Foreign Minister (1910–16); Prince Karl Lichnowsky was German Ambassador in London (1912–14).

8. *England on the Witness Stand* (1915) and *The Awakening of Public Opinion in England* (1915).

9. 2 July 1915, p. 9d.

10. Letters from A. J. Butler (Brasenose College), J. T. Cunningham (former Fellow of University College), who considered people like Conybeare 'cowards as well as traitors', G. W. Prothero, who wrote of 'virulent and libellous attacks' on Grey: *Morning Post*, 19 June 1915 (p. 9e), 21 June 1915 (p. 6e), 22 June 1915 (p. 6g), 24 June 1915 (p. 6d).

11. Raleigh to G. W. Prothero, 30 June 1915, Prothero Mss., PP.3/IV. See also letters of 1 and 3 July 1915, and the letters published in *Letters of Sir Walter Raleigh*, II, 429–30, 434 to W. Mcn. Dixon and Meyer.

12. *Oxford Mag.*, XXXIII, 24 (18 June 1915), 396 (also 378–9); *Morning Post*, 21 June 1915 (p. 6f), 23 June 1915 (p. 6d).

13. *Sir Edward Grey*, 1971, p. 300.

14. *Open Court*, XXIX, vii (July 1915) 393n. (letter to the editor), 402. See also *ibid.*, viii (Aug. 1915), 506.

15. VI, xxiii (2 June 1917), 661.

16. 'A Message from Aristophanes', *Open Court*, XXX, i (Jan. 1916), 41–59.

17. 'In a word it was Russia's war and we had to consent to all her wishes.' Conybeare to E. D. Morel, 8 Jan. 1921, Morel Mss. F.9.

18. 'It seems clear to me on his own evidence that Sir E. Grey must bear a large share of the catastrophe, whether he acted as he did consciously or stupidly. He steadily refused to give Germany any assurance of neutrality on any conditions, until he produced a belief that he meant England to fight, and Germany thereupon ran 'amok'. But the evidence shows that she was willing to bid high for our neutrality [Lichnowsky's offer] .... It is sickening to think that this deluge of blood has been let loose in order that the tyranny of the Tsar shall be extended over all the world.' Schiller to Russell, 19 Aug. 1914, *cit.* Russell, *Autobiography*, II, 44–5. Schiller was very probably at the meeting of tutors referred to by Conybeare.

19. H. G. Johnston, 'Arthur Cecil Pigou, 1877–1959', *Canadian J. of Economics and Political Science*, XXVI, i (Feb. 1960), 153.

20. XV, xix (6 Feb. 1916), 591. Cf. a report of a Cambridge Union debate in which Pigou took part: *Cambridge Mag.*, IV, xvii (13 Mar. 1915), 336.

21. 15 Feb. 1915 (p. 6c) and 27 Feb. 1915 (p. 6e). For critical letters and Pigou's reply, see *ibid.*, 17 Feb. 1915 (p. 6f), 23 Feb. 1915 (p. 6g), 27 Feb. 1915 (p. 6e).

22. W. Cunningham (Fellow of Trinity College), *The Nation*, XVI, xx (13 Feb. 1915), 619. Cunningham was to be one of Pigou's persecutors. Cf. H. S. Jones (Trinity), *Morning Post*, 23 Feb. 1915 (p. 6f), who argued that Germany had to be 'absolutely ground to powder'.

23. XVI, xix (15 May 1915), 222.

24. 'The Conditions of a Permanent Peace', *War and Peace*, III, 28 (Jan. 1916), 54–55.

25. 26 Nov. 1915, p. 6d.

26. 30 April 1916, n.p.

27. See entries for 30 April; 6, 8, 10, 19, 22–23, 25–26, 29–30 May; 13, 19–22 June 1916; 25 and 29 April 1917. J. N. Keynes Mss.

28. The entry gives details of the vote.

29. *Cambridge Daily News*, 4 May 1916, p. 4a. On Foxwell and the National Party, see W. D. Rubinstein, 'Henry Page Croft and the National Party', *J. of Contemporary History*, IX, i (Jan. 1974), 139.

30. *Cambridge Mag.*, V, 22 (27 May 1916), 490; J. N. Keynes Diary, 10 and 19 May 1916; *Cambridge Daily News*, 22 May 1916, p. 4a–b.

31. J. N. Keynes Diary, 19 May 1916.

32. M. Cole, *Life of G. D. H. Cole*, 1971, p. 48. Magdalen under Sir Herbert Warren (whose snobbery was equalled only by that of Oscar Browning in Cambridge) was a rather 'aristocratic' college.

33. R. P. Arnot in *Historical Bulletin of the Society for the Study of Labour History*, 13 (Autumn 1966), 11. The Society had split off from the University Fabian Society.

34. Letter to the *Oxford Mag.*, XXXVI, 16 (15 Mar. 1918), 231–2; M. P. Ashley and C. T. Saunders, *Red Oxford*, Oxford, [1933], p. 25.

35. Arnot, *loc. cit.*

36. L. P. Carpenter, *G. D. H. Cole*, Cambridge, 1973, p. 36.

37. M. Cole, p. 72.

38. 31 Mar. 1918, *cit.* M. Gilbert, *Plough My Own Furrow*, 1965, p. 111.

39. Diary, vol. 33, 18 Mar. 1916.

40. Letter to G. Murray (18 May 1916) asking him to attest to his (Cole's) conscientious objection. Murray Mss. Box 57.

41. M. Cole, p. 71.

42. Diary, *loc. cit.*

43. *Daily Chronicle*, 5 June 1915, p. 5b; 7 June 1915, p. 5b; 9 June 1915, p. 6c.

44. Letter to Leonard Huxley, 10 Mar. 1916, in *Letters*, pp. 92–4.

45. His entry in *Who's Who* reads: 'First Class Honours Moderations, 1916; First Class Literae Humaniores, 1918; imprisoned as socialist war-resister, 1916; sent down from Oxford for Socialist anti-war propaganda, 1917'.

46. V. G. Childe to G. Murray, 27 May [1918?] to 17 Nov. 1918, Murray Mss. Box 57.

47. *Oxford Mag.*, XXXIV, 15 (10 Mar. 1916), 256 and 16 (17 Mar. 1916), 273.

48. *Autobiography*, I, 146.

49. *Experiment in Autobiography*, II, 762–5.

50. Undated [1912?], *cit.* Clark, p. 244.

51. *Autobiography*, II, 16. Massingham was editor of *The Nation*.

52. To Lucy Donnelly, 22 Aug. 1914, *cit.* B. Feinberg and R. Kasrils, *Bertrand Russell's America*, 1973, I, 51.

53. *Autobiography*, II, 17–18.

54. *Ibid.*, 18–19.

55. To R. F. Hoernle, 11 June 1916, *cit. Bernard Bosanquet and His Friends*, p. 174.

56. Clark, p. 257.

57. *Ibid.*, p. 269. Russell was not happy with the title *Why Men Fight*.

58. West, *Diary of a Dead Officer*, Oxford, 1919, p. 50 (19 Aug. 1916). Siegfried Sassoon apparently made his (more successful) decision before meeting Russell. See *The Complete Memoirs of George Sherston*, 1932, pp. 477ff. Here Russell appears as Thornton Tyrrell.

59. Letter to F. P. Bulmer, 21 Feb. 1915, Wedd Mss.

60. 17 Sept. 1915, p. 9e. See also letters from R. W. Seton-Watson (18 Sept. 1915, p. 9e) and Russell (20 Sept. 1915 p. 9e).

61. J. G. Slater, 'Bertrand Russell and the *Tribunal*', *Russell*, I (Spring 1971), 6–7.

62. Hardy, p. 15.

63. 27 May 1915, *cit. Autobiography*, II, 52.

64. C. P. Snow, 'Foreword' to G. H. Hardy, *A Mathematician's Apology*, Cambridge, 1967, p. 39.

65. Russell, 'Some of my Contemporaries at Cambridge', *Portraits from Memory*, 1956, p. 67. On McTaggart, 'the most curious combination imaginable of Dr. Johnson, Hegel, and Robert Browning', see Dickinson, *Autobiography*, p. 143.

66. *Portraits from Memory*, p. 93. Cf. the letter from Whitehead, 4 June 1916, *cit.* Russell, *Autobiography*, II, 65.

67. A. E. Housman to E. H. Neville, *cit.* Wood, *Bertrand Russell*, p. 89.

68. Letters to Sir. G. O. Trevelyan, 20 Mar. 1917 and 12 Mar. 1916, in R. St. J. Parry, *Henry Jackson*, Cambridge, 1926, pp. 94, 107 (see also pp. 96, 101–2). The Librarian at Trinity College had similar views. See H. F. Stewart, *Francis Jenkinson*, Cambridge, 1926, p. 76.

69. Hardy, pp. 25–9, 43–4. Russell got his two terms' leave only with difficulty.

70. See *Rex v. Bertrand Russell*, 1916. The pamphlet (*The Case of Ernest F. Everett*) is reprinted in Russell, *Autobiography*, II, 63–4. See also Boulton, pp. 182–5.

71. *Cit.* Holroyd, p. 622.

72. H. McL. Innes to Russell, 11 July 1916, *cit. Autobiography*, II, 68. Russell seems to have realised that he could lose the lectureship (see his letter to Ottoline Morrell, *ibid.*, p. 67).

73. Hardy, pp. 43–6 (a remarkably charitable view of the Council's action).

74. Letter to N. Wedd, 12 Nov. 1916, Wedd Mss. Box. III.

75. Letters from S. Alexander and F. M. Cornford, *cit.* Russell, *Autobiography*, II, 68.

76. 3 Sept. 1916, *cit. ibid.*, 71.

77. *The Nation*, XIX, 19 (5 Aug. 1916), 568; 20 (12 Aug. 1916), 596–9 (from three mathematics Fellows: G. H. Hardy, J. E. Littlewood, S. Chapman); 25 (16 Sept. 1916), 759 (D. S. Robertson).

78. Letter of 23 July 1916, *cit.* Russell, *Autobiography*, II, 69.

79. Hardy, p. 43.

80. Proofs of the manifesto in J. M. Keynes Mss. Box. 17 (Ec.2).

81. Five other Fellows approved but did not sign, including Ward who had no wish to sign 'anything that would whitewash the action of the Council' in dismissing Russell. See Hardy, pp, 49–51, 53.

82. Lord Chorley, 'Academic Freedom in the United Kingdom', *Law and Contemporary Problems*, XXVIII (Summer 1963), 662.

83. See J. R. Mock, *Censorship 1917*, Princeton, 1941, pp. 32–3; Hofstadter and Metzger, pp. 495–506; Gruber, chapter V.

84. W. Zuelzer, *The Nicolai Case*, Detroit, 1982, pp. 186, 26.

85. *Ibid.*, p. 26 and generally chapter 1. Förster retained his chair during the war.

86. *Ibid.*, chapters 9–14; R. Rolland, *The Forerunners*, 1920, pp. 140–74 (which incorrectly has Nicolai imprisoned); G. F. Nicolai, *The Biology of War*, 1919, pp. v–vi, 9–11.

87. C. H. Herford in *The Nation*, XIX, 17 (22 July 1916), 503. Herford was a former Fellow of Trinity College, now Professor of English at Manchester University.

88. *Ibid.*, XIX, 18 (29 July 1916), 537 (Dickinson) and 26 (23 Sept. 1916), 790–1 (Murray).

89. 'The German Peace Offer', *Tribunal*, 90 (3 Jan. 1918), 1 (reprinted in Russell, *Autobiography*, II, 79–81) and 72 (30 Aug. 1917), 2.

90. *Hansard*, Ser. 5, LXXXVI (Oct.–Nov. 1916), 538–40. For subsequent debate see *ibid.*, 863–82, 1127–8 and LXXXVIII (Nov.–Dec. 1916), 146, 288–300.

91. *Cit.* Feinberg and Kasrils, pp. 60–1.

92. See the file in the J. M. Keynes Mss (30.12) on the attitude of the National Council for Civil Liberties.

93. Manifesto amongst Keynes-Russell letters, J. M. Keynes Mss. 32.2 (also in Murray Mss. Box 57). Signatories were S. Alexander, H. W. Carr (Secretary of the Aristotelian Society), G. D. Hicks (Professor of Philosophy, University College, London), T. P. Nunn (Professor of Education, London), A. E. Taylor, J. Ward, A. Whitehead. See various letters to Murray, 7–20, Sept 1918, Murray Mss.

94. Taylor to Murray, 4 Sept. 1918, Murray Mss. Box 57. According to Lowes Dickinson, this was also a consideration when Trinity College Council dismissed Russell in 1916. See his letter to N. Wedd, 4 Nov. 1916, Wedd Mss. Box 3.

95. Murray to Russell, 27 Mar. 1918, *cit.* Russell, *Autobiography*, II, 82 (and 34). Also letters of Murray to Russell, 10 Feb. 1918 to 7 April 1918, Murray Mss. Box 46; Russell to H. W. Carr, 29 Mar. 1918 to 17 April 1918, *cit.* M. R. Thompson, 'Some Letters of Bertrand Russell to Herbert Wildon Carr', *Coranto* (1976), 15–18.

96. A. W. Chapman (former University Registrar) to the writer, 26 July 1973.

97. For Max Freund, see T. W. Moody and J. C. Beckett, *Queen's Belfast, 1845–1949*, 1959, II, 457 and n.6, 611.

98. Records of Reading University College Council, 27 Oct. 1914; Minutes of St. Andrews University Court, 19 Oct. 1914 and 10 May 1915; Annual Report of the Vice-Chancellor, Liverpool University (courtesy Mr. A. Allen, University Archives); Edinburgh University Senatus Academicus Minutes, 5 Nov. 1914.

99. W. T. S. Sonnenschein (now Stallybrass) continued to be affectionately known as 'Sonners'. H. G. Hanbury in *DNB, 1941–50*, p. 816.

100. See Walston to N. Wedd, 12 May 1918, Wedd Mss. Box 3.

101. Oliver Lodge, *The War and After*, 1916, pp. 152–3. Haldane had been Lord Chancellor, and was the author of several philosophical works.

102. A. Hassall, '*Just For A Scrap of Paper*', Oxford, 1914, p. 4.

103. 14 May 1915, p. 10d. The signatories were K. H. Breul (Cambridge), H. G. Fiedler (Oxford), A. W. Schüddekopf (Leeds), K. Wichmann (Birmingham), R. Priebsch (London).

104. *The Times*, 19 May 1915, p. 10b and L. Oppenheim, 'On War Treason', *Law Quarterly Rev.*, XXXIII, cxxxi (July 1917), 266.

105. Letter to the Secretary, Certificates of Naturalisation (Revocation) Committee, 21 Oct. 1918 (courtesy of Birmingham University Archives).

106. See M. Sanderson, *The Universities and British Industry, 1850–1970*, 1972, pp. 221–3, 229–30.

107. Letter to the writer from Ms. C. L. Penney, 26 July 1973.

108. *Hansard*, Ser. 5, LXXIII (July 1915), 185–6. Butcher had been a Fellow of Trinity College, Cambridge (1875–84).

109. Information supplied by the German Department, University of Leeds, June 1973.

110. E. L. Ellis, *The University College of Wales, Aberystwyth, 1872–1972*, Cardiff, 1972, p. 171.

111. C. H. Herford in *The Times*, 6 Nov. 1916, p. 10c.

112. A certain Dr. Harries seems to have taken the lead against Ethé. The Professor of History (E. Edwards) who was present at the meeting strongly defended Ethé. *The Times*, 13 April 1916, p. 11d.

113. Herford, *loc. cit.*

114. Ellis, p. 173.

115. See E. M. W. Tillyard, *The Muse Unchained*, 1958, pp. 29, 35, 61.

116. For the offending article, see *The Varsity*, XIV, 340 (9 Feb. 1915), 1. See also: XIV, 341 (16 Feb. 1915), 1–2; 343 (2 Mar. 1915), 5 and 344 (9 Mar. 1915), 11. For the protest, see *Oxford Mag.*, XXXIII, 15 (5 Mar. 1915), 248 and 16 (2 Mar. 1915), 263.

117. *Oxford Mag.*, XXXIII, 20 (21 May 1915), 328 and 21 (28 May 1915), 342. After the war Hazel became Principal of Jesus College.

118. One definition (by a founder of the A.A.U.P.) is: 'the freedom ... to investigate or discuss' a subject and to express 'conclusions, whether through publication or in the instruction of students, without interference from political or ecclesiastical authority, or from the administrative officials' of the university — unless the methods employed 'are found by qualified bodies' of the profession 'to be clearly incompetent or contrary to professional ethics'. A. O. Lovejoy, 'Academic Freedom' in *Encyclopedia of the Social Sciences*, N.Y. 1930, I, 384. Before 1914 American academics were attempting to include extramural freedom of speech into a broader definition of academic freedom. This was reflected in the 1915 Report of the Committee on Academic Freedom and Tenure of the A.A.U.P. See Hofstadter and Metzger, pp. 403–12.

119. Chorley, 664. Cf. E. Ashby, *Universities British, Indian, African*, 1966, p. 292.

120. *Cit.* R. H. Tawney, 'Introductory Memoir' to Unwin, *Studies in Economic History*, 1927, pp. lii–liii.

121. The lead being taken by the fellow-historian Professor Tait. See Winter, p. 152, n.19.

122. See Tawney, 'Introductory Memoir', pp. liii–liv and Rae, pp. 199–200.

Chapter 10

1. 'Inaugural Lecture on the Study of History' (1895), reprinted in Acton, *Lectures on Modern History*, 1906, p. 2.

2. 20 Aug. 1914, p. 3b.

3. Smith Mss. Box I, Group I.

4. Letter to A. Schuster, 15 Oct. 1915, Smith Mss Box I, Group I, Cf. R. H. Tawney to A. L. Smith, 27 Dec. 1917, *cit.* Winter, p. 170.

5. Pp. vii–viii. The joint authors were R. W. Seton-Watson, J. Dover Wilson, Alfred Zimmern and Arthur Greenwood.

6. Letter to F. Cunliffe, 25 Aug. 1914, Smith Mss. Box I, Group I. Cf. Prothero to W. H. Dawson, 15 Mar. 1915, Dawson Mss. WHD/268.

7. See Smith Mss. Box I, Group I.

8. *Memories of Four Score Years*, 1946, p. 153. On the political colouration of Extension lecturers, see S. Rowbotham, 'The Call to University Extension Teaching, 1873–1900', *U. of Birmingham Hist. J.*, XII, i (1969), 57–71.

9. Marwick, *The Deluge*, p. 45.

10. Dicey's *How We Ought To Feel About The War* (1914) was originally a lecture at the Working Men's College, London; Ashley's *The War and Its Economic Aspects* (1914) was originally a W.E.A. lecture at Birmingham.

11. Letter to *The Times*, 5 Sept. 1914, p. 9d. See also letters from T. B. Strong (Vice-Chancellor, Oxford University) and L. R. Farnell (Rector of Exeter College), *ibid.*, 31 Aug. 1914, p. 4b. Also from the historians J. H. Rose and C. G. Robertson, *ibid.*, 21 Aug. 1914 (p. 4c), 26 Aug. 1914 (p. 5a) and 27 Aug. 1914 (p. 7e).

12. *The Times*, 5 Sept. 1914, p. 9d (Sonnenschein) and 26 Aug. 1914, p. 9a (Marshall).

13. *Ibid.*, 22 Aug. 1914, p. 7e. Cf. *Memorials of Alfred Marshall*, 1925, pp. 490-1.

14. *The Times*, 25 Aug. 1914, p. 7d and 31 Aug. 1914, p. 4b.

15. Letter to C. P. Scott, 10 Mar. 1915, C. P. Scott Mss. Cf. J. M. Keynes, 'Alfred Marshall' (1924), reprinted in *Collected Writings*, X, pp. 226-7.

16. *The Times*, 28 Aug. 1914, p. 5b-c.

17. See M. L. Sanders, 'Wellington House and British Propaganda during the First World War'; *Historical J.*, XVIII, i (1975), 119-46; also M. L. Sanders and P. M. Taylor, *British Propaganda During the First World War*, 1982, for a general picture.

18. D. G. Wright, 'The Great War, Government Propaganda and English Men of Letters, 1914-16', *Literature and History*, 7 (Spring 1978), 82-4.

19. I. N. Nicholson, 'An Aspect of Official British Wartime Propaganda', *Cornhill Mag.*, N.S. LXX, 5 (May 1931), 594. The civil servants included Ernest Gowers, later author of *Plain Words*.

20. Letter to J. D. Squires, 20 Jan. 1933, *cit.* Squires, *British Propaganda at Home and in the United States from 1914 to 1917*, Cambridge, Mass., 1935, p. 57. See also S. P. Mews, Religion and English Society in the First World War, Cambridge Ph.D. thesis, 1975, p. 12.

21. S. Gaselee, 'Prefatory Note' to G. W. Prothero, *Select Analytical List of Books Concerning the Great War*, 1923, p. iii. Cf. the material in the Prothero Mss., esp. correspondence with informants on neutral opinion: Countess Martinego in Italy (pp. ii) and Miss S. Norton in the United States (pp. iii); also letters from American academics (pp. 3/VI/1-3) and from Wellington House (pp. 3/VI/4). Also J. Ward to F. von Hügel, 16 Oct. 1914, von Hügel Mss. 3126.

22. H. W. B. Joseph, 'Harold Henry Joachim, 1868-1938', *PBA*, XXIV (1938), 405.

23. Kemp Smith had moved from a lectureship at Glasgow University to the chair of psychology at Princeton (1906), followed by the McCosh chair of Philosophy (1914). He worked in propaganda 1916-18 and then went on to the chair of Logic and Metaphysics at Edinburgh (1919).

24. See Smith, *Our Common Conscience* (1918) and Butler, *International Law and Autocracy* (1917), both products of the lecture circuit in the United States.

25. National Board announcement, *cit.* Gruber, p. 125. On propaganda in the United States generally see: Gruber, chapter IV; J. R. Mock and C. Larson, *Words That Won the War*, Princeton, 1939, chapter 7; L. Gelfand, *The Inquiry*, New Haven, 1963, p. 44.

26. Letter to F. J. Jameson, 21 Nov. 1917, *cit.* L. F. Stock, 'Some Bryce-Jameson Correspondence', *AHR*, L, 2 (Jan. 1945), 268.

27. *Propaganda Technique in the World War*, 1927, p. 32.

28. See Sanders, 122-9 and A. Headlam-Morley, 'Introduction' to J. W. Headlam-Morley, *A Memoir of the Paris Peace Conference, 1919*, 1972, p. xx. Alfred Zimmern had been a Fellow of New College, Oxford (1904-9) before joining the Board of Education in 1912. After the war he had a distinguished academic career.

29. Masterman, *cit.* Sanders, 120; J. M. Read, *Atrocity Propaganda, 1914-1919*, New Haven, 1941, p. 38 and n.76; A. Ponsonby, *Falsehood in Wartime*, 1928, pp. 102-12; Sanders and Taylor, pp. 146-8.

30. Sanders, p. 140.

31. Presidential Address to the British Academy, *PBA*, 1915–16, p. 24.

32. Bryce had studied law at Heidelberg in the 1860s. Later he received honorary degrees in law from Jena (1908) and Leipzig (1909).

33. *Cit.* H. C. Peterson, *Propaganda for War*, Norman, Oklahoma, 1939, p. 58. Cf. E. R. May, *The World War and American Isolation, 1914–17*, Chicago, 1966, p. 180. E. S. Ions, *James Bryce and American Democracy 1870–1922*, 1968, indicates generally the reputation Bryce enjoyed in the United States.

34. Fisher, *Bryce*, II, 126–7.

35. *The Attitude of Great Britain in the Present War*, 1916, p. 26.

36. Letter to B. Henry, 5 April 1917, *cit.* Fisher, *Bryce*, II, 159.

37. Letter of 21 Mar. 1917, *loc. cit.*

38. Letter to C. W. Eliot, 25 June 1915, *cit. ibid.*, II, 155. Eliot had written on behalf of the Union cause during the Civil War.

39. J. M. Read, p. 64. Like many other U.S. historians of the interwar period, Read emphasises the role of Allied propaganda in American entry to the war.

40. *Goodbye To All That*, Harmondsworth, 1960, pp. 152–3.

41. E.g. the Belgian report of 1915 carried the names of three professors of the University of Brussels (Catier, Nys, Wodon). See Belgium, *Report on the Violations of the Rights of Nations . . .*, 1915, I, xxxiv–xxxv. Prince Max of Baden suggested to the Kaiser 'a Report on atrocities, no longer issued as heretofore, by our official authorities, but endorsed by the responsible signatures of well-known German jurists and philanthropists'. *Cit.* J. M. Read, pp. 142–3. Cf. Peterson, pp. 38, 40.

42. Sir John Simon (Home Secretary) to H. A. L. Fisher, 15 Dec. 1914, Fisher Mss. Box 3/2.

43. G. B., Home Office, Committee on Alleged German Outrages, *Report*, I, 3–4.

44. *Loc. cit.* They were instructed 'not to 'lead' the witnesses, or to make any suggestions to them, and also to impress upon them the necessity for care and precision in giving their evidence'. However, they were encouraged to cross-examine them.

45. *Propaganda for War*, pp. 53–4.

46. *Atrocity Propaganda*, p. 204.

47. 22 Aug. 1914, p. 7e.

48. *The Times*, 28 Oct. 1914, p. 9d.

49. *Loc. cit.* and Marshall to C. P. Scott, 10 Mar. 1915, Scott Mss. B.M. Add. 50908.

50. *Letters to 'The Times' Upon War and Neutrality (1881–1920)*, 1921, pp. 77–8.

51. 'The Legal Relations Between an Occupying Power and the Inhabitants', *Law Quly. Rev.*, XXXIII, 132 (Oct. 1917), 370.

52. For international lawyers and the war, see Appendix 2.

53. Farnell, p. 329.

54. *Cit.* M. B. Lowndes, *Diaries and Letters of Marie Belloc Lowndes, 1911–1947*, 1971, p. 73.

55. J. M. Read, p. 26. Read was making a point about all atrocity propaganda, not just the Bryce Report.

56. A. S. Link, *Wilson: The Struggle for Neutrality, 1914–1915*, Princeton, 1975, p. 41 n.11. Cf. Ions, pp. 250, 327 n.19 and E. L. Woodward, *Great Britain and the War of 1914–18*, p. 210 n.2. However, D. M. Smith, *The Great Departure*, N.Y., 1965, p. 4 repeats the view of 'revisionist' historians of the 1930s.

57. G. F. A. Best, *Humanity in Warfare*, 1980, pp. 224–31, 235–7.

58. See pp. 37–41 of the Report for some of the most sensational evidence, and p. 6.

59. Best p. 236.

60. 6 Mar. 1916, Bryce Mss. Box UB57. Cf. Fisher to Bryce 7 Mar. [1915?] and 11 Mar. 1915, *loc. cit.*

61. See his 'A League of Peace' in *For the Right*, 1916 (pp. 130–40), a publication of the 'For the Right' movement of which he was a leading member.

62. 18 Sept. 1914 and 23 Sept. 1914, Bryce Mss. UB/23.

63. *Report*, pp. 6–7.

64. Fisher, *Bryce*, II, 132 n.2. J. H. Morgan's claim that he approached the evidence with initial scepticism does not convince in view of his readiness to give credence to atrocity stories even more lurid than those in the Report. See Lowndes, pp. 75–6 for his disclaimer.

65. *Report*, p. 31.

66. P. Schöller, *Das Fall Löwen u. das Deutsche Weissbuch, cit.* Best, pp. 236–7.

67. *Report*, pp. 34–5.

68. Reprinted from the *Westminster Gazette*.

69. 'Opening Address' in *International Crisis: The Theory of the State*, pp. 6–7.

70. *German Atrocities*, pp. 52–3, 57, 114–5. Cf. his letter to *The Times*, 2 Aug. 1916, p. 7d. Typical of Morgan's tales of girls 'abused by hordes of savage and licentious' German soldiers was one from Richebourg l'Avoué where advancing British soldiers had apparently found a naked girl lying on the ground 'pegged out in the form of a crucifix'. Morgan, *Dishonoured Army*, 1916, p. 19. Such a story was calculated to suggest blasphemy as well as rapaciousness as a German trait.

71. See Best, pp. 146, 344 n.25. Cf. Morgan's remarks in *The German War Book*, 1915, pp. 1–11.

72. *German Atrocities*, pp. 44–5, 118–9, 60.

73. Gwatkin, pp. 8–9.

74. *The Method in the Madness*, p. 243. Cf. the reaction of L. P. Jacks, 'An Interim Religion', pp. 65–8.

75. Letter to G. S. Gordon, 17 Dec. 1914 in Raleigh, *Letters*, II, 409.

76. Pollard, *The War: Its History and Morals*, p. 13.

77. J. W. Allen, *Germany and Europe*, p. 46.

78. J. H. Rose, *Origins of the War*, pp. 21–2.

79. 'The Ethics of Retaliation', in *Ad Clerum*, Dublin, 1918, p. 183.

80. *Ibid.*, pp. 178–84.

81. E.g. D. Cairns, J. E. Carpenter, L. P. Jacks, J. Oman, J. H. Muirhead, A. S. Peake, W. B. Selbie, H. G. Wood, W. Temple in *Goodwill*, II, 8 (23 June 1917).

82. *The War and Its Causes*, p. 30.

83. *The Times*, 1 Sept. 1914, p. 12a–b; Holland, *Letters to 'The Times'*, pp. 69–72.

84. See correspondence in *The Times*, 16 Oct. 1915 (p. 9d), 22 Oct. 1915 (p. 9c–d), 18 Oct. 1915 (p. 9d), 19 Oct. 1915 (p. 10f), 7 Feb. 1916 (p. 9c), 11 Feb. 1916 (p. 7e), 16 Oct. 1917 (p. 9c), 28 Dec. 1917 (p. 4b) from A. F. Pollard, Bryce, W. Sanday, W. B. Selbie, A. Marshall. See also Dicey, *How We Ought To Feel About the War*, p. 11 and E. M. Sidgwick, 'The Morality of Strife in Relation to the War', *International Crisis . . . Ethical and Psychological Aspects*, pp. 19–21.

85. XXXVI, 906 (19 May 1915), 326.

86. *The Times*, 30 Mar. 1917, p. 7e. Cf. J. A. Stewart (Professor of Moral Philosophy at Oxford), *ibid.*, 10 Aug. 1916, p. 8b and 16 Aug. 1916, p. 5c. For the failure to institute war-crime trials after the war, see Best, pp. 178 and 349 n.88; J. H. Morgan, *Assize of Arms*, [1945], I, chapter VIII.

87. See P. Kerr to Curzon in Lothian Mss. GD 40/17/43 and A. Marwick, *Britain in a Century of Total War*, Harmondsworth, 1970, p. 112.

88. Pp. 5, 8.

89. *Belgian Deportations*, p. 55.

90. Including the conservative German historian Gerhard Ritter. See his *The Sword and Scepter*, 1973, III, 358–72.

91. *The Destruction of Poland*, 1916, p. 30.

92. E.g. France, Ministère des Affaires Etrangères, *Germany's Violations of the Laws of 1914–15*, 1915 and Belgium, *Report on the Violation of the Rights of Nations*.

93. See R. T. Shannon, *Gladstone and the Bulgarian Agitation, 1876*, p. 36.

94. R. G. Hovannisian, *The Republic of Armenia*, Berkeley and Los Angeles, 1971, I, 11–15; U. Trumpener, *Germany and the Ottoman Empire, 1914–1918*, Princeton, 1968, chapter VII; M. Ferro, *The Great War, 1914–1918*, 1973, pp. 100–1; F. G. Weber, *Eagles on the Crescent*, Ithaca, 1970, pp. 144 ff.

95. See E. Ettinger, 'The Jew in Russia at the Outbreak of the Russian Revolution', in *The Jews in Soviet Russia Since 1917*, 1970, pp. 18–19; L. Greenberg, *The Jews in Russia*, New Haven, 1951, II, 94–103; E. Zechlin, *Die deutsche Politik u. die Juden im Ersten Weltkrieg*, Göttingen, 1969, chapters 5–10, 23.

96. *Acquaintances*, p. 149.

97. Letter to Bryce, 27 June 1916, *cit.* p. xxxi.

98. Letter to Bryce, 2 Aug. 1916, *cit.* p. xxix.

99. P. 14. But a year earlier Bryce had written to an American friend that reports suggested that German officials *had* done this. See Fisher, *Bryce*, I, 153.

100. *Armenian Atrocities*, 1915, pp. 106–8, 110, 115–6. This was based on the official report.

101. Toynbee, 'The Position of Armenia', *New Europe*, IV, 50 (27 Sept. 1917), 329–35.

102. 'The War State', reprinted in *Essays and Addresses in Wartime*, 1918, p. 52.

103. '*The Murderous Tyranny of the Turks*', N.Y., 1918, pp. 7, 23–4. The title came from the Allied reply (Jan. 1917) to President Wilson's request for a statement of war aims (one of the latter being the liberation of subject nationalities in the Ottoman Empire).

104. The German Government 'was not only unwilling to irritate its Turkish allies [by interceding] but actually wished them to clear its prospective colony from the most formidable competitors on the spot. The German public learned little and late of what was afoot in Turkey.' W. W. Gottlieb, *Studies in Secret Diplomacy During the First World War*, 1957, p. 110.

105. Trumpener, pp. 204–5.

106. See V. H. Rothwell, *British War Aims and Peace Diplomacy, 1914–1918*, Oxford, 1971, pp. 179–84 and (for the public war aims) pp. 64–5.

107. 'Preface' to Toynbee, '*The Murderous Tyranny . . .*', pp. iv–v. Cf. Bryce, 'The Future of Armenia', *Contemporary Rev.*, CXIV, 6 (Dec. 1918), 604–11.

108. Rothwell, pp. 25–30, 117–8.

109. See H. and C. Seton-Watson, *The Making of the New Europe*, 1985; G. Glasgow, *Ronald Burrows*, 1924; G. P. Gooch, *Harold Temperley, 1879–1939*, 1939.

110. Toynbee, *Experiences*, 1969, p. 72 and *Acquaintances*, pp. 228–30.

111. See *The Times*, 5 Mar. 1924, p. 10c.

Chapter 11

1. *War The Offspring of Fear*, 1915, p. 3.

2. Mayer, p. 888.

3. E.g. J. B. Bury and E. G. Browne. See N. H. A. Baynes, *A Bibliography of the Works of J. B. Bury*, Cambridge, 1929, p. 39 and E. D. Ross, p. xv.

4. It has been estimated that 1062 congresses met in international assembly between 1900 and 1910. F. S. Northedge, 'International Intellectual Cooperation Within The League of Nations', London Ph.D. thesis, 1953, p. 242. Cf. F. S. L. Lyons, *Internationalism in Europe, 1815-1914*, Leyden, 1963, pp. 202-8, 223-37.

5. *Cit.* H. Bosanquet, pp. 131-3. Cf. Muirhead, *Bernard Bosanquet*, p. 165 and *Reflections*, p. 181.

6. *PAS*, N.S. XX (1919-20), 304-6.

7. T. F. Tout, 'National and International Cooperation in Historical Scholarship', *TRHS*, Ser. 4, X (1927), 1-20.

8. *Proc. of the 19th International Congress of Americanists*, Washington, D.C., 1917.

9. F. Kenyon, *The British Academy*, p. 21.

10. *PBA*, VII (1915-16), 3-4.

11. 10 May 1918, p. 9d. Cf. the letter from E. A. Sonnenschein, *ibid.*, 29 Nov. 1918, p. 11f.

12. Germany applied for membership of the League of Nations in Feb. 1926, but faced opposition from Brazil, Poland and Spain (a controversy over the composition of the League Council). Germany was finally admitted in Sept. 1926. Austria and Bulgaria had joined in 1920, Hungary in 1922 and Turkey was to join in 1932.

13. J. A. Stewart (Professor of Moral Philosophy, Oxford), *The Times*, 13 May 1918, p. 11d.

14. C. Dampier Whetham (Trinity College, Cambridge), *ibid.*, 24 Aug. 1918, p. 4b.

15. The Advisory Council for Scientific Research (1915), later the Department of Scientific and Industrial Research (1918), the University Grants Committee (1919).

16. J. J. Sheehan, *The Career of Lujo Brentano*, Chicago, 1966, pp. 188-9 (but see p. 189, n.49 for Sheehan's doubts about Brentano's conversion).

17. *The Times*, 7 Nov. 1918, p. 5f.

18. Sheehan, *loc. cit.* He had not changed his mind when he published his memoirs in 1926. See *My Recollections, 1848-1914*, 1930 (first English translation), pp. 382-3.

19. Bryce to J. F. Rhodes, 22 Aug. 1919, *cit.* Fisher, *Bryce*, II, 223-4; E. A. Sonnenschein, 'The German Professors', *19th Century*, LXXXVI (Aug. 1919), 322; H. Wehburg, *Wider den Anruf den 93!*, Charlottenburg, 1920, pp. 8-13. The latter shows that by 1919, of the 93 signatories, 18 were dead, 16 unchanged in their views, 42 claimed to have been deceived (most had not seen the text) or mistaken, 17 had not replied (from a sense of shame, Wehburg surmised). On the atmosphere of the postwar University of Berlin, see Zuelzer, chapters 17-19.

20. *The Times*, 3 Nov. 1919, p. 13e and 6 Nov. 1919, pp. 14d, 18a-b.

21. Barker, *Age and Youth*, p. 136; *The Times*, 10 June 1921, p. 8c and 7 June 1921, p. 10f.

22. *The Times*, 2 July 1921, p. 12e.

23. The lectures were published in English as *Christian Thought* (1923).

24. *Nature*, CII (5 Sept. 1918), 4. Cf. H. H. Godwin-Austen, *ibid.* (26 Sept. 1918), 64.

25. *Science*, N.S. XLIX (21 Feb. 1919), 193.

26. CIV (30 Sept. 1919), 172 (Lankester) and (23 Oct. 1919), 154 (Thompson).

27. *The Times*, 27 Oct. 1920, p. 13e (Bridges). Cf. critical letters from L. R. Farnell (30 Oct. 1920, p. 11e) and B. W. Henderson (19 Oct. 1920, p. 13e), both of Exeter College.

28. *Ibid.*, 20 Oct. 1920, p. 13e.

29. 18 Oct. 1920, p. 12b–c.

30. 18 Oct. 1920, p. 8c. For a list of signatories, see Appendix 6.

31. Sir Frederick Pollock, *The Times*, 26 Oct. 1920, p. 11e (cf. letter of the same date from Arthur Hassall).

32. *International Scholarship*, pp. 5–7.

33. E. D. Ross, p. xv.

34. H. Koht, *The Origins and Beginnings of the International Committee of Historical Sciences*, Lausanne, 1962, pp. 2–4. Pirenne had been imprisoned on suspicion of being a leader of the campaign of passive resistance to German occupation. See J. Pirenne, 'Preface' to H. Pirenne, *A History of Europe*, N.Y., 1958, I, xxiii–xxxii.

35. Kenyon, *The British Academy*, p. 26.

36. *A Description of the I.C.S.U.*, Cambridge, 1950, pp. 2, 114–5. Cf. *Nature*, CVII (17 Mar. 1921), 72 and (24 Mar. 1921), 108; Forster, *Goldsworthy Lowes Dickinson*, pp. 154–6.

37. *The Times*, 28 Oct. 1926, p. 9b. The Board included Gilbert Murray, Ernest Barker, Sir William Beveridge, C. G. Robertson, Sir Michael Sadler, A. C. Seward (Master of Downing College, Cambridge). G. Foster (Provost of University College, London), P. Giles (Master of Emmanuel College, Cambridge), Sir T. Morrison (Principal of Armstrong College, Newcastle).

38. See R. Simpson, *How the Ph.D. Came to Britain*, 1983, chapters 5–6. In 1913, due to overcrowding, restrictions had been imposed on the admission of foreign students to German universities (Simpson, pp. 115–6).

39 See the correspondence reprinted in *Heidelberg and American Universities*, N.Y., 1936, which (despite its title) is concerned with the response of British universities to Nazism.

Postscript

1. Pp. 54–5.

2. *Ibid.*, pp. 53–4.

3. *Peace with Patriotism*, p. 9.

4. See Stromberg, *Redemption By War*, Lawrence, Kansas, 1982 and R. Wohl, *The Generation of 1914*, Cambridge, Mass., 1979.

5. See C. Lasch, *The Agony of the American Left*, 1970, Chapter 3.

6. *Times Higher Education Supplement*, 21 Oct. 1983, p. 5.

Appendix 2

1. E. A. Whittuck, 'International Law Teaching', *Trans. Grotius Soc.*, III (1917), 55. In 1910 there were ten professors, readers and lecturers in international law in Britain, compared with more than double the number in France, and one or two professors in each German and Swiss university. A. P. Higgins, *The Binding Force of International Law*, Cambridge, 1910, p. 48, n.12.

2. 18 Sept. 1914 speech at Edinburgh, *cit.* Ginsburg, p. 34. But for the relative unimportance of international law in policy-making, see C. Parry, 'Foreign Policy and International Law', in *The Foreign Policy of Sir Edward Grey* (ed. F. H. Hinsley), Cambridge, 1977, pp. 89–99.

3. H. E. Richards, 'The Issues at Stake in this War', pp. 202–3.

4. J. Joll, 'Politicians and the Freedom to Choose: The Case of July 1914', in A. Ryan (ed.), *The Idea of Freedom*, Oxford, 1979, pp. 102–3.

5. *The Binding Force of International Law*, p. 22.

6. *Does International Law Still Exist?*, Oxford, 1914, pp. 8, 13–17. Cf. L. Oppenheim, *The League of Nations*, 1919, p. v.

7. See I. Abrams, 'The Emergence of the International Law Societies', *Rev. of Politics*, XIX, 3 (July 1957), 361–80.

8. 'Introduction' to *Trans. Grotius Soc.*, I (1915), 1–2.

9. Best, pp. 247–8. The Declaration was designed to cover sea war as the Hague Regulations covered land war. Rules on blockade were left substantially unaltered (hence British approval), while those on contraband were 'refined and extended', offering neutrals 'a better prospect of continuing to do business with belligerents in not absolutely contraband goods'. Cf. Parry *op. cit.*, pp. 104–5.

10. Best, p. 248. Because thus Britain failed to ratify the Declaration, to which it was a signatory, other states also refused to ratify it.

11. *Ibid.*, p. 212. Cf. Parry, pp. 103–8.

12. Holland, pp. 87–92, 154.

13. *Does International Law Still Exist?*, pp. 14–15. The distinction between 'absolute' and 'conditional' contraband was a traditional one which had been preserved in the 1909 Declaration. The former included all articles (e.g. guns, ammunition) which could only be used for military purposes, and could be condemned by mere proof of destination to enemy territory. The latter included everything of practical use in peace or war (i.e. everything else), but could only be defined as 'conditional contraband' after further proof of its consignment directly to enemy government or military forces.

14. Macdonell was a member of the Anglo-German Friendship Society, Lawrence of the Church of England Peace League. Both were members of the National Peace Congress (see Appendices 3–4). On Lawrence's reputation, see D. H. N. Johnson, *The English Tradition of International Law*, 1962, p. 25.

15. *Report of Proceedings*, 1912, pp. 89–90.

16. 'Present Policy', p. 15. We need to distinguish 'the exemption of neutral shipping from interference, whether carrying contraband, however defined, or goods of enemy origin or ownership' from 'the exemption of private property from capture, whether carried in neutral or enemy bottoms and with or without exceptions in case of contraband character, however defined, or of destination to a blockaded place'. Parry, *op. cit.*, p. 104. The second would clearly change the status of belligerent ships and their cargoes; the first would not. Both were proposed as solutions before 1908.

17. Lawrence, 'The Inviolability of Private Property at Sea in Time of War', *Peace Yearbook 1913*, pp. 6–9. Cf. Lawrence, *The Third Hague Conference and Innocent Commerce in Time of War*, 1912 and his contribution to the 'Understanding Conference' (1912) in the Report of Proceedings.

18. *Some Plain Reasons for Immunity from Capture of Private Property at Sea*, 1910, pp. 9–10.

19. *International Problems and the Hague Conferences*, 1908, pp. 106–7.

20. *The Society of Nations*, p. 83.

21. See E. Castren, *The Present Law of War and Neutrality*, Helsinki, 1954, pp. 21–2, 358–9, 535 and J. W. Garner, *International Law and The World War*, 1920, I, 30. Britain formally abandoned the Declaration of London in 1916.

22. Best, p. 248.

23. 'The War and the Empire', *Law Quly. Rev.*, XXXIII, 131 (July 1917), 215–6.

24. Best, p. 250.

25. P. 1.

26. 'Contraband and Continuous Transport', *Contemporary Rev.*, CVII, 2 (Feb. 1915), 177.

27. Castren, p. 314.

28. 'The New Blockade', *The Nation*, XVI, 25 (20 Mar. 1915), 793–4.

29. 'Some Notes on the Blockade', *Trans. Grotius Soc.*, I (1915), 108–9.

30. Best, pp. 250–1. Advances in naval technology now made effective blockade a long-distance form of warfare, with Britain (by use of mines) virtually able to enforce use of certain sea lanes if necessary. Cf. the detailed account by A. Marsden, 'The Blockade', in *British Foreign Policy Under Sir Edward Grey, op. cit.*, pp. 488–515.

31. Best, p. 254.

32. 'The True Freedom of the Sea', *19th Century*, CXXXII, 479 (Nov. 1917), 1017. Cf. de Montmorency, 'The Barbary States in International Law', *Trans. Grotius Soc.*, IV (1918), 87–94.

33. Defended, however, by A. P. Higgins, *Defensively-Armed Merchant Ships and Submarine Warfare*, 1917. Cf. his *Studies in International Law and Relations*, Cambridge, 1928.

34. *International Problems ...*, p. 197.

35. *Ibid.*, pp. 121–7, 155, 174–7, 190–1 and *Society of Nations*, pp. 91–110.

36. 'Contraband and Continuous Transport', p. 177.

Appendix 5

1. For the First World War there is Edward Shanks, *The Old Indispensables: A Romance of Whitehall* (1919).

2. Oman, *Things I Have Seen*, 1933, pp. 220–4.

3. W. M. Johnston, *The Formative Years of R. G. Collingwood*, The Hague, 1967, p. 10.

4. Collingwood, *Autobiography*, p. 42.

5. J. R. H. Weaver, *Henry William Carless Davis, 1874–1928*, 1933, pp. 36–42; Obituary in *The Times*, 29 June 1928, p. 11b; Headlam-Morley, *Memoir ...*, p. 4; Letter of Lord Southborough (Chairman of Restriction of Enemy Supplies Committee) to *The Times*, 30 June 1928, p. 10a.

6. Cf. his inaugural lecture as Regius Professor of History at Oxford, 'The Study of History' (Nov. 1925), in Weaver, esp. pp. 70–4.

7. *Beatrice Webb's Diaries, 1912–1924*, 1952, p. 85 (3 June 1917). However, two articles by Adams on the international control of disputes show real grasp of the difficulties involved. See his *International Control* (1915) and 'The Basis of Constructive Internationalism', *Annals A.A.P.S.S.*, LXI (Sept. 1915), 217–29. On Adams see also the obituary in *The Times*, 1 Feb. 1966, p. 123; Stubbs, 734; Jones, *Whitehall Diary*, I, 31.

8. H. V. Wiseman in *DNB 1951–60*, pp. 429–31.

9. See D. W. Dean, 'H. A. L. Fisher, Reconstruction and Development of the 1918 Education Act', *British J. of Educational Studies*, XVIII, 3 (Oct. 1970), 259–76; L. O. Ward, 'H. A. L. Fisher and the Teachers', *ibid.*, XXII, 2 (June 1974), 191–9; G. E. Sherrington, 'The 1918 Act: Origins, Aims and Development', *ibid.*, XXIV, 1 (Feb. 1976), 66–85 and 'H. A. L. Fisher and the Teachers', *ibid.*, XXIV, 2 (June 1976), 171–6.

10. See C. Harvie, *The Lights of Liberalism*, 1976.

11. 9 Dec. 1916 and 12 Dec. 1916, Fisher Mss. Box 7.

12. To F. A. Keynes, 13 Jan. 1916, in *Collected Writings*, XVI, 161–2.

13. 14 Jan. 1917 and 15 Dec. 1917, Keynes-Grant correspondence, J. M. Keynes Mss.

Index